URBAN DESIGN:
STREET AND SQUARE

To Kate

URBAN DESIGN: STREET AND SQUARE

Third Edition

Cliff Moughtin
Miquel Mertens

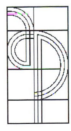

AMSTERDAM BOSTON HEIDELBERG LONDON NEW YORK OXFORD PARIS
SAN DIEGO SAN FRANCISCO SINGAPORE SYDNEY TOKYO

Butterworth-Heinemann is an imprint of Elsevier
Linacre House, Jordan Hill, Oxford OX2 8DP, UK
30 Corporate Drive, Suite 400, Burlington, MA 01803, USA

First edition 1992
Reprinted 1995
Second edition 1999
Reprinted 2001
Third edition 2003
Reprinted 2004, 2005, 2006, 2007

British Library Cataloguing in Publication Data
A catalogue record for this book is available from the British Library

Library of Congress Cataloging-in-Publication Data
A catalog record for this book is available from the Library of Congress

ISBN–13: 978-0-7506-5717-4
ISBN–10: 0-7506-5717-0

For information on all Butterworth-Heinemann publications
visit our website at books.elsevier.com

Printed and bound in *Great Britain*

07 08 09 10 10 9 8 7 6 5 4

CONTENTS

PREFACE TO THE FIRST EDITION

My interest in urban design began in the mid 1950s with Professor McCaughan's history of planning lectures given in the then Department of Civic Design, University of Liverpool. At those lectures 'Mac' made it quite clear that he was a follower of Camillo Sitte, a Viennese architect whose main work dated from the last decade of the nineteenth century. After a five-year education in architecture where the heroic dimension of modern architecture was stressed, it came as a refreshing tonic to read the works of a scholar, Sitte, who analysed urban form to distil from it the principles of good design. After Sitte, the writings of Le Corbusier and those of like mind could be seen for what they were - polemical manifestos. This is not meant to denigrate the work of Le Corbusier, he is one of the great architects of this century, nothing can destroy that reputation. However, as a planner and urbanist Le Corbusier, and more particularly followers of lesser stature, are responsible for much environmental damage through-out European cities - vandalism would not be too strong a word for such developments.

The early years of my professional career were spent in developing countries, Singapore, Ghana, Nigeria and the Sudan. Those years living and working with people of diverse life-styles gave a valuable insight into the relationship of built form and culture. Again under the influence of 'Mac' I read works in social anthropology and made studies of traditional settlement form and architecture. Walking in Singapore's China Town or exploring the wonderful mud cities of the Hausa, Nigeria together with readings in anthropology convinced me of the aridity of much contemporary urban design.

From the mid 1960s onwards I worked closely with 'Mac', first at Liverpool University, then at the Queen's University of Belfast and latterly at Nottingham University. During 25 years 'Mac' and I collaborated on many European student field trips exploring a rich urban heritage with our students. This book is an introduction to our common European urban design heritage and the reader is advised to visit the places mentioned in the text as the printed word, drawings and photographs are no substitute for the excitement of personal discovery. The following text is a starting point which may help the development of the reader's own critical faculties and so lead to a greater appreciation of the European street and square.

The need for a book of this type was made apparent to me on my recent visits to universities in the developing world. For example, during a two-month visit to Nairobi University, where I was teaching the urban studio, I undertook to develop the workshop lectures and seminars into some form of useful publication. Eight years later that task is now complete. Three further volumes on urban design have now been published entitled *Urban Design: Ornament and Decoration*, *Urban Design: Green Dimensions*, *Urban Design: Method and Techniques*.

PREFACE TO THE SECOND EDITION

This is the preface to the second edition of *Urban Design: Street and Square*, in which a new chapter, 'Seafront, River and Canal,' is incorporated. An additional case study of riverside regeneration has been added to the last chapter of the book to illustrate the role of water in urban design. The chapter and its case study are intended to fill a gap in the original text; they are concerned with the design of public space close to urban waterways.

Urban design is closely linked to both architecture and planning, yet is a quite distinct subject area. The main concern of urban design is the design and structuring of public space in cities, towns and also in the smaller settlements that comprise urban regions. In the Introduction to *Urban Design: Street and Square* it is maintained that the main component of urban design is the city quarter: 'Certainly, it could be, and has been, argued that clearly defined city quarters about 1.5 kilometres (1 mile) across will be a major preoccupation of urban designers in the coming decade.' The Introduction does go on to suggest that the urban designer may, nevertheless, be involved in smaller scale developments in street and square. This preface to the second edition reaffirms this definition of the core activity of urban design.

Urban design, however, is a large subject area which this book deals with in part only: it does not pretend to be a manual of good practice in urban design, nor is it prescriptive. The aim of the book is much more modest: it is to examine precedent to see if general principles can be deduced which may at some future date form the basis for a more definitive theory of urban design. Until such time the content of this book is presented as part of the ongoing discussion about the nature of this most absorbing art form.

Since the first edition of this book was published there have been, in this country, a number of far reaching developments in the practice of urban design. The Government has prepared or is preparing Planning Policy Guidance and other documents which have elevated urban design to a central position in the process of planning and regeneration. The importance of urban design is also confirmed by the report of Rogers and his Urban Task Force. An alliance of professional bodies with an interest in urban design has been formed which includes The Urban Design Group, the Royal Institute of British Architects, the Royal Town Planning Institute, the Landscape Institute, the Royal Institution of Chartered Surveyors, the Institution of Civil Engineers together with The Civic Trust: the formation of such a group provides a vehicle to promote and lobby for the recognition and development of the subject. While much development in this country still fails to achieve high standards of urban design there are, nevertheless, notable exceptions many of which are being documented in *Urban Design*, the quarterly journal of the Urban Design Group.

PREFACE TO THE THIRD EDITION

Since the publication in 1992 of the first edition of this book there has been considerable development in the understanding and practice of urban design. These developments have been gathering momentum since the publication of the second edition in 1999. Many of the ideas in the Report of Lord Rogers and his Urban Task Force *Towards an Urban Renaissance*, also published in 1999, have been absorbed into Government thinking and may in part be responsible for the recent Planning Green Paper. Ideas in the Green Paper could, if implemented, lead to an innovative planning system where urban design is elevated to a central role.

In 2001, Lomberg's book *The Skeptical Environmentalist* was translated into English and published by Cambridge University Press. The optimistic, almost complacent, view of the state of the global environment presented in his book has been rebutted by most of the reputable scientists in the field. Nevertheless, this thought-provoking book and its assessment that conditions on earth are generally improving for human welfare, has encouraged those advocating an 'environmental free for all', particularly those to the right of American politics. Fortunately, here in Britain and indeed in Europe, sustainable development still seems to be a goal of urban planning. In his response to some of the criticisms of the Green Paper, Lord Faulkner promised to give more weight to sustainability as a goal of development in a future planning agenda. This book, and the others in the series, will continue to advocate 'the precautionary principle' as a guide for environmental design; this principle is fundamental to the theory of sustainable development. Until the Scientific Community decides otherwise it is sensible to propose development strategies, which reduce, as far as possible, the pressures on a fragile global environment.

The types of development and planning tasks that have involved urban design skills have increased over the past decade. For example, they now include tasks of urban restructuring over large sub-regional areas. If the ideas encompassed by the Green Paper on planning are implemented, then it is likely that the workload of the urban designer will increase; he or she will also be engaged in a wide variety of tasks, once thought to be the province of other disciplines. To some extent urban design can quite simply be defined as the work carried out by urban designers. However, throughout this series of books on urban design the core of the subject is considered to be the planning and design of the city quarter, district or neighbourhood. The nature of urban design is discussed elsewhere in this book.

Here, I wish to reaffirm that the main concern of urban design is the creation of sustainable quarters of environmental quality. This book deals with only part of this subject area: its theme is the design of street and square, that is, the design of the major components of the urban realm.

There are four main additions to this third edition. A chapter has been included which examines in outline, the theories of sustainable development in order to bring the contents of the book into line with current thinking: it deals specifically with the relationship of these theories to the design of street and square, taking into consideration the probable changes to transportation systems in the city. A chapter, Visual Analysis, has also been introduced to explain the practical significance of the theoretical contents of the book, and to clarify how the techniques of visual analysis can be used to achieve greater understanding of the form, function and meaning of the streets and squares that make up the major part of the urban realm. A new case study on regeneration of the seafront in Barcelona has been included in Chapter 9. This case study illustrates a major urban design achievement, emphasising the importance of the waterfront and its relationship to the cities network of streets and squares. Finally, there is a short concluding chapter, which brings together the main themes of the book, asking the question - why were so few great streets or squares developed in the twentieth century?

ACKNOWLEDGEMENTS

My greatest debt is to my friend and teacher the late Reginald Ellersley Manifold McCaughan, 'Mac' or 'Mek' to his colleagues, friends and students. 'Mac' was Senior Lecturer in Civic Design at Liverpool University for many years. Later, after his retirement, he became Special Professor in the History of Planning and the History of Architecture at The University of Nottingham. 'Mac' taught many generations of architectural and planning students in Liverpool, Nottingham and also in his native city of Belfast. I was fortunate to be one of his students from 1953 when I first heard him lecture until 1989 when he died. It was 'Mac' who introduced me to the delights and mysteries of urban design and it is to his teaching and his ideas that this book owes its origins; while the mistakes are my own, the inspiration is 'Mac's'.

This book would not have been completed if my wife Kate McMahon had not given great support and put pressure on me when other academic matters appeared to occupy both my mind and time. Kate read the manuscript and being an English graduate, she ensured that it both made sense and could be read easily. I also wish to acknowledge the help given by Dr Taner Oc and Dr Peter Tregenza: both read early versions of the text and gave valuable criticism. The students in my department at Nottingham and those at other universities where I have taught, particularly in Third World countries, have provided most useful feedback on the material for urban design as it has developed over the years. One particular student group gave great moral and intellectual support during a critical stage in the development of the text: Dave Armiger, Rafael Cuesta, Alison Gee, June Greenway, Persephone Ingram and Christine Sarris accompanied me on visits to Italian hill towns, indeed their work appears in the text. It was the enthusiasm of this student group which gave final impetus to the completion of this manuscript.

The drawings in the text were prepared by Peter Whitehouse. Peter is both a student and technician in the Institute of Planning Studies, University of Nottingham. Though performing both these roles, he found time to complete the lovely drawings which illustrate the text and without which it would lose so much meaning. I am also indebted to Glyn Halls, the senior technician in the School of Architecture, University of Nottingham. Glyn took my negatives and turned them into the photographs which also illustrate the text. This was a mammoth undertaking - the illustrations used here are the 'tip of the iceberg', representing barely a quarter of those produced and less than ten per cent of the negatives.

Last but by no means least, I wish to thank the secretarial staff in my department - Linda Francis, Liz Millward and Jenny Chambers. They prepared the final manuscript for publication, which as it turned out was the sixth draft. Linda Francis, in addition to organizing work on the manuscript, typing much of it herself, also managed my professional work (no mean feat!) so that as much time as possible remained for work on this book.

INTRODUCTION

The subject matter of this book is urban design or *City Planning According to Artistic Principles* as Camillo Sitte entitled his seminal work in 1889.[1] It is intended to begin after the manner of the theorist Sebastiano Serlio who in *The Five Books of Architecture* wrote:

> In the beginning of this book, I observed the comedians order, who (when they intend to play any comedy) first send out a Prologue, who in a few words giveth the audience to understand what they intend to entreat of, in their comedie. So I, meaning in this Booke, to entreat of the manner of buildings, viz Thuscan, Dorica, Ionica, Corinthia and Composita, have thought good, that in the beginning thereof, men should see figures of all the several kinds where I propose to entreat of.[2]

In the case of urban design the main actors in the play presented here are the square, the street and the buildings that make up the public face of towns and cities. The meaning and role these elements play in urban design, the ways in which they are arranged, designed and detailed is the subject matter of the remaining chapters.

Urban design is an important though often neglected aspect of planning and a topic which has not always received due recognition in architectural education. Urban design is at the interface between architecture and planning but is quite distinct from both disciplines.

There are a number of definitions of planning, in fact, almost as many as there are planners. At its broadest planning can be defined as the process by which resources are distributed.[3] Indeed some planners would see the planners' role as one which is deeply committed to redistribution of resources in favour of those less well-off sections of society.[4] These definitions elevate planning to the political arena, that is, deciding who gets what, where and when. Other more technical definitions of planning restrict the subject to the organization of land uses, transportation and infrastructural networks both for efficient functioning and the creation of a pleasant and well-ordered environment. This narrow definition of planning does not free the discussion entirely from politics, for land itself is a resource and all developments bring benefits to some and incur costs for others. It is, therefore, concerned with the distribution and allocation of resources, as such it is an activity of government. Planning periods are often long, possibly twenty years and may cover large urban and rural regions. On the other hand action plans requiring entrepreneurial skills from the planners may have a timescale of five to ten years and cover only small parts of a town.

Architecture is concerned with the design and construction of individual buildings. Usually the architect designs for clearly identifiable clients. The designs are made for particular sites. The construction period, for the most part, covers short term projects of one to five years' duration. However, an architect involved in hospital design or other large scale developments would be working on a building complex covering many acres of ground which would take ten or more years to build. The knowledge and expertise of the planner are as necessary as the professional skills of the architect for the successful execution of such a project. Hence, in practice, there is no precise differentiation between the domain of the architect and that of the planner. Since the boundary between these subject areas is blurred there can be no clear and precise subject definitions.

Urban design is allied to architecture and planning. For its practice it requires some of the skills and knowledge of both disciplines. The subject matter of urban design is the arrangement of many buildings so that they form a single composition. The designs may cover more than one site and involve many owners, users and government agencies. Since more than one owner is usually involved the time horizon is longer than that of a single building and usually varies between five and twenty years, though many of the finest urban designs such as the Piazza Annunziata, Florence, have taken centuries to complete. For the purpose of this book urban design is the study of the design of the urban realm as opposed to the private domain. By public realm is meant the streets, boulevards, squares and public parks together with the building façades that define them. Clearly, the design of the private domain, both as a study and as a professional activity, is the proper function of the architect. The planner and the urban designer are concerned with the private domain of individual properties only so far as it affects the public realm.

For example, developments exceeding certain densities or volumes may put excessive strain upon roads and services, or indeed, may destroy the visual quality of the environment. The internal subdivision of a building is a problem for the owner and his designer. Such internal planning may have to satisfy by-laws, health and safety regulations, but it is not a matter for the planner and nor does it fall within the normal province of urban design. Nevertheless, the relationship between internal and external space, as depicted on Nolli's map of Rome, is a facet of design which should be an important consideration of all those working in the field of city construction and reconstruction.

It has been suggested by some writers that the city quarter is the main component of urban design.[5] Certainly the scale of development since the Second World War has increased significantly, first in the public then latterly in the private sector. It is now possible to consider whole urban quarters as single design problems undertaken by a single group of developers and a single design team. In the case of urban development corporations concerned with inner-city regeneration, major components of the city such as the Isle of Dogs, London, are managed and developed by specially constituted authorities. Certainly, it could be, and has been, argued that clearly defined city quarters about 1.5 kilometres (1 mile) across will be a major preoccupation of urban designers in the coming decade. Other smaller-scale groupings of urban design elements forming the urban realm, such as the area comprising the precinct around St Paul's, London, will, nevertheless, remain central to the professional interests of the urban designer. Indeed, the consideration of the design of small-scale developments in conservation areas is very much within the field of urban design.

Over the last decade there has been considerable development in the understanding and practice of urban design. The types of development and planning tasks in this country that have involved urban design skills have increased – for example, urban design now includes tasks of restructuring large subregional areas. Ideas in the *Planning Green Paper*, produced in 2002 by the former Department of Transport, Local Government and the Regions for Her Majesty's Government, could lead to an innovative system of planning where urban design is elevated to a central role. If these ideas are implemented then it is likely that the workload of the urban designer will increase: he or she will be engaged in a wide variety of tasks once thought to be the province of other disciplines. The complex nature, however, of most urban development requires the skills of, amongst others, the planner, architect, urban designer, landscape architect and traffic planner.[6] The successful completion of these complex tasks requires that the urban designer exhibits ability and skill to work with these professionals from other disciplines.

City builders, architects, town planners and transportation engineers are in disarray, attacked, seemingly, from all sides. The gulf between the design professions and client group, those who live in or use the cities, is witnessed by critical press coverage and unsympathetic television programmes. Community destruction, demolition of pleasant, nineteenth-century terrace housing, inner-city blight, memories of new-town blues, high-rise development, all appear on the long menu of violations thought to be caused by the planner, a term used to cover a multitude of participants in the development process. The successes of the development professions are not given the same publicity. City conservation schemes, the protection of the green belt, the creation of national parks and the movement towards public participation in planning do not make headlines. Environmental success is not news, but planning and design disasters appear frequently on television and are fully documented. These negative views on the state of the city design professions are best articulated by Prince Charles. His pithy remarks about the 'monstrous carbuncle' or the 'giant glass stump' whether given in a lecture to the RIBA or made on a television programme

have the immediacy and quality of the eye-catching headline.[7] These views do, however, appear to be closely in tune with those of the lay person.

This general discontent with city planning closely parallels conditions a century ago as Sitte, a Viennese architect saw them. Sitte, in the preface to the first edition of his book, *Der Stadte-Bau*, after noting the general approval at the time, in 1889, with the technical aspects of city planning, wrote:

> In contrast there is almost as prevalent a condemnation of the artistic shortcomings of modern city planning, even scorn and contempt. This is quite justified; it is a fact that much has been accomplished in technical matters, while artistically we have achieved almost nothing, modern majestic and monumental buildings being usually seen against the most awkward public squares and the most badly divided lots.[8]

Sitte's great seminal work is the starting point and the inspiration for this present study. He studied in detail magnificent civic design achievements of the past so that he could glean from them the principles that contributed to the quality of their composition. Sitte has been described, quite erroneously, as the founder of modern city planning. Even a cursory reading of his book *City Planning According to Artistic Principles* reveals quite clearly that the subject matter is not planning as it is defined and practised in Britain today.

Sitte's main preoccupation was the artistic design and decoration of streets and squares and, as such, he would more accurately be described as the founder of urban design. This present study follows Sitte's method using historical precedent to establish the ground rules for composition in the field of urban design. Though drawing heavily on historical examples, this is not a history of urban form and should not be confused with work in that field. The examples of streets and squares chosen for the text are ones that are generally accepted as fine city building and, indeed, are well-known tourist attractions, places thought worthy of visiting by many people. It is argued here that if we can analyse the properties that made fine city streets and squares in the past it may be possible to reproduce some of those qualities in future development, not by outright copying, but by employing the underlying principles of composition.

The theoretical literature of western architecture starts with Vitruvius, the Augustan architect, and his treatise *De Architectura*. It was with Vitruvius that this present search for a theoretical understanding of urban design appropriately began. More important for urban design however, are the works of the Renaissance scholars, Leone Battista Alberti, Filarete, Serlio and Andrea Palladio. *De re aedificatoria* begun by Alberti in the 1430s was presented to Pope Nicholas V in 1452. With this great work Alberti established architecture as a learned discipline based upon principles articulated and structured by reason. In his text Alberti dealt also with elements of city design, streets, roads and piazze. Antonio Averlino, known as Filarete, was the first author to write a treatise on architecture, *Libro architettonico*, in a modern language. The book is of interest to the urban design student mainly for its description of a capital city, Sforzinda, and a port city, Plousiapolis: explanations are given not only for planning, design and construction of the city but also for its institutional organization. *Tutte l'opere d'architectura*, by Serlio, is probably best known for its exhaustive treatment of the five orders of architecture and the splendid illustration of their proportions and use.

It was, however, Palladio who wrote the most influential architectural treatise of the sixteenth century, *I Quattro Libri dell'Architettura*. It was frequently republished in Italy and other European countries and had an unprecedented impact on architects and architecture in the centuries following its publication. The book covers the general principles of architectural design, the Classical orders, the design of palaces, villas, bridges, civic buildings, temples and churches. Like Alberti a century before him, Palladio discussed the design of streets and piazze. There is little abstract theory in Palladio, most of the text discusses actual buildings and the problems of design they raise. The drawings of Palladio's own buildings with their great economy of form, simple symmetry and proportional regularity were probably the main reasons for the book's influence, an influence that can still fire the imagination of the young architect.[9]

Sitte reacted against a debased Classical tradition as it had been incorporated into design dogma at the large scale of the city. His counter proposals to the poor and mechanical imitations of Hausmann's axial planning of Paris were based largely on an exhaustive study of medieval towns. The opposing view of city design, the Beaux Arts, is represented by writers such as Julien Guadet and his *Elements et Théorie de l'Architecture*.[10] More important for this study, however, is the school of urban design stemming directly from Sitte and those he influenced through the many translations of his book into other European languages. In Britain, Raymond Unwin, a key figure in the Garden City movement, was an early convert to Sitte's influence. His own book *Town Planning in Practice*, an immense work on the design aspects of city planning, was of profound influence on the planning profession during the early part of the twentieth century.[11] Meanwhile, in the United States, there were Werner Hegemann and Elbert Peets, who, early in the last century, wrote *The American Vitruvius, An Architect's Handbook of Civic Art*. It was an important contribution to the development of urban design, and is still a delight to read.[12]

The writers associated with the Modern Movement in architecture, represented particularly by Le Corbusier or the manifestos of CIAM, were following dictates other than the concerns of Sitte. One of the foremost apologists of the Modern Movement, Sigfried Giedion, dismissed Sitte's ideas as palliatives and, instead, advocated mass housing, vast engineering roadworks and comprehensive city-centre development – now the subject of popular criticism. It may, however, be too soon to write an objective critique of the pre-Post-Modern architectural styles current during the first part of the last century. Time and distance from those events may be necessary for them to be seen with any clarity. Giedions' *Space, Time and Architecture* however, is still a book well worth the attention of the student of architecture and urban design; of particular interest is the section dealing with the planning of Rome by Pope Sixtus V.[13]

The interest in urban design continued after the Second World War. As a result of this a number of important books were published in the 1950s. Frederick Gibberd's *Town Design* is still a standard text book on the design of elements that form the town.[14] He is clearly indebted for many of his ideas to Sitte, particularly in his analysis of the town square. Paul Zucker in *Town and Square*, like Gibberd, builds on the work of Sitte, but introduces a much broader typology of public squares. These two books are complemented by *Towns and Buildings*, by Steen Eiler Rasmussen, which, like Zucker, relies heavily on the analysis of urban groupings set in an historical setting.[15]

Three important works on the perception of cities appeared in the late 1950s and early 1960s. They were, *Experiencing Architecture*, by Rasmussen, *Townscape* by Gordon Cullen and *The Image of the City* by Kevin Lynch.[16] Rasmussen's main concern in his book is to try to show how we react to internal and external architectural space and the ways in which we appreciate forms, colours and textures. Cullen, by contrast, takes up the idea of serial vision which is also a feature of Sitte's work. With the aid of fine perspective sketches, Cullen dissects in great detail the form of the urban realm as the viewer moves through it. Clearly many of the towns and cities most admired are picturesque, in the sense that they are capable of analysis using Cullen's techniques for expressing serial vision. Lynch, too, was interested in the way in which the city is perceived. For his evidence Lynch conducted a survey among city residents analysing the drawings and mental maps made for him. From this analysis Lynch formulated the theory of 'Imageability', that is, the elements of urban structure which need to be present to create a strong visual image in the eye or mind of the beholder. Lynch's theories of urban form are probably the single most important contribution in the field of urban design in the twentieth century.

Christopher Alexander is among the most prolific writers on architecture and urban design. An early essay, 'The city is not a tree' is a well-argued critique of current planning concepts for the hierarchical distribution of facilities and services.[17] In support of his case, he pointed out the complexities and diversity of connections in the real world. Two other of Alexander's works will be mentioned here: *A Pattern Language* and *A New Theory of Urban Design*. In both works Alexander seeks to establish a natural or organic way of designing and building.[18] First he established a set of 253 patterns, such as the organization of an entrance or a window place: the criteria arrived at to define and describe these patterns, Alexander argued, applied to all similar cases. The designer, armed with this set of patterns from sleeping area to outdoor meeting place, is able to reproduce universally acceptable solutions forming part of an all-pervasive organic unity. In his theory of urban design, Alexander goes one step further by attempting to establish a natural or organic design process by which means the unity of the traditional town can be recreated. Alexander's work is challenging and it is a body of theory with which the urban design student must come to terms.

Two works which considerably affected architectural thinking both appeared in 1966. They are Aldo Rossi's *L'Architettura della Citta*, and Robert Venturi's *Complexity and Contradiction in Architecture*.[19] Rossi set the intellectual agenda for neo-Rationalism, while Venturi, with a preference for richness of meaning rather than clarity of meaning, gave further support to an empirical and flexible approach to city design.

Colin Rowe and Fred Koetter, in their enigmatic mid-1970's work *Collage City*, aimed to illuminate the complex process of city building using a language often as obscure as poetry.[20] The book is a warning against the Utopian vision, whether populist or elitist. Instead, they put forward a pluralist view of city form, a collage city that accommodates a range of ideas and visions. In similar fashion, Christian Norberg-Schulz lays stress upon the unique qualities of place and the importance of symbolism in all that man creates.[21] Symbolism, like so many aspects of a rich and stimulating environment, was completely overlooked or considered unimportant by architects of the so-called 'heroic age' of modern architecture. Amos Rapoport with his seminal work *House Form and Culture*, and his later book *Human Aspects of Urban Form*, brought the close relationship between built form and culture to the attention of architects and planners.[22] The idea that architecture is applied social anthropology broadens the scope of urban design from 'architecture writ large' to a subject that now includes the social sciences. Urban form is clearly seen as resulting from the interplay of a number of factors such as location, transportation networks, land value and topography. A discussion of settlement form as the physical manifestation of culture is not a major theme in this present study, it has been explained elsewhere in, for example, *Hausa Architecture*.[23]

The other major theme to be found in the Post-Modern reaction to the hegemony associated with modern architecture is 'new rationalism' given, as we saw, its intellectual stimulus from Rossi. The creed of the new rationalists is *The Third Typology*.[24] The new rationalists, turning their attention to urbanism, reacted against the anti-historicism of the Modern Movement as encapsulated in the Charter of Athens. Architects such as Leon and Rob Krier turned instead to the city for typological components. Said Leon Krier: 'The history of architectural and urban culture is seen as the history of types. Types of settlements, types of spaces (public and private), types of buildings, types of construction. The bourgeois concept of architectural history - basically concerned with the monument - is extended to include the typological

complexity of the urban fabric, of the anonymous buildings forming the flesh of the city, the skin of the public space.'[25] The prime concern of urbanism for the new rationalist is the design of the urban realm. Leon Krier again: 'In these new projects the form of the public realm is the prime concern. The public realm as a finite, unitarian, rational space.'[26] For those in the planning profession who have followed people like Sitte rather than worshipping at the feet of the false gods of the architectural profession this all sounds rather old fashioned producing a feeling of *déjà vu*.

The tension between the rational and empirical wings of the Post-Modern era is captured by the debate *Reconstruction Deconstruction, My Ideology is better than Yours*, in which Peter Eisenman and Leon Krier discuss architecture and city building in terms of 'presentness' and 'tradition'.[27]

The cudgels for rationalism are taken up by Alexander Tzonis and Liane Lefaivre who, using Classical architecture as a model, articulate a growing concern in some quarters for the poetics of order in architecture.[28] Reading once again about the canon of Classical design, emphasizing, as it does, order analysis and composition, is a refreshing return to sanity after some of the more whimsical excursions or architectural fashions in the 1980s. Tzonis and Lefaivre do not advocate a return to the glories of a past style, the dead hand of 'copyism' is not the message of this scholarly work. It is, however, a timely reminder of a systematic thought process that has produced many fine buildings in the past.

Deconstructionists following the writings of Jacques Derrida aim to deconstruct aesthetics. Derrida attempts to free philosophy from in-built constraints: centuries of thinking have, according to him, stultified the thought processes. In his literary and philosophical criticism, Derrida aims to deconstruct, among other things, the belief that logic and rational argument will provide the key to understanding - all things will become clear from rational explanation. Derrida, therefore, hopes to show that by applying rational methods rationalism cannot work.[29]

Geoffrey Broadbent, in *Emerging Concepts in Urban Space Design*, presents an exhaustive account of the main contributors in the field of urban design.[30] This useful and extensive annotated bibliography deals in greater detail with the Post-Modern philosophical debate and is complementary to the foregoing, more selective, range of authorities chosen for their relevance to, and importance for, the thesis presented in the following chapters. For the moment, the last word will he left with Broadbent and his attempt to connect Venturi, Derrida and Rationalism:

> Venturi likes walls to be good and solid; obvious containers, protectors of internal space with trans-parent holes for windows. He cannot abide the Modem Movement idea of 'flowing space'; of outside and inside opening into each other through glass walls which 'can be discounted by the eye'. Inside and the outside are and must be different. Which is exactly what Derrida says of words. Spoken words, he says, are too transparent' - like Venturi's glass walls - which is why he, Derrida, gives such priority to writing.

Broadbent goes on to say that Derrida demonstrates:

> the impossibility of conceiving the inside prior to the outside. Only an outside can define an inside! So whilst Derrida may have 'stunned' rationalism, he gives even more authority to Venturi's kind of Empiricism![31]

So has Rationalism been dealt the *coup de grâce?* While agreeing the primacy of the outside (which followers of Sitte wouldn't) this writer will cling irrationally to the rational process of testing ideas in the world of empirical fact: the idea or concept comes first, the test later. Those ideas are generated by theory, even Derrida's! The present text is firmly in the tradition of Sitte and that tradition's latest manifestations, the New Rationalism. There is, here, however, no attempt like that of David Gosling in 'Definitions of Urban Design', 'to discover whether there is indeed a shift away from The Third Typology towards new directions.'[32] The new rationalists publicized and brought back onto the urban design agenda the need to design using the main formal elements found in the city.

Three interconnected themes seemed to inform the discussion about 'urbanism' or urban design during the last decade of the twentieth century: they were participation, context, and sustainable development. With the growing awareness of the importance of urban design amongst the development professions, environmental quality became an important goal of city planning, a quality ultimately judged by the user. Participation was therefore thought to be a key component in the delivery of fine city development, which was both accepted and owned by its citizens. The impetus for this movement to politicize the planning and design process was generated by a number of books appearing in the 1960s, which were critical of the development process. Books such as Jacobs' seminal work, *The Death and Life of Great American Cities* published in 1965 and Gans series of essays in *People and Plans* published in 1968, were highly influential in changing the attitudes of architects and planners. Goodman's *After the Planners* published in 1972, with its suggestions for 'guerrilla architecture' and 'squatter environments in which the community as a body lays down what it requires', gave a positive architectural dimension to the critique of the then formal process of city development.[33]

The pursuit of environmental excellence is now equated with 'contextualism' or the design of development, which is suited to the local context as defined by environment and culture. As Tibbalds wrote in *Making People Friendly Towns,* 1992 'Places need to offer variety to their users. They need to be unique and different from one another - each rooted in their own particular historical, geographical, physical or cultural context'.[34] Context as a generator of environmental excellence in the public realm has its roots in 'critical regionalism.' According to Frampton, who is also associated with the development of the concept, Alexander Tzonis and Liane Lefaivre first coined 'Critical Regionalism' in 1981.[35] The first International Seminar on the topic, however, was not until 1989, the University of Pomona - the proceedings were published later in 1991. According to Amourgis who edited the proceedings 'the intentions behind the use of the word "regionalism" are to express natural and social context, essential factors in the shaping and evolution of life and civilization.'[36]

The rest of this book is composed of ten chapters. Chapter one deals with the method of urban design and programme formulation, a fundamental study for establishing discipline. It poses the question: 'Where do design ideas orig1nate?' concentrating on creative thinking as outlined by Edward de Bono, and Bryan Lawson.[37] The urban design programme, or the social and economic needs of society, is shown to be the generator or foundation of city building activities. Urban form is defined as a physical expression of culture and, as such, it is related directly to user satisfaction and, ultimately, to public participation in the design process.

Chapter two examines the laws of composition in architecture in order to determine how and in what ways they apply at the larger scale of urban design. Composition at the scale of urban design is used in a similar way to its use for music or literature; a musical composition has a beginning, an end, theme, movements, chords and notes; similarly, a novel has a beginning, an end, theme, chapters and words. This chapter examines the grammar and syntax of urban design.

Chapters three to nine form the core of the text. Chapter three examines the ways in which buildings can be arranged, both within space and to form space. It develops an idea for a general typology of built form. Chapter four discusses the design of the square or plaza. It starts with an outline of the role and function of the square in the built environment and goes on to analyse, through examples, its form.

Chapter five discusses the design of the street - the other main element in urban design. It follows the structure of chapter four starting by outlining the role and function of the street in the built environment, then going on to analyse its form using examples. Chapter six specifically examines the role of water in the design of public spaces: it discusses the form and function of the river, canal and seafront with a particular concern for the spaces formed along the edge of such water courses.

Chapter seven introduces the principles of sustainable development as they affect the design of street and square. The second part of the chapter concentrates on public transport in street and square and pays particular attention to the architectural settings for the tram or light train. Chapter eight concentrates on the use of visual analysis as a tool for understanding the role of street and square in the urban quarter. The chapter starts with an outline of the principles of visual analysis, which is followed by a study of Tavira, a small town in the Algarve, Portugal: it concludes with a summary of the ways in which the technique of visual analysis can inform the urban design process for the better understanding and design of streets and squares. Chapter nine has five case studies, bringing together the main ideas in the previous chapters, namely the design of the public realm and, in particular, its streets and squares.

Chapter ten, a short concluding chapter, examines why it proved so difficult in the twentieth century to design and develop lively streets and squares of real quality. The chapter returns to the issues raised in previous chapters in order to learn both from past mistakes and also from the great achievements of earlier generations.

NOTES

1   Sitte, Camillo. *Der Stadte-Bau*, Verlag Von Carl Graeser and Co. Wien, 1889

2   Serlio, Sebastiano. *The Five Books of Architecture*, an unabridged reprint of the English edition of 1611, Book 4, Folio 3, Dover Publications, New York, 1982

3   Eversley, David. *The Planner in Society*, Faber & Faber, London, 1973

4   Davidoff, Paul. Working towards redistributive justice. In *Journal of the American Institute of Planners*, Vol 41, No 5, September 1975, pp.317-318

5   Gosling, D. and Maitland, B. *Concepts of Urban Design*, Academy Editions, London, 1984, p.7

6   Department for Transport, Local Government and the Regions, *Planning Green Paper, Planning: Delivering a Fundamental Change*, DTLR, London, 2002.

7   HRH, The Prince of Wales. *A Vision of Britain*, Doubleday, London. 1989

8   Collins, G.R. and Collins, C.C. *Camillo Sitte: The Birth of Modern City Planning*, Rizzoli, New York, 1986, p.138

9   Wiebenson, Dora. *Architectural Theory and Practice from Alberti to Ledoux*, University of Chicago Press, Chicago, 1982

The following are the English translations used in this text:

Vitruvius. *The Ten Books of Architecture*, Dover Publications, New York, 1960

Alberti, Leone Battista. *Ten Books on Architecture* (trns Cosimo Bartoli (into Italian) and James Leoni (into English) Tiranti, London, 1955

Filarete (Antonio di Peiro Averlino). *Treatise on Architecture* (trns J.R. Spencer) Yale University Press, New Haven, 1965

Serlio, Sebastiano. *The Five Books of Architecture* (an unabridged reprint of the English edn of 1611), Dover Publications, New York, 1982

Palladio, Andrea. *The Four Books of Architecture*, Dover Publications, New York, 1965

10 Guadet, J. *Elements et Théorie De L'Architecture,* Vols I to IV, 16th edn, Librarie de Ia Construction Moderne, 1929 and 1930

11 Unwin, Raymond. *Town Planning in Practice*, Benjamin Blom Inc. New York, 1971 (first published 1909)

12 Hegemann, Werner and Peets, Elbert, *The American Vitruvius, An Architect's Handbook of Civic Art*, Benjamin Blom, New York, 1922

13 Giedion, Sigfried. *Space, Time and Architecture*, Harvard University Press, Cambridge. Mass., 3rd edn, 1956

14 Gibberd, Frederick. *Town Design*, Architectural Press, London, 2nd edn, 1955

15 Rasmussen, S.E. *Towns and Buildings*, Liverpool University Press, Liverpool, 1951

16 Rasmussen, S.E. *Experiencing Architecture*, MIT Press, Cambridge, Mass., 1959

    Lynch, Kevin. *The Image of the City*, MIT Press, Cambridge, Mass., 1960

    Cullen, Gordon. *The Concise Townscape*, Architectural Press, London, 1986 (first published 1961)

17 Alexander, Christopher. A city is not a tree. In *Architectural Forum*, New York, April 1965, pp.58-62 and May 1965, pp.58-61

18 Alexander, C., et al. *A Pattern Language*. Oxford University Press, Oxford, 1977

    Alexander, C., et al. *A New Theory of Urban Design*, Oxford University Press, Oxford, 1987

19 Rossi, A. *L'Architettura della cilta* (ed. Macsilio), Padua, 1966

    Venturi, R. *Complexity and Contradiction in Architecture*, Museum of Modern Art, New York, 1966

20 Rowe, C. and Koefler, F. *Collage City*, MIT Press, Cambridge, Mass., l978

21 Norberg-Schulz, Christian. *Existence, Space and Architecture*, Studio Vista, London, 1971, and *Genius Loci, Towards a Phenomenology of Architecture*, Rizzoli, New York, 1980

22 Rapoport, A. *House Form and Culture*, Prentice-Hall, Englewood Cliffs, New Jersey, 1962, and *Human Aspects of Urban Form*, Pergamon Press, Oxford, 1977

23 Moughtin, J.C. *Hausa Architecture*, Ethnographica, London, 1985

24 Vidler, A. The third typology. In *Rational Architecture*, Archives d'Architecture Moderne, Bruxelles, 1978

25 Krier, L. The reconstruction of the city. In *Rational Architecture*, Archives d'Architecture Moderne, Bruxelles, 1978, p.41

26 Ibid, p.42

27 Eisenman, P. and Krier, L. Reconstruction deconstruction, my ideology is better than yours. In *Architectural Design*, vol 59, No 9-10, 1989 pp.7-18

28 Tzonis, A. and Lefaivre, L. *Classical Architecture, The Poetics of Order*, MIT Press, Cambridge, Mass., 1986

29 Derrida, J. *Of Grammatologie* (trns G.C. Spivak) Johns Hopkins University Press, Baltimore, 1976; *L'Ecriture et la Difference* (trns A. Bass) Chicago University Press, Chicago, l978; *Speech and Phenomena*, Northwestern University Press, Evanston, 1973 and *Derrida and Deconstruction* (ed. H.J. Silverman) Routledge, London, 1989

30 Broadbent, G. *Emerging Concepts in Urban Space Design*, Van Nostrand Reinhold, London, 1990

31 Ibid, p.320

32 Gosling, D. Definitions of urban design. In *Architectural Design, Urbanism* (ed. David Gosling) Vol 54, No 1/2, 1984, pp.16-25

33 Jacobs, J. *The Death and Life of Great American Cities*, Penguin, Harmonsdworth, 1965. Gans, H. *People and Plans*, Basic Books, New York, 1968. Goodman, R. *After the Planners*, Penguin, Harmondsworth, 1972

34 Tibbalds, F. *Making People-friendly Towns*, Longman, Harlow, 1992

35 Tzonis, A. and Lefaivre, L. Critical regionalism. In *Critical Regionalism: The Pomona Meeting Proceedings* (ed. A. Amourgis) California State Polytechnic University, California, 1991

36 Amourgis. S. ' Introduction', in *Critical Regionalism*, ibid

37 de Bono, E. *Lateral Thinking*, Penguin Books. Harmondsworth, 1977, and Lawson, B. *How Designers Think*, Architectural Press, London, 1980

URBAN DESIGN AND PEOPLE

1

INTRODUCTION

The title of this chapter presents a dilemma. This dilemma is caused by the tension between the desire to practise an art form based upon method and principle, while, at the same time, involving people actively in the design process. The tension can be summed up in the phrase 'professionalism versus populism'. HRH Prince Charles is engaged with this dilemma by supporting public participation in planning and architecture while advocating, at the same time, a form of Classical design: 'Buildings should reflect these harmonies, for architecture is like a language. You cannot construct pleasing sentences in English unless you have a thorough knowledge of the grammatical ground rules. If you abandon these basic principles of grammar the result is discordant and inharmonious. Good architecture should be like good manners and follow a recognized code. Civilized life is made more pleasurable by a shared understanding of simple rules of conduct.'[1] Later he writes: 'People should be involved willingly from the beginning in the improvement of their surroundings. . .but participation cannot be imposed: it has to start from the bottom up.'[2]

In any dispute between the views of the 'people' and the 'professionals' which takes precedence? In Bath this dilemma was made manifest when an individual occupying a property in The Crescent wished to paint her door yellow. The professional view considered that all doors in John Wood junior's great piece of Classical urban architecture should be white. The law in this case upheld the individual's right to express her own taste.

The aim of this chapter is not to solve this dilemma but, more simply, to make it apparent and to set theoretical ground rules for incorporating public participation into the urban design process. The dilemma will not disappear, but it may be that the resolution of the tensions will stimulate creative design.

AN ANALYTICAL FRAMEWORK FOR PUBLIC PARTICIPATION

Urban design, or the art of building cities, is the method by which man creates a built environment that fulfils his aspirations and represents his values.[3] This he does in his own likeness, The sixteenth-century theorist and architect John Shute likens the city to the human figure: 'A city ought to be like the human body and for this reason it should be full of all that gives life to man.'[4] Urban design, like its sister art architecture, is a people's use of an accumulated technological knowledge to control and adapt the environment for social, economic, political and religious requirements. It is the method learned and used by a people to solve the total programme of requirements for city building. The city is an element of a people's spiritual and physical culture and, indeed, it is one of the highest expressions of that culture.

Central to the study of urban design is man, his values, aspirations and power or ability to achieve them. The task of the city builder is to understand and express, in built form, the needs and aspirations of the client group. How does the city builder design to best serve the community's needs? How can the designer ensure that the end product is culturally acceptable? These and other similar questions are important issues for those in the city designing professions.

Experience from the recent past, in this and many other countries, is littered with well-intentioned, but totally unsuitable, developments. Developments that range from the faceless mass housing of the 1960s to the large-scale office blocks or commercial areas which totally destroy the intimate fabric of the city. As a reaction the conservation movement grows apace. Timidity, the fear of further mistakes, prevents even the replacement of mediocre buildings from the past. Yet Shute, one of the country's earliest theorists and author of the first English architectural book, recognized that all buildings have a natural lifespan then they need to be replaced, sometimes with reluctance: 'You can say one eats, and even so dies. The building must also decline through time just as one person dies sooner than another or has better or poorer health.'[5] Copying features from past architectural styles is once again in vogue among city builders around the world, as if the planting of an onion dome, a minaret or horseshoe arch will, of themselves,

convert a barren design into culturally acceptable development.

The anarchy of the Post-Modern movement in architecture, with its dependence upon cliché and eclectic use of symbols from the past, must, if progress is to he made, give way to a more rational approach to architectural design steeped in discipline and method. Urban design, too, requires a return to its roots in method. Central to such a return to method is the relationship between designer and client.

It is evident that the architect has lost touch with his client. In traditional practice the architect worked for an individual or a small group representing a landed proprietor, the Church Commissioners, a company or government department. The individual client is a vestige of the past: a time when architect and client shared the same culture, values and may even have been on the same 'grande tour'. Growth of democracy and mass culture now requires the architect and city builder to recognise a wider client group. This wider client group includes the church congregation, the ordinary voter and the general user of the buildings. Many in this expanded client group do not share the values of the designer group. It is frequently possible that a wide cultural gap separates the city builder and the new client – the man and woman in the street.

The chasm between city designer and client can be bridged when the problem is recognized as existing and its nature defined: when the complexity and heterogeneity of the client group is admitted and when the designer realizes that culture is never static: it is in a constant state of change and to some extent, he or she – the designer – is an agent for those changes. Finally, it is necessary to develop methods and techniques for use when working with community groups.

For evidence of the gulf between the design professions and lay people one need only turn to the outpourings of the press or the many critical programmes appearing on television where planners and architects alike receive rough treatment. These views are best summarized by Prince Charles's remarks at the Festival of Architecture held at Hampton Court in early 1984. In his blistering attack on architectural practice in Britain he compared the Ahrends, Burton and Koralek design for the National Gallery extension to 'a monstrous carbuncle on the face of a much loved and elegant friend' and he called the Mies van der Rohe design for Mansion House Square 'a giant glass stump better suited to Chicago'.[6] These views are important not only because they were expressed by a member of the Royal family but because they appear to be closely in tune with those of the lay person.

The reasons for the present public antipathy to much recent urban development lie squarely with the training of architects and planners. To a large extent architects, urban designers and planners have been trained in a rarefied atmosphere where the subject is taught with little or no reference to the public for whom the product is intended. Education in city building in the recent past has been dominated by the posturings of the avant-garde, a break with sound tradition and the pursuit of novel, but empirically untested, theory. The result is that we have a very special subculture designing with its own peer group in mind. The internal validating process in our subject area of urban design has produced a class of people out of touch with the general mass of users. There are notable exceptions to this general rule. There are also movements within the professions which espouse a more populist approach, but, generally speaking, the gap between designer and client is wide and goes unnoticed or disregarded by many.

The communities inhabiting towns and cities, and therefore the focus of our subject, are complex heterogeneous groups made up of diverse subcultures with differing values and aspirations. The understanding of an alien culture or subculture poses great difficulties. In our understanding of the world around us, we all start from our own cultural framework modified by a personal frame of refer-
ence. Such an analytical framework so deeply embedded in culture, while necessary for structuring thought can, in the process, limit understanding. Culture can be viewed as a filter, acting between the outside environment and the receiver. Understanding others requires, primarily, an understanding of the limitations of one's own cultural and personal frame of reference.[7] The modest approach to design advocated here is somewhat at variance with the egocentric attitudes inculcated in the great designer. I suggest that a change in attitude on the part of the design professions is essential for understanding a community's needs and aspirations and for working with people.

Culture is never entirely static, it is in a constant state of change. The world is getting smaller and there is increasing contact between peoples. As a result, cultures are changing. What is more, they appear to be changing at an increasing rate. Urban designers are forward looking; we plan and design, not only for the here and now, but also for the future. A backward looking or even static view is, therefore, a highly mischievous occupation. It is the dynamic of cultural change that must be the urban designer's primary concern. As anthropologists would say, it is the process of acculturation - the way in which new ideas and mores are grafted onto existing cultures - that should be the prime concern of those engaged in designing for the future.[8] It is the agents of change, those actors or processes that drive the engines of change, which have to be discerned and harnessed. The situation is further complicated when the architect, urban designer or planner realizes that he or she is an important agent of change. The designer even when working with people is not a neutered, objective observer, but a significant actor in the process of culture change.

An important aspect of the designer's skill is the development of a menu of techniques for incorporation into the design process. These techniques range from anthropological studies establishing essential cultural data, user studies, and planning surveys, through informative techniques, the exhibition and

1. Techniques of Participation
1. Community Administration
2. Self-Build
3. Community Planning & Design
4. Political Manifesto
5. Public Meeting
6. Public Enquiries
7. Planning Appeals
8. The Exhibition
9. Press Release
10. Planning Survey
11. User Study
12. Anthropological Study

Figure 1.1 Techniques of participation

2. Levels of Participation	
1. Citizen Control	Degrees of Citizen Power
2. Delegated Power	
3. Partnership	
4. Placation	Degrees of Tokenism
5. Consultation	
6. Informing	
7. Therapy	Non-participation
8. Manipulation	

Figure 1.2 Levels of participation

press notices, to administrative procedures such as public enquiries and planning appeals. People's views can also be elicited at public meetings or sought through the electoral process by including planning matters in political manifestos. Finally, there is the group of more active forms of participation such as community design exercises, self-build operations and community administration and control. The menu of techniques, Figure 1.1, has limited utility without the ability to predict the type of technique most useful in any given situation or, conversely, the changes in context necessary to facilitate the use of a technique.

Participation can have different meanings for different people. Fortunately for those working in this field Sherry Arnstein has described the shades of meaning attached to this term.[9] Her ladder of participation, Figure 1.2, though now 30 years old, is still a good tool for a preliminary analysis of participation. Her typology ranges from illusory forms of participation, which she terms manipulation and therapy, through degrees of tokenism such as informing, consulting and placating. The top rungs of the hierarchy are partnership, delegated power and citizen control, all of which infer a degree of citizen power, that is, they require some redistribution of power if they are to be realized.

The Arnstein typology makes it easy to understand the communication gap between the 'planned' on the one hand, the planner, urban designer and politician, on the other. The former, having had his or her expectation of participation raised, often thinks in terms of having the final word in the decision-making process while, to the professional and politician it usually means publicity and consultation. A phrase such as 'more participation' can mean to the public a more intensive form of participation, that is, moving up the ladder, while to the professional and politician it may mean greater consultation in the form of more publicity.

From Figures 1.1 and 1.2 it can be seen that in Arnstein's terms, the more intense forms of participation, that is participation of a type close to the top of the ladder, requires techniques which actively involve the individual in plan making, design, constructional work, and responsibility for estate administration including participation in any economic gains from development. The mid-range levels of participation, the more usual conditions found in western democracies, suggest the use of bureaucratic techniques usually advocated and organized by the professionals in any administration. Towards the lower end of the scale, which Arnstein defines as non-participation, are the more objective and scientific methods of information gathering which can inform the planning and design process but, at best, result only in a more sympathetic and human form of administration, still in all its essential features paternalistic.

The higher levels of participation require a redistribution of power, that is, power has to be removed from some sectors of society and placed in the hands of others. The higher one moves in Arnstein's ladder the greater is the degree in the shift in power. For example, the professional planner, urban designer and architect in a participatory situation lose much of their ability to decide the outcome of the development process. This line of argument brings the planning, design and development process directly into the political arena.[10]

American scholars in their writings have made it abundantly clear that planning decisions by their very nature are political and cannot be considered simply technical. For example, Paul Davidoff states:

'The essence of politics is who gets what. Or call it distributive justice. The public planning process as a part of the political system is inextricably related to the distributional question facing communities in which planners work.'[11] This point has also been made by writers such as David Eversley in Britain, who says:

But it must be made clear that since the planner, as defined here, is the person who determines where people shall build, and where they shall not build, where there shall be new or expanded towns, or growth areas, and where national parks or Areas of Outstanding Natural Beauty shall prevent building, where power stations shall be sited and canals reopened, motorways built and railways shut down, he is in fact responsible for the allocation of this very large part of the national product and the benefits it confers.[12]

It can be argued that urban design is akin to planning in many respects and, since it deals with large parts of towns and cities, it too is concerned with distribution of resources and wealth. It would be advisable, for the urban designer wishing to remain within the safety of a technical design process, not to dabble with participation that confronts the designer directly with the issue of the distribution of power and wealth and, hence, takes the subject right to the centre of politics.

Figure 1.3 shows in simplistic form a scale of political structures, ranging from anarchy through various forms of democracies to the varieties of dictatorship which exist in the world. From the viewpoint of participation in development it is convenient to concentrate on the middle portion of the range. A state of anarchy, though an ideal among some thinkers and activists, in its more extreme forms does not last long before being replaced by a more disciplined regime. Totalitarian government, by definition, does not permit general and widespread participation.

Democracy according to Carole Pateman has three main definitions.[13] These are: first, representative or modern democracy; second, classical democracy associated with the writings of the eighteenth-century political philosophers and, finally, participatory democracy based upon a reinterpretation of the writings of Jean Jacques Rousseau to take regard of an industrialized society.

The theoretical basis of representative democracy has been developed by Joseph Schumpeter and others. Schumpeter states that: 'The democratic method is that institutional arrangement for arriving at political decisions in which individuals acquire the power to decide by means of a competitive struggle for the people's vote.'[14] Competition for votes is similar to the operation of the economic market. Voters choose between the policies offered by competing political entrepreneurs. Political parties are analogous to trade associations in the economic sphere and regulate competition. 'Participation' for the majority in a representative democracy is, therefore, only participation in the choice of decision makers.

Representative democracy does not require high levels of participation and interest in political affairs except from a small minority. Pateman points out that 'the apathy and disinterest of the majority play a valuable role in maintaining the stability of the system.'[15] Planners and urban designers should be aware of the shortcomings of this rather cynical view of the political process whereby plans are legitimized and development is implemented. Dealing with problems such as where and how people live, work and educate their children, should lead us to question the necessity and desirability of decisions in these fields being handed over to 'representatives of the people'. To remove people's right to make these decisions removes also their self respect and lessens their dignity as human beings.

For the followers of Rousseau and participatory democracy, 'participation' is an essential element of the decision-making process and is also a method of protecting private interest. This theory is also concerned with the psychological effect of social and political institutions. The central function of Rousseau's theory is educative and his chief concern is that the political system should develop responsible individuals. In effect, he is saying that as one can only learn to swim by swimming so too one can only learn to be democratic by being involved in democratic processes. These democratic processes, according to Rousseau and his twentieth-century followers, should permeate all aspects of society, and that, of course, includes planning and developmental decisions.

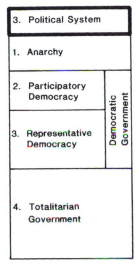

Figure 1.3 Political system

4. Spatial Unit
1. Room
2. Home
3. Street
4. Neighbourhood
5. District Quarter
6. Town
7. City
8. Region
9. Nation

Figure 1.4 Spatial unit

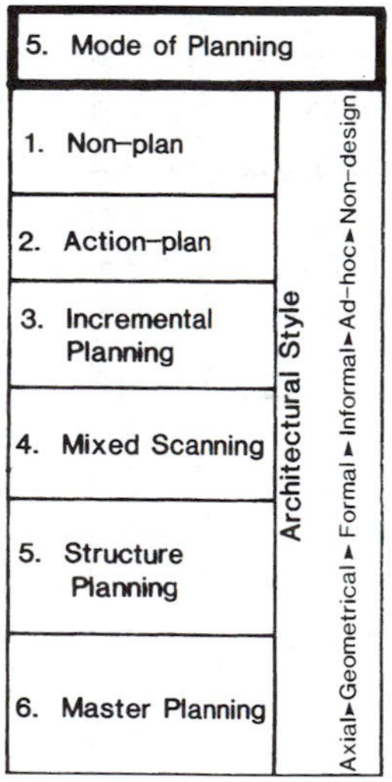

5. Mode of Planning	
1. Non–plan	
2. Action–plan	
3. Incremental Planning	Architectural Style
4. Mixed Scanning	
5. Structure Planning	Axial ► Geometrical ► Formal ► Informal ► Ad–hoc ► Non–design
6. Master Planning	

Figure 1.5 Mode of planning

Comparing Arnstein's ladder of participation, Figure 1.2, with governmental types, Figure 1.3, one would expect higher intensities of participation to be found in situations of near anarchy where group decision making is an amalgam of the total of individual decisions. It could also be predicted that the normal form of participation in a representative democracy would be tokenism to use Arnstein's terminology. Referring to Figure 1.1 the most usual techniques used in such politics tend to lie in the mid-range, that is, those administrative procedures defined and devised by the bureaucracy. It would appear that the use of techniques which represent the more intensive styles of participation requires a highly politicized and active population together with a high degree of tolerance for forms of local democracy by the central government.

Figure 1.3 is extremely simplistic; it takes no account of the administrative system or even relationships between central and local governments within any representative democracy which are both of great importance. Even within the same country, relationships may differ between central and local government. In Britain, for example, the 1980s saw a movement of power from the periphery to the centre. In the late 1990s, however, there seems a movement towards devolution of power to Scotland, Wales, Northern Ireland and the English Regions.

For full participation it could be postulated that it is necessary to have devolution of power to local communities; decision making in fields such as housing and local community services being placed in the hands of the residents of such communities. Such decentralization of power presupposes an active and highiy politicized population.

Figure 1.4 depicts a hierarchy of spatial units adapted from Constantinos Doxiadis: it is a simplified version of his Ekistic scale.[16] Moving down the scale involves greater numbers of users with an interest in the outcome of any decisions affecting the form of the element. Comparing Figure 1.4 with Figures 1.1 and 1.2 it would appear that techniques associated with citizen control, planning and

decision making at the larger spatial scales are unrealistic despite any other favourable conditions which might prevail in the political or administrative climate. When coordination of services, infrastructure and the economy at higher spatial levels is advisable it may be necessary to forgo full citizen participation and to delegate power to elected representatives. At town scale and above, those bureaucratic procedures such as public meetings, enquiries and appeals, together with the enlightened use of the political manifesto, may be the best that can be achieved regardless of the political system involved. Increasing the level and intensity of participation in any large spatial unit requires its subdivision into small planning and design units the size of the neighbourhood and street block; each such unit having appropriate responsibilities delegated.

Figure 1.5 illustrates a range of planning styles. The scale ranges from the less formal types of planning, starting with the non-plan where economic forces determine settlement form through various types of ad hoc decisions, where short-term projects are pragmatically woven into the existing situation, to the more rigid planning methods culminating in the master plan, a blueprint for a desired future end state. A similar range could be devised for architectural style. Such a scale would range from the worst forms of entirely cost-oriented speculative housing, through incremental, additive and irregular design concepts and eventually to geometrically dominated design and highly formal axial compositions. Comparing these notions of planning and design with previous figures it can be seen that high levels of citizen participation are more compatible with less formal architectural and planning styles. In non-planning situations, however, the level of an individual's ability to participate is dependent upon his ability to pay. The physical result ranges from the large detached house in a wealthy European suburb to the temporary tin hut on the periphery of Nairobi. At the other extreme the blueprint for long-term city development and the rigid axial composition, almost by definition, are not conducive to high levels of citizen participation.

Figure 1.6 is a composite of the scales so far discussed. It indicates some of the ways in which the participation process can be analysed. The diagram can be imagined as a type of complicated slide rule where each scale can be moved up or down in relation to its neighbours. It is then possible to outline or describe the sort of conditions likely to operate in any situation.[17] There may,

however, be factors not represented on the scale which have to be taken into consideration.

Where high levels of participation are thought desirable then the planner/designer must think in terms of community administration, self-build together with community planning and design. This situation would also presume high levels of participatory democracy together with some form of decentralization of power and decision making. Such

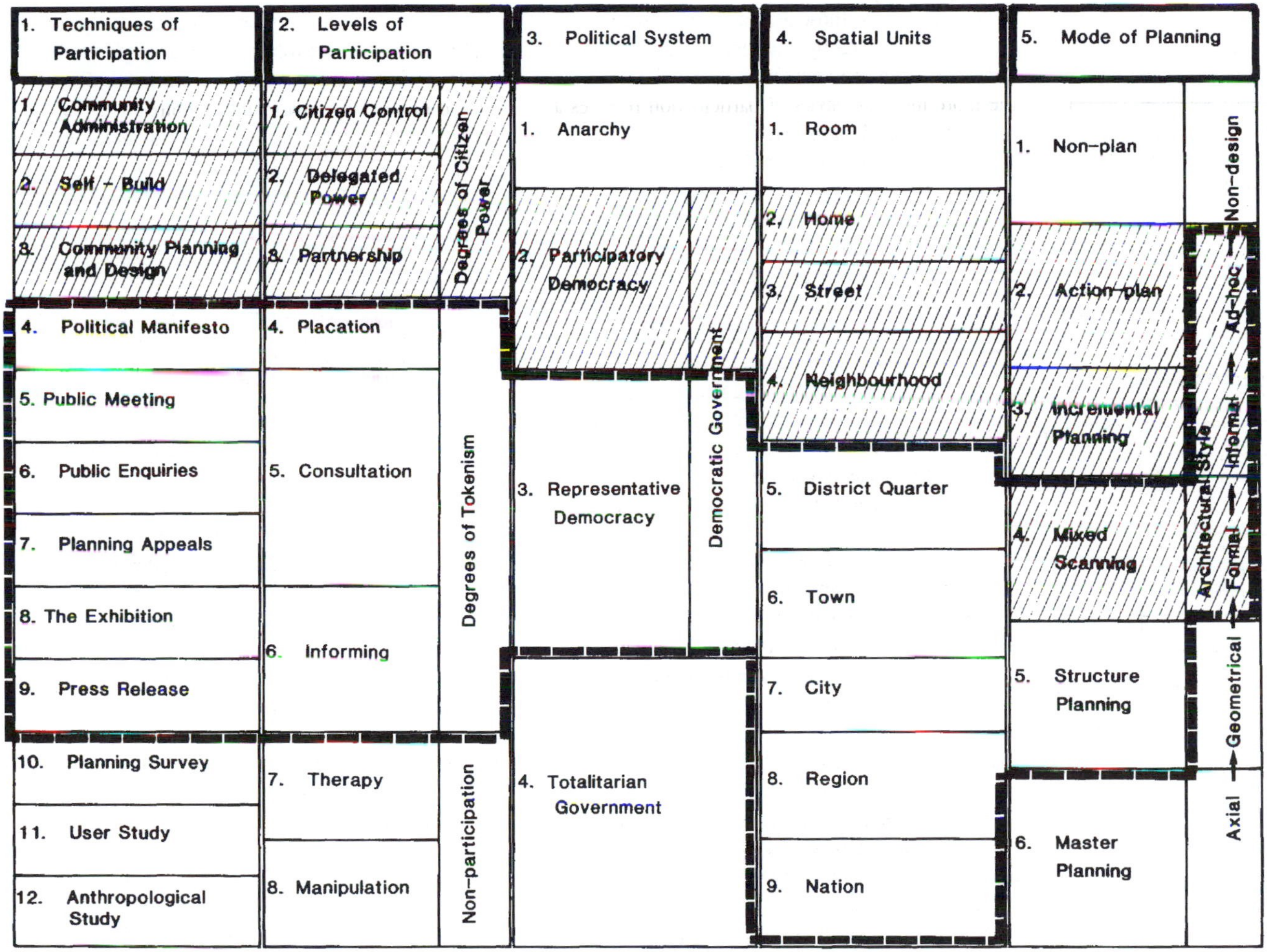

Figure 1.6 Analytical scale of participation

1. Techniques of Participation	2. Levels of Participation		3. Political System		4. Spatial Units	5. Mode of Planning	
1. Community Administration	1. Citizen Control	Degree of Citizen Power	1. Anarchy		1. Room	1. Non-plan	Non-design
2. Self - Build	2. Delegated Power				2. Home		
3. Community Planning and Design	3. Partnership		2. Participatory Democracy	Democratic Government	3. Street	2. Action-plan	Ad-hoc
4. Political Manifesto	4. Placation				4. Neighbourhood	3. Incremental Planning	Informal
5. Public Meeting		Degrees of Tokenism					Architectural Style
6. Public Enquiries	5. Consultation		3. Representative Democracy		5. District Quarter	4. Mixed Scanning	Formal
7. Planning Appeals					6. Town		
8. The Exhibition	6. Informing					5. Structure Planning	Geometrical
9. Press Release					7. City		
10. Planning Survey	7. Therapy	Non-participation	4. Totalitarian Government		8. Region	6. Master Planning	Axial
11. User Study					9. Nation		
12. Anthropological Study	8. Manipulation						

conditions would apply only to the planning of the home, the street and the neighbourhood. The room, it is assumed, is a purely personal space and requires little or no community action, while the district or quarter may be too large for effective community action. The sort of planning most suitable for such conditions would be incremental and ad hoc, probably resulting in less formal architectural solutions (see shaded section of Figure 1.6).

Conversely, the techniques of participation most suited to the planning of towns, cities, regions and for national planning would seem to be the political manifesto, public meetings, public enquiries, planning appeals, the planning exhibition and media releases. Arnstein would define this participation as tokenism but it would require some form of democratic structure. At these scales, mixed scanning or structure planning would be most appropriate. Presumably the architectural style would be determined by the amount of genuine citizen control exerted at local levels (see area in Figure 1.6 outlined with heavy dotted line).

THE URBAN DESIGN PROCESS

Urban development is the result of a process. It is, therefore, a little simplistic to discuss participation in planning or design unless one is specific about the type of participation and the techniques used at each stage in the process.

Planning method was for some time based upon Sir Patrick Geddes' dictum: 'Survey. Analysis. Plan.' However, in making a planning survey it is necessary to know what sort of information is required and for what purpose it is to be analysed. Others have since amplified Geddes' method inserting

additional intermediate steps. One such amplification is shown in Figure 1.7. Descriptions of the planning method indicate that the process is not a simple linear progression where each phase is completed before proceeding to the next step. The planning process is deemed to be cyclical having intermediate loops. For example, after an evaluation of alternative plans it may be necessary to redefine goals, or to collect additional data, or to analyse the data in a different way.

Design methods advocated by architects are similar in nature to those prepared by planners. The RIBA practice and management handbook divides the design process into four phases:[18]

Phase 1 *Assimilation:* The accumulation of general information and information specially related to the problem.
Phase 2 *General study:* The investigation of the nature of the problem: the investigation of possible solutions.
Phase 3 *Development:* The development of one or more solutions.
Phase 4 *Communication:* The communication of chosen solution/s to the client.

Thomas Markus and Thomas Mayer take the description of design method a little further.[19] They argue that the designer goes through a decision sequence – analysis, synthesis, appraisal and decision at increasingly more detailed levels in the design process (see Figure 1.8). During the analytical stage, goals and objectives are classified and patterns in information are sought. Synthesis is the stage where ideas are generated. It is followed by a critical evaluation of the alternative solutions against objectives, costs and other constraints. Decisions are made depending upon the findings of the evaluation,

Figure 1.7 Planning method

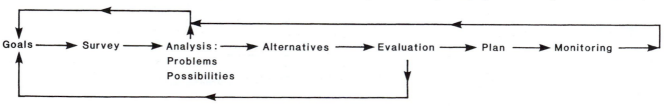

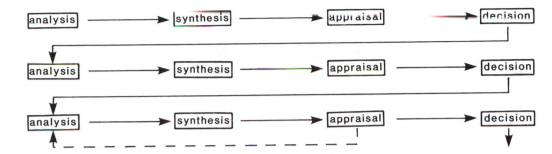

SITE PLANNING

analysis → synthesis → appraisal → decision

INTERNAL PLANNING

analysis → synthesis → appraisal → decision

DETAIL PLANNING

analysis → synthesis → appraisal → decision

though, as with any other design method, return loops between stages are important.

This way of looking at the design process for an individual building can be extended to include urban design, town planning and regional planning (see Figure 1.9). In this case decisions at the higher level should inform the design process at the next, lower order of design, for example, from regional to town planning. It makes most sense when each component of the environment fits consistently within the framework of a higher order plan, for example, a building designed to fit within an urban design scheme which is determined by an urban structure plan based upon proposals for the region. It is, however, not simply a one-way process from large to small scale. It could, quite correctly, be

argued that the design of each individual building should have some effect upon the design of the larger urban grouping and that this three-dimensional design of large city areas should inform the higher level of city planning. Hence in Figure 1.9 there are return loops between the distinct facets of the development process for city planning.

In the planning and design methodologies so far discussed there has been no mention of theory. Facts without theory are meaningless pieces of information. They take on meaning when related to each other by some theoretical construct. Solutions to urban design problems, alternative ways of organizing space in a city, ideas about the relationship of function and urban structure have their origins in theory. In order to insert theory into the design

Figure 1.8 Architectural method

Figure 1.9 Integrated design process

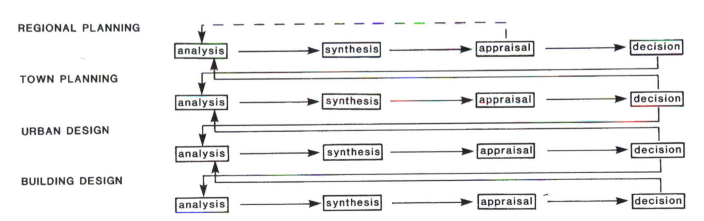

REGIONAL PLANNING

analysis → synthesis → appraisal → decision

TOWN PLANNING

analysis → synthesis → appraisal → decision

URBAN DESIGN

analysis → synthesis → appraisal → decision

BUILDING DESIGN

analysis → synthesis → appraisal → decision

Figure 1.10 Scientific
process: information sets

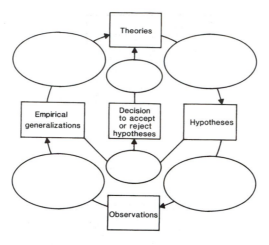

acceptance or rejection of hypotheses (see Figure
1.10). The six methods or techniques of transformation are shown in Figure 1.11. Theory, the most
general type of information, is transformed into
hypotheses through the method of logical deduction. The hypotheses are transformed into observations by interpretation into observables,
instrumentation, scaling and sampling. The observations are transformed into empirical generalizations
through the process of measurement, sample
summarization and parameter estimation. The
hypotheses can then be tested for conformity with
the generalizations. From the test is derived the final
information set, the decisions about the validity of
the hypotheses. The last action in the process is the
confirmation, modification or rejection of the theory
through the processes of logical inference or
concept formation, proposition formation and
proposition arrangement.

process a direct analogy can be made with scientific
method. According to Walter Wallace: 'The scientific
process may be described as involving five principal
information components whose transformations into
one another are controlled by six principal sets of
methods...'[20] The five sets of information are: the
body of theory, hypotheses, sets of unique observations from the surrounding environment, empirical
generalizations derived from the unique observations
and finally the body of decisions relating to the

While this outline of scientific method appears
clear, precise and systematic, it is open to endless
variation. Some elements of the process are more
important for some research projects, some scientists practise a high degree of rigour while others
behave quite intuitively and informally.

However, there appear to be two main
constituents of science, theory construction and
empirical research. The left-hand side of Figure 1.12
represents inductive construction of theory from an
understanding of observations, while the right half
represents the deductive application of theory to
observations. The top half of the diagram represents
the process of theorizing using inductive and deductive logic while the bottom half illustrates the
process of carrying out a piece of empirical
research.[21]

Figure 1.11 Scientific
process: techniques of
transformation

Figure 1.13 is a diagrammatic representation of
design method incorporating theory and structured
according to the analysis of scientific thinking by
Wallace.[22] Entry into the design circle is possible at
three points, design theories, ideas, or directly into
the investigation stage. It is theoretically possible to
move directly from problem definition to ideas for

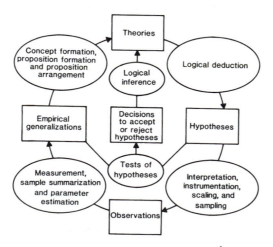

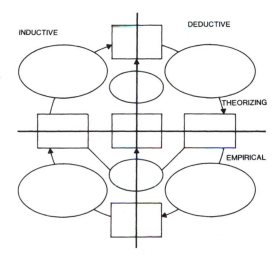

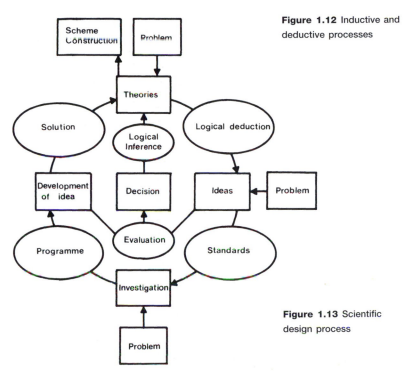

Figure 1.12 Inductive and deductive processes

Figure 1.13 Scientific design process

its solution or to the search for data that will assist with finding the solution. Nevertheless, both of these procedures require some preliminary notions about theory however ill formed or inexplicit they may be; it is only through theory that ideas and data can be related to form a pattern. The more usual, the more classic procedure, is to move from problem definition to a theoretical understanding of the problem then to proceed through the steps in a clockwise direction.

At the core of scientific method is asking the right question or questions. We are all aware of the home truth that asking a silly question will result in a silly answer. The same is true of design. Posing the problem is the art of design. There is a school of thought, now somewhat out of fashion, which infers that the application of method results in good design. The 'method school', in its more extreme forms would have us believe that a study of the problem, followed by logical analysis of all possible solutions will result in the best solution being chosen to solve the problem. In complex design situations it is not always possible to define the problem, nor to collect all the facts, nor to generate all possible solutions. This is to misunderstand the

design process where the problem is explored through the examination of solutions. An application of design method may result in the redefinition or clarification of the problem initiating a whole new round of investigation.

The design process is not linear but dialectical, taking the form of an argument between problem and solution. As Bryan Lawson says: 'It is clear from our analysis of the nature of design problems that the designer must inevitably expend considerable energy in identifying problems confronting him. It is central to modern thinking that problems and solutions are seen as emerging together rather than one following logically upon the other.'[23] Following this view of design the nature of the problem becomes clearer as the process develops. Lawson also goes on to say that: Since neither finding problems nor producing solutions can be seen as predominantly logical activities we must expect the design process to demand the highest levels of creative thinking.'[24] Design, urban design included, does involve creative thinking, it would, however, be misleading to assume that this does not apply equally in the field of scientific investigation. It would also be misleading to think that design solutions cannot be generated through logical deduction from theory or inductively from the data or evidence, or indeed, that problem exploration is not the outcome of standard design procedures. It is, however, reasonable to suggest that the designer explores the nature of the problem through the examination of solutions or partial solutions.

While theory is an important source for the development of urban design ideas, it is not the only one. Ideas can be generated in other ways which fall outside the scope of inductive or deductive reasoning. Artists and designers often resort to the use of analogies in their work. Analogy is one of the most useful tools of the creative artist. Analogies offer a convenient technique for removing a thought block, a way of reviving design method instead of waiting patiently for inspiration to find new ways of looking at a situation. De Bono suggests that: 'The main usefulness of analogies is as vehicles for functions, processes and relationships which can then be transferred to the problem under consideration.'[25]

Ideas or concepts used in urban design can be generated by reference to general theory through a process of deduction, or from the facts by a process of inductive logic. Ideas, however, may be generated by a process of lateral thinking; these ideas can be evaluated later using techniques of logic. This all sounds very far from the life of the man in the street. How then can the community be involved in the process? At what point, therefore, do people take part in the design and development process?

The notions of the great architect and the 'big idea' that sets architectural fashion in new directions run deep in our profession. The planner is also loath to relinquish to the layman control over the creative part of plan making, the search for solution. Ideas are thought to be the province of the professions. Starting the design process from a theoretical foundation and from abstract notions does give to the professional, with his or her long period of education and experience, great advantages over the layperson. If, however, a positive form of participation is desired, these notions that the professions know best must be abandoned.

The layperson, too, has knowledge and experience. He or she is the expert on his or her family, its needs and aspirations. This is a highly specialized knowledge about the sort of housing, educational, health care and recreational facilities the family needs and can afford; it is his or her daily preoccupation. The layperson is well able to extend this personal knowledge and to form accurate ideas about his neighbours' needs also. The layperson then is the expert on the problems of the neighbourhood in which he or she lives. The professional when carrying out surveys into user requirements estimates in crude terms this knowledge, whereas the layperson's knowledge in this field is immediate and first hand. The ordinary citizen also has ideas about the ways in which these problems can be solved and how to capitalize on any possibilities that exist. For corroboration of this statement one has only to examine the self-help housing built in Third World cities or return to the roots of tradition when settlements were developed without the aid of the professional.[26]

Making the most of this wealth of experience requires starting the design process; either by investigating the problem, permitting the community to outline its problems, or by their posing solutions to problems already intimately known to them, then examining these solutions in the light of an evaluation. Experiments in Belfast, Nottingham and Newark confirmed that residents are perfectly capable of organizing their own survey and are also able to generate planning and architectural solutions.[27]

The professional's role, in citizen-participant dominated design, is not defunct. On the contrary, it becomes more delicate and subtle requiring patience and, above all, skills in listening. It also requires of the designer the humility to be able to offer advice only when requested.[28] The professional's advice on technical matters is supreme, experience shows that it is well respected by the layperson. The professional's role, however, is not so narrowly drawn; it is also one of education. The layperson can offer solutions only from within his or her own experience. The professional can open up a new world of experience to the client group through knowledge of many other similar situations. Sharing this knowledge with the client has always been part of the professional's role; it remains so in the process of participation.

The layperson's knowledge and experience of planning and design matters beyond the immediate neighbourhood decreases as does his or her interest. These wider issues, and their implications for the locality, have to be interpreted and made clear to the community by the professional. If, however, high levels of participation are thought desirable then the planning and design process should give emphasis to a bottom-up order rather than working from the region or city down to the neighbourhood and the street. The higher levels of planning then become an amalgam of small-scale plans co-ordinated to ensure that higher level services are not inhibited.

Culturally appropriate development may or may not result from deep, introspective, self-discovery by the designer or from a sensitive approach to the client group and its communal needs. Clearly, however, people associate more closely with an environment that they can make their own through their own actions. To facilitate the active participation of communities with the planning and development of the environment requires a whole range of approaches and a full menu of techniques. These approaches are likely to vary with the type of political and administrative system, the spatial unit being designed, the current mode of planning and the stage in the design process. Citizen participation is maximized when there is a democratic form of government with high participatory levels in many fields of administration, where much of the decision making is decentralized and where the form of planning is incremental in style. Even in such an ideal situation the greatest levels of participation could be expected to occur at the small scale of the group of families in the street, or the small community occupying a small neighbourhood. It is in such residential areas where the general public's knowledge and experience is paramount.

NOTES

1. HRH, The Prince of Wales. *A Vision of Britain*, Doubleday, London, 1989, p.80

2. Ibid, p.96

3. Rapoport, A. *House Form and Culture*, Prentice-Hall, Englewood Cliffs, New Jersey, 1969

4. Shute, John. *The First and Chief Grounds of Architecture*, published by John Shute, printed by Thomas Marshe, London, 1563, Book IV, p.45

5. Ibid, Book I, p.14

6. *Architect's Journal*, 6 June 1984, p.30

7. See for example the work of Rapoport, A. *Human Aspects of Urban Form: Towards a Man Environment Approach to Urban Form and Design*, Pergamon Press, New York, 1977

8. Moughtin, J.C. and Shalaby, T. 'Housing design in Muslim cities: towards a new approach'. In *Low Cost Housing for Developing Countries*, Vol II, Central Building Research Institute, New Delhi, 1984, pp.831-851

9. Arnstein, Sherry R. A ladder of citizen participation. In *Journal of the American Institute of Planners*, Vol 35, No 4, July 1969, pp.216-224

10. Moughtin, J.C. *Planning for People*, Queen's University, Belfast, 1972

11. Davidoff, Paul. Working towards redistributive justice. In *Journal of the American Institute of Planners*, Vol 41, No 5, September 1975, pp.317-318

12 Eversley, David. *The Planner in Society*, Faber & Faber, London, 1973

13 Pateman, Carole. *Participation and Democratic Theory*, Cambridge University Press, Cambridge, 1970

14 Schumpeter, J.A. *Capitalism, Socialism and Democracy*, Allen and Unwin, London, 1943

15 Pateman, C. Op cit, p.7

16 Doxiadis, C.A. *Ekistics: An Introduction to the Science of Human Settlements*, Hutchinson, London, 1968

17 Moughtin, J.C. Public participation and the implementation of development. In *Town and Country Summer School Report*, London, Royal Town Planning Institute, 1978, pp.81-84

18 RIBA, *Architectural Practice and Management Handbook*, RIBA Publications, London, 1965

19 Markus, T.A. The role of budding performance measurement and appraisal in design method. In *Design Methods in Architecture* (eds. G. Broadbent and A. Ward), Lund Humphries, London, 1969

    Mayer, T.W. Appraisal in the building design process. In *Emerging Methods in Environmental Design and Planning* (ed. G.T. Moore), MIT Press, Cambridge, Mass., 1970

20 Wallace, Walter. An overview of elements in the scientific process. In *Social Research: Principles and Procedures* (eds. John Bynner and Keith M. Stribley), Longman, Harlow, 1978, pp.4-10

21 Ibid (Figures 1.10, 1.11 and 1.12 are taken from Wallace)

22 Ibid

23 Lawson, Bryan. *How Designers Think*, Architectural Press, London, 1980

24 Ibid

25 De Bono, Edward, *Lateral Thinking*, Penguin, Harmondsworth, 1977

26 Moughtin, J.C. *Hausa Architecture*, Ethnographica, London, 1985

27 Moughtin, J.C. Markets areas redevelopment. In *Built Environment*, February 1974, pp.71-74

    Moughtin, J.C. and Simpson A. Do it yourself planning in Raleigh Street. In *New Society*, 19 October 1978, pp.136-137

28 Gibson, Tony, *People Power*, Penguin, Harmondsworth, 1979

BASIC DESIGN CONCEPTS

2

INTRODUCTION

A number of concepts have been used to analyse architectural compositions in order to gain an understanding of the qualities which determine good or beautiful form. The ways in which these basic design concepts are used, and their relative importance. differ from architect to architect. Vitruvius, the fountainhead of architectural theory, thought that '. . . architecture depends on Order, Arrangement, Eurhythmy, Symmetry, Propriety and Economy . . .'[1] Since Vitruvius wrote those words in the first century AD the language of compositional analysis has changed mainly in the number and range of criteria used for quality description. Writings on aesthetics and architectural criticism are often left confused by the number and vagueness of the terms used. Zevi lists the following attributes of architecture that are frequently used with little clear specification of their precise meaning, 'truth, movement, force, vitality, sense of outline, harmony, grace, breadth, scale, balance, proportion, light and shade, eurhythmics, solids and voids, symmetry, rhythm, mass volume, emphasis, character, contrast, personality, analogy'.[2] Some of the more important basic design concepts will be discussed here in

order to determine their utility for the study of urban design.

ORDER

Order, the first quality on the Vitruvian list appears to have universal acceptance. Few designers, if any, appear intent on the creation of disorder; deliberate chaos, it seems, is not a legitimate goal of architecture. Definitions of order, however, differ. Vitruvius defines order as giving '. . . due measure to the members of a work considered separately, and symmetrical agreement to the proportions of the whole. It is an adjustment according to quantity. By this I mean the selection of modules from the members of the work itself and starting from these individual parts of members, constructing the whole work to correspond.'[3]

Writers of the Renaissance follow Vitruvius in their definition of order, for example, Alberti writes: '. . . for everything must be reduced to exact measure, so that all the parts may correspond with one another, the right with the left, the lower parts with the upper, with nothing interfering that may blemish either the order or the materials, but everything squared to exact angles and similar lines'.[4] Later, Andrea Palladio, the sixteenth-century architect and one of the great exponents of orderly design uses almost the same terms as Alberti in his definition of beauty as resulting from '. . . the form and correspondence of the whole, with respect to the several parts with each other, and of these again to the whole; that the structure may appear an entire and complete body, wherein each member agrees with the other, and all are necessary to compose what you intend to form'.[5]

A commonly held view among architectural theorists maintains that order in architecture is part of the much grander scheme of nature. The argument goes something like this; the evidence accumulated by science conforms with the idea of a rational world, or perhaps more importantly, the world and the cosmos we occupy is perceived by human beings as rational. The current view is the belief in an ordered universe; it confirms man's idea of rationality and requires rational behaviour for effective living. Effective architecture like any other human behaviour conforms to the order of the universe; the model for architecture is the design of the universe.[6]

For those who believe that the universe has a designer in God, then such theorists can call upon this higher authority to confirm their position. Architecture is of God or at one with nature when it conforms to harmony – disorder and unrest are its antithesis. Alberti called upon the ancient world for his authority: 'The Ancients . . . did in their Works propose to themselves chiefly the imitation of Nature, as the greatest Artist at all Manner of Compositions; and for this Purpose they Laboured, . . . to discover the Laws upon which she herself acted in the Production of her Works, in order to transfer them to the Business of Architecture.'[7] This theme was taken up later by Palladio who declared '. . . that architecture, as well as all other arts, being an imitatrix of nature, can suffer nothing that either alienates or deviates from that which is agreeable to nature, . . .'[8]

Writers of the last century, steeped in this philosophy inherited from Vitruvius and his Renaissance followers, repeated its phrases as support for an architectural style quite different from one based on the Classical language of the Renaissance.[9] Eliel Saarinen, for example, speaks of fundamental principles: 'When we speak of fundamental principles we do not mean "man made ones", but those that are from the beginning of all time.'[10] He also writes of '. . . the universal principle of architecture in all creation' and: 'Art of nature and art of man thus are closely inter-related.'[11] Walter Gropius, a leader of the much criticized Modern Movement in twentieth-century architecture, wrote: 'For unless we choose to regard the satisfaction of those conditions which alone animate and so humanise a room - spatial harmony, repose, proportion - as an ideal of some higher order, architecture cannot be limited to the fufilment of its structural function.'[12] Order in architectural design is taken as a fundamental quality and is seen by most theorists as related to a larger order, that of nature.

Many crimes against humanity are committed in the name of religion, so too, many architectural transgressions are created in the name of order. Prince Charles has lighted on several popular examples in his attacks on some modern architecture in Britain. 'Look at the Bull Ring. It has no charm, no human scale, no human character except arrogance. It is a planned accident,' said the Prince of the Birmingham development. Though striking a chord with the common sense of the layman, these remarks have brought no act of contrition from the profession.[13]

Prince Charles's views of the Bull Ring are reminiscent of Pugin's attacks over a century earlier on the vulgarity of Birmingham's products. He described them as 'those inexhaustible mines of bad taste'. And of the non-Christian architecture of the day he wrote in these terms: 'Neither relative scale, form, purpose, nor unity of style, is ever considered by those who design these abominations.'[14] Many such 'abominations' are now enthusiastically

Figure 2.1 Bijlmermeer

conserved. Nevertheless, while caution must be used in judging contemporary or recent buildings, it is difficult to conceive of anything less human or more out of scale than Bijlmermeer in Amsterdam (Figure 2.1). It was designed on the principles of Le Corbusier, an avid proponent of rationality and order in design, who said: 'An inevitable element of Architecture. The necessity for order. The regulating line is a guarantee against wilfulness. It brings satisfaction to the understanding.'[15]

A large section of the architectural profession has understandably turned its back on the immediate past. Says Charles Jencks: 'The Modern Movement proved simply too limited, provincial and impoverished - like *cuisine minceur*, very good every third day but hardly a full diet.'[16] Robert Venturi calls for the recognition of complexity in design, a calculated ambiguity of expression based upon the confusion of experiences - he does not abandon the concept of order but extends its meaning: 'A valid order accommodates the circumstantial contradictions of a complex reality. It accommodates as well as imposes. It thereby admits "control *and* spontane-

ity", "correctness *and* ease" - improvisation within the whole.'[17] Venturi criticizes orthodox modern architects for their almost religious zeal in proselytizing design dogma: 'In their role as reformers, they puritanically advocated the separation and exclusion of elements, rather than the inclusion of various requirements and their juxtapositions.'[18] Much of Post-Modern writing appears as intolerant of rival theories as the 'young lions', the avant-garde of the early Modern Movement. The statements of the Post-Modernists have the same high-flown, moral tone, the same claim to the justness of the cause: 'Total styles are the product of simple societies or totalitarian regimes. Eclecticism - not necessarily historical in form - is the vernacular of sophisticates, the language of freedom.'[19]

The freedom cited as a reason for the new eclecticism may prove illusory with sinister overtones of visual as well as political anarchy. For an understanding of Post-Modernism it must be seen in part as a product of North American culture from which it grew and from which it takes its nourishment. Its forms derive from the desire to show off the power of the international corporations, monopolies seeking a formal image, uncontrolled and perhaps uncontrollable by democratically elected governments - here is the unacceptable face of big business operating in the international jungle of money markets. This is the style of freedom, but only for those with untrammelled power. From this viewpoint some forms of Post-Modernism mean new façades for old concepts, dressing the skyscraper, or the vast supermarket in the garb of the tart - 'all fur coat and no knickers'.

Many would agree with Joseph Mordaunt Crook when he asserts that '. . . eclecticism in some form or other is surely here to stay'.[20] Basing designs on past experience is a legitimate and respectable procedure for the architect. Many of our finest buildings owe their existence to a model from the distant past, the Parthenon perhaps, with its timber detailing fossilized in stone being one of the great examples of this process. However, in the writing of some modern eclectics there appears to be a loss of clarity in the presentation of theoretical ideas, a weakening of rationality, the basis of reasonable behaviour. It seems that all is well with architecture if it is 'fun', 'cute', 'paradoxical', 'meaningful' and a whole host of other attributes which defy precise definition and are therefore impossible to make generally applicable. Such lack of rigour holds out little prospect for the development of the discipline of architecture. And yet, if architecture is to return to its roots, re-establish contact with the client group, the man and woman in the street, then it is patently obvious that eclecticism and building within the traditions of the general population is essential.

The discipline to give structure and order to the potential anarchy and chaos of eclecticism is urban design. Since most buildings are seen from the street, square or civic landscape then the public face of building is the prime consideration. This is the public realm and it is by establishing order here that buildings may take their place within a disciplined framework. The eighteenth-century

designs for the city of Bath are a wonderful example of the use of such a framework. John Wood the Elder and his son, also called John Wood, organized the land holdings and made the overall three-dimensional design including elevations. Individual plots were then sublet to other developers who were obliged to conform to the master plan but were free to design the interior to suit individual clients. The result is one of the masterpieces of European civic design (Figures 2.2–2.5). Giving primacy to the public domain or the context for buildings is the foundation of good city building and a very necessary discipline for the architect.

For too long architects have been designing buildings from the inside outwards, Le Corbusier's adage: 'The plan is the generator,'[21] is mischievous. The city context is the generator, that is, the streets and squares should condition the form of buildings. Werner Hegemann and Elbert Peets, writing as long ago as 1922, made this point succinctly: 'Only under rare circumstances will a fine piece of work be seen to advantage if thrown into a chaos, and dignity, charm and unassuming manners are preposterous when the neighbours are wantonly different or even obnoxious. The hope that good work will show off better for being different from its surroundings which are to act as a foil, is an illusion. The noise produced at county fairs by many orchestras simultaneously playing different tunes is a true symbol for the architectural appearance of the typical modern city street. The fact that one of the orchestras plays Beethoven will not resolve the chaos.'[22] Very little seems to have changed since then: we are still searching for the tools to bring order to our cities.

Hegemann and Peets place architecture in its proper perspective, they say: 'And the greatest of those ideals [of the Vitruvian tradition] though in these days of superficial individualism it is often forgotten, is that the fundamental unit of design in architecture is not the separate building but the whole city.'[23] Alberti, following the Vitruvian tradition, describes the city as 'no more than a great house'.[24] Gibberd stresses that the most essential

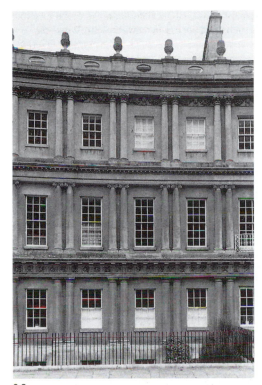

2.2

2.3

Figure 2.2 Details of The Circus, Bath

Figure 2.3 Queen's Square, Bath

2.4

Figure 2.4 View from The Circus towards The Crescent, Bath

2.5

Figure 2.5 The Crescent, Bath

characteristic of the design of this large house, the city is '. . . the combination of different objects into a new design: the designer must consider not just the design of the object itself, but its co-relation with other objects . . . Now whilst fine architecture is all important for a satisfactory urban scene, the architect has to realise that the forms of his buildings react on adjacent forms . . . he needs to discipline his urge to self-expression in the interests of the scene as a whole'.[25] Here Gibberd is writing of a larger order of the urban scene and not the order involved in the design of separate buildings. The neglect of this principle is a major failure of much modern architecture.

Urban designers like their counterparts, the architects, write about organic order, the order of nature as it applies in urban or civic design; they too see orderly design as being part of larger order as represented in the cosmos. For example, Christopher Alexander writes: 'Let us begin with the idea of organic order. Everyone is aware that most of the built environment today lacks a natural order, an order that presents itself very strongly in places that were built centuries ago. This natural or organic order emerges when there is perfect balance between the needs of the individual parts of the environment, and the needs of the whole.'[26] This statement about city design in the late twentieth century echoes very closely the views of the great theorists of the Renaissance.

The look of something, particularly a complex artefact like a city or part of a city, cannot be separated from its function. However well ordered and structured the city may be, it is only valued when, as Sir Henry Wotton maintains, it 'consists of commoditie, firmness and delight'.[27]

Jane Jacobs in her forthright critique of modern planning, *The Death and Life of Great American Cities*, makes a similar point and one apparently forgotten by the planners of the twentieth century: 'The look of things and the way they work are inextricably bound together, and in no place more so than cities . . . It is futile to plan a city's appear-

ance, or speculate on how to endow it with a pleasing appearance of order, without knowing what sort of innate, functioning order it has. To seek for the look for things as a primary purpose or as the main drama is apt to make nothing but trouble.'[28] This is undoubtedly true, but to seek only functional solutions is equally short-sighted. Despite the strictures of Jacobs, the analysis of city form has engaged the attention of designers for many centuries. The failure of some large-scale city projects may have resulted from neglect of this important principle linking beauty, utility and durability. As Palladio points out: 'That work cannot be called perfect, which should be useful and not durable, or durable and not useful, or having both these should be without beauty.'[29]

City order is related to the ways in which people perceive or read and understand the environment. This perceptual order is related to the legibility of the environment or the ease with which its parts can be recognized and organized into a coherent pattern. Kevin Lynch, for example, claims that: 'A vivid and integrated physical setting, capable of producing a sharp image, plays a social role as well. It can furnish the raw materials for the symbols and collective memories of group communication.'[30] If this is so, then the urban designer has the task of creating areas with a strong image, that is an environment which has the quality of 'imageability', defined by Lynch as, 'that quality in a physical setting which gives it a high probability of evoking a strong image in any given observer'.[31] The main elements, according to Lynch, for achieving imageability or perceptual order are paths, edges, districts, nodes and landmarks.

UNITY

The role of design is to bring some sort of order out of chaos. However, the results of the activities performed by architects or those involved in urban design are widely different. Even those products which could be described as orderly exhibit widely different qualities. The development of a theory of urban design requires the use of analytical concepts other than, or in addition to, order, with which to define either good architecture or good urban design.

In their search for tools with which to analyse good architecture, writers on theory turn to the other arts for useful analogy. Language has become an important source of ideas about architectural composition; for example: 'An understanding of functional design, the study of the building and its various parts, cannot however, be satisfactorily translated in an architectural creation unless it is accomplished through a comprehension of the Laws of Composition, through knowledge of the grammar of design.'[32] Like language, architecture has its vocabulary and its grammar, 'but while it has several distinct vocabularies all covering the same field of expression, it has only one grammar.'[33] Alexander extends this idea of an architectural pattern language to include a visual language for a town: 'Such a language is, in principle, complex enough and rich enough to be the language of a town.'[34]

In this search for general principles of abstract composition an attempt must be made to distinguish those qualities in good urban design compositions that can be analysed: 'It should be one of the analyst's functions to try to satisfy himself as to whether a building is a success or a failure as a piece of composition, and for that he must look above all for the application of sound first principles,'[35] wrote Howard Robertson.

The perfection of grammar, however well this technique is mastered, does not of itself produce a great work of literature. In much the same way that a great book has a theme or idea and grammar is merely the vehicle of expression for that idea, so too, the test of good architecture is the quality of the idea that the designer is trying to express. Architecture, then, is the concrete expression of an abstract idea. Here, to remind you, we are analysing only the third of Sir Henry Wotton's trilogy of archi-

tectural qualities, 'delight'.[36] Any idea in any medium must *a priori* be complete; it cannot be composed of scattered elements with no relation to each other. A haphazard collection of such scattered architectural or urban design elements represents a weak and incomplete idea. The full realization of an idea in architecture and urban design must express complete unity. Unity is the first and most important of the basic design concepts in the grammar of formal architectural composition.

The clearest expression of this concept of unity is found in Renaissance Italy. Alberti stated: 'I shall define beauty to be a harmony of all the parts, in whatever subject it appears, fitted together with such proportion and connection, that nothing could be added, diminished or altered, but for the worse.'[37] The Tempietto of S. Pietro in Montorio, Rome, by Donato Bramante and completed in 1502, epitomizes in built form this philosophy of Alberti (Figure 2.6).

Figure 2.6 The Tempietto of S. Pietro in Montorio by Bramante

The building is complete in itself; no part is unnecessary for the composition, every element is in its correct position and is of a predetermined or almost pre-ordained size: '. . . a building that appears as nearly pure volume as a Greek temple'.[38] In the ideal plans for Renaissance new towns this same thought process is evident. The first fully planned, ideal city of the Renaissance appears in the *Treatise on Architecture* by Filarete.[39] In Filarete's drawing of the city of Sforzinda he enclosed it in the Vitruvian circle but based the plan of the town on an eight-point star made of two intersecting quadrangles. Vincenzo Scamozzi was a sixteenth-century Italian

theorist able to put into practice his ideas for ideal city plans. The small fortified town of Palma Nova, started in 1593, is usually attributed to him.[40] Like so many of the other ideal town plans of the time, it is strongly influenced by the writings of Vitruvius, his follower Alberti and the quest for the perfect form (Figure 2.7).

'All serious architecture aims at an effect of unity.'[41] In this statement Roger Scruton probably expresses the view of most of those who have practised or who are still practising the art of architecture. As an example Bruno Zevi said: 'The aim of every artist is to express a single idea in his work.'[42] This, however, is not quite the universal proposition it appears at first sight. Venturi advocates '. . . messy vitality over obvious unity. I include the non sequitur and proclaim the duality'.[43] He favours elements which are 'hybrid' rather than 'pure', 'distorted' rather than 'straightforward', 'ambiguous' rather than 'articulated', 'boring' as well as 'interesting', and so on. Without offering a coherent theory he does come down eventually on the side of unity though his definition is strange: 'It must embody the difficult unity of inclusion rather than the easy unity of exclusion.'[44] As Arthur Trystan Edwards, however, points out there is no such animal as a style in architecture without exclusion; style implies that there are certain things that the designer, or the building exemplifying the style, is not permitted to do.[45] Breaking these prohibitions, ignoring the self-imposed discipline, leads to laxity and sloppy designs. Paradoxically, it is only by acceptance of discipline that energy can be channelled in creative directions. Without discipline there is only chaos. In criticisms of the style of architecture associated with the first half of the twentieth century care should be taken not to dismiss the wealth of tradition gained over 2,000 years or longer. The concept of unity is one of the pillars of our discipline.

Lynch and others who have tried to come to terms with the complexity of the concept of unity, particularly when it is applied in the field of urban design, have turned, in part, to the study of human

Figure 2.7 Palma Nova (1593)

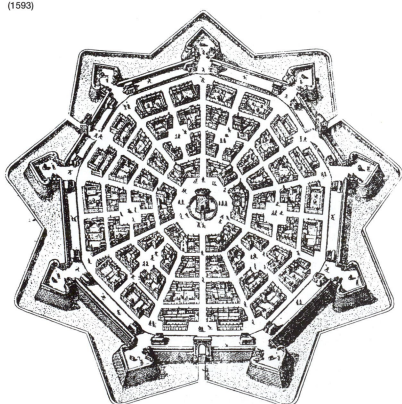

perception.[46] Lynch points out that '. . . observers will distort complex facts to simple forms'.[47] He uses concepts such as 'figure-background', in the sense that these are used by the Gestalt school of psychology, to explain his thesis.[48] Simplicity of visible form in the geometrical sense is particularly important in producing figure-background clarity or 'singularity' in urban design, he claims. Man, in order to orientate himself in the city, of necessity reduces the enviromnent to an understandable pattern of signs and clues. In the words of Norberg-Schulz: 'If we want to interpret these basic results of perception psychology in more general terms, we may say that the elementary organizational schemata consist of the establishment of *centres* or places (proximity), *directions* or paths (continuity) and *areas* or domains (enclosure).'[49] Composition in urban design is the art, firstly, of creating visual unity for each of these components of the city out of a diversity of elements. This is done to reinforce the normal tendency to see, understand and respond to vivid and coherent images. Secondly, it is to bring together these lesser unities into a city or town structure which itself is a visual and organizational unity. The goal of urban design has been given by Lynch as the development of a strong urban image This is the lacuna of much modern city planning.

PROPORTION

An examination of the concept of unity leads to a study of the characteristics of unified composition, that is, to the manner in which components may be arranged in a coherent manner. Using once again the analogy of language, the mere juxtaposition of words without composition into meaningful and connected statements is unthinkable; so, too, in architecture and urban design, the elements are arranged to form a coherent visual statement. The method by which visual order and unity is established is through the use of proportion, or giving

due weight to the compositional elements. The Renaissance writers provide a good model for the understanding of this broad principle. As Heinrich Wölfflin notes: 'The Renaissance took delight in a system of greater and lesser parts, in which the small prepared one for the large by prefiguring the form of the whole.'[50] To maintain unity in a composition it is necessary that 'some central or focal idea . . . should be clearly apparent'.[51] The visual element or group of related elements should clearly dominate the whole composition; it is often referred to as the dominant. This focal point dominates the architectural composition as does a thematic tune in an orchestral work or the thematic plot in a play. In urban design it may be the main town square around which the civic buildings are arranged, or it may be a group of related squares serving the same civic function.[52] Unity may be achieved through the use of one main local building material, the repetition of roof pitch, eaves and ridge details or the constant use of similar windows or doors. Chipping Campden and other Cotswold villages are lovely examples of unity achieved in this way through the constant repetition of a particular set of local building patterns developed by many hands over a number of generations.[53]

Some exaggerated claims have been made for particular proportional systems. One principle of proportion, however, appears universally held to be true; since unity is the recognized aim of every designer, any composition which breaks down into two equal parts is to be avoided. The first of Edward's three principles 'that of number . . . declares that both nature and art abhor a duality which has not in some measure been modified so that it may partake of the character of unity'.[54] Later in the same work Edward's language is even stronger: 'Now a building is an atrocity and an abortion if it is split down the centre by a narrow vertical dividing member into two equal symmetrical parts.'[55] Duality often occurs with the ubiquitous British semi-detached house (Figure 2.8). In any element divided into two equal parts, and with

2.8

Figure 2.8 Semi-detached
house, Nottingham
Figure 2.9 Minaret of the
Grand Mosque, Kairouan
Figure 2.10 Basilica di S.
Antonio, Padua
Figure 2.11 Low
Pavement, Nottingham

equality of proportion, the original unity will be
weakened. Geometric forms which can easily be
divided into two equal parts are, therefore, to be
used with care. For this reason some writers have
suggested that the double square is a weak form to
be avoided. The eye, it is argued, conditioned to see
simple shapes, detects the presence of the two
squares and divides the original unit into two
definite and equal single units so creating a duality.

The double square has, however, been used to
great effect, for example, it is the basis of Japanese
house planning. As a proportion for use on a façade,
the double square gave Alberti no problems: 'If the
length of the platform be twice its breadth: then
where the roof is to be flat, the height must be
equal to the breadth.'[56] The apparent proportion of
an architectural element is affected by the context
in which it is placed, that is the way in which it is
related to adjacent elements. A door, for example, is
seen against the surrounding wall and a wall against
an abutting wall and the floorplane on which it sits
(Figures 2.9-2.10). The apparent size or proportion
of an element is also changed by its detailing (Figure
2.11). While many riders and qualifications can be
added, the general principle holds true that the

2.9

2.10

2.11

2.12

presence of an unresolved duality or the splitting of a unity into two equal subdivisions is a defect in composition which is to be avoided. Venturi, for one, probably could not accept such a clear and unambiguous statement on the role of duality in architectural composition. He does insist that: 'An architecture of complexity and accommodation does not forsake the whole.'[57] Later he qualifies his position with statements such as: 'However, the obligation toward the whole . . . does not preclude the building which is unresolved.'[58] Even writers such as Robertson hesitate to be dogmatic on the subject of duality. In a helpful note to his text he introduces the idea of an exception to the rule: 'A duality may be intentionally introduced on account of its very weakness, to split up, for example, some element in a composition which might otherwise be overpowering.'[59] He cites the example of the Treasurer's House at York where the projecting wing, if treated as a perfect unit, might have been too dominant and destroyed the balance of the whole building (Figure 2.12).

The small town or village dominated by one church spire when seen in the general landscape presents a unified picture. Boston in Lincolnshire,

2.13

Figure 2.12 The Treasurer's House, York

Figure 2.13 The Stump, Boston

dominated by a tower known as 'The Stump', which is seen as a beacon from great distances, is just such an example of unity (Figure 2.13). Two such elements in the scene would cause confusion and a duality. However, the repetition of the many spires of Stamford in Lincolnshire and the towers of San Gimignano once again present a unified theme and, with it, the feeling of a balanced composition (Figure 2.14). The duality of the twin churches of S. Maria dei Miracoli and S. Maria di Montesanto in the Piazza del Popolo, Rome, has been resolved through their subordinate visual role in relationship to the dominant space of the piazza with its obelisk at the centre and the town gate. The churches take their place as incidents in the overall theme of portal or gateway to the *corso*. In urban design the unity sought is in terms of town mass or urban space. As Walter Bor points out: 'The designer's task will be to unify floor and walls into spaces which will meet all the functional requirements and are pleasing and attractive.'[60]

SCALE AND PROPORTION

At its most basic level, the proportions of a room or a public square mean the relation of the height to width to length. For a two-dimensional object, such as a door, the proportion is the height to width. The definition of proportion that permeates architectural thinking is a little more complex; it is the relation of the parts to each other and to the building as a whole. In other words, it is a system of proportion applied to the whole building or group of buildings. Scale, in contrast to proportion, depends upon the comparison of one set of dimensions and proportions with another set. The architect and urban designer are most concerned with human scale. Human scale is a measure of real size. The dimensions of buildings, squares and streets are compared with the proportions of the human figure. Man, therefore, is the measure used for the built environment: 'It is commonly recognised that

Figure 2.14 San Gimignano

buildings should take account of the scale of the human figure, and should if possible express this dimension by its own subdivisions.'[61] For example, the proportions of a man, his overall width to height, indicate the natural proportions of a normal door. We expect the normal door to be about 2 m (6 ft 6 ins) high × 0.75 m (2 ft 6 ins) wide; this is the opening we can move through in comfort and we are accustomed to its proportions. We expect larger doors to repeat this proportion. The method of scaling-up the door is to project the diagonal of the rectangle of the normal door. A door which is too wide for its height looks wrong, it will be out of scale and badly proportioned[62] (Figure 2.15).

When we speak of scale in city planning two analogies from the allied fields of economics and sociology immediately spring to mind. Economists discuss 'economies of scale' where size of manufacturing unit is related to efficiency of production and marketing. Judging from the rash of company takeovers it appears that maximizing size assures survival in the global market of the twenty-first century. The idea that 'small is beautiful' for the moment, at least, is a concept to which few successful industrialists would subscribe. At the other extreme, many believe that the revival of the dying inner city can only be achieved through the creation and stimulation of the small business enterprise; much emphasis has been placed in the Britain on the development of the enterprise culture. In social terms human scale is defined as a series of groups where every person knows every other. Plato proposed that the good city should have a population of 5,040 citizens.[63] Aristotle was a little more circumspect, he is content to suggest only empirical guidelines for determining the maximum and minimum size of the state: '. . . if it has too few people it cannot be self-sufficient . . . but not so large that it cannot be easily surveyed'.[64] Aristotle, of course, was considering political life in fifth century BC Greece. His concern was for a group not too large to make decisions 'on matters of justice, and for the purpose of distributing offices

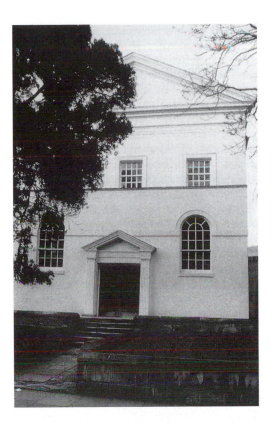

Figure 2.15 Doorway, Oxford

on merit, it is necessary that the citizens should know each other and know what kind of people they are'.[65] Such ideas of social scale have been accepted into planning dogma, perhaps uncritically, but have been rejected again all too hastily. It is generally acknowledged that the complexity of modern urban life, with its diversity of social structures, stimulates the development of non-spatial communities.[66] Communities of interest span beyond narrow, parochial boundaries to include metropolitan-wide and even international networks of association. There is, nevertheless, the need for local neighbouring communities of a few hundred families sharing the same locality and basic facilities.

Figure 2.16 Duomo, S. Maria del Fiore, Florence

Figure 2.17 Duomo, S. Maria del Fiore, Baptistery, Florence

Figure 2.18 Duomo, S. Maria del Fiore, Campanile, Florence

Figure 2.19 Duomo, S. Maria del Fiore, Florence

There may, as Lynch suggests, also be a need for small governmental units of 20,000 to 40,000 people where citizens 'can be active in politics if they wish, feel connected to an identifiable political community, and sense some control over public affairs, constrained as small town moves may be by regional, national, and corporate decisions'.[67] The range of scales, from the human and intimate social and economic organizations to the large metropolitan structures, have physical parallels in the field of urban design; each scale having its appropriate use in the repertoire of the urban designer.

Beauty, as Aristotle states, 'commonly arises in a context of size and number . . . there is a normal size for . . . animals, plants, instruments and so on'.[68] For example, if the weight of a fly exceeds certain limits it can no longer function as a fly. So too with a model aeroplane, it has a weight-to-power ratio and functions within fixed limits – this is called a 'scale effect'. There is a limit to the size of anything and when that limit is broken it can survive only by becoming something else, that is by a change of function. This question of scale and proportion is important in the fields of architecture and urban design. There are structural and functional limits to the size of buildings. So, too, are there thresholds for the support of urban services, as well as physical limits which determine the ways in which we perceive and appreciate the urban landscape. It is the visual quality of the built environment which is the prime concern of this text and, in this matter, the correct scaling of the urban landscape from the intimate human scale of the housing cluster to the extra human scale of the metropolitan area is of great importance for the way we appreciate our surroundings.

Taking man as the measure of scale then for scale to be determined man must be visible. The mathematics for the measurement of scale was related to building design by H. Maertens when in 1877 he published his book, *The Optical Scale in the Plastic Arts*.[69] This work has formed the basis for many studies of scale by urban designers since then.[70] It is

to these works that the following section is indebted. The part of our field of vision occupied by any object is defined by the rays from the outline of the object to the eyes. This general field of vision is of two overlapping irregular conical shapes, about 30° above the eyes, 45° below and 65° to each side. In addition to the general field of vision there is a detailed field of vision which is a very narrow cone within the larger one. The smallest discernible difference is determined by this narrow cone measuring one minute which means that we cannot distinguish any object at a distance more than about 3,500 times its size. It is the limitations set by this geometry that defines the varieties of urban scale. For example Maertens suggests that the nasal bone is a critical feature for the perception of the individual. At a distance of about 35 m (115 ft) the face becomes featureless. Using the analogy of the nasal bone Maertens also suggests that it is this size that dictates the dimensions of the smallest parts of a building of human scale. We can distinguish people at 12 m (40 ft) and a person can be recognized at 22.5 m (75 ft). Body gestures can be discerned at 135 m (445 ft). This is also the maximum distance that a man can be distinguished from a woman. Finally we can see people and recognize them as such up to about 1,200 m (4000 ft).

If we follow Aristotle and the Renaissance theorists in thinking it desirable to perceive the unity and wholeness of a building, it means that it should be perceived at a glance. The maximum angle at which a building can be seen clearly in this way is at 27° or at a distance which is about twice its height. The limitation is most apparent in the vertical plane where in addition only two-thirds of the normal field of vision are above the eye. At 22 m (72 ft), according to Hans Blumenfeld, the maximum height of a building should therefore be about 9 m (30 ft) or three storeys.[71] For the more intimate scale of recognizing one's neighbour, using as a measure the closer-knit community or group of people known to each other, then facial expression is important. In this instance the horizontal distance should be 12 m

(40 ft) and the buildings of two storeys. A street width of 21 to 24 m (70-80 ft) for streets three storeys high and 12 m (40 ft) for streets of two storey buildings appears to coincide with the dictates of a common-sense definition of human scale.

The distance at which it is still possible to perceive a human being may be important for the successful design of monumental layouts. There are few, good, uninterrupted urban vistas which extend beyond 1.5 km (1 mile). The distance, for example, from the Washington obelisk to the Lincoln memorial is just over 1,200 m (4,000 ft). The distance to the Capitol from the same spot is about 2.4 km (1½ miles), it remains impressive mainly because of its elevated siting on a hill. The great vistas of baroque Rome do not exceed 1.5 km (1 mile) which may represent the limit of public human scale; to break this barrier requires a different method of perception, understanding and design. An urban form, such as a medieval town, usually having a maximum total dimension of 800 m (½ mile) can be seen as a whole from the critical distance of 1.5 km (1 mile) and therefore still retains a human scale. If sited on a hill it, too, can impress its form upon the viewer.

The metropolis is quite another animal requiring a totally different set of principles for its organization and structuring. Monumental scale can take two forms; either as in the case just discussed, where the normal rules of proportion apply and design is related to human dimensions, or where development can break the bounds of this discipline and move onto a superhuman plane, a scale of gods, kings and dictators. Monumental works of this type can be either ennobling and spiritually uplifting or overpowering, oppressive and destructive of human dignity.

The grandeur of the Gothic cathedral is appreciated with the senses: entering, one hears and feels the hard metallic sound of one's steps on smooth worn paving; hears the vast reverberations of chanting choir or thunderous organ; feels the chill of massive stone piers and, with a movement of the head, admires the soaring height of delicately

2.16

2.17

2.18

2.19

Figure 2.20 Duomo, S. Maria del Fiore, Florence

balanced vaulting. Finally one processes along with the rhythmic nave arcade through shafts of coloured light towards the distant choir, high altar and great east window. Appreciation of scale in the environment is sensual as well as cerebral. The appreciation of the Duomo, S. Maria del Fiore, in Florence, is of this type. The cathedral is larger than life, too big for the space that surrounds it. Nowhere can one get a decent photograph even if traffic were banished from the square. The building can be seen only in parts, revealed as one moves round it; looking upwards with awe at the great cupola of Brunelleschi, a daring piece of engineering; then on to the Campanile of Giotto with its massively projecting cornice (Figures 2.16–2.19). This is urban design

on a monumental scale. It is, however, of limited extent and set contrastingly within a framework of streets which brings the scale of the town back down to earth and to the level of man (Figure 2.20).

Buildings and spaces designed on these two scales, the human and the superhuman may reinforce each other by their contrast as long as the superhuman can be related back to human scale otherwise the composition becomes colossal. Gigantism is usually associated with art in decline and, perhaps, also society in decline. Compare, for example, the use of the superhuman scale of the religious buildings of the Middle Ages in Europe with those compositions associated with the totalitarian regimes of Germany and Italy in the 1930s where the human dimension has been rejected for the glorification of state power: the dead hand of authority. The ponderous layout of colonial New Delhi is saved only by the impressive architecture of Edwin Lutyens. As a layout for people it has none of the untidy charm of Old Delhi nor the spiritual calm of the Taj Mahal (Figures 2.21–2.23). Fortunately, New Delhi has lost much of its oppressive connotations with Indian independence and the daily use by the Indian people of the great, grassed areas of the Raj path. Such compositions come to life on great state occasions such as the funerals of Mahatma Gandhi, Nehru and Indira Gandhi, the purpose for which they are most suited.

At the extreme of the hierarchy of urban scale is what George Banz defines as 'Megascale'[72] and Blumenfeld calls 'extra-human scale'.[73] Blumenfeld distinguishes it from the inhuman scale of the overgrown complex of flats or the colossal public building with Classical details expanded five times life size; for him it is equated with the great bridges, airfields, dams, reservoirs, power stations and modern motorway networks (Figure 2.24). As Blumenfeld says: 'It is a scale more related to the phenomena of nature, . . . than to any creation on the "superhuman scale", even though some of these may be just as big.'[74] These works of extra-human scale are usually utilitarian, often controlling the

2.21

2.22

2.23

forces of nature or used for rapid communication. They are seen at a distance or from a rapidly moving vehicle. They are not associated with the leisurely pace of the pedestrian. The scale is that of the mountain range, the vast forest and the sea, as such they are accessible to the human senses in part only. Total metropolitan form may be conceptually defined in terms of images, pattern, routes and systems but its definition by the senses is limited to incomplete sequences of spatial impressions received from objects and places less than 1.5 km (1 mile) distant. Compositional form based on the principles derived from the architectural theorists has no meaning at the extra human scale of the metropolis nor for those elements of cities seen from the moving car.

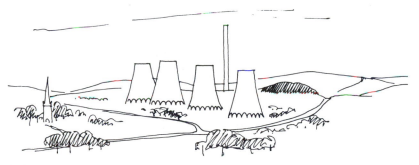

2.24

Figure 2.25 Temple, Paestum

Urban design is concerned with analysing metropolitan form and designing for future development using a hierarchy of scales - the intimate human scale where 12 m (40 ft) is a critical horizontal measure; normal human scale where this horizontal dimension is about 21-24 m (70-80 ft); public human scale where 1.5 km (1 mile) dictates the limit of perception; the superhuman or spiritual scale of monumental design; and finally the extra-human scale of untamed natural landscape together with those structures or technologies used to subdue its expanse and harness its resources. The art of urban design is to use these scales appropriately: to invent mechanisms for the smooth transition between scales - the equivalent of the clutch for gear change - so that change of scale is achieved with elegance, avoiding the visual chaos, for example, of the large shopping precinct introduced into the fine grain of an inner city street pattern. The design of the city quarter with a 800 m (½ mile) radius is, however, the main challenge for urban design. It is at this scale that man can fully appreciate the visual qualities of his environment.

2.25

absolute in regard to man (Figure 2.25). In the Classical building the number of elements such as columns, entablature and doors remains constant, their size varies; the elements in a medieval building remain constant in size but their number varies. A comparison of the façade of a Greek temple and a Gothic cathedral clearly illustrates these different concepts of scale (Figure 2.26).

HARMONY AND PROPORTION

Figure 2.26 Notre Dame, Paris

In western architecture there are two broad approaches to the ordering of architectural elements. The Classical school of design is the first of these approaches. It is derived from the theories of the Greek designers as interpreted by Vitruvius and his Renaissance followers. The second is derived from the master builders of the Middle Ages. The great works of Gothic architecture are made up of elements or characteristic parts which bear a fairly constant size related to man and are absolute in regard to the building as a whole. The scale of the Classical order is relative to the entire order, columns, entablature and mouldings expand and shrink with the height of the building. The parts of the building are related to the size of the column base therefore the scale of the building is

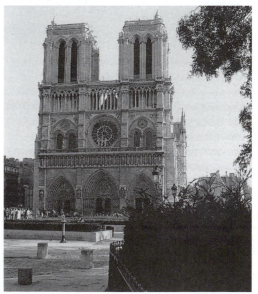

2.26

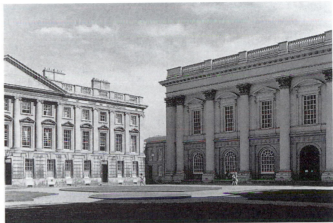

The differences between the two approaches to scale, while starting from a different premise, have much in common and each can result in harmonious compositions. In the great buildings of the Classical and Gothic schools the concept of scale characteristic of the other method was not entirely rejected. The Gothic cathedral has a clear module of structural members and its west façade can be seen as a whole with clearly articulated elements. Bernard George Morgan suggests that it was the use of the mason's square which contributed both to the obvious regularity of the Gothic cathedral and to the proportional system he finds in work of this period: 'The mason's square - the instrument with which he had been familiar since his early days of apprenticeship - alone provided the designer with a means of regulation of his work, ensuring the "recurrence of similar relations" and infusing the design with "some harmony" in all its parts.'[75] The temples of Classical Greece never lost touch with human scale. Temples did not exceed 20 m (65 ft) in height, could be seen as a whole from normal viewing distance, the module was related to normal human size and details could be related directly to parts of the human body; the fluting on the column, for example, is related to the width of the arm. This system of modular design can and did lead to gigantism both in ancient Rome and in Baroque buildings. It can also lead to confusion when two buildings using a different module are placed adjacent to each other (Figure 2.27). If, however, the module and overall building size are both determined by a viewing distance of 21-24 m (70-80 ft) then the building naturally takes on a human scale in addition to being harmoniously proportioned.

The theory of harmony in architecture is largely derived from the classical writers of the Renaissance. According to John Summerson: '. . . the aim of Classical architecture has always been to achieve a demonstrable harmony of parts. Such harmony has been felt to reside in the buildings of antiquity and to be to a great extent "built in" to the principal antique elements - especially to the "five orders" '[76] (Figure 2.28). The module or measure used to achieve harmony through proportion was the radius of the column at its base which was divided into 30 parts. All elements of the structure were multiples of this module. The five orders of architecture each had their own system of proportion, for example, in the Tuscan order the column height was fourteen modules, the Ionic and Corinthian nineteen times and the Composite twenty.[77] All other parts of the orders varied in a similar manner. The purpose of such proportions is

Figure 2.27 Peckwater Quad, Christ Church College, Oxford

Figure 2.28 The five orders

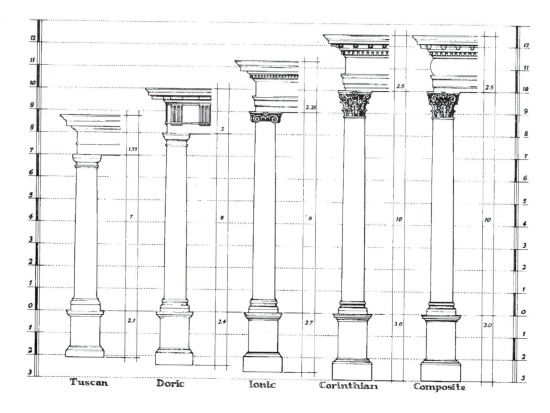

Tuscan   Doric   Ionic   Corinthian   Composite

to establish harmony throughout the building. The harmony is appreciated through the use of one or more of the orders as dominant components of the building or more simply by the use of dimensions repeating simple ratios: 'It is the property and business of the design to appoint to the edifice and all its parts their proper places, determinate number, just proportion and beautiful order; so that the whole form of the structure be proportionable.'[78] Again, Alberti writing about proportion, states: 'Variety is without dispute a very great beauty in everything, when it joins and brings together, in regular manner, things different, but proportionable to each other; but it is rather shocking, if they are unsuitable and incoherent. For as in Music, when the bass answers the treble, and the tenor agrees with both, there arises from that variety of sounds a harmonious and wonderful union of proportions which delights and enchants the senses . . .'[79] Beauty according to Alberti and other Renaissance theorists is a harmony inherent in the building imbued with a system of proportion which does not result from personal whim but from objective reasoning. The key to the correct proportion for the Classical designer is 'Pythagoras' system of musical harmony'.[80]

Alberti, following a tradition from classical times, equates music and geometry, to him they are one and the same thing; music is geometry translated into sound while architecture is frozen music. The same audible harmonies account also for harmonious composition in architecture. Alberti makes this point quite simply and effectively in a number of passages, 'from whence I conclude, that the same numbers, by means of which agreement of sounds effects our ears with delight, are the very same which please our eyes and mind. We shall therefore borrow all our rules for the finishing of our proportions, from the musicians . . .'[81] In his specific recommendations for the proportion of rooms Palladio uses the arithmetic, geometric and harmonic means to calculate the heights of rooms from their lengths and breadths;

1. 'But if those which are longer than they are broad, it will be necessary from the length and breadth to seek for the height, that they may bear a proportion to each other. This height will be found in adding the breadth to the length, and dividing the whole into two equal parts, because one of the halves will be the height of the vault.' (arithmetic mean)
2. 'As for example, if the place that we intend to vault be nine foot long and four foot wide, the height of the vault will be six foot; and the same proportion that nine has to six, six also has to four, that is the sesquilateral.' (geometric mean)
3. 'The height being found from the length and breadth of the room according to the first method, the length, breadth and height must be placed as they are in the figure, then nine is to be multiplied with twelve and six, and that which will proceed from twelve is to be placed under the twelve, and the product of six under the six; afterwards the six is multiplied by the twelve, and the product which is seventy two, placed under the nine; then a number being found which multiplied by nine amounts to seventy two, which in our case would be eight, we'll say eight foot to be the height of the vault.'[82]

$$
\begin{array}{ccc}
12 & 9 & 6 \\
108 & 72 & 54 \\
& 8 &
\end{array}
$$

In all cases the ratios used for the sides of two dimensional elements are simple and commensurable with the exception of the √2 rectangle. This, the diagonal of the square, is the only irrational

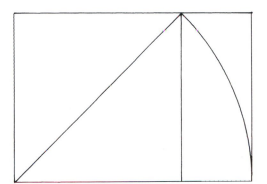

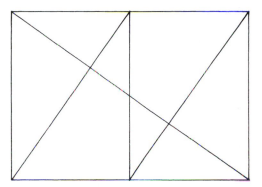

Figure 2.29 √2 Rectangle

number in Renaissance theory of architecture.

The √2 rectangle with sides in the ratio 1:√2 is considered by many architects to have a pleasing proportion. The sides of the rectangle are in the ratio of 1:1.412. It has the property of producing two further √2 rectangles when divided in half (Figure 2.29). The product of this proportional system is a continuous series of rectangles related by the same ratio of their sides. It is this system which is used for A sized paper and as a proportional system it has often been used for building purposes. The Golden Section has also been used to relate the parts of a façade. The continuous proportional series of the Golden Section is derived from the formulae:

$$\frac{a}{b} + \frac{b}{a+b}$$

Figure 2.30 Golden Mean

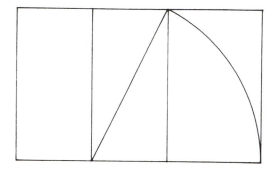

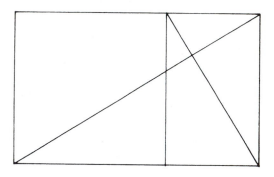

That is, where a and b are two segments of a straight line, c. The resulting rectangle is shown in Figure 2.30. In this case b is equivalent to the hypotenuse of the half square. If the side of the square is one unit the hypotenuse of half the square is $\sqrt{5}/2$, the sides of the rectangle are then in the ratio of 1:1.618. Matila Ghyka points out that 'the Golden Section also plays a dominating part in the proportions of the human body, a fact which was probably recognized by the Greek sculptors, who liked to put into evidence a parallelism between the proportions of the ideal temple and the human body, or even to trace harmonious correspondence (a proportion or analogia, in fact between the terms Universe - Temple - Man)'.[83] Further on he emphasizes the 'preponderance in botany and living organisms in general' of the Golden Section.[84] Jay Hambridge early in the twentieth century was saying

much the same thing as Ghyka. In 1919 he first put forward his theory of Dynamic Symmetry; on the opening pages of a reprint of this work he says: 'The basic principles underlying the greatest art so far produced in the world may be found in the proportions of the human figure and in the growing plant. . . . The principles of design to be found in the architecture of man and of plants have been given the name "Dynamic Symmetry". This symmetry is identical with that used by Greek masters in almost all art produced during the great classical period.'[85]

Le Corbusier took the Golden Section and Greek mathematical proportions as the starting point for his own modular system. He, however, related the actual dimensions for the scale back to the human figure; taking the 1.8 m (6 ft) man with upstretched arm as the basis of the Fibonacci scale which resulted: 'Take a man-with-arm-upraised, 2.2 metres in height; put him inside two squares, 1.1 × 1.1 metres each, superimposed on each other; put a third square astride these first two squares. This third square should give you a solution. The *place of the right angle* should help you to decide where to put this third square. With this grid for use on the building site, designed to fit the man placed within it, I am sure you will obtain a series of measures reconciling human stature (man-with-arm-upraised) and mathematics.'[86] With these enigmatic and mystical instructions he left an assistant Hanning to produce the first result, a combination of the $\sqrt{2}$ and the $(1 + \sqrt{5})/2$ rectangles (Figure 2.31).

Ultimately, Corbusier derived his red and blue series of dimensions for use in building design. According to Danby, Corbusier's architecture is not the product of this system 'but that of a creative artist using the system to help him relate many different factors, both practical and aesthetic, to a balanced and integrated solution of an architectural problem'.[87] Judging from the dimensions on the scales it would be difficult not to find one that suits the occasion. Perhaps for some the palette is too wide and would require further restriction for the discipline necessary for harmonious design.

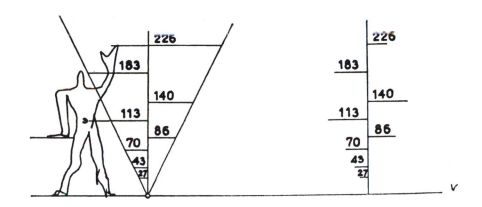

Figure 2.31 The Modulor

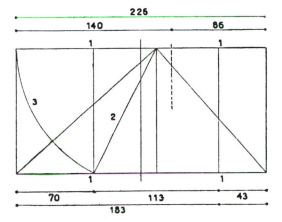

Searching for a secret mathematical harmony behind every form of architectural beauty is not confined to the Renaissance. According to Scruton this has been the most popular conception of architecture from the Egyptians to Le Corbusier.[88] The fundamental concept is simple. Certain shapes and their arrangement seem harmonious and pleasing, others appear disproportionate, unstable and unsatisfactory. There is a general conviction that harmony in architecture results only if the shapes of rooms, windows, doors and, indeed, all elements in a building conform to certain ratios which relate continuously to all other ratios. It is doubtful if such rational

systems of proportion do produce the effects which the eye and mind consciously see and understand. As Rasmussen points out: 'The truth is, however, that a person listening to music has no idea of the lengths of the strings that produce it ... there are no visual proportions which have the same spontaneous effect on us as those which we ordinarily call harmonies and disharmonies in music.'[89] Wittkower agrees with this general stance: 'It is obvious that such mathematical relations between plan and section cannot be correctly perceived when one walks about in a building. Alberti knew that, of course, quite as well as we do.' He goes on to add that the harmonic order produced by such proportions represents an absolute value above subjective perception: '... this man-created harmony was a visible echo of a celestial and universally valid harmony'.[90] Summerson reduces the whole argument to a more common-sense and practical viewpoint: 'To what extent rational systems of this kind do produce effects which eye and mind can consciously apprehend I am extremely doubtful. I have a feeling that the real point of such systems is simply that their users (who are mostly their authors) need them: there are types of extremely fertile, inventive minds which need the tough inexorable discipline of such systems to correct and at the same time stimulate invention.'[91]

The techniques used in building automatically lead to the use of standardized units. Architecture has its own inbuilt method of proportioning. The basic building material in many constructions is the brick, usually of standard dimensions, which leads to a system of standard lengths for walls. The timber, stonework and window frames are often made to finished dimensions away from the building site; they have to fit into predetermined positions in the structure. In some cases the proportions of rooms are often determined by some practical necessity, for example, the room size in Klint's Hospital, Copenhagen, is determined by the bed size and its efficient arrangement.[92] An extreme example of this form of modulation is the Japanese house based upon the size of the sleeping mat which is 1.8 m × 0.9 m (6 ft × 3 ft). There is a variety of combinations of this rectangle; the size of each room being known by the number of mats used. The wall panels are also based on this rectangle. The house consists of a framework of timber panels related in three dimensions by the 1.8 m × 0.9 m (6 ft × 3 ft) module.[93] Plan shapes can also be determined by the structural qualities of the material used for spanning between supporting walls and piers. The material used to support the heavy mud roofs of the traditional Hausa building, Nigeria, for example, has a maximum span of 1.8 m (6 ft). The Hausa using a complicated system of corbelling and arches are limited by the structural strength of

azara, the joist material, to a number of fairly standard plan shapes.[94] (Figure 2.32)

There is some doubt about the ability of the normal viewer to see and appreciate the subtleties of the more esoteric forms of proportional systems used in building. Modular design, however, when related back to human dimensions is probably a natural way of seeing the world. It may also be possible to appreciate the deliberate, non-trivial,

Figure 2.32 Modular construction in mud, north Nigeria

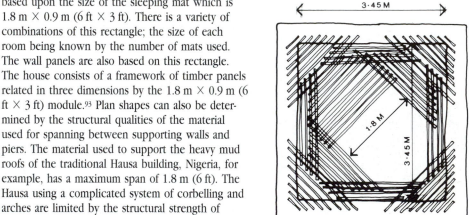

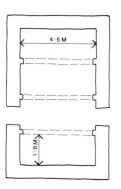
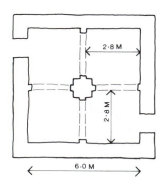
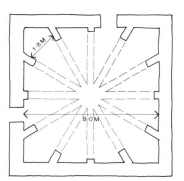
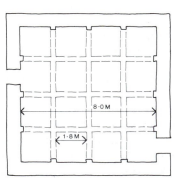

2.33

2.34

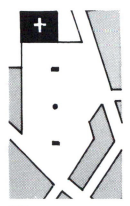

2.35

2.36

While we have seen that architecture has a natural module derived from the constructional process, so too urban areas are structured by the normal module for site development for specific functions. A good example was the development of the central area of old Singapore for the Chinese

Figure 2.33 Piazza S. Maria Novella, Florence
Figure 2.34 Piazza S. Maria Novella, Florence
Figure 2.35 Piazza S. Maria Novella, Florence
Figure 2.36 Piazza S. Maria Novella, Florence
Figure 2.37 Singapore Ordnance Survey

almost grave proportions of a villa by Palladio. One cannot, of course, appreciate the exact measurements of his elegantly proportioned rooms, but it is possible to receive an impression of an integrated composition where each room is so much a part of the greater whole. It may or may not be possible for all to feel or experience relationship in size between rooms in a building, but certainly these relationships are not so clear or apparent in the urban scene. Indeed, distinguishing an irregular from a regular piazza is almost impossible. Standing at any point in the Piazza S. Maria Novella, Florence, it is impossible at first glance to tell that this is a five-sided space. To all intents and purposes it is a regular square (Figures 2.33-2.36).

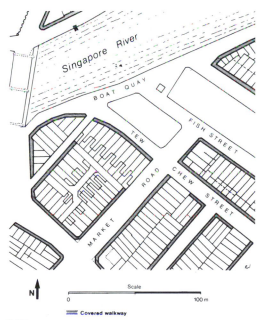

2.37

2.38

Figure 2.38 Singapore
Figure 2.39 Maid Marian
Way, Nottingham
Figure 2.40 Maid Marian
Way, Nottingham
Figure 2.41 Maid Marian
Way, Nottingham

the urban quality of the city (Figures 2.39-2.41). Reducing the scale of Maid Marian Way with tree planting is one small step currently being undertaken by the city council in an effort to ameliorate the worst effects of insensitive, out-of-scale development dating from the 1960s.

2.39

2.40

community. Here the standard arcaded shop front with three-storey development was repeated over many acres which lent a unity and modulation to the city (Figures 2.37-2.38). A similar effect can be found in many of the small English market towns where the parcels of land abutting the street were of similar dimensions, giving scale and proportion to the ground plan. Vertical dimensions until recently retained a human scale being two, three or at the most four storeys; such heights being determined, in part, by the comfortable height to which it is possible to climb on foot. This normal harmony of similar proportions has been disturbed by the ever increasing size of developments. Landholdings are amassed and organized into large parcels to suit developers' needs. The result is usually a loss of intimate human scale similar to the effect of the development of Maid Marian Way in Nottingham once described as the 'ugliest street in Europe'.[95] Maid Marian Way severed the natural small-scale grain of the street pattern connecting the old Saxon town where St Mary's now stands and the Norman town centred on the castle. Here we get the juxtaposition of conflicting scales which add nothing to

2.41

The city must be experienced to be appreciated, preferably the experience should be on foot and at a leisurely pace. The city is not simply an artefact to be viewed. The viewer is part of the city. He or she experiences the noise of distant bells, the babble of fellow pedestrians, the delicious smell of roasting coffee beans, the reflected heat from hot pavements. He or she explores dark alleyways and experiences the sudden brightness of the market square and the bustle of business. The module for this experience is the footstep; distances are measured in paces, this is the module that gives proportion to the city. The area that can be appreciated in this way is about a twenty minute walk or an area of 1.5 km (1 mile) across; this is the largest unit of urban design and the one that demands most attention. Scale and proportion have social connotations for urban design. A domain becomes 'home' only if it is small; the settlement and its parts must remain within an imaginable scale for it to become home. As Norberg-Schulz points out: 'The limited size of the known places naturally goes together with a concentrated form. A centralized form primarily means "concentrated". A place, therefore, is basically "round". '[96] Oscar Newman in his study of defensible space in the USA found that project size affects crime rate: 'If the two variables of building heights and project size are coupled, the probability of crime increases to the extent that it is possible to guarantee a higher crime rate in virtually all projects of excessive height and size.'[97] Alice Coleman's findings in Britain paralleled those of Newman. She found that crime and vandalism increased with size and resulted from anonymity. 'Anonymity,' she said, 'is the impersonal character of areas where a community structure has failed to develop and people know few other residents, even by sight. This makes criminals feel secure in the knowledge that they will not be identified, and hence free to prowl through the buildings and grounds looking for illicit opportunties.'[98] There may, of course, be reasons other than physical arrangement for crime patterns. A simple physical

determinism is not the meaning to be construed from this paragraph. However, adopting the right scale in urban design is critical in establishing due proportion certainly in the physical world and possibly also in social environment where the parts of the city are a microcosm of the whole.

SYMMETRY, BALANCE AND RHYTHM

Symmetry has come to mean the identical disposition of elements on either side of an axis. This type of symmetry was given its grandest form of expression during the Beaux Arts movement at the beginning of this century. As a static form of design it is quite different from the ancient Greek or Renaissance use of the concept. Hambridge with Ghyka following him, call this other more subtle form of ordering architectural elements, 'Dynamic Symmetry'.[99] These ideas, as we have seen, have their origin in the mathematics and aesthetic theory of Greece, and indeed may owe something to the tradition handed down from the great builders of Pharaonic Egypt. Just as Plato conceived of the 'Greater Ordering One' arranging the cosmos using pre-existing eternal archetypes or ideas, so too the artist, according to this Classical ideal, orders his work to conform with this timeless, God-given, system of proportion ruled by a spatial dynamic symmetry corresponding to musical eurhythmy.[100] Vitruvius provides the key to understanding the use of this particular conception of symmetry in architecture: 'Symmetry is a proper agreement between the members of the work itself, and relation between the different parts and the whole general scheme, in accordance with a certain part selected as standard. Thus in the human body there is a kind of symmetrical harmony between forearm, foot, palm, finger and other small parts.'[101] Later in the text he says the principles of symmetry '. . . are due to proportion in Greek (*analogia*)'.[102] Eurhythmy is defined by Vitruvius as '. . . beauty and fitness in the adjustment of the members. This is found when the members of a work are of a height suited to their breadth, of a breadth suited to their length, and, in a word, when they all correspond symmetrically'.[103] Translating the Classical concept of symmetry into modern English is difficult now that the term is used for compositions more rigidly arranged. Perhaps the term 'balance' is the simplest and clearest expression for this idea.

There are two common sayings in the English language – 'a sense of proportion' and a 'balanced outlook' – both of which, when used about someone, convey the impression of a reasonable and well-adjusted human being. Similarly a building which achieves balance is well adjusted, exhibiting a reasonable distribution of its component parts. Weighing scales are the symbol for justice, it is a symbol that designates the gravity of attaching due measure to the evidence so that the outcome of deliberation is both rational and just. In the case of the simple scales, the force of gravity ensures that equal weights placed at equal distances from the fulcrum will balance. This idea of physical balance is extrapolated to the world of visual forms and is important in architecture structurally and also visually; the idea of balance is used as analogy in the world of design. An obvious imbalance looks awkward, top-heavy, lop-sided or positively drunk. Symmetry, in its modern usage, is the balance of formal axial buildings or urban design groups. It can be applied to the front of the Parthenon in Athens, the Taj Mahal, or to the great space in front of St Peter's, Rome. Symmetry of this type implies an axis of movement. Most creatures or man-made objects which move directionally are symmetrical about an axis of movement, whether they be flies, birds, mammals or aeroplanes and ships. Symmetrical arrangements about an axis in architecture, together with other man-made structures uses this analogy of movement from nature. Consequently the symmetrical building composition is best appreciated while moving along this central axis.

A strictly symmetrical appearance in nature does not entirely reflect a similar, symmetrical, internal arrangement of the working parts. While the heart and liver, for example, in man are asymmetrically arranged, the external features for a frontal view if noticeably unbalanced would be considered less than pleasing in any individual. Some theorists developed these ideas about the lack of correspondence between external symmetry and internal functions and see them as a useful analogy for architectural design. Such ideas were challenged by theorists of the functional school of modern architecture who insisted on honestly expressing the functions of a building. The Pompidou Centre is an example of designers thinking along these lines. By exhibiting the mechanical services, the Pompidou Centre could be likened to a man, his skin removed, with guts and other working organs exposed. Buildings like the Pompidou Centre, however interesting or stimulating they may be, can only act as exceptions to the rule or to the general principles of good composition. This is not, however, to detract from the reputation of a fine building, but simply to point out that if the experiment were repeated often, buildings like this would lose the power to shock and to stimulate thought.

Formal symmetry is a type of balance which is easy to see and understand, but it involves great difficulties in achieving a balance between the internal functions and the highly disciplined exterior. Robertson provides a good illustration of some problems of achieving unity using symmetry as the unifying concept.[104] It is Robertson's simple explanation of this concept which is used here. A composition produced by two equal buildings (Figure 2.42) has balance but also dual centres of interest. Since duality is to be avoided, it is necessary to examine ways in which unity can be restored. The problem facing the designer in such circumstances is how to create one main centre of interest for the whole composition. The link which is introduced becomes a third element in the composition. As Plato recommends: 'But it is not possible to combine two things properly without a third to act as a bond to hold them together.'[105] Any device which shifts the dual

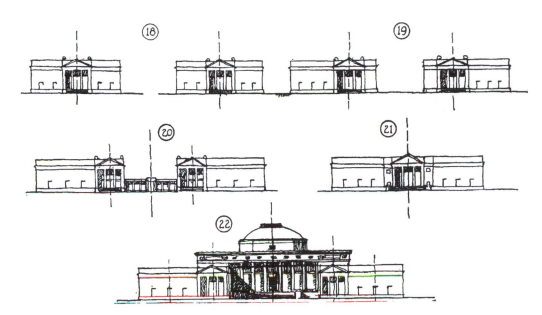

Figure 2.42 Formal symmetry

centres of interest in a direction which brings them closer together assists in establishing unity in a symmetrical composition (Figure 2.42).

Christopher Wren achieved a measure of unity in his designs for Greenwich Hospital. He was unable to replace the small Queen's House by Inigo Jones with a bigger building which would have unified the whole scheme, nor could he block the view of this important building with another structure. Wren, therefore, settled for a less satisfactory method of establishing unity. He moved the centres of interest of the flanking buildings, the twin domes, away from the centres of their own mass towards the axis of the total composition (Figure 2.43).

Figure 2.43 Greenwich Hospital, London

Figure 2.44 Taylor Institute and University Galleries, Ashmolean Museum, Oxford, 1839–45 before enlargement

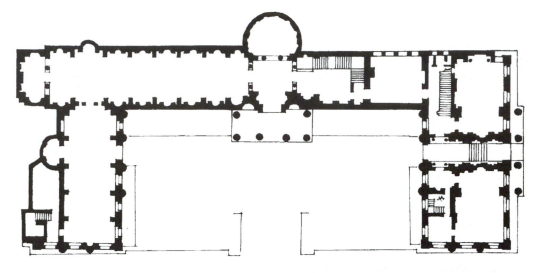

Figure 2.45 Ashmolean Museum, Oxford

Introducing a third element to tie together the centres of interest, and so complete the composition, improves the sense of unity (Figure 2.42). Having the main masses on the wings of the composition however, weakens the total effect of unity. The Ashmolean Museum and Taylor Institute by C.R. Cockerell in Oxford, exhibits this weakness

2.45a

2.45b

of composition along its main front: 'The two wings are higher than the centre, always a visual risk to take, and here particularly so, as the difference is not great.'[106] (Figures 2.44–2.45).

Better methods of achieving unity can be seen in Figure 2.42. In the first case the two buildings are merged into one to form a complete composition. The second method introduces a third building which completely dominates the other two. Here we have a composition formed of a plurality of elements with three centres of interest, but the central element forms the dominant necessary for unity. It has been argued that the plans for Government House and the adjoining secretariat building by Lutyens and Baker in New Delhi were fatally flawed by the lack of dominance of Government House as seen from important axial view points[107] (Figures 2.21–2.23). 'Approaching Government House on the King's Way (Raj Path), the visitor begins to lose sight of the monumental portico a half-mile from the brow of Raisina Hill, while at the Great Place he sees merely the palace dome above the rise. Finally even this is wholly obliterated until he reaches the crest of the inclined way leading to Government Court and its flanking secretariat blocks.'[108] According to the editorial of the *Town Planning Review* the composition had nothing akin to the 'majestic dominance' of the Capitol building in Washington: 'Rather than a single satisfying whole, a unified

2.45c

Figure 2.46 The notion of asymmetrical balance: the Church of San Francesco, Assisi

conception, the crowning feature at Delhi presented two perversely severed halves.'[109]

Asymmetry is the informal balance of non-axial architecture. It corresponds to the human figure in profile, which is capable of balanced positions of great complexity compared with the more static frontal symmetry. In simplistic terms a great weight close to the fulcrum of a balance will be balanced by a lesser weight at a greater distance. Similarly the notional weights of architectural masses can also achieve a complex balance. There are no limits to the number of elements which form a composition providing they resolve themselves round a point of balance or a dominant focal point of interest. It is to this point that the eye is first attracted, and to which it returns after an examination of the rest of the composition. The effect of compositional grouping is similar to the resolution of forces in mechanics. Just as the forces acting on a body can be resolved into a single, resultant force, so too can the various weights of the elements comprising a visual composition; the composition achieves balance when these resolved, notional weights pass through its centre of gravity. It is only when asymmetrical buildings obey the law of equilibrium and balance that they correspond to the 'canon of unity'[110] (Figure 2.46).

2.47

more complex matter and one requiring great sensitivity, the visual forces cannot be calculated, as in mechanics, they can only be 'felt'. Buildings, town spaces and landscape, with the exception of distant views, are appreciated as one moves through the composition. The town presents an ever-changing series of different pictures each one of which is a separate composition. Designing infill for an existing town or designing an urban group on a green-field site requires of the urban designer the imagination to see all these pictures and arrange the buildings to create, support or complete a series of balanced compositions. Gordon Cullen in his book *Townscape* has given the designer both a method of analysing and designing the town using the tool of serial vision.[111] Examples of wonderful, balanced compositions can be found in any of the great medieval towns of Europe, the Piazza del Campo,

Figure 2.47 The Church and Convent of San Francesco, Assisi
Figure 2.48 The Church and Convent of San Francesco, Assisi
Figure 2.49 Piazza del Campo, Siena

2.48

The picture of asymmetrical balance so far presented is rather static and best suited, in some ways, to the analysis of a two-dimensional design. It should be remembered, however, that in a building group the apparent relationship between masses changes with changing viewpoint. Each viewpoint of the building presents to the viewer a different picture or composition (Figures 2.47–2.48). Asymmetrical balance in urban design is an even

2.49

Siena is a particularly fine example (Figures 2.49-2.50).

A badly composed picture can look top heavy' or 'lop sided'. To avoid this fault the balancing line should not be awkwardly situated, say at the extreme edge of the composition. It should be somewhere close to the centre of the composition: as a rough and ready rule it should be within the middle third. In a similar manner, the focal point of an urban composition whether it is a building or a space should be somewhere near the middle of the group. In the design of an area, a district, neighbourhood or housing group, the climax should be towards its centre so that all routes lead to it.

RHYTHM, HARMONY AND CONTRAST

The mysteries of rhythm have to be experienced; rhythm is a basic characteristic of our nature. Children in the dark, listening to the tick-tock of the clock magically turn the sounds into a rhythmic

Figure 2.50 Piazza del Campo, Siena

beat, a pattern imposed by the mind. The great dancer moves rhythmically to the music both controlling and controlled by the motion, carried along by the experience. The ritualistic dances of Africa are imbued with heightened energy and the whirling-dervish dance quite transports participants to another plane. Rhythm in architecture has similar properties. It can be explained by reasoned analysis; to understand its stimulating and insistent effect is beyond reflection. In the last resort it is experiential.

Rhythm in architecture is the product of the grouping of elements; of emphasis, interval, accent and direction. It is the sense of movement achieved by the articulation of the members making up the composition: 'A single column is just, well a point on a plan; or rather, a very small circle on a plan – it gives you the module of an order but nothing more. But two columns give you at once an inter-columnation, a rhythm, and there with the module, you have the germ of the whole building.'[112] The importance of inter-columnation in Classical build-ings has its counterpart in the spacing of the giant piers of the medieval cathedral. It is the heart beat of architecture. The fossilized memory of ancient Rome preserved in the *Forma Urbis* records a pulsating rhythm at city scale. The great basilica, fora and arcades beat the steady time of the colum-nar structures: truly a frozen music. The rhythm of Amsterdam lives on in narrow, gabled properties marching side by side along canal banks, a testa-ment to the value of water frontage and the prac-tical necessity of servicing from the canal. The steady pace of the main structural land divisions are accompanied by the quicker, but still regular, pace of upper-floor windows, the whole street composi-tion in sweeping curves following and reflected in the accompanying canal.

The triumph of unity over chaos, or the victory of order, is the condition of aesthetic success both in architecture and urban design. Good design, however, should avoid monotony and, therefore, it should have interest and accent. Some of the great pleasures in life derive from the contrasts found in nature, sunshine and shadow, the cliffs of Moher rising sheer from the Atlantic, the granite inselbergs protruding like giant black warts from the red plains of Hausaland. In architecture much of the pleasure derives from similar contrasts. Entering the bright amphitheatre of the Piazza del Campo, Siena, from dark cavernous streets incised in the urban fabric is a marvellous urban experience, the contrast of horizontals and verticals in the Palazzo Communale confronts the visitor with further delight. If such contrasts were eliminated our lives would lose much intensity and vitality. Contrasts have generally to be kept within proportion to avoid perceptual overload. The correct balance between complexity and repose in architecture is the key to order: 'Aesthetic success is conditional upon the victory of order, but there has to be sufficient complexity to make the victory worthwhile.'[113]

Good composition is harmonious composition. Good composition, to recapitulate, is dependent upon achieving unity through the use of proportion. Harmonious design includes within its definition due consideration of contrast, an essential ingredient of harmony in architectural composition. Harmony, however, is not another term for conformity; achiev-ing consistency through such devices as repetition of materials, details and even height is only the first thought in the design process leading to unity in urban compositions. Without the elements of contrast and surprise delight would be diluted to bland repetition of existing conditions.

Contrast in architecture and urban design is applied over an almost limitless field. There is contrast, of form and antiform, that is, of building and space, of street and square or soft and hard landscape. In buildings there can be contrast in form, such as, the sphere and the cube, the dome and the spire. In details there is contrast of line or the contrast of objects in silhouette, contrast in direction, vertically and horizontally, or in colour and texture. Whatever the forms of contrast used the main lines of the building or townscape should produce an effect of decision, all the elements of the composition should themselves be imbued with a similar quality.

In the design of fenestration, for example, either the wall area or the window area should clearly be seen to dominate the façade. In the use of simple shapes the same principle should be followed. A square should be an actual square not a slightly smaller or bigger rectangle, an ellipse should not be a circle with a bulge and it should maintain its ellipse shape unequivocally. Generally speaking, it is preferable to have complete decision and clarity of form in architectural composition. If this quality is maintained then contrast can be achieved with harmony: 'Wherever there is a juxtaposition or clash in two information networks, the mind seeks to establish an orderly relationship. When it succeeds there is a basis for harmony, but when it fails there is dissonance. Thus the concept of harmony can be extended to include any success in extracting order-liness from complexity.'[114]

A difficulty facing the designer lies in the attain-ment of the right degree of contrast. Taken to extremes such contrast can only produce discord. This occurs when the proportions of contrasting elements are so individually insistent that they compete rather than act as a foil to each other. The Golden Section (*phi*) may he a useful tool in testing the appropriateness of the contrasting element. The ratio of the *phi* rectangle 1:1.618 is the point at which there is least uncertainty about the relation-ship of the sides of the rectangle. There is a clear dominant in the relationship of the sides while the subordinate side retains its significance.

Applying the *phi* rule of thumb to the problem of fenestration design, the most harmonious balance occurs in Classical terms when the wall accounts for 60 per cent of the visual weight and the windows for 40 per cent. There is some doubt, however, about the general ability to distinguish the *phi* rectangle from others close to it in size. There is also a problem in calculating the apparent weight of design elements which often depends upon architec-

tural detailing, colour, texture or symbolic impor-tance attached to them. In the end the calculation of the right amount of contrast in harmonic compo-sition is a question of design intuition and feeling. The rule of thumb, however, would seem to indicate the need for a clear dominant theme with contrasts of a compatible order. Extreme contrasts may produce disorder and lack of clarity.

CONCLUSION

Some of the concepts for the analysis of architec-tural composition have formed the subject matter of this chapter. Order, unity, balance, symmetry, scale, proportion, rhythm, contrast and harmony are among the important tools used to define good architecture. These concepts overlap and are mutually reinforcing and, as such, they have been connected in the foregoing paragraphs. Individual concepts do not, and cannot, stand alone but if one stands out as paramount it is unity. These concepts can be used to analyse the aesthetic qualities of urban form though they are not used in precisely the same way for large scale urban developments. These and other analytical concepts will be used in the next chapter to examine the methods of arrang-ing buildings and, more specifically, the design of street and square.

NOTES

1   Vitruvius. *The Ten Books of Architeclure*, Dover Publications, New York, 1960, Book 1, Chapter 2, p.13

2   Zevi, Bruno. *Architecture as Space* (trns. M. Gendel), Horizon Press, New York, 1957, p.21

3   Vitruvius. Op cit., p.13

4   Alberti, Leon Battista. *Ten Books of Architecture* (trns. Cosimo Bartoli into Italian, and James Leoni into English), Tiranti, London, 1955, Book VI, Chapter 5, p.119

5   Palladio, Andrea. *The Four Books of Architecture*. Dover Publications, New York, 1965, First Book, Chapter 1, p.1

6   Allsopp, Bruce. *A Modern Theory of Architecture*, Routledge & Kegan Paul, London, 1977, p.18

7   Alberti, Leon Battista. *Ten Books of Architecture* (1955 Leoni edn). Dover Publications, New York, 1986. Book IX, Chapter 5, p.195

8   Palladio, A. Op cit. First Book, Chapter 20, p.25

9   Summerson, Sir John. *The Classical Language of Architecture*, Thames and Hudson, London, 1963

10 Saarinen, Eliel. *The Search for Form in Art and Achitecture*, Dover Publications, New York, 1985, p.70

11 Ibid, p.27

12 Gropius, Walter. *The New Architecture and the Bauhaus* (trns. P. Morton Shand with introduction by Frank Pick), MIT Cambridge, Mass., 1965, p.44

13 *The Guardian*, 29 October 1988, p.1, and *The Observer*, 30 October 1988, p.18

14 Pugin, A.W. *The True Principles of Pointed or Christian Architecture*, Henry G. Bohn, London, 1841, p.22

15 Le Corbusier, *Towards a New Architecture*, Architectural Press, London, 1946, p.9

16 Jencks, Charles. *Language of Post-Modern Architecture*, Academy Editions, London, 4th edn, 1984, p.5

17 Venturi, Robert, *Complexity.and Contradiction in Architecture*, Moma, New York, 1966, p.46

18 Ibid, p.23

19 Crook, J.M. *The Dilemma of Style*, John Murray, London

20 Ibid, p.270

21 Le Corbusier. Op cit, p.45

22 Hegemann, W. and Peets, E. *The American Vitruvius, An Architect's Handbook of Civic Art*, Benjamin Bloom, New York, 1922, p.1

23 Ibid, p.2

24 Alberti. Op cit, Book I, Chapter 9, p.13

25 Gibberd, Frederick. *Town Design*, Architectural Press, London, 2nd edn, 1955, p.11

26 Alexander, Christopher, et al. *The Oregon Experiment*, Oxford University Press, New York. 1975, p.10

27 Wotton, Sir Henry. *The Elements of Architecture*, Gregg, London, 1969

28 Jacobs, Jane. *The Death and Life of Great American Cities*, Random House, New York, 1961, p.24

29 Palladio. Op cit, First Book, Chapter 1, p.1

30 Lynch, Kevin. *The Image of the City*, MIT Press, Cambridge, Mass., 1960, p.4

31 Ibid, p.9

32 Robertson, Howard. *The Principles of Architectural Composition*, Architectural Press, London, 1924, p.1

33 Edwards, A.T. *Architectural Style*, Faber and Gwyer, London, 1926, p.17

34 Alexander, Christopher. *A Timeless Way of Building*, Oxford University Press, New York, 1919, p.336

35 Robertson, H. Op cit, p.2

36 Wotton, Sir H. Op cit

37 Alberti, Op cit, Book VI, Chapter 2, p.113

38 Pevsner, Nikolaus. *An Outline of European Architecture*, Penguin, Harmondsworth, 7th edn, 1977, p.204

39 Rosenau, Helen. *The Ideal City*, Studio Vista, London, 1974, p.51

40 Morris, A.F.J. *History of Urban Form*, George Godwin, London, 1972, p.117

41 Scruton, Roger. *The Aesthetics of Architecture*, Methuen, London, 1979, p.11

42 Zevi, Bruno. *Architecture as Space* (trns. M. Gendel), Horizon Press, New York, 1957, p.193

43 Venturi, R. Op cit, p.22

44 Ibid, p.23

45 Edwards, A.T. Op cit, p.13

46 Lynch, K. Op cit

47 Lynch, K. Op cit

48 Katz, David. *Gestalt Psychology*, Ronald Press, New York, 1950 and Kofka, K. *Principles of Gestalt Psychology*, Harcourt, Brace and World Inc, New York, 1935

49   Norberg-Schulz, C. *Existence, Space and Architecture*, Studio Vista, London, 1971, p.18

50   Wölfflin, Heinrich. *Renaissance and Baroque*, Collins, London, 1964, p.43

51   Robertson, H. Op cit, p.5

52   Collins, G.R. and Collins, C.C. *Camillo Sitte: The Birth of Modern City Planning*, Rizzoli, New York, 1986, p.181

53   Alexander, Christopher, et al. *A Pattern Language*, Oxford University Press, New York, 1977

54   Edwards, A.T. Op cit, p.29

55   Ibid, p.32

56   Alberti. Op cit, Book IX, Chapter 3, pp.190-191

57   Venturi, R. Op cit, p.89

58   Ibid, p.101

59   Robertson, H. Op cit, p.13

60   Bor, Walter. *Making Cities*, Hill, London, 1972, p.164

61   Edwards, A.T. Op cit, p.127

62   Danby, Miles. *Grammar of Architectural Design*, Oxford University Press, London, 1963, p.121

63   Plato. *The Laws* (trans. Trevor J. Saunders), Penguin, Harmondsworth, 1988, Book 5, p.205

64   Aristotle. *The Politics* (trns. T.A. Sinclair, revised by Trevor J. Saunders), Penguin, Harmond.sworth, 1986, Book VII, Chapter 4, p.404

65   Ibid, p.405

66   Webber, Melvin M. 'The urban place and nonplace urban realm.' In *Explorations into Urban Strurture*, Oxford University Press, London, 1967, pp.79-153

67   Lynch, Kevin. *A Theory of Good City Form*, MIT Press, Cambridge, Mass., 1981, p.245

68   Aristotle. Op cit, p.404

69   Maertens, H. *Der Optische Masstab in der Bildenden Kuenster*, 2nd edn, Wasmuth, Berlin, 1884

70   Blumenfeld, Hans. Scale in civic design. In *Town Planning Review*, Volume XXIV, April 1953, pp.35-46

Spreiregen, P.D. *Urban Design: The Architecture of Towns and Cities*, McGraw-Hill, New York, 1965

Banz, George. *Elements of Urban Form*, McGraw-Hill, San Francisco, 1970

Lynch, Kevin. *Site Planning*, MIT Press, Cambridge, Mass., 2nd edn, 1971

71   Blumenfeld, H. Op cit

72   Banz, G. Op cit, p.99

73   Blumenfeld, H. Op cit, p.43

74   Ibid, p.43

75   Morgan, B.G. *Canonic Design in English Medieval Architecture*, Liverpool University Press, Liverpool, 1961, p.97

76   Summerson, Sir John. Op cit, p.8

77   Palladio. Op cit, Book IV

78   Alberti. Op cit, Book I, Chapter 1, p.1

79   Ibid, Book 1, Chapter 9, p.14

80   Wittkower, R. *Architectural Principles in the Age of Humanism*, Tiranti, London, 1952, p.29

81   Alberti. Op cit, Book IX, Chapter 5, pp.196-197

82   Palladlo, Op cit, Book I, Chapter 13, pp.28-29

83   Ghyka, Matila. *The Geometry of Art and Life*, Dover, New York, 1977, p.16

84   Ibid, p.17

85   Hambridge, Jay. *The Elements of Dynamic Symmetry*, Dover Publications, New York, 1967, p.11

86   Le Corbusier. *The Modulor*, Faber & Faber, London, 1951, p.37

87   Danby, M. Op cit, p.122

88   Scruton, K. Op cit, p.60

89   Rasmussen, S.E. *Experiencing Architecture*, John Wiley, New York, 1959, pp.104-105

90   Wittkower, R. Op cit, p.7

91   Summerson, Sir J. Op cit, p.112

92   Rasmussen, S.E. Op cit, p.123

93   Danby, Miles. Op cit, p.129

94   Moughtin, J.C. *Hausa Architecture*, Ethnographica, 1985, pp.99-115

95   This is a statement attributed to Professor Arthur Ling, first Professor of Architecture at the University of Nottingham

96   Norberg-Schulz, C. Op cit, p.20

97   Newman, Oscar. *Defensible Space*, Macmillan, New York, 1972, p.27

98   Coleman, Alice. *Utopia on Trial*, Hilary Shipman, London, 1985, p.14

99   Hambridge, Jay. Op cit and Ghyka Matila. Op cit

100 Plato. *Tinaeus and Critias* (trns. Desmond Lee), Penguin, Harmondsworth, 1987

101 Vitruvius. Op cit, p.14

102 Ibid, p.74

103 Ibid, p.14

104 Robertson, H. Op cit, pp.13-17

105 Plato. Op cit, p.44

106 Sherwood, Jennifer and Pevsner, Nikolaus. *Oxfordshire*, Penguin, Harmondsworth, 1974, p.268-269

107 Editorial, *Town Planning Review*, Volume 4, No. 3, October 1913, pp.185-187

108 Irving, RG. *Indian Summer, Lutyens, Baker and Imperial Delhi*, Yale University Press, New Haven and London, 1981, p.143

109 *Town Planning Review*. Op cit

110 Zevi. Op cit, p.194

111 Cullen, Gordon. *Townscape*, Architectural Press, London, 1961

112 Summerson, Sir J. Op cit, p.92

113 Smith, P.F. *Architecture and the Principle of Harmony*, RIBA publications, London, 1987, p.14

114 Ibid, p.71

TOWNS AND BUILDINGS

3

INTRODUCTION

There are two quite distinct architectural concepts for the town or city. In the first concept the town or city is visualized as an open landscape into which buildings have been introduced as three-dimensional objects, pieces of sculpture sitting within a parkland. The second concept is of a town or city where public space, that is, the streets and squares appear to be carved from an original block of material. In the first concept, buildings are the positive solid elements and space is the general background against which they are seen. In the second way of looking, the city space itself is the positive element with three-dimensional properties and the buildings are two-dimensional façades framing the space. It will be argued here that the second concept, derived as it is from wonderful cities like Florence, Assisi and Oxford, if used as the model for future development, holds out the greatest promise for a European urban lifestyle in keeping with a long and distinguished cultural heritage.

Irrespective of general architectural form, whether the city is composed of buildings sitting in space or of spaces formed within building mass, urban design aims at a cohesive and unified composition. In the last chapter it was shown that unity in built form, in part results from the use of a common building material, the repetition of architectural details and the employment of a constant, preferably human scale. For example, the cities, towns and villages most admired in this country are those like the older parts of Lincoln, King's Lynn and the Cotswold villages; they have in common a long history and exhibit many of the unifying qualities so far discussed. In contrast, there is little delight in much twentieth-century development. A visit, for example, to the town centre at Skelmersdale does not compare with the experience of walking through the Mediaeval Gate, in Lincoln, on past the twelfth-century Jews House, up Steep Hill to Castle Hill, through the Exchequer Gate and out before the great west front of the cathedral. The walk through this part of Lincoln presents an urban architecture; spaces, detailing, floor plane, which is all of a piece, a unified experience, one of the reasons for Lincoln's attraction (Figures 3.1–3.4).

Unity in urban design is also dependent upon the form of the layout adopted and the consistency with which it is developed. There are five broad techniques for use in achieving unity in large-scale

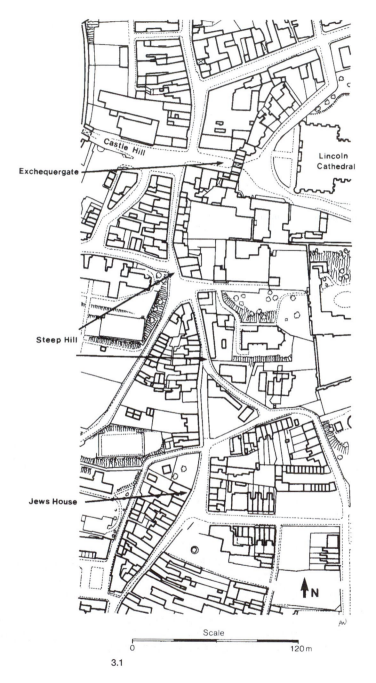

3.1

3.2

3.3

3.4

buildings need space around them so that they can be appreciated as unique compositions. The building standing in isolation within a landscape is appreciated in the same way as sculpture, that is, by walking round it and viewing from all sides.

There are two basic forms taken by buildings designed to be seen in the round and appreciated as sculpture. The first is the informal model composed of free sculptural forms which give maximum flexibility for internal planning. At its highest expression this building type conforms to and enhances the landscape setting. The formal Classical model of the building appreciated as a three-dimensional object demands a disciplined adherence to a symmetrical arrangement of internal space. While it is often more useful than the informal model for an urban setting, it is confined to architectural programmes requiring few simple internal volumes.

The informal, sculptural building is exemplified by the chapel at Ronchamp, Notre Dame Du Haut designed by Le Corbusier. It is sited at the top of a hill in a wooded clearing.[1] The building has the sculptural qualities of the little church in Mykonos, a possible inspiration for its design[2] (Figure 3.5). Geoffrey Baker's analysis shows how the building embraces, through its structural forms, the total

urban design projects. First, landscape can be used to unify an otherwise disparate group of buildings. Second, the use of simple geometric shapes for buildings may lead to a unified composition. Third, the right angle is effective as a unifying discipline in large developments. Fourth, buildings can be arranged about a series of axes and sub-axes. Finally, urban space itself can form the basis of an urban design discipline.

BUILDINGS IN LANDSCAPE

Buildings of great individuality when placed close together are almost certain to conflict. Such

3.5

landscape setting so that it is at once the focus of attention while at the same time an outward viewing station for the panoramic setting[3] (Figure 3.6).

In this country the isolated cottage seems to be the English person's ideal home - a building aloof from neighbours and set in its own garden (Figure 3.7). The lovely Cotswold cottage with thatched roof, neatly manicured hedge, garden gate and protected entrance has its roots deep in the English psyche; for social origin it has as a model the isolated detached country house. The building is set within its own landscape; individuality being emphasized with sculptural shapes. The possibilities for architectural form are manifold. The space around a building designed in this way should be sufficient for it to be seen in total, that is, at a distance of twice the height. Often the building and landscape form one composition with soft landscape elements and architectural forms changing relative positions

to form picturesque views as the observer walks around and through the complex.

The Tempietto S. Pietro in Montorio by Bramante is an ideal model for the formally designed, freestanding building; it probably represents this sculptural form in all its perfection.[4] Renaissance architects interested in developing the perfect shape for the building seen in its totality turned to the Temple of Vesta (arguably, according to Summerson, plausibly assigned to Portumnus) as their model.[5] The Tempietto, built for Ferdinand and Isabella of Spain in the place associated with the martyrdom of St Peter, was originally planned to stand in the centre of a much larger circular cloister.[6] Here in this small building the ideals, set out by Alberti, for perfection based on ideas derived from Classical traditions were put into practice. This truly is a building where all the parts are related to each other and to the whole using the discipline of proportion

Figure 3.6 Ronchamp

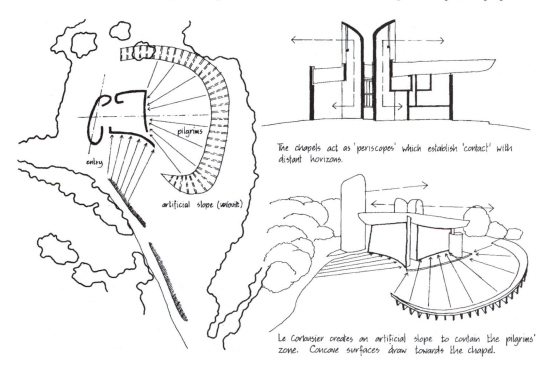

The chapels act as 'periscopes' which establish 'contact' with distant horizons.

Le Corbusier creates an artificial slope to contain the pilgrims' zone. Concave surfaces draw towards the chapel.

Figure 3.7 Cottage, Chipping Campden

Figure 3.8 The Tempietto of S. Pietro in Montorio by Bramante

based on the module; all parts of the building are necessary for its completion. nothing can be added, subtracted or changed without destroying the unity. This discipline, this perfection of form was intended, by Bramante, to encompass also the space occupied by the building, its urban setting - the perfect model for this type of development (Figures 2.6 and 3.8).

In Britain, at Oxford, the Radcliffe Camera by James Gibbs was based on this Classical model of the centralized plan. Dr John Radcliffe decided in 1712 to endow the university with a library, originally to be added first to the west end of the Bodleian and later to the south of the Schools Quadrangle. In both cases the new library, though round in plan form, was attached at one side to the existing structures. The original design, or rather designs, for the library are by Wren's student Nicholas Hawksmoor. It was,

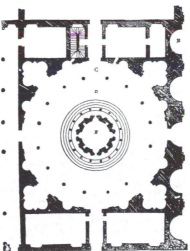

Figure 3.9 The Radcliffe
Camera, Oxford

Figure 3.10 Hampstead
Garden Suburb, London

however, Gibbs who was finally commissioned to design the building. It was he who detached the Radcliffe from neighbouring buildings so that the sculptural form could be seen in the round, a splendid sight and surprise as one enters the square from either end of Catte Street to be faced by the mass of the great Rotunda[7] (Figure 3.9).

Landscaping is one tool by which unity is achieved when buildings of great individuality are placed in close proximity. Trees, bushes and lawns placed between buildings of different form, materials and colour isolate them by a mass of vegetation. The landscape in this case becomes the dominant element in the composition, the buildings playing the minor and contrasting roles. In England for example, the normal method of siting the detached house is well back from the road and approached along a drive through trees and bushes. Each home is cocooned in its own isolated world where neighbours are excluded; it presents the barest discreet views of the building through thick foliage. Buildings having little or no architectural relationship are in this way held together by the landscape; garden design fusing buildings, roads and footpaths into a larger unity[8] (Figure 3.10).

In the suburbs of North American cities such as Roland Park, Baltimore, designed by John Charles and Frederick Law Olmsted, large detached villas stand in their own grounds but the fronts face onto a lawn with foliage acting as the foil between buildings. Large flowing areas of neatly mown grass is the landscape element which unifies buildings of disparate architectural form and style[9] (Figure 3.11).

This type of layout requires large areas of land for its successful implementation. For example, the density in housing areas following this pattern is as low as eight dwellings per hectare. Only at such density is there sufficient garden area to support mature trees and dense planting. At higher densities one has to turn to the garden cities of Letchworth and Welwyn or the garden suburbs such as Hampstead to study the role of landscape in unifying neighbourhoods of higher densities. In the

Figure 3.11 Roland Park, Baltimore

Figure 3.12 The superblock, Letchworth

garden suburbs the ubiquitous semi-detached house
and groups of terraced cottages arranged around
communal lawns are developed at 24 houses to the
hectare. These early attempts at mass housing set
the pattern for the Englishman's ideal home – the
country house in parkland, but brought within the
means of the many. Later developments with
increased density left no space for landscape and so
debased the idea. It may be time to return to the
ideas of architects like Raymond Unwin and Barry
Parker who had developed mass housing design in
the early decades of the century[10] (Figure 3.12).

There appears a tendency today for the development of business parks, entertainment centres and
other similar developments. Such parks and centres
usually comprise buildings of little architectural
merit scattered within a desolate sea of car parking;
the often-shoddy development is then densely
planted with saplings in the hope that the vegetation will disguise the poverty of the original concept
(Figures 3.13–3.15). Such overtly North American
imports with ubiquitous drive-in burger bars are a
poor substitute for the culturally rich streets and
squares of the European city. Indeed, if repeated *ad
infinitum* across European cities it would lead to a
waste of land and resources on a massive scale.
Today, when focus is given to energy conservation,
because of concerns about the fragile political
climate in the Middle East and the effects of pollu-

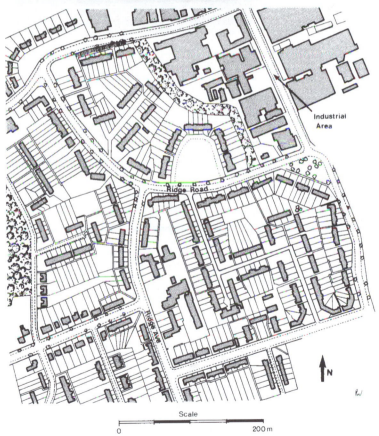

Figure 3.13 Development in Nottingham

3.13

Figure 3.14 Development in Nottingham
Figure 3.15 Development in Nottingham

3.14

3.15

Figure 3.16 Pisa
Figure 3.17 Pisa

tion on the environment, it seems outrageously foolish to be following land-use policies which increase, through dispersal, the time and cost of travel. Even if a substitute for the petrol engine is found, so permitting the development of a cheap vehicle for personal travel, the congestion on roads is likely to produce gridlock. The mere palliative of building more roads is no solution. This is the time for traffic calming, congestion charging and the eventual weaning of the public from the car back to public transport. In such circumstances dense urban developments will become the pattern of the future.

BUILDINGS OF SIMPLE GEOMETRIC SHAPE

Buildings having simple geometric volumes when placed together can present to the viewer a unified composition provided that certain conditions are met. The dynamic nature of the way building groups of this type are appreciated requires sufficient space around the buildings so that the ever-changing composition is seen from many viewpoints. It is particularly important for buildings in a group of this type to be linked strongly by a similar architectural treatment so that all components are clearly seen as members of the same family. Successful composition is also dependent upon one building dominating the rest by its sheer size and bulk.

PIAZZA DEL DUOMO, PISA

It is unusual, particularly so today when architectural programmes are complicated and functional requirements dominant, for groups of buildings to be unified using only a combination of simple form and a strong architectural treatment. The group of buildings in the Piazza Del Duomo, Pisa, is one of the few successful examples of this type of development, but it is still a legitimate design model for an urban area where a contrasting form would enliven the scene (Figures 3.16-3.20).

In the Piazza Del Duomo there are three important religious buildings – the cathedral

3.16

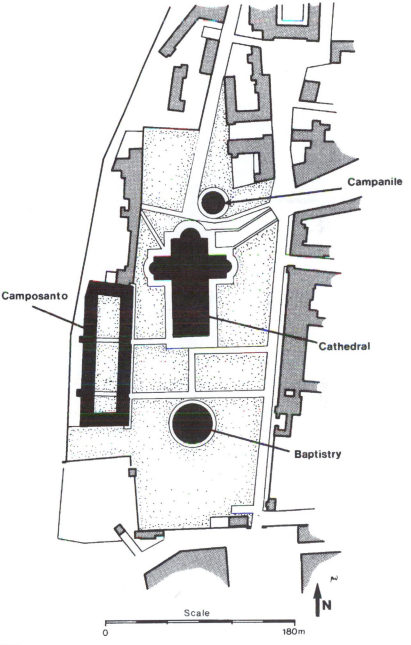

3.17

(1063-92), the baptistry (1153-1278) and the campanile (1174). The piazza is quite unlike most other Italian squares. At Pisa there is no attempt to create a sense of spatial enclosure. The site is so large compared with the ground coverage of the

main buildings that the cathedral, baptistry and campanile stand out as plastic compositions on a broad grassy plane. The surrounding walls of the piazza are low in comparison with the principal buildings; they act as visual links between the three main compositional elements rather than enclosing walls. This is particularly true of the Campo Santo (1278-83) the other great building associated with the group. It is designed with restraint externally; the blank walls being arcaded with arch and column motif. A door inserted in one such bay together with a small dome are its only distinctive features as seen from the outside. The principal views of the group are from the road which flanks the eastern wall of the piazza. From here the Campo Santo forms a rhythmical link between the three main building forms. It never sets up a visual conflict with its grand neighbours remaining as a quiet backcloth for the more lively foreground. It is only when one enters the Campo Santo that the full delight of a quiet, geometric, enclosed space is revealed - a cool contrast to the open piazza beyond.[11]

Approaching the town, the group rises above the wall and is silhouetted against the sky. It is on entering the town gate that the visitor receives the first glimpse of this magnificent composition - civic design at its best. Passing through the gateway and into the piazza, the three main buildings are arranged in line following the direction of the road. First there is the baptistry, then the cathedral and finally the campanile forming a visual stop to the group. The Christian symbolism of the composition can be read with the same clarity as the spatial organization. Entry to the civilized, inner world of Christian fellowship is through the portal, the first step. Profanity and the chaos of the outside world is left behind. Baptism ensures full membership of the church community on earth celebrated by mass and communion in the main body of the cathedral. The final gesture of the campanile points upward to the promise of membership of the greater kingdom above.

3.18

3.19

Figure 3.18 The Cathedral, Pisa
Figure 3.19 The Baptistry, Pisa
Figure 3.20 The Campanile, Pisa

3.20

The baptistry is placed on the major axis of the cathedral, facing the south front, but the campanile is placed off-centre and closer to the road. The cylindrical forms of the baptistry and campanile never conflict visually with the more massive and cubic volumes of the cathedral. In fact, as the viewer moves around the piazza and between the buildings, they form important contrasting elements in an ever-changing series of compositions. The pictures formed include those where buildings fuse together, those where elements are seen isolated from each other or positions where the viewer can take in one part of a building and explore the elevation in detail. The simple but contrasting forms of the buildings are unified further by the use of the recurring theme of arch and column in continuous arcading, and also by the use of a limited number of materials, the terracotta roof tiles, marble walls, broad marble surrounds set in a continuous level grass surface.

Compositions of the type epitomized by the group at Pisa require, for success, sufficient space for the buildings to be seen both individually and as a group. Also of paramount importance is the need for buildings to be of simple geometric form and having a unified architectural treatment. Architectural programmes demanding few internal divisions may also be important to achieve a successful urban composition of this type.

SPATIAL UNITY AND THE USE OF THE RIGHT ANGLE

Building forms can be co-ordinated using the right angle to relate them in space. The buildings retain a three-dimensional quality, that is, they remain as plastic solid forms resting on a two-dimensional floor plane but in this case they are related in plan by the right angle and all horizontal lines vanish to common points. Walking round the group the buildings are appreciated as solid form, but order is maintained by the firm, spatial anchor of identical vanishing points. Buildings placed off parallel, as Gibberd notes, produce an irregular layout in space and are almost certain 'to produce a chaotic appearance, because each building sets up different vanishing points.'[12] Gibberd later discusses the methods of arranging slab-like blocks in an orderly and unified manner and suggests that the technique 'is to devise plan types suitable for any orientation and to place them at right angles to each other . . . instead of one set of street or space pictures, we can have a complexity of views closed by buildings in all directions'[13] (Figure 3.21).

Relating building groups using the right angle has been a common method of organizing urban development particularly on flat sites or in the

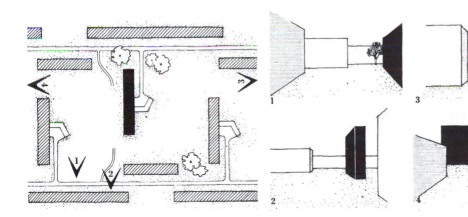

Figure 3.21 Orthogonal layout

planning of new settlements. In Paestum, the early Greek colony of Poseidonia, a regular rectangular layout was used for the whole town. Here some form of regular planning may have been used well before Hippodamus is said to have introduced the grid plan to the Greek world at Piraeus and Miletus. At the southern end of the gulf of Salerno, on a broad flat plane, are the remains of the city. The city plan is organized on an orthogonal grid with a large centrally placed rectangle for the agora and sacred precincts. Three well-preserved temples remain on the site. Two dedicated to Hera (550 BC and 450 BC) are placed close together and, according to Vincent Scully, create a special perspective towards a sacred landscape feature, a conical hill to the east.[14] The third temple, to Athena and dating from about 510 BC, is a little way off on higher ground to the north but is still strongly related visually to the other two temples. The temple to Athena rises above the general level of the town to be seen, from ships in the bay, against the mountain backdrop, as a signal of the town's existence. The temples are slightly offset from the town's orthogonal grid but still maintain a tight visual relationship; this is particularly true of the two dedicated to Hera. The relationship of temples to each other and to distant mountain range is strongly heightened at setting sun when the orange stone comes to life and long shadows are cast eastwards orientating spectator and temple alike towards the sacred landform, a strongly conical hill lying in advance of the encircling mountain range (Figure 2.25).

As a method of setting out development the use of the right angle was particularly popular during the decades immediately after the Second World War. Following on from Le Corbusier and the ideals of the Modern Movement in architecture the city was to be destroyed and a new world built on its ashes. One such post-war, mass-housing scheme in Britain which employed the right angle as the organizing framework was a 12.95 ha (32 acre), bomb-damaged site alongside the Thames opposite Battersea Power Station. Westminster City Council, in 1946, promoted an open competition for the site's development which was won by Philip Powell and John Moya. They developed the site at 494 persons per hectare (200 per acre) so conforming to Patrick Abercombie's density requirements.[15] At this density 62 per cent of the dwellings were flats in nine- to eleven-storey slab blocks, 37 per cent in four- to seven-storey maisonette blocks and 1 per cent in three-storey terraced houses. According to Ernest Scoffham: 'It was a cubic layout that was clearly connected in inspiration to Gropius's Siemenstadt project, and it became a layout form later applied in many LCC schemes.'[16] Here, at Churchill Gardens, the blocks form a series of courts for gardens, trees, lawns and children's play areas, but, nevertheless, they are appreciated as blocks standing isolated in space with three-dimensional volume clearly expressed (Figure 3.22).

Comprehensive housing schemes have received their due measure of criticism. But this style of urban design was not confined to housing. For example, the University of Liverpool, where many of the country's important architectural practices have

Figure 3.22 Churchill Gardens, London

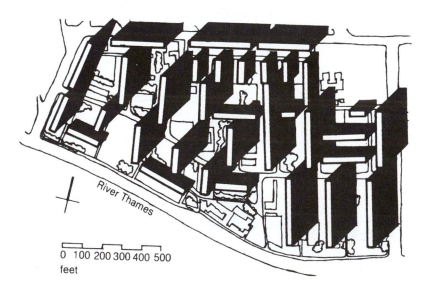

River Thames

0 100 200 300 400 500
feet

been engaged, the master plan used the design discipline of the right angle in a brave attempt to unify many buildings with a wide range of architectural treatment.[17] The street was abandoned as a three-dimensional design discipline though the main street lines and land boundaries, which in places took the form of a rectangular grid, have conditioned the geometry of the new-built form. For example, buildings cross the former streets to break the continuity but they remain at right angles to them; others step back from the pavement, but remain parallel to the original street. The spatial volume of the street has been destroyed but the memory of its original geometry retained. The design discipline of the right angle in this case at Liverpool has not quite achieved the desired result, unity over a large site. The juxtaposition of buildings of a highly individual character in close proximity creates neither street nor square but rather an amorphous space saved, in some areas, by fine landscaping (Figures 3.23–3.26).

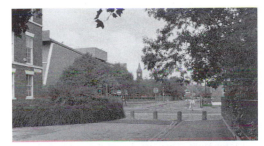

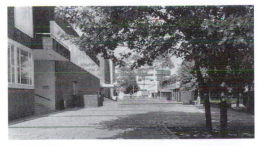

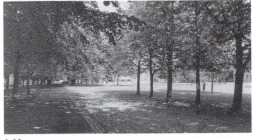

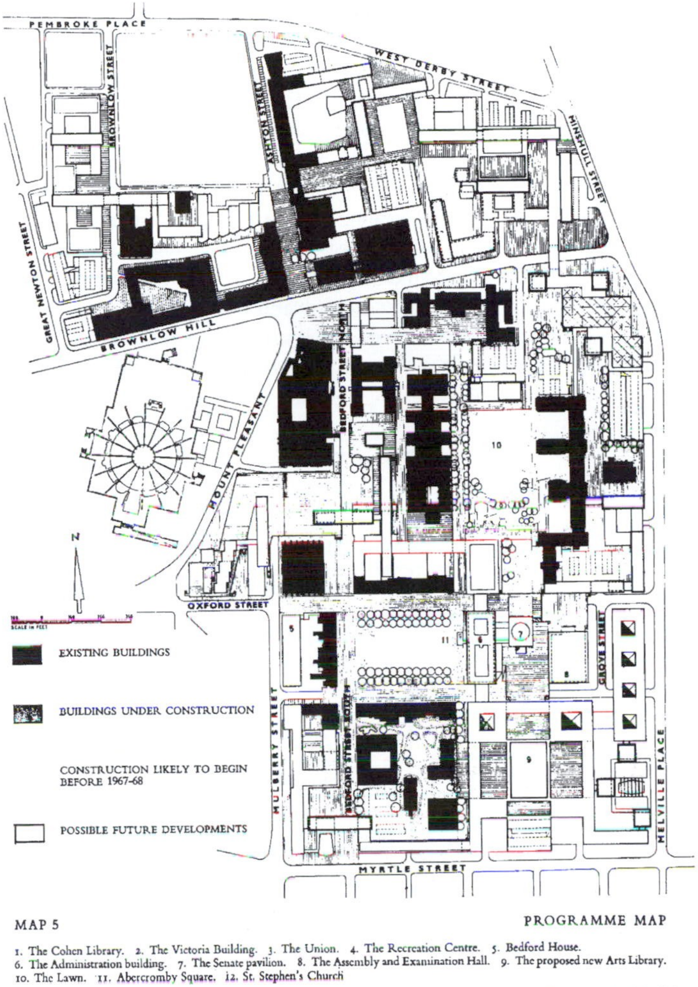
PEMBROKE PLACE
WEST DERBY STREET
HINSHULL STREET
BROWNLOW STREET
ASHTON STREET
GREAT NEWTON STREET
BROWNLOW HILL
MOUNT PLEASANT
BEDFORD STREET NORTH
OXFORD STREET
MULBERRY STREET
BEDFORD STREET SOUTH
GROVE STREET
MELVILLE PLACE
MYRTLE STREET
N
EXISTING BUILDINGS
BUILDINGS UNDER CONSTRUCTION
CONSTRUCTION LIKELY TO BEGIN BEFORE 1967-68
POSSIBLE FUTURE DEVELOPMENTS
MAP 5
PROGRAMME MAP
1. The Cohen Library. 2. The Victoria Building. 3. The Union. 4. The Recreation Centre. 5. Bedford House.
6. The Administration building. 7. The Senate pavilion. 8. The Assembly and Examination Hall. 9. The proposed new Arts Library.
10. The Lawn. 11. Abercromby Square. 12. St. Stephen's Church

3.23

3.24

3.25

3.26

Figure 3.23 Liverpool University
Figure 3.24 Liverpool University
Figure 3.25 Liverpool University
Figure 3.26 Liverpool University

Figure 3.27 Axial planning

This method of city building, using the right angle as design discipline, is also one that requires sufficient space for the building to be seen to best advantage. The clarity of this type of composition is sharpened considerably where the buildings are simple in shape. Where buildings of different heights occur in close groupings some form of regular architectural treatment, such as arcading around the lower floors, assists in visual continuity. However, where there is a multiplicity of ownership or where designers of individual buildings insist on pandering to their own egos it may be the only way of organizing a city landscape which has any coherence.

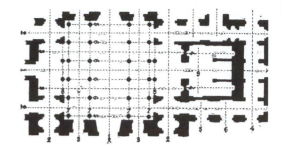

Figure 3.28 Baphuon, Temple at Angkor (c. eleventh century)

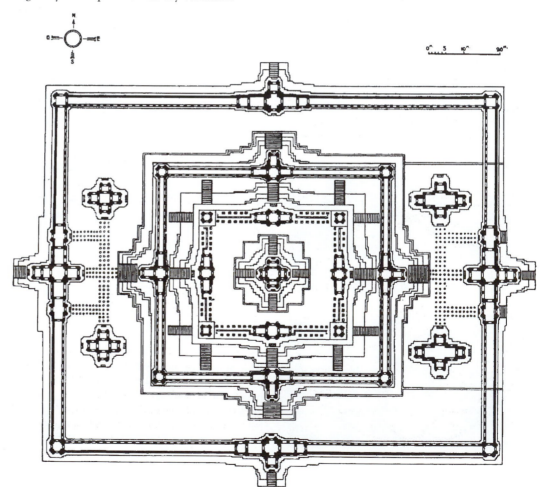

AXIAL COMPOSITIONS

A strong axis as the organizing discipline for grouping buildings is a common method of layout which has been used in many periods in the past and is not confined to any particular cultural grouping. With this generic layout form buildings and landscape elements are arranged symmetrically about an axis; unity being established through the presentation to viewer of controlled viewpoints along an axial vista. In the simpler forms of the system the orthogonal grid is developed so that some points on the grid gain added significance setting up axes and subsidiary axes which determine the location of compositional elements. As a method of spatial planning it was most common in the nineteenth century, particularly for civic groups. It was raised to the status of dogma in Beaux Arts theory; see for example the four-volume work, *Elements et Théorie de L'Architecture*, by Julien Guadet.[18] In this design system, building elements within the building and externally on the grand scale of the city, face each other in such a way that their centre lines coincide to form an axis (Figure 3.27).

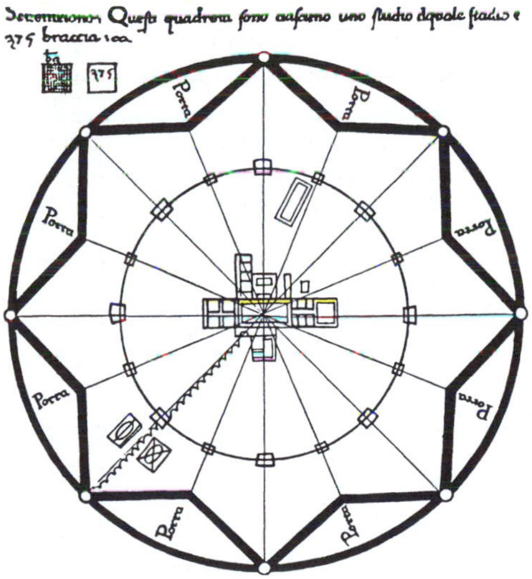

In this way the elements within buildings, doors, windows, rooms, and so on, all bear a spatial relationship to each other. This discipline, when extended beyond the bounds of the building, produced layouts where the buildings also bear a spatial relationship to each other determined by the vista down the common axis. Minor axes at right angles to the main axis are introduced to relate buildings across the main direction of movement. In this way the whole city or part of a city is ordered using a special form of the orthogonal grid (Figure 3.28).

When more than four axes converge on a terminal point a whole new pattern emerges. Avenues radiate from the central terminal building, a rotunda. This was the ideal town form advocated by Renaissance theorists who themselves were following the ideas set out by Vitruvius.[19] Many models of the Renaissance centralized town, such as Filarete's Sforzinda, were never realized. However, one such fortified town, Palma Nova, attributed by some to Vincenzo Scamozzi was indeed built in the sixteenth century[20] (Figure 2.7). Scamozzi, in 1615, published *L'Idea dell'Architettura Universale*, a ten-volume work outlining his architectural experience; included in the book is a detailed plan for a fortified city. The plan is similar to Palma Nova except for the street system which, in this case, is based, in part, upon an orthogonal grid (Figure 3.29). The vistas in Palma Nova however, terminate at one building which means it has to be completely symmetrical - a centralized form or rotunda was rarely achieved in all its perfection even in the High Renaissance. Despite the thought given, by Leonardo da Vinci among others, to the problem of the centralized building, the Tempietto S. Pietro, Montorio, by Bramante is one of the few successful projects of its kind.[21] It is more usual for the point at which several axes meet to be marked by a monument or landmark such as the Arc de Triomphe de l'Etoile in Paris, the All-India War Memorial Arch, or the graceful sandstone Baldachin - set in a raised circular basin at the centre of a

Figure 3.29 Sforzinda

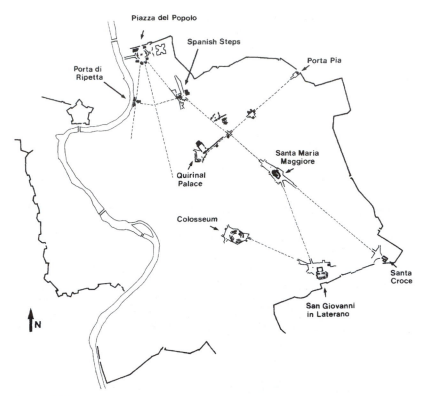

rectangular pool – which marks the terminus of a dozen converging vistas in New Delhi.[22]

Pope Sixtus V during the five years of his papacy between 1585 and 1590, and with the assistance of his architect Domenico Fontana, transformed the face of medieval Rome. The technique he used to create ordered development out of the chaos of the medieval city was the long vista. Using wide, straight roads he connected the seven main churches, the holy shrines which had to be visited by pilgrims in the course of a day. The city planning of Sixtus V was not simply concerned with the building of great religious processional routes; he was a practical man and part of his development plan was to bring water to the higher and under-utilized parts of Rome, a daring feat requiring great engineering and surveying skills. Part of the plan was to open up for development new tracts of land previously unoccupied. Incorporating the work of previous popes he developed a whole new communication network of major access routes through the city. According to Giedion it was in Rome that 'the lines of the traffic web of a modern city were first formulated, and were carried out with great assurance'.[23]

Figure 3.30 Rome and Sixtus V
Figure 3.31 S. Maria, Maggiore

Using the vista as the guiding principal for urban structuring Sixtus V set the pattern for Rome's future development. At the termination of his great vistas obelisks were raised and around these and other important nodes along the routes wonderful squares were later to develop (Figures 3.30-3.32).

One further important example of axial planning is the work of Georges-Eugène Haussmann in Paris. From 1853 to 1869 Haussmann, under the patronage of Napoleon III, transformed the face of the French capital using the great vista and a system of axial planning on a grand scale to restructure large areas of the city. An important objective of the plan was to facilitate the control of street fighting and insurrection among the population. The medieval streets of Paris proved difficult to police in times of unrest, however, the new boulevards between the main areas of the city were to provide easy movement of troops in times of riot. Other aims of the plan were to improve the appearance of the city,

to afford easy access to public buildings in times of celebration and also to improve '. . . the state of health of the town through the systematic destruction of infected alleyways and centres of epidemics'[24] (Figure 3.33).

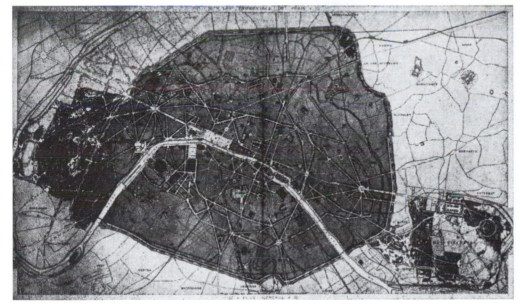

Figure 3.32 The Spanish Steps, Rome

Figure 3.33 The transformation of Paris by Haussmann

Haussmann broadened boulevards into squares with buildings surrounding parks like the Place des Arts et Metiers in Boulevard Sebastopol, or, where several boulevards meet, a great space was developed such as the Place de l'Etoile, Place de la Concorde or Place de l'Opéra; these boulevards and great squares were the main elements of city design. There remains in Paris, a most magnificent heritage from the nineteenth century which, incidentally, was

Figure 3.34 Bloomsbury, London

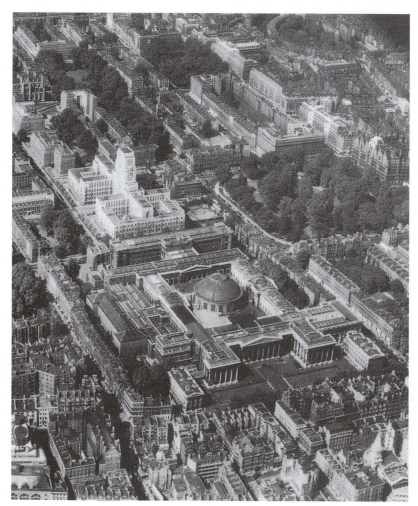

to influence town planning thought for a number of generations including people like Lutyens and Baker in Delhi (Figures 2.21–2.23).

Urban structure disciplined by the vista is usually most successful when the uninterrupted view is no greater than 1.5 km (1 mile). It was shown in Chapter two that this distance is the maximum at which it is still possible to see and recognize the form of a human being. Axes extending beyond this length require some added points of visual interest along the route. As Gibberd points out, vista or axial planning is not compatible with design for traffic speeds and densities of present day cities: 'The radial focal point system breaks down with modern road design because the line of the vista is now the path of rapid movement, . . .'[25] The main government building in Islamabad, Pakistan, is placed in the axis of an important vehicular route. The road carries heavy traffic in two directions and gaining access to the sanctuary of the central divide for a photograph of the government complex, from the axial viewpoint is a hazardous business. The vista is nevertheless part of the urban designer's repertoire. Many a town scheme is dependent upon a dominant structure placed at a strategic place along a tree-lined vista. Such axial compositions, if small in extent, and where the axis passes through a number of urban spaces of different use, can lend character to the townscape.

SPACE AS THE ORGANIZING CONCEPT IN URBAN DESIGN

Late in the nineteenth century the Viennese architect Camillo Sitte reacted against the poor imitations, throughout Europe, of Haussmann's schemes for Paris in the mid-century.[26] Many nineteenth-century groupings are dull mainly because they were designed about a few ideal viewing points without the subtleties of spatial composition of the greater works. Axial planning degenerated into the unimaginative use of the straight edge and the stereotyped employment of compact solid building blocks as the primary element of urban design. Furthermore these building blocks of city planning were often set out on a major axis, as for example in South Kensington, London, described by Gibberd as being '. . . like meat on a skewer'[27] (Figure 3.34). Within such developments the main architectural relationship is the correspondence of adjacent entrances. Sitte reversed current urban design dogma by emphasizing the square and the street as the elements of city development. In other words, according to his theory it is the spaces in the city which should receive the attention of the designers. This theory of urban design places emphasis on the outdoor rooms and corridors of the city; they are the volumes to be designed and the buildings are merely two-dimensional enclosures - the walls of the spaces.

Following Sitte's pattern of city development buildings are designed in such a way that the scene becomes more important as urban design while architecture is relegated to a subsidiary supporting role. The façades of buildings, which stand alone in space, meet an an external angle and are seen by the observer as a mass. Reversing the process, buildings arranged around a space have façades which meet at an internal angle and there is an effect of volume.

Relating building forms seen in mass at urban densities requires some form of rectangular or regular layout and preferably this should occur on a flat site. When buildings form the walls of squares and streets this is not nearly so important. The multitude of vanishing points are not so apparent.

Figure 3.35 Geraci, Reggio Calabria

Figure 3.36 Geraci, Reggio Calabria

Figure 3.37 Geraci, Reggio Calabria

3.36

3.35

3.37

Figure 3.38 St Mark's
Square, Venice
1 = Piazza San Marco
2 = Piazzetta San Marco
3 = San Marco
4 = Doges Palace
5 = Campanile
6 = Library

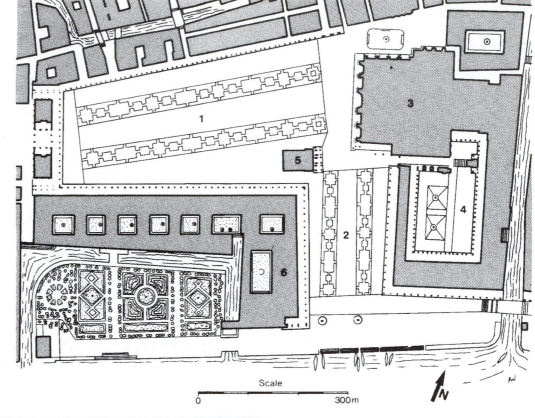

Scale

0   300m

Figure 3.39 Entrance to
the Piazzetta San Marco,
Venice

An irregular spatial layout is not obvious to the
spectator apart from very obtuse angles in an
awkward triangular space. Even when irregularities
are apparent the scene is often thought quite
picturesque with adjacent planes eliding to form a
single element containing the space (Figures
3.35–3.37).

Sitte's suggested method of organizing building
groups is best illustrated by the Piazza and Piazzetta
San Marco in Venice (Figures 3.38–3.42). His own
words describe most eloquently his views:

> So much beauty is united on this unique little patch
> of earth, that no painter has ever dreamt up

3.40

3.41

3.42

Figure 3.40 Piazza San
Marco, Venice
Figure 3.41 San Marco
from the Piazzetta, Venice
Figure 3.42 Piazzetta San
Marco, Venice

anything surpassing it in his architectural
backgrounds; in no theatre has there ever been seen
anything more sense-beguiling than was able to arise
here in reality. This is truly the sovereign seat of a
great power, a power of intellect, of art, and of
industry, which assembled the riches of the world
on her ships, and from here exercised dominion
over the seas, relishing her acquired treasures at
this, the loveliest spot in the whole wide world. Not
even Titian or Paolo Veronese could invent anything
more magnificent for the imaginative city views in
the backgrounds of his large paintings of weddings
and other occasions. If we were to examine the
means by which this unexcelled grandeur was
achieved they would, indeed, prove to be
extraordinary: the effect of the sea, the
accumulation of superlative monumental structures,

the abundance of their sculptural decoration, the
rich polychromy of S. Marco, the powerful
Campanile. However, it is the felicitous arranging of
them that contributes so decidedly to the whole
effect. There is no doubt that if these works of art
were disposed separately according to the modern
method, straight in line and geometrically centred,
their effect would be immeasurably decreased.
Imagine S. Marco isolated, with the Campanile set
on the axis of its main portal in the middle of a
huge modern square - the Procuratie, library, etc,
standing about separately in the modern "block
system" instead of forming a tight enclosure - and

to top it all, a boulevard of almost 200 feet in width running past this so-called plaza. One cannot bear the thought.[28]

CONCLUSION

There are two main ways in which buildings can be arranged in space. The buildings themselves can be the positive object designed as a three-dimensional mass, the 'figure' in the composition, while the space in which they stand is the 'ground'. The alternative method advocated by Sitte and his followers is a reversal of this process. Space itself becomes the 'figure', the positive element, the volume to be designed and buildings are relegated to a supporting role, the 'ground'. As the background of the urban scene the buildings are the stage setting for the activities of daily life taking place within the spatial volumes they define.

There are a number of techniques by which buildings of three-dimensional mass can be unified; with the use of landscaping, through the unified architectural treatment of simple volumes and by the use of the right angle, axis or vista. Axial or vista planning takes on an added dimension and greater subtlety when used in conjunction with a spatial composition following the prescriptions of Sitte. In any system of categorization there will always be the possibility of overlap, the use of two or more basic concepts together with the deliberate and successful application of principles to achieve particular effects. It does appear, however, that in any given composition one method, one concept should be the dominant idea if unity is to be achieved.

For the remainder of the text it will be assumed that urban areas in the future will be constrained by the imperative of resource conservation both in terms of land allocation and the husbanding of energy. Such an imperative would place a premium on the development of a tightly grained urban fabric as opposed to prairie planning associated with the North American suburban ideal. This is not to suggest that suburban expansion will cease to exist in the twenty-first century. Though in Europe particularly there may be a return to urban form more in keeping with our cultural heritage. It is assumed that over large areas of European cities urban designs will he required for projects where land will be intensively used with little space being available for massive landscaping schemes. Certainly, there will be parts of cities such as industrial estates where buildings will sit on their own site surrounded by car-parking space. But for the major parts of the city the ideas of Sitte will take on added importance. These ideas will be considered in detail in the following chapters. They will examine spatial composition using squares, streets and the methods used for their combination.

NOTES

1 Boesiger, Willy. *Le Corbusier*, Thames and Hudson, London, 1972, pp.116-119

2 Le Corbusier. *The Chapel at Ronchamp* (trns. Jacqueline Cullen), Architectural Press, London, 1957

3 Baker, G.H. *Le Corbusier, An Analysis of Form*, Van Nostrand Reinhold, Wokingham, Berkshire, 1984, pp.186-211

4 Murray, Peter. *The Architecture of the Renaissance*, Thames and Hudson, London, 3rd edn, 1986, pp.123-127, and Burckhardt, Jacob, *The Architecture of the Italian Renaissance* (ed. Peter Murray), Penguin, Harmondsworth, 1985, pp.61-63

5 Summerson, John. *The Classical Language of Architecture*, Thames and Hudson, London, 1980, p.49

6 Serlio, Sebastiano. *The Five Books of Architecture* (an unabridged reprint of the English edition of 1611), Dover Publications Inc, New York, 1982, Book 3, Chapter 4, Fol. 18

7 Downs, Kerry. *Hawksmoor*, Thames and Hudson, London 1969, pp.92-94, and Kersting, A.F. and Ashdown, John. *The Buildings of Oxford*, Batsford, London, 1980, pp.22, 64 and 65

8   Gibberd, Frederick. *Town Design*, Architectural Press, London, 2nd edn, 1955 pp.216-217

9   Tunnard, Christopher. *The City of Man*, The Architectural Press, London, 1953

10 Unwin, Raymond. *Town Planning in Practice*, London, 1909

11 Norberg-Schulz, Christian. *Existence, Space and Architecture*, Studio Vista, London, 1971, pp.171-177 and Gibberd, F. Op cit, pp.125-127

12 Gibberd, F. Op cit, p.75

13 Ibid, p.252

14 Scully, Vincent. *The Earth, The Temple and The Gods: Greek Sacred Architecture*, Yale University Press, New Haven and London, 1962, p.65

15 Abercrombie, Patrick. *Greater London Plan*, HMSO, London, 1945

16 Scoffham, E.R. *The Shape of British Housing*, Godwin, London and New York, 1984, p.56

17 University of Liverpool, Recorder, *Report of the Development Gommittee to the Council of the University for the Years 1959-1964*, The University of Liverpool, Liverpool, January 1965

18 Guadet, J. *Elements et Theorie de L'Architecture*, Vols I to IV, 16th edn, Librairie de la Construction Moderne, Paris, 1929 and 1930

19 Vitruvius. *The Ten Books of Architecture* (trns. by Morris Hicky Morgan), Dover Publications, New York, 1960, pp.24-32

20 Morris, A.E.J. *History of Urban Form*, George Godwin, London, 1972 pp.117-118

21 Popham, A.E. *The Drawings of Leonardo da Vinci*, Jonathan Cape, London, 1964, pp.161. 312-314

22 Irving, R.G. *Indian Summer, Lutyens, Baker and Imperial Delhi*, Yale University Press, New Haven and London, 1981, pp.259-260

23 Giedion, S. *Space, Time and Architecture*, Harvard University Press, Cambridge. Mass., 3rd edn, 1956, p.76

24 Ibid, p.648

25 Gibberd, F. Op cit, p.77

26 Sitte, Camillo. *Der Stadte-Bau*, Carl Graeser & Co. Wien, 1901

27 Gibberd, F. Op cit, p.75

28 Quoted from the translation of Sitte in Collins, G.R. and Collins, C.C. *Camillo Sitte, The Birth of Modern City Planning*, Rizzoli, New York, 1986, pp.196-197

THE SQUARE OR PLAZA

4

INTRODUCTION

One of the most important elements of city design is the square or plaza. It is possibly the most important way of designing a good setting for public and commercial buildings in cities. This has led some writers to equate architectural grouping of buildings with, and identical to, plaza design.[1] A square or plaza is both an area framed by buildings and an area designed to exhibit its buildings to the greatest advantage. Great civic compositions such as St Mark's Square, Venice, St Peter's Square, Rome, and the group of squares in Bath by John Wood and his son are unique in the relationship between space, the surrounding buildings and the dome of the sky; they demand an emotional and cerebral response and, as such, compare with any other art form.

There are two main methods of categorizing squares – by function and by form. There are numerous examples of recent plaza design where one or other of these two equally important criteria of excellence have been neglected. The empty windswept place surrounded by under-utilized buildings is all too common in the modern city, while its opposite or counterpart, the busy traffic island or faceless car park around which are scattered collections of non-related buildings, is also endemic in the urban scene.

FUNCTION AND THE SQUARE

Activity in a square is important for its vitality and, therefore, also for its visual attraction. Vitruvius when writing about the design of the forum said it 'should be proportionate to the number of inhabitants, so that it may not be too small a space to be useful, nor look like a desert waste for lack of population'.[2] The Renaissance theorists followed and expanded such statements found in Vitruvius. For example, Alberti tells us that '. . . there ought to be several squares laid out in different parts of the city, some for the exposing of merchandises to sale in time of peace; and others for the exercises proper for youth; and others for laying up stores in time of war, . . .'.[3] He goes on further to detail the various types of market square and associates these with zones in the city: 'The squares must be so many different markets, one for gold and silver, another for herbs, another for cattle, another for wood and so on; each whereof ought to have its particular place in the city, and its distinct ornaments.'[4] Sitte takes up this point in a number of places in his treatise '. . . that in the Middle Ages and the Renaissance there still existed a vital and functional use of the town square for community life and also, in connection with this, a rapport between square and surrounding public buildings. . . In short, we miss activity exactly where in Antiquity it was most animated, that is, around the great public buildings.'[5]

A word of warning is necessary at this point. There is some danger in attempting to transfer design concepts which may be effective at one particular time, or at one place or in one culture to a quite different setting. The great wealth of wonderful squares in Italy may be explained in part by a combination of climatic conditions conducive to outdoor living and the temperamental attitudes characteristic of Italian culture. These conditions and the outgoing nature of the Mediterranean peoples led to a public life which in turn gave form to street and square. The evening parades in cities like Florence, together with the many other outdoor community activities, demand the concentration of design effort in the development of the public domain. In more northern climes such as our own in Britain the covered street, the arcade, the covered atrium, provided it is in community ownership, and, of course, the public house are important in the life of the city. Nevertheless, even in countries like Britain the square and the street still have an important function in the context of urban design.

The types of space needed in a city are: the setting for a civic building; the principal meeting places; places for great ceremonial occasions; spaces for entertainment around buildings such as theatres, cinemas, restaurants and cafes; spaces for shopping, shopping street, arcades and markets; spaces around which offices are grouped; spaces of a semi-public nature around which residential accommodation is arranged; and, finally, the spaces associated with urban traffic junctions.

Some spaces will take on heightened meaning as the centres or portals for places, while others may serve a number of overlapping functions. Exhortations for the isolation, separation and expression of individual functions associated with the philosophy of the Modern Movement, in architecture and city planning. has indeed proved to be a great disservice to the art of city building. The products of such thinking, the massive office complex or the equally extensive shopping precinct dying when its sole activity ceases, sterilize large areas of the city making them 'no-go' areas in the evening. The most successful city squares, though they may have a dominant function for which each is known and by which they may be classified, are often those that sustain activity through the diversity of uses in the surrounding buildings.

The single most important function of an element in the city is the symbolic meaning attached to it. All great civic art is in tune with the profound depths of our emotions. The great plaza, like the great building, is linked with the world of fantasy, the context of feeling. There is in all-aesthetic experience, a deep core of valuation, which owes little to critical judgement. This primitive reaction to the world around, including the built environment, is intimately and irrevocably connected to the ways in which we perceive the human body. This is the basic building block of urban design. As Scruton points out, it is to Melanie Klein's theory of 'the good and bad breast' that the designer must turn for a greater understanding of aesthetic appreciation.[6] If, as Klein postulates, human reactions can be analysed in terms of infantile views of the breast, towards the 'bad breast' which removes and disintegrates, and the 'good breast' which nurtures and restores, then all artistic creation is a re-creation of the once-cherished whole. The artist's role, and in this the urban designer is no exception, is the rebuilding of the once-ruined object, or the 'advancement from childish resentment and loss, to mature acceptance of a world where giving and taking, receiving and losing, good and evil, comingle irredeemably'.[7] Acceptance of this principle means the recognition of symbolism as central to the design process and also a willingness to manipulate urban form to achieve meaning.

The concept of the centre is probably the single most important idea with which the urban designer works. Without an understanding of its importance to man's perception of the environment only damage can be inflicted upon the city. Le Corbusier in his book *The Radiant City* was advocating the opposite proposition: 'Demolition of the centre. That is what we have been insisting upon for years. And now you are actually doing it! You are actually doing it! Because it is inevitable.'[8] The unholy alliance of architect, planner and road engineer together with blind market forces have, in many instances, sapped the vitality of existing centres in the process of decentralization and surburbanization of city life. In the words of the poet Yeats: 'Things fall apart; the centre cannot hold; Mere anarchy is loosed upon the world.'[9]

If civilization is defined as the culture of living in cities then Corbusier's prophesy could well be self-fulfilling and so strike the death knell of Europe's proud legacy of great city building and, with it, the passing of our distinctive culture, to be replaced by the 'linear Coca-cola belt' stretching from Liverpool to the Ruhr with individuals isolated in Frank Lloyd Wright's bland sea of super suburbia, Broadacre City.

Man's perception of space is centred upon himself. The development of schemata for the general organization of space based upon this subjective idea of centre is extended into the notion of externalized centre as a point of reference in the environment. This idea of centre is applied to the 'known' and friendly' world, as opposed to the undifferentiated outside and often hostile world. Each group has its own centre; the centre of the Muslim world is Mecca; that of the Catholic world is the Vatican in Rome; while the world of Judaism is centred in Jerusalem. At the opposite pole to the concept of public 'World Centre', is the home or the personal family centre or, in the words of Norberg-Schulz: 'If the centre of the world thus designates an ideal, public goal, or "lost paradise", the word "home" also has a closer and more concrete meaning. It simply tells us that any man's personal world has its centre.'[10] Within these extremes of world and home centres is a continuum or hierarchy of overlapping centres serving different communities or groups. It is the design, physical definition or reinforcement of these centres which is at the core of the disciplines of architecture, urban design and planning.

In considering the centre two architectural theorists are particularly important; Lynch and Alexander. In his study of the perception of urban structure, *The Image of the City*, Lynch found the node to be one of the elements by which a city is recognized and understood. In short, the node is an important element which gives the city 'imageability' or a strong image.[11] As he says: 'Nodes are points, the strategic spots in a city into which an observer can enter, and which are the intensive foci to and from which he is travelling.'[12] Or in other words the nodes are '. . . the conceptual anchor points in our cities'.[13] Alexander makes much the same point: 'Every whole must be a "centre" in itself, and must also produce a system of centres around it.'[14] He considers that the centre tends towards a symmetrical arrangement, '. . . especially bilateral symmetry, similar to that which the human body has . . .'.[15] In this process of centre formation each new centre endeavours towards symmetry but never quite achieves it. This struggle towards a relationship of the centre to the complexities of the surrounding urban field is an effort to unite it or make it whole. This tendency towards 'unity', or the 'making of wholes', Alexander sees as the inevitable outcome of an 'effort to be true'. In Alexander, centre formation takes on an almost natural, self-determining goal. If this view holds then the urban designer is simply working with the grain of natural forces. Following Lynch's theories leads also to a similar position, though he does not stress the inevitability only the desirability of the process. Nor does he stress the symmetrical tendency of centres but he advocates the achievement of identity for the node by the continuous quality of the walls, floor, detail, lighting, topography or skyline as the main prerequisite of perceptual support.

In any composition there is a need to emphasize some parts and subordinate others; this is the art of design. As Unwin says, the best way to achieve this in town planning is '. . . to have definite centres'.[16] It is only in this way that a relationship and proportion can be established between the different parts of the town design. The dramatic effect of the main civic buildings is lost if they are haphazardly scattered throughout the town. By grouping them around the central place as a dominant element in the urban scene, the town takes on a unified form. Sitte in his investigations of plaza design found that '. . . in each town a few major squares are, as a group, decidedly the largest, the rest having to content themselves with a minimum expanse'.[17]

This then, is the centrepiece of the 'public realm', the place where the major public works, the major public expenditure and the greatest civic art is located. It is only when the main square of most old towns is reached that one has really 'arrived'; all the streets lead naturally to this focal point. The centre dominates the town in size and grandeur; it gives meaning to its existence as a place distinct from other places. It is easy to overlook just how great a part the centre played in the life of the ancient city. Here much of the life was conducted in the open air. It was here that ideas and produce were exchanged. To some extent this still occurs in some European cities; even a city such as Nottingham has its centre, Market Square, or 'Slab Square' as it is affectionately known by locals. It is still the hub of social life and place of great and diverse activities.

ST PETER'S SQUARE, ROME

The square or plaza is for the city what the atrium represents for the family home. It is the well-equipped and richly appointed main hall or reception room. St Peter's Square in Rome is a prime example of such a place. St Peter's Square is, however, something more than an important node in Rome's urban fabric; it is the centre of the Catholic universe. Symbolically it represents the fountainhead of Christ's kingdom here on earth. Gianlorenzo Bernini's great elliptical colonnade sweeps outwards in two vast protective arms, encircling, enfolding and welcoming the Christian pilgrim (Figures 4.1–4.5).

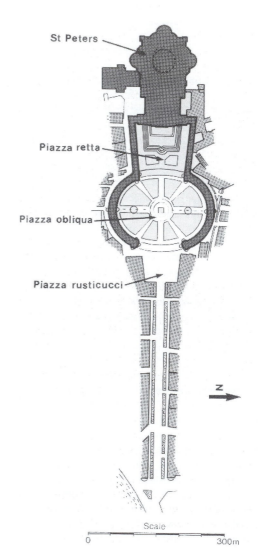

Figure 4.1 St Peter's, Rome

Figure 4.2 St Peter's, Rome
Figure 4.3 St Peter's, Rome
Figure 4.4 St Peter's, Rome

4.2

4.3

The trinity of Vatican, St Peter's and the great piazza, as an urban complex are indivisible. As a unity they have had bestowed upon them the attention of many of the great artists of Christendom, particularly during the Renaissance and Baroque. The history of the building of St Peter's is a complex affair centred around the debate about the liturgical and symbolic merits of the Latin and Greek cross for

4.4

Figure 4.5 St Peter's, Rome

church planning. The present building was begun in 1506 and was completed in 1626. It received the attentions of some of the great architects of the time including Bramante, Raphael, Peruzzi, Sangallo, Michelangelo, Giacomo della Porta, Fontana and Maderna with the square completed by Bernini; the list is impressive by any standards. The unified result, one of the world's great masterpieces of civic art is amazing considering the fundamental changes in architectural style, the debate about the ideal church form and the very different personalities involved during the period of its completion. It was somewhat marred during the last century by the intervention of Mussolini and his architects in the extension of the axial approach.

Pope Julius II appointed Bramante as capomaestro to St Peter's and in 1506 the foundation stone was laid for the building. From the Bramante drawing in the Uffizi, it appears that his proposal was for a centralized church based upon the Greek cross and a similar concept to his Tempietto of S. Pietro in Montorio though more closely modelled on ideas that inspired churches like S. Biagio in Montepulciano by Antonio da Sangallo the Elder.

For Bramante and his generation of architects the Latin or elongated cross when used for the plan was a rather obvious form of symbolism. Instead they opted for the mathematical perfection of the centralized plan of the Greek cross with its theological symbolism as a reflection of the perfection of God. According to Murray: 'The earliest Christian churches were of two types, the *martyrium* and the *basilica*. Martyria were almost always small and almost always centrally planned. They were erected in places with some religious association, such as the spot where a martyrdom had taken place'.[18] What more natural form than the martyria is there for both the Tempietto where St Peter is thought to have been martyred and the cathedral whose dome marks the place of his tomb. Despite vicissitudes in the fortune of the building between the replacement of Bramante by Giuliano da Sangallo, Fra Giocondo and Raphael in 1513 and the appointment of Michelangelo in 1546 the guiding principle for the completion of St Peter's remained basically a centralized structure.

There were, however, alternative suggestions for St Peter's completion during the period between Bramante and Michelangelo, for example, Raphael proposed a plan in the shape of the Latin cross and Antonio da Sangallo the Younger attempted a design which proposed an 'awkward compromise between central plan and longitudinal form . . .'[19] Michelangelo on the death of his immediate predecessor Sangallo the Younger returned to Bramante's purer centralized form of the Greek cross. Michelangelo increased the size of the main piers to take the weight of the huge dome and reduced the overall space between the piers and the outside walls. The spatial composition was very much more dynamic but used fewer elements. The external expression of the Greek cross changed from the simplicity of the forms associated with Bramante and the High Renaissance to those associated with Mannerism or the transition to Baroque. Where Bramante's plan is square with entrances in the four straight sides Michelangelo, by standing the square on its corner, obtained a diamond shape. The main façade which gives direction to the plan is formed by blunting one corner of the diamond and replacing it with a large portico.

On the death of Michelangelo in 1564 much of St Peter's was standing in the form we know today, Michelangelo had completed the drum of the dome as far as the springing and the rear elevations with their giant order of Corinthian pilasters were complete. The dome was completed between 1585 and 1590 by Giacomo della Porta and Domenico Fontana. The plan, however, was once again modified by Carlo Maderna in the first half of the seventeenth century. He extended the plan by the addition of a long nave and the present main façade. The Latin cross finally won the day partly because of its many liturgical advantages including the greater space it provides for processions. Just as important for this dramatic change in plan form were the deliberations of the Council of Trent after which time the medieval cruciform type of church came once more to be preferred and with it a change in architectural taste.

In competition with other leading architects Bernini developed a number of designs for the completion of St Peter's Square. Pope Alexander VII commissioned Bernini to complete the project which he did between 1656 and 1667. In preparing the final design Bernini had to include the gigantic obelisk erected in 1586 by Domenico Fontana for Pope Sixtus V and the fountain on the right-hand side erected by Maderna in 1613; the matching fountain on the left hand side being finished on the completion of the square. Bernini also had to minimize the design faults in the great cathedral notably Maderna's much too broad front (the width to height ratio being 2.7:1) and his elongation of the nave which in perspective means that the dome appears to sit awkwardly on the roof without intervening drum. The specific purpose of the square was therefore designed as a huge enclosed forecourt; it is a parvis or atrium for the cathedral.

The façade of St Peter's with its colossal columns together with the obelisk were the points of reference for the proportions of Bernin's square. Bernini conceived the parvis as three connected units; the *piazza retta* in front of the church façade, the *piazza obliqua* consisting of two half circles and a rectangle but appearing as an oval through the floorscaping, and the *piazza rusticucci* not completed by Bernini but now part of Mussolini's avenue which links St Peter's and the River Tiber. The function of the *piazza rusticucci* was to collect and direct visitors towards the *piazza obliqua*. Some of the original drama of the composition can still be gained by entering the *piazza obliqua* through the surrounding colonnade. The surprise and contrast in moving from small-scale streets to this great parvis has been muted by the overlong avenue from the Tiber and the steady march of faceless buildings of ordinary office scale.

The main axis of the *piazza obliqua* does not lead directly to the main façade of the church. It is parallel to it: another surprise. The movement towards the church is arrested by this change of direction of the axis. The long, north-south axis of the *piazza obliqua* is emphasized by the main sculptural elements of the square, fountain-obelisk-fountain and also by the dishing of the floor plane towards the centre. The main features of the space are the two colonnades; columns 15 m (50 ft) high and standing four deep. In all there are 560 free-standing columns in rows of four and arranged in two great arcs; a forest of columns through which the light penetrates between gigantic cylinders and from which one can see the sweeping dish of the floor. The pavement descends past the fountain to the obelisk and beyond the second fountain up to a similar ceremonious crescent of columns. The floor pattern of eight radial spokes centred on the obelisk ties it strongly with the other vertical elements, the fountains and sweeping colonnades whose insistent rhythm, Summerson says, '. . . is steadied by columns standing out at the ends and again, in coupled pairs, at the centre - sentinels'.[20] There is some doubt about the order to which the colonnade belongs, variously described as Doric or Tuscan. The capital is Doric, the base Tuscan and the entablature a form of Ionic. Summerson sums it up in this way: 'Doric? Well, yes; except that they have Tuscan bases and are a trifle taller than the conventional Doric and they carry an entablature which is not Doric at all but more or less Ionic. In other words for this particular occasion, Bernini has taken the law into his own hands and designed his own order.'[21] This deliberate architectural confusion, or blurring at the edges, a feature of the Baroque, is repeated in the spatial composition of the whole complex of piazze that form the parvis.

Where the colonnades meet the closed corridor framing the *piazza retta* the space narrows, creating a second visual stop, but blurred by the intrusion of the oval floor pattern. The *piazza retta* rises towards St Peter's, the rhythm and pace of the rise quickened by the many-stepped platform projecting about 76 m (250 ft) or halfway from the entrance of the church and the *piazza obliqua*. Both side wings of the *piazza retta* diverge towards the church façade also losing height with the change of floor level. Those approaching St Peter's imagine the wings to be at right angles to the building and also imagine a flat floor plane; the result is an optical illusion caused by false perspective. Maderna's much too broad front is naturally perceived as narrower than it actually is and closer to an ideal proportion.[22]

A centre is a place of arrival but it is also the point of departure. The pilgrim having visited St Peter's stands on the threshold of Maderna's vast portico over 70 m (230 ft) wide and more than 12 m (40 ft) deep: he or she surveys the complex of piazze and the world beyond. It is from here that the message of the Gospels radiates to the Catholic world. The 'narrows' between *piazza retta* and *piazza obliqua* appears as wide as Maderna's portico. In consequence the great *piazza obliqua* with its wide encircling arms 198 m (650 ft) apart, takes on added scale induced by false perspective. The effect is heightened by the fall in the pavement, 3.5 m (12 ft) over the *piazza rette* and a further 2.5 m (8 ft) to the obelisk. The floor level of the cathedral protrudes over 243 m (800 ft) into the square then drops dramatically in steps to the receding floor plane – a further enhancement of the dramatic landform. From this stage the full theatrical effect of the expansive composition is revealed; scores of statues of gigantic scale look down from the colonnade to view the teeming life within the square below. Bernini originally planned to part-close the space with an added length of colonnade, an idea, it seems, he later abandoned. Carlo Fontana's later project for a triumphal arch and clock tower opposite St Peter's at the termination of the *piazza rusticucci* and at an equal distance from the obelisk was also unfortunately abandoned. Instead, there is the Mussolini over-long vista leading nowhere in particular and as a result the centre peters out with no real termination.

St Peter's Cathedral and piazze is the centre of a world community. It is therefore on a grand scale. But each community, each physically distinct area, in order to be given proper definition requires its centre. Centres of small communities will not be on the scale of St Peter's and its piazze but nevertheless in establishing the identity of the district, neighbourhood or area they will have important aesthetic and symbolic meaning. Each centre should have the unified form of a place, an enclosure, somewhere that denotes arrival and forms the springboard for departure.

THE PORTAL

A place has a dual function. It becomes a centre because it is a goal, a place of pilgrimage, or more mundanely, somewhere to get the weekly shopping. Just as significant is that function of a place as a point of departure; the home is left daily for work while, at the grand scale, Mecca, when a pilgrimage is complete, is left behind for home and the daily routine of life. This tension between centripetal and centrifugal forces is most pronounced in the portal, a point made clear by Alberti: 'Now if there is any other part of the city that falls in properly with the subject of this book, it is certainly the haven, which may be defined as a goal or proper place from where you may begin a voyage, or where having performed it you may put an end to the fatigue of it, and take repose.'[23]

The door has been one of the most important elements in architectural design since antiquity. We can speak of a door as 'inviting' or 'gaping'. The entrance of the Palazetto Zuccari in Rome is actually formed as 'the gaping jaws of a giant'.[24] The transition from one domain to another is also a critical design problem in structuring the city: '. . . we must not forget the gateway and the importance of marking in some way the entrances of our towns, our suburbs, our districts. . . For example, some little forecourt of green surrounded by buildings and led up to by an avenue of trees would strike at once the necessary note . . .'[25] Alexander, in his search for design patterns, also found the gateway to be of great importance, making it one of his design principles: 'Mark every boundary in the city which has important human meaning – the boundary of a building cluster, a neighbourhood, a precinct – by great

gateways where the major entering paths cross the boundary.'[26] His prescriptions include the need to mark the transition along all paths which penetrate the boundary of any distinctive place or quarter in much the same way as Alberti many centuries before: 'The principal head and boundary of all highways, whether within or without the city, unless I am mistaken, is the gate for those by land, and the haven for those by sea.'[27] The function of the city portal may now indeed be quite different from the ancient gateway, the prime purpose of which was exclusion. The entrance to the housing cluster may however be designed to deter those who may disturb the privacy of the residents. The organization of the traditional Islamic city into clearly defined culs-de-sac is a particularly good example of this type of entrance definition to semi-private space, so important for Islamic family life (Figure 4.6).

PIAZZA DEL POPOLO

The Piazza del Popolo is a particularly fine example of the city portal. For many centuries, until the age of the railway, the Piazza del Popolo was the main

Figure 4.6 Islamic housing layout

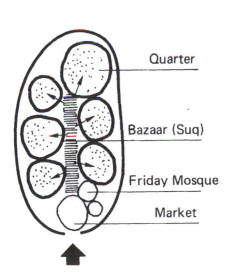

Quarter

Bazaar (Suq)

Friday Mosque

Market

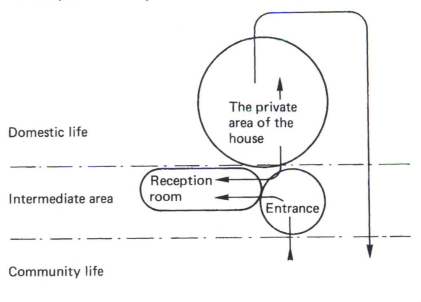

Domestic life

The private area of the house

Intermediate area

Reception room

Entrance

Community life

Figure 4.7 Piazza del
Popolo, Rome
Figure 4.8 Piazza del
Popolo, Rome

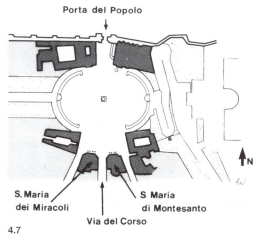

Porta del Popolo

S. Maria
dei Miracoli

Via del Corso

S Maria
di Montesanto

N

4.7

Figure 4.9 Twin churches,
Piazza del Popolo, Rome

4.8

4.9

Figure 4.10 The entrance
to the Strada de Corso,
Piazza del Popolo, Rome
Figure 4.11 The Porta del
Popolo, Rome

4.11

4.10

entrance to Rome for all visitors coming from the north; it was also the departure point for those travelling northwards (Figures 4.7–4.11). Since the closure of this gateway, the Porta del Popolo, to all through-traffic except for taxis, and also its partial pedestrianization, it now forms just another square in Rome's urban structure. Today, it is a pleasant entrance to Pincio Gardens and a termination of three streets. The present traffic restrictions, while preserving the form of the square and improving its local environment, have denuded it of a once-proud meaning as a city entrance. It is almost a museum piece, an historic anachronism, a quiet backwater away from the mainstream of modern life. Though still a pleasure to see and to visit, it needs new activities, new purpose, to breathe life into this old city entrance.

First impressions of any place are important. The great city is no exception. It deserves a splendid entrance. The grandeur and spacious welcome of the Piazza del Popolo, the most important historic gate of Rome, has been recorded by many travellers to the city: 'Such an august entrance cannot fail to impress a stranger with a sublime idea of this venerable city,' said Smollett. Beckford commented on the city entrance in this way: 'Shall I ever forget the sensations I experienced . . . when I entered an avenue between terraces and ornamented gates of villas, which leads to the Porta del Popolo, and beheld the square, the domes, the obelisk, the long perspective of streets and palaces opening beyond, all glowing with the vivid red of sunset.'[28] Some of the splendour described by Beckford may still be recalled at sunset in the piazza when it is enveloped by long shadows and the sunlight is reflected in the red granite of the obelisk; but where now is the entrance to this or indeed to most modern cities?

Like many other examples of civic art the Piazza del Popolo has a long development. It is, nevertheless, extraordinary that the many additions made by so many hands have resulted in such a unified composition. It is probably to the papacy that we must give credit for the ultimate guardianship of the long, slow development.[29] Over this long period the main structuring elements were the gateway itself, the church of S. Maria del Popolo, the obelisk erected by Fontana for Pope Sixtus V in 1586, the twin churches begun by Carlo Rainaldi in 1662 and the scheme to unify the piazza by the French architect-planner Giuseppe Valadier in 1816–20.

The present layout of the piazza is determined by the existing topographical features and the solutions to the problems caused by the existence of buildings, monuments and road constructions of such importance and permanence that they demanded preservation. The Piazza del Popolo is situated between the Tiber on the west and the steep slopes of Monte Pincio on the east. The main approach to ancient Rome crossed this narrow area between the river and the hill passing through the Porta del Popolo built into the Aurelian wall of AD 272.[30] The great north road, the Via Flaminia, now the Strada de Corso, continued undeviating from the gate to the foot of the Capitol; this determined the main axis in the most important direction. The next great influence was the church of S. Maria del Popolo, built just within the gateway and founded by Pascal II in 1099 to counter the evil said to pervade the place where tradition placed the tomb of Nero. The church was rebuilt in the thirteenth century and again by Sixtus IV and it is to this period, 1480, that the present simple Renaissance façade, attributed to Baccio Pontelli, in the main belongs.

One of the most important factors which determined the later development of the form of the piazza was the making of the third radial road to the east of the Corso. The new road was made to repeat the angle to the main axis of the Via del Ripetta which, along with the Corso, were the two main roads entering the piazza during Roman times. The new road, now called Via del Babuino, was planned by Leo X in 1516 and built to the line determined by Raphael and Antonio de Sangallo the Younger. This branching out of three roads from the gateway, though the product of centuries of development, was a rational piece of urban design. The Corso as we have seen is the main approach to the centre of the city. The Via del Babuino follows the natural line of the Pincio and connects the south east part of the city, now the Piazza di Spagna and the Spanish Steps. The third road, the Via di Ripetta, follows the line of the Tiber connecting with the south-western part of the city via a ferry crossing where 'an architectural arrangement of terraces and stairs led down to the river'.[31] This arrangement of three streets radiating from a square became a common feature of town planning in later centuries; examples include Versailles, Place de Ia Concorde and Letchworth town centre.

The Egyptian obelisk of red granite is the focal point of the piazza; it is from the XIX dynasty in the time of Set I and Rameses II. The obelisk was first brought from Heliopolis by Augustus and erected in the Circus Maximus. It was rediscovered in 1587 and transported to the Piazza del Popolo by Sixtus V and used as a focal point in his reconstruction of Rome. Domenico Fontana placed it in its present position where the axes of the Corso, Via del Babuino and Via di Ripetta meet. From this point it has both dominated the piazza and dictated decisions about later developments.

The Porta del Popolo itself underwent many developments since medieval times. The outer façade was probably designed by Vignola in 1561-2 and the inner face completed by Bernini in 1665. In the late nineteenth century the two side gates were made in the flanking walls converting the gate into a triple entrance. Despite almost continuous remod-elling, the gateway itself remained in virtually the same position throughout the slow development of the piazza; it was the foundation for the form of the square and created its whole essence from the outset.

The impressive entrance to the Corso is a stroke of pure genius in terms of urban design. As Giedion so aptly says, Carlo Rainaldi's twin churches stand '. . . like ecclesiastical sentries guarding the three main arteries of the city . . .'.[32] Rainaldi's original scheme was for two identical churches. The first, S.

Maria dei Miracoli was begun under Alexander VII in 1662 but was completed later, together with the second church S. Maria di Montesanto, after his death. The building of both churches was carried out by Berini and Carlo Fontana. Only the façades facing the Piazza del Popolo are identical; the plans being different necessitated domes of different heights and shapes. The two campanili are different in design and were added at the end of the eighteenth century. Being on either side of the Corso they give emphasis to its importance. The churches are part of both the square and the streets and link the square streets and the obelisk of Sixtus V.[33]

Valadier, the architect who worked for Pius VI and Pius VII, prepared a plan for the Piazza del Popolo which was approved in 1813. His plan completed the three sides of the square facing the twin churches. The east and west sides are great hemicycles or sweeping exedras; the one to the east, Valadier designed in conjunction with a great stairway, ramp and cascade. He transformed the garden of the Augustinian monastery into a public garden through which the ramp winds and cascades to the lower level of the piazza. There is a large terrace on the high point of the Pincio. The propor-tions of the substructure for the terrace Valadier related to the other buildings he built next to the twin churches to enclose the square: 'Thus, despite its being on a much higher level, it fits within and makes a unity of his whole spatial composition.'[34]

At the entrance to the square Valadier regularized the design, repeating the basic form of S. Maria del Popolo on the western side of the Porta del Popolo. He also remodelled the dome over the cibo chapel of the church. This dome, which is on the axis with the Via di Ripetta and the obelisk, he repeated on the other side thus providing a contrasting background for the obelisk from the Via di Ripetta and the Via del Babuino. The Piazza del Popolo is a fine model for the city entrance, a statement of both arrival at the haven and the point of departure for the outside world.

THE FORM OF THE SQUARE

There have been a number of attempts to classify the form that squares may take. Two of the most influential theories were outlined by Paul Zucker and Sitte. From his work on squares Zucker was able to distinguish five archetypal forms: the closed square where the space is self-contained; the dominated square where the space is directed towards the main building; the nuclear square where space is formed around a centre; grouped squares where spatial units are combined to form larger compositions; and the amorphous square where space is unlimited.[35] For Sitte, enclosure was taken as the prerequisite of the square and he concluded that there were only two types of square in formal terms, the character of either being determined by the nature of the dominant building. The two categories of square distinguished by Sitte were, 'the deep type and the wide type . . . whether a plaza is deep or wide usually becomes apparent when the observer stands opposite the major building that dominates the whole layout'.[36] For Sitte both the amorphous square and the space formed around a central object being outside his definition of the subject matter would have little meaning for him. Grouped squares on the other hand were the object of much attention by Sitte. They were, however, not thought by him to be a generic form but more simply one manner in which squares could be related to each other and to the urban fabric in general.

THE ENCLOSED SQUARE

For the purpose of this analysis the 'closed' square of Zucker and also his 'dominated' square which equates with Sitte's 'deep' and 'wide' squares are brought together as variants of the same type under the heading 'enclosed'. The overriding quality of this spatial type is a sense of enclosure. The enclosure of space in this manner is the purest expression of a sense of place, the centre. It is here that order is created out of the undifferentiated chaos of the world beyond. The square is an outdoor room and with the room it shares the quality of enclosure.

The key to enclosure in the square is the treatment of its corners. Generally speaking, the more open the corners of the square the less the sense of enclosure, the more built up or complete they are, the greater the feeling of being enclosed. Many recent urban spaces have two streets meeting at the corners; the space in this case disintegrates. Each building block is isolated and retains its own three-dimensional properties. As Sitte points out: 'Precisely the opposite rule was followed in former days: if possible, only one street opened at each point, while a second one would branch off further back on this street out of sight from the plaza.'[37] Sitte goes on to suggest his own ideal of leading the streets off the plaza in the fashion of turbine blades so that from any point in the square there is no more than one view out. A further strengthening of the sense of enclosure is achieved by a complete building up of the corner as for example in the main square at Salamanca. Alternatively the corner can be closed using an arch for completion: 'Arches give a very great ornament to piazze that are made at the head of streets, that is, in the entrance into the piazza,'[38] declared Palladio.

Other important qualities of squares and their surrounding buildings affect the degree of enclosure. These include the nature of the enclosing buildings' roof line, the height of the enclosing buildings in relation to the size of the space, the degree of their three-dimensional modelling, the presence or absence of a unifying architectural theme and the overall shape of the space itself.

The top surface of an internal space is usually completed by a flat ceiling; it is the lid for the room. The dome of the sky is the ceiling for the plaza. Zucker believes that the height of the sky above a closed square is '. . . imagined as three or four times the height of the tallest building on the square'.[39] This lid or dome to the square appears to sit more securely when the roofline is more or less of equal height throughout its length. Indeed a strongly defined eaves line serves the same purpose as the cornice and frieze in the room, a finish or edge to the vertical element of the space. However, there are many wonderful medieval squares which gain their charm, in part, from the picturesque nature of the roofline. The variations in height in these cases are normally within the same magnitude of scale. The other end of the continuum which describes degree of enclosure occurs when there is a wide divergence of building heights between the sides of the square; enclosure is progressively diminished as the size of the variations in height increase.

The design guide prepared by Essex County Council states: 'The relationship between the *effective height' of the buildings* and the width of the space is critical if a harmonious urban place is to be created. If too high in relation to width, a feeling of oppression may result; if too low, a feeling of exposure and vulnerability.'[40] The guide goes on to suggest the maximum harmonious proportion of height to width as being 1:4. Ideas about the relationship between the height of buildings and the width of public spaces, like many other urban design theories can be traced back to Alberti, who, writing on this subject suggested: 'A proper height for the buildings about a square is one third of the breadth of the open area, or one sixth at the least'.[41] According to Hegemann and Peets, Palladio endorses Alberti's ideas about the proportions for the height of buildings around the square but goes on to narrow down the range by quoting the width adopted in a typical Roman Forum as between 1¾ and 2½ times the height of the buildings. Hegemann and Peets, together with Spreiregen, independently come to similar conclusions: they separately conclude that seeing the detail of a building is best achieved at a distance equal to the largest dimension of the building.[42] Since we are mobile and the eye can be moved horizontally the critical dimension is the height. The minimum width of a piazza is therefore determined by an angle of 45° from the eaves. The building however, is seen best as a

whole, that is as a total composition, at a distance of about twice its height or at an angle of 27°. Seeing more than one building requires a viewing distance of three times the height or at an angle of 18°. Below the threshold of 18° the object loses predominance in the field of vision, objects beyond the space are perceived and the square loses its enclosed feeling.[43] Sitte's extensive survey of public squares seems to accord with the lower end of the scale of proportion. He states quite categorically that 'the height of its principal buildings, taken once, can be declared to be roughly the minimum dimension of the plaza, the absolute maximum that still gives a good effect being double that height. . .'. He adds the proviso, 'provided that the general shape of the building, its purpose, and its detailing do not permit exceptional dimensions'.[44] Despite the findings of the last authors there are many successful town squares that fall outside these strict proportional limits. It must also be remembered that Sitte was most influenced by the small-scale medieval square. A good example of the larger town square is in Nottingham which as it recedes from the Council House attenuates into the form of a narrow neck. Such squares may owe their success to their still relatively small absolute dimensions and the strong symbolic meaning they have for the community. What they may lack in enclosure they make up for in their sense of place and the lively activity they support.

The absolute size of the urban space also has a bearing on its resulting degree of enclosure. Sitte, the most specific of those writing on this topic, found the largest plazas in ancient cities on average were only 57 m × 143 m (190 ft × 470 ft). Many of the delightful intimate squares in the older parts of our towns and cities may be as small as 15-21 m (50-70 ft), which now is barely wide enough for a road reserve through a housing area. There is no doubt that the small cosy medieval square found in cities like York or towns like Stamford are a safe haven where people can stop, relax and escape from the mad bustle of modern urban life. They contrast vividly with the 'modern gigantic plaza, with their yawning emptiness and oppressive ennui, . . . Overly large plazas have a most pernicious influence on their surrounding structures. The latter can, in turn, never be large enough'.[45] At best the buildings surrounding a large, windswept plane take the form of three-dimensional villas; better far, to treat them as such and create a parkland edged by fine buildings as, indeed, John Nash did at Regent's Park, London.

The work of Maerteus and the limitations set by optical geometry upon urban scale bear out many of the findings of Sitte and the more intuitive beliefs of other writers in the field. Around 135 m (450 ft) is the upper limit where body gestures can be distinguished and approximates closely with the recommendations of Sitte for the maximum size of a plaza. Of course the distance at which one can appreciate a tank, intercontinental missile, marching troops or massed bands is much greater than the gestures of a single human being. Such reasoning may give the justification for Red Square in Moscow and other great spaces for ceremonial occasions. These, however, do not fall within the classification of town or city square.

As previously mentioned, the maximum angle at which a building can be seen clearly according to most theorists is 27°, or at a distance which equals about twice its height. A viewer at the centre of a space could therefore rotate and appreciate all sides of the space if the proportion of its width to height is 4:1, that is, the size as recommended by the Essex design guide.[46] A three-storey square would then be about 36–45 m (120–150 ft) across and a four-storey square would be about 48–54 m (160–180 ft). If, however, the aim is to appreciate the full composition of the wall of the square, or several buildings, the distance from it should be three times the height. An appreciation of all the sides of the square from its central point requires a size of square in the width-to-height ratio of 6:1, or the maximum dimension recommended by Alberti. Using this module the size for a three-storey square would be 73–91 m (240–300 ft) and a four-storey square

97–109 m (320–360 ft). The maximum permissible size square of 137 m (450 ft) would require buildings of about seven storeys. Using the upper range of Alberti's formulae means that movement of the observer within the square permits an appreciation of the composition as a whole, the proportions of individual buildings and also details from a closer range, but there is a consequent reduction in the sense of enclosure. The last word on this matter of the proportion of squares must, however, be left with Sitte: 'The relationship between buildings and plazas cannot be established as definitely as, for instance, the relationship between columns and entablatures has been defined in handbooks.'[47]

The closer the walls of the square or plaza resemble the two-dimensional quality of the internal room, the greater will be the feeling of enclosure. The greater the three-dimensional modelling of surrounding buildings the greater will be the reduction in this sense of enclosure in the public space. Enclosure is lost, for example, if the sides of the space are designed as individual villas standing in isolation as three-dimensional pieces of architectural sculpture. Rob Krier makes some play with the wealth of treatment open for choice in the design of the walls for urban space. Many examples he cites would, however, destroy enclosure. They may be used for other purposes but should be avoided when designing public enclosed space.[48] The ideal for enclosure, let it be said again, is the two-dimensional plane. There is room for a sculptural surface, and indeed decoration of an essentially two-dimensional surface; the essence of the wall however, is its two dimensionality which is quite the opposite of the use of sculptural forms throughout. The three-dimensional element in urban space is the void between buildings, in the case of the public square this is a simple contained shape.

The buildings around an enclosed space should form a continuous surface and present to the viewer an architectural unity. The effect of the mass of individual buildings has to be reduced in order to preserve continuity. The effect of continuity is heightened if there is a repetition of individual building or house types facing the enclosure. The medieval gable front if repeated around the square, or the measured and carefully modulated terrace of Georgian fronts - though giving a different scale and character to the square, serve the purpose of enclosure equally well. The enclosure of the space can be further strengthened using either the colonnade or arcade as a continuous feature linking the ground floors of individual buildings in a covered walkway. This is an architectural feature mentioned first by Vitruvius: 'The Greeks lay out their forums in the form of a square surrounded by very spacious double colonnades, adorn them with columns set rather closely together, and with entablatures of stone or marble, and construct walks above the upper storev.'[49] Both Alberti and Palladio repeat this point made by Vitruvius for the adornment of the piazza: 'The Greeks made their Forums or markets exactly square. and encompassed them with large double porticoes, which they adorned with columns and their Intablatures, all with stone, with noble terraces at the top, for taking the air.'[50] And: 'Porticos, such as the ancients used, ought to be made round the piazze . . .'[51] Salamanca and other Spanish town squares use this feature of the covered walkway as a unifying element in spatial composition (Figure 4.12). There is also a good functional reason

for using the colonnade or arcade as in hot climates it protects from the sun and in the northern parts of Europe it protects from the rain.

In Platonic terms the ideal form, basic concept, or idea for the town square would approximate to Zucker's 'closed square' having a simple geometrical volume built from a square, rectangular, or circular ground plan. In practice, such perfection is rarely, if ever, achieved. Some writers, Sitte being among them, suggest that 'it suffices to mention in passing that square plazas are rare and do not look very good. . .'[52] It is a view not supported by Renaissance theorists such as Alberti. The perfect square, it is probably true to say, does not exist except in the mind as a concept. However delightful squares abound; they take shapes that come to terms with the exigencies of site, the practicalities of a long-

Figure 4.12 Main square, Salamanca
Figure 4.13 Place des Voges, Paris
Figure 4.14 Place des Voges, Paris

4.13

4.12

4.14

term building process and a multiplicity of individual ownership decisions. The idealized type, as Zucker points out, '. . . without being bound to specific periods or definite architectural styles, appears in its most perfect form in the Hellenistic and Roman eras and then again in the seventeenth and eighteenth centuries'.[53] Models of this type of square are Place des Voges in Paris, Inigo Jones's plan for Covent Garden, London, The Queen's Square and the Circus at Bath, and the Agora in Priene (Figures 4.13–4.14).

PIAZZA DELLA SANTISSIMA ANNUNZIATA, FLORENCE

This piazza takes its name from the Basilica Santissima Annunziata, Florence, which terminates the axis at one end of a long street, the present Via del Servi. The street is closed at the other end by Brunelleschi's great dome. The loggias on three sides of the square make it probably the best example of a Renaissance piazza. Broadly speaking the piazza as it now appears represents the general ideas of town planning of Brunelleschi and his contemporaries. Indeed it was Brunelleschi himself who designed the major building in the square, the Ospedale degli Innocenti or the Hospital of the Innocents (Figures 4.15–4.19).

The piazza is a small, intimate rectangular space. The floor plan between the external faces of the loggias is about 60 m × 75 m (197 ft × 246 ft). If, however, the back wall of the loggias is used as the plan form then it approximates closely to a perfect square. The ratio of the effective height to width between loggias in the short direction is about 1:3.3, in the long direction towards the church it is 1:5.4 and in the direction towards the cathedral it is 1:3.8.[54] All ratios are within the ideal range Alberti advocated. The whole of the Hospital of the Innocents can be seen from the opposite side of the square within a ground-plan angle of 60°, and can be seen comfortably as a total composition. The vertical viewing angle of the hospital from the bottom of the steps of the Confraternity of the servants of Mary is approximately 18°, the minimum angle some

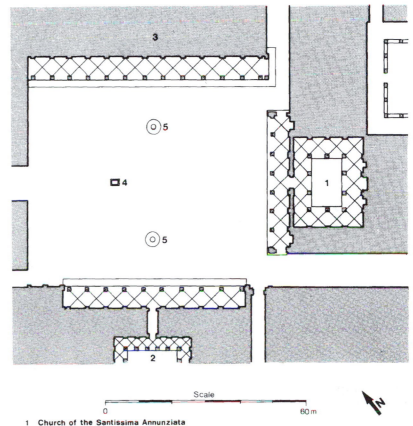

Scale

0   60 m

1 Church of the Santissima Annunziata
2 Foundling hospital
3 Servi di Santa Maria Brotherhood
4 Equestrian figure of Grand Duke Ferdinand I
5 Fountains

theorists believe necessary to maintain enclosure. Here in this piazza the strong visual structure of the architectural composition holds the space together maintaining a tremendous sense of enclosure and completeness. The loggias with their simple architectural elements of column and arch unify the composition and almost completely mask the function of the surrounding buildings. The arcades of the loggias set a lovely rhythm to the square and the simply vaulted roof permits the space to expand to the walls of the surrounding buildings.

Figure 4.15 Piazza Annunziata, Florence

Figure 4.16 Basilica
Santissima Annunziata,
Florence
Figure 4.17 Ospedale Degli
Innocenti, Florence
Figure 4.18 Statue of the
Grand Duke Ferdinand,
Piazza Annunziata, Florence
Figure 4.19 Corner detail,
Piazza Annunziata, Florence

4.16

4.17

4.19

4.18

Three of the corners of the piazza are open, one,
indeed, having two roads in a manner frowned upon
by Sitte. Nevertheless, the outlets are narrow and the
buildings visually linked so strongly, using arches on
two exits, that enclosure is maintained and the eye
is not encouraged to wander beyond the space. The
statue of the Grand Duke Ferdinand the First is
placed on the centre line of the major axis. So large
is it in mass that it is in proportion to the space in
which it stands. It is also firmly related to the piazza
by the backdrop of the loggia of the church and the
drum of its rotunda which terminates the axis. There

are also two small, identical fountains by Pietro Jacca
placed on the centre line of the entrance to the
Foundling Hospital which emphasize the minor
secondary axis at right angles to the main movement.
The triangular disposition of the three pieces of
sculpture furnishing the piazza form an extremely
subtle spatial composition and complete the decoration of one of the great squares of Europe.

The development of the piazza is the result of
many centuries of effort involving many fine artists.
The building of the great dome for Florence
Cathedral gave the city a magnificent centre and the
focal point of civic pride. It also gave direction for
new developments in the city. One such
development preceding the building of the dome
was the new street laid out by the Servite monks
through their property to the north-east of the
cathedral. This street, possibly from as early as the
late thirteenth century, linked Santissima Annunziata
the church of the Servite monks to the cathedral[55]
This initial regulating line set in motion the orderly
planning of this part of the city which culminated in

the building of the piazza and its most important building the Foundling Hospital in the early fifteenth century by Brunelleschi.[56] Its elegant arched arcade set the architectural pattern for the later completed square. The centre arch for the church was designed by Antonio Sangallo the Elder in the mid-fourteenth century while Michelozzo Michelozzi was rebuilding the fabric of the church.[57] The loggia was enlarged by Giovanni Battista Caccini some 200 years later still employing the arch and column motif. The final form of the square, however, was determined by Sangallo the Elder who was commissioned to design the building opposite the hospital. In the early sixteenth century nearly 90 years after Brunelleschi had completed the hospital arcade, Brunelleschi's façade was repeated in almost exact detail. From his analysis of the development of the Piazza Della Santissima Annunziata, Edmund Bacon formulated the 'principle of the second man'. From this principle he deduced that 'it is the second man who determines whether the creation of the first man will be carried forward or destroyed'.[58] In this case Sangallo the Elder must be given great credit for completing the masterpiece of civic design set in motion by Brunelleschi. However, from the thirteenth to seventeenth centuries a number of artists were involved in the planning of this part of Florence. Each followed the imperative of place inherited from his predecessors. The art of civic design is founded upon the reading of, and the reaction to, seminal forces inherent in particular locations. Understanding and appreciating the context for development, the *genius loci* is a lost art and fundamental to great city building. In Florence this art was demonstrated by those involved in the creation of this piazza.

THE DOMINATED SQUARE

According to Zucker the dominated square 'is characterized by one individual structure or a group of buildings toward which the open space is

4.20a

directed and to which all other surrounding structures are related'.[59] Sitte distinguished only two types of public square the 'deep' and the 'wide' plaza; both fall into Zucker's category of the 'dominated' square - 'whether a plaza is deep or wide usually becomes apparent when the observer stands opposite the major building that dominates the whole layout'.[60]

As an example of the deep type, Sitte quotes the piazza in front of Santa Croce in Florence (Figure 4.20). All the main views lead towards the church and it is usually seen from this direction; the main streets lead to the church, the sculpture and street furniture are arranged with this in mind. As Sitte pointed out, the building that dominates the deep piazza, to be effective, should have dimensions similar to the space it faces. In the past it was the façade of the church which fitted this requirement most readily. The square in front of the church, the medieval parvis, was an expansion of the function of the church's main entrance. It was here that the church community gathered before and after the mass; here occasional outdoor sermons were given and through it passed

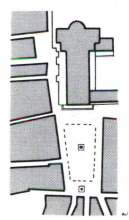

4.20b

Figure 4.20 Santa Croce, Florence

great processions. The buildings around the church were often functionally related to it and naturally subordinate to the main structure.

The ideal distance for viewing one dominant building at the end of a plaza lies somewhere between equalling the height of the building and twice that dimension. Since it is the detail of a Gothic building including its statuary which is so important the shorter of these two dimensions is often found in the older medieval church squares. The parvis is not a common feature of the English medieval cathedral. It is more usual to find the English cathedral set in a landscaped area, Canterbury being a fine example and Southwell Minster with its green to the west is also typical (Figure 4.21). At Lincoln, however, there is such a

parvis before the great west entrance to the cathedral (see Figures 3.1 and 3.4). Entrance to the parvis is through the Exchequer Gate. From behind the gate rise the two western towers to a height of 60 m (200 ft). The complete view of the façade, symbolic entrance to the Kingdom of God, is seen as one enters the courtyard through the arched gateway; the distance is about the same height as the main part of the front. The lower part of the west front is a mass of fine sculptural detail, a maze of interlaced arcading, dating largely from the twelfth and thirteenth centuries. The composition, some say, is marred by the lack of resolution caused by the twin towers. The strong horizontal line below the fourteenth century towers and the lack of dominance of the central feature of door, west window and nave gable produce a disturbing effect in compositional terms. This defect in composition, if so it is, is not so apparent through forced concentration on detail and the amazing richness of its rhythm. The towers which rise above the main mass of the façade are best viewed from beyond the gateway.

Figure 4.21 Southwell Minster

Figure 4.22 Modena

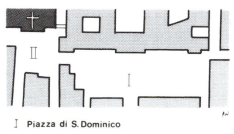

I   **Piazza di S. Dominico**

II **Piazza Reale**

As an example of a wide square Sitte cites the Piazza Reale in Modena (Figure 4.22). Here the square is dominated by a palace - long in elevation when compared to its height. The bulk of the dominant building having similar proportions to the square in which it stands. It contrasts sharply with the adjacent Piazza S. Domenico to which it is connected by a short street. The Piazza S. Domenico having a church as its dominant element is, according to Sitte's classification, a deep square.[61]

Sitte found no evidence to indicate that there are preferred relationships between the length and width of a square, nevertheless he noted that 'overly long plazas in which the ratio of length to width is more than three to one already begin to lose charm'.[62] This is the way Paul David Spreiregen accounts for this loss of charm in the excessively long piazza, '... the cornice at the far end would be too far below the eye's field of vision'.[63] Alberti's ideal was a 'square twice as long as broad',[64] while Vitruvius, his teacher, suggested a ratio of 3:2.[65]

PIAZZA NAVONA, ROME

A square which defies all these rules is the Piazza Navona, Rome, whose sides are in the ratio of approximately 1:5 (Figures 4.23–4.25).

The shape of the Piazza Navona recalls that of a stadium and in fact it is built over the foundations of

4.24

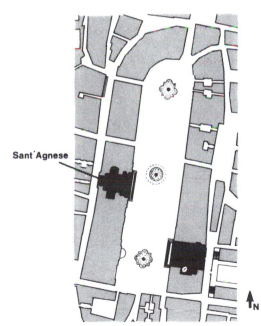

Sant´Agnese

N

4.23

4.25

Figure 4.23 Piazza Navona, Rome
Figure 4.24 Piazza Navona, Rome
Figure 4.25 Piazza Navona, Rome

the Roman Stadium of Domitian which stood there before; the walls of the present square closely following the shape of the original structure. It was converted into its present magnificent space during the seventeenth century. The Church of San Giacomo degli Spagnuoli from the mid-fifteenth century is subordinated by the Church of Sant' Agnese (1652-77) on the opposite long side of the square designed by Girolamo and Carlo Rainaldi in collaboration with Francesco Borromini. More importantly it was the furnishing of the square by Bernini with his magnificent fountains which actually defines the form and rhythm of the square. There is an emphasis on the length of the space which is reflected in the bold, horizontal treatment of the façade of Sant' Agnese. The forward position of the cupola, between the twin towers of the façade, also encourages oblique views of this imposing feature in the square as opposed to the more usual frontal perspective. Bernini's Fountain of the Rivers composed round the ancient obelisk of Domitian is placed on the longitudinal axis of the square but off its central axis. The curved façade of the church in

this way is not diminished but enhanced. Bernini is responsible for the other two fountains in the square both on the longitudinal axis. The southernmost Fountain of the Moor was remodelled by the addition of sculptures by Bernini, and the Fountain of Neptune, executed in the nineteenth century, is based on Bernini's original design.

The Piazza Navona is a square dominated by the fountains of a great civic artist who gave to it its essential character. He changed the direction of movement of those using the piazza by directing attention away from the long axis and towards the façade of the church. Apart from Sant' Agnese, the architecture of the rest of the piazza is subdued and contrasts with the movement of Bernini's fine sculpture set within a cascade of water. The whole piazza must have taken on the appearance of an exotic stage set when flooded in the eighteenth century for a theatrical naval spectacle.

A public square can be dominated by a vista or void rather than a building or piece of great sculpture. Many of the lovely hill towns of southern Italy or Sicily have examples of public squares where the

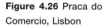

Figure 4.26 Praca do Comercio, Lisbon

surrounding buildings on three sides form the space. The fourth side of the square is a belvedere giving magnificent views of the countryside. The main market square of San Giorgio Morgeto in the province of Calabria, southern Italy, is such a piazza with one side open to the view (Figure 5.38). It is approached by narrow streets which widen out into a space surrounded by two- and three-storey buildings. It is here that the main market takes place once a week around a lovely ornamental fountain. The Praca Do Comercio, on the River Tagus in Lisbon, with an open vista of a large, flat surface of water is possibly the most impressive square in the Iberian peninsula; it has all the magnificence of the Place Royale in Paris (Figures 4.26–4.28). The square has a rhythmic arcade on three sides, enclosed corners and a main central arch indicating the position of the Rua Augusta, the

spine road leading to the Praca de Dom Pedro and the city. It fulfils all the requirements for a haven set out by Alberti: 'The haven is adorned by broad porticoes, . . . with spacious squares before it.'[66] Again Alberti writing about the haven says: 'And from the port straight through the heart of the city ought to run a large street.'[67]

THE CAPITOL, ROME

The piazza as a place of arrival and departure is given its fullest expression in the Capitol in Rome designed by Michelangelo. Michelangelo in this piazza, through the architectural treatment of the square, created a unified composition dominated in one direction by the main civic building, the Palazzo del Senatore, and in the opposite direction, by the views across Rome (Figures 4.29–4.33).

4.27

4.28

Figure 4.27 Praca do Comercio, Lisbon
Figure 4.28 Rua Augusta, Lisbon

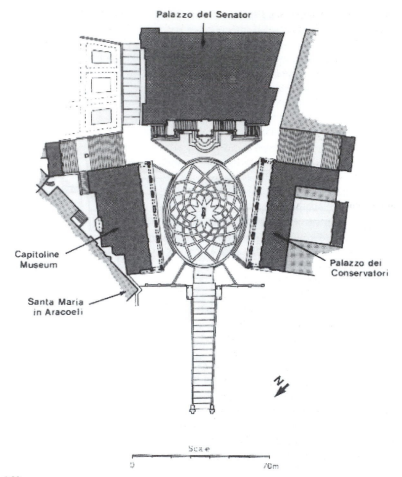

Palazzo del Senator

Capitoline Museum

Santa Maria in Aracoeli

Palazzo dei Conservatori

Scale

0   70m

4.29

4.30

4.31

Figure 4.29 Piazza del Campidoglio, Rome
Figure 4.30 Piazza del Campidoglio, Rome
Figure 4.31 Piazza del Campidoglio, Rome

The history of the development of Capitol Hill in Rome is long and is a story of alternating periods of greatness and decline. This history is well documented by Thomas Ashby.[68] The Capitol was one of the seven hills of ancient Rome. From early times it was an important political and religious centre serving the city as a whole. The Capitol also acted as a political centre in medieval Rome, a palace existing on the site in 1145, and which was rebuilt a number of times during the Middle Ages, acted as the town hall. The neighbouring church,

Santa Maria in Aracoeli, dates from 1250 and its imposing stairway from 1348. The first building on the site of the Palazzo del Senatore dates from the early fifteenth century though it was not transformed into a palace until the time of Pope Nicholas V.

It was during the papacy of Paul III, in 1537, that Michelangelo was commissioned to design a monumental square on Capitol Hill. Final completion of the square was, however, not until some hundred years after Michelangelo's death.[69] When Michelangelo started work on Capitol Hill he found a confusion of buildings, mounds of earth and sculptures.

The Campidoglio is one of the masterpieces of civic art, a full account of its master plan being given in Giorgio Vasari's *Lives of the Artists*.[70] It forms a link between the early Renaissance piazza such as Piazza Della Santissima Annunziata in

4.32

4.33

Florence and the later, Baroque developments of Rome. The design was conditioned by the two existing buildings on the site, the Palazzo del Senatore and the Palazzo del Conservatori. Michelangelo retained both buildings but gave them a new architectural form. The first development was the levelling of the hilltop and the placing of the famous equestrian statue of Marcus Aurelius on the centre line of the Palazzo del Senatore According to Bacon: 'By a single act of will he established a line of force . . . which in effect became the organizing element that pulled chaos into order.'[71] The new building, the Capitoline Museum was sited at the same angle to the Palazzo del Senatore as that of the Palazzo dei Conservatori. It seems eminently sensible to conclude, as Ashby does, that the resulting shape of the square is largely determined by the practical exigencies of a cramped site flanked, on one side, by the ancient and important church of Santa Maria in Aracoeli and on the other by two existing buildings of antique significance.[72] The effect of the false perspective forced on Michelangelo by the existing building alignments accentuates and makes monumental the Palazzo del Senatore. The actual splay of the buildings also ensures an uninterrupted view of the main building when approaching from the grand stairway.[73] Here in the Capitol is an example of a development where the restrictions of an unprepossessing site can be used to create a great work of urban design without destroying existing cultural heritage. A fine lesson for today.

The shape of the Capitol is a trapezoid, a break with the regular geometric figures of the Renaissance. It is a small space, 55 m (181 ft) at its widest and 40.5 m (133 ft) at its narrowest between the two flanking buildings. The piazza is not a completely enclosed space. In addition to the open side, the two main corners are open contrary to the method of forming corners advocated by Sitte. When standing in the piazza, however, it appears rectangular so skilfully has the irregularity been counteracted by the pattern of the pavement which is a large sunken oval with a star pattern radiating from the statue of Marcus Aurelius. Bacon writes: 'Without the shape of the oval, and its two-dimensional, star-shaped paving pattern, as well as its three-dimensional projection in the subtly designed steps that surround it, the unity and coherence of the design would not have been achieved.'[74] The pavement and the great statue at the centre of the space together with Michelangelo's architecture hold together what, otherwise, may have been a formless space leaking in all directions. The last word on this space is left with Norberg-Schulz: 'The project has been interpreted as expressing the idea of the Capitoline Hill as the *coput mundi*. The oval, thus, would be nothing less than the very top of our globe . . . Michelangelo here succeeded in symbolizing the essense of place, as perhaps nobody else in the history of architecture.'[75]

Figure 4.32 Capitoline Museum, Piazza del Campidoglio, Rome
Figure 4.33 Piazza del Campidoglio, Rome

LINKED SQUARES

The city is seen and experienced as the observer moves about either on foot or by some other means of transport. The quality of the observer's experience

Figure 4.34 Piazza Della Signoria, Florence

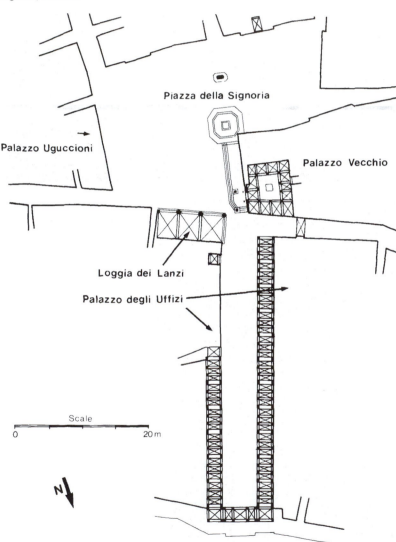

Piazza della Signoria

Palazzo Uguccioni

Palazzo Vecchio

Loggia dei Lanzi

Palazzo degli Uffizi

Scale

0   20 m

N

depends on the speed at which he or she moves. The faster he or she travels the less detail is perceived - from a car it is only the general massing of buildings and major landscape features which impinge on the perception. At walking pace it is possible to take in greater detail both of the buildings around and the spaces passed through. The scenery in the town is presented to the pedestrian not as a constant evolving motion picture, but more like a series of clips or snapshots of memorable events on the route. Gordon Cullen terms this feature of perception ' "Serial Vision" . . . although the pedestrian walks through the town at a uniform speed, the scenery of towns is often revealed as a series of jerks or revelations.'[76] Sitte was one of the first architectural writers to adopt this picturesque method of analysing a townscape. It was he who pointed out some of the delights of medieval towns where narrow lanes open out into a town square and where one space leads on to another: '. . . one should keep in mind the special effect that results from walking about from one plaza to another in such a cleverly grouped sequence. Visually our frame of reference changes constantly, creating ever new impressions.'[77] Zucker takes up this theme likening a sequence of squares to the relationship of successive rooms in a Baroque palace - 'the first room preparing for the second, the second for the third, etc., each room meaningful as a link in a chain, beyond its own architectural significance'.[78]

There are numerous methods by which links between squares may be formed, A public square may be of complex shape so that it consists of two or more overlapping or interpenetrating spaces: quite clearly defined spaces may open onto each other; a series of spaces may be physically connected by streets or alleyways; one or two major public buildings may be surrounded by a series of spaces which use the walls of the buildings for definition; great civic squares have been designed to unfold along a predetermined axis; and, finally, spaces may be related by an external reference point, a dominant element such as a tower.

PIAZZA DELLA SIGNORIA, FLORENCE

After the civil war in the thirteenth century between the Guelphs and Ghibellines the houses and towers of the vanquished Ghibellines on the site of the Piazza Della Signoria, Florence, were razed and the area designated as an open space. Other neighbouring sites were amassed to complete the space and to accommodate the new palace. The Palazzo Vecchio, the seat of medieval government, designed by Arnolfo de Cambio, was built largely between 1288-1314. The Piazza Della Signoria remained the civic centre of Florence for over six centuries (Figures 4.34-4.39).

The square is essentially medieval in shape with streets entering informally at different angles. There are, however, no direct views through the square. Therefore, using Sitte's definition, the square maintains a complete sense of enclosure. There are three important buildings in the civic centre, the Palazzo Vecchio protruding into the main square, the Loggia dei Lanzi attributed to Andrea Orcagna and dating from the late fourteenth century, and to the north of the square, the Palazzo Uffizi built for administrative offices by Vasari between 1560 and 1574.

The main square forms two distinct, but interpenetrating, spaces their boundary being defined by an optical barrier of sculpture; Michelangelo's David, Bandinelli's Hercules and Cacus group, Donatello's Judith, Ammanati's large Neptune fountain and the equestrian statue of Cosimo Medici by Giovanni da Bologna. Using this device a formless, medieval space was converted into two spaces with proportions corresponding more closely to Renaissance ideals. The process was started with the placing, in 1504, of Michelangelo's David to the left of the palace entrance, a decision receiving much deliberation by many experts. The line of sculpture was completed in 1594 by the placing of the equestrian statue at the centre point of the imaginary border line of both squares. The line of statues parallel to the east façade of the Palazzo Vecchio continues to the dome of the cathedral while the subtle placing of the Neptune fountain, at 45° to the corner of the

Figure 4.35 The Uffizi from the Arno, Florence
Figure 4.36 The Piazza Degli Uffizi, Florence

4.37

Figure 4.37 Equestrian statue of Cosimo, Florence
Figure 4.38 Palazzo Vecchio, Florence
Figure 4.39 Corner closure, Piazza Signoria, Florence

4.38

4.39

palace, acts as a fulcrum about which both spaces pivot.[79]

The Loggia dei Lanzi which heralds the opening of the small space formed by the Palazzo Uffizi, originally designed for staging ceremonies in front of the citizens of Florence, has become a magnificent exhibition space for fine sculpture. Among the sculptures exhibited beneath the arcade are the bronze statue, Perseus, by Cellini and the marble group, Rape of the Sabines by Giambologna.[80]

The third space in the group, opening off one side of the main square, is formed by the Palazzo Uffizi. This narrow shaft of space, in one direction, dramatizes the contrasting forms of the palace tower and the great dome by Brunelleschi. In the other

direction it leads through arches to the River Arno 'giving the effect of seizing the flow of space along the river's course, and pulling it into the Piazza della Signoria'.[81]

LUCCA

Sitte's drawing of medieval Lucca clearly indicates the variery of spatial composition open to the city designer; here individual façades appear to have determined to some extent the size and shape of adjacent squares so that the buildings can be seen to full advantage. Buildings often form the sides of adjacent spaces and spaces flow into each other or are separated by narrow linking passageways (Figures 4.40–4.44).

4.40

4.41

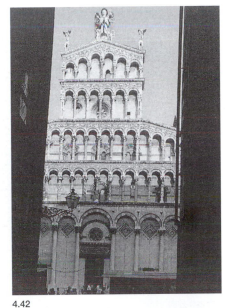

4.42

SAN GIMIGNANO

San Gimignano is another such example of the
juxtaposition of contrasting spatial forms (Figures
4.45–4.50). The main entrance to the town is the
Porta San Giovani, a constricted opening in the
powerful mid-thirteenth century town wall – a wall
that still forms a hard visual edge between town and
fine landscape. The gateway leads to the narrow St
John's Street flanked by three-storey, cliff-like
thirteenth- and fourteenth-century buildings. The
street widens into the lovely Cugnanesi Square
dominated by the Cugnanesi Tower. The little
square, a vestibule for the main civic square,
prepares the visitor's entry through the Becci Arch,
portal in the city's first defensive wall. The main
square, Piazza della Cisterna, is a triangular space
with sloping herringbone pattern pavement and
lovely fountain. The square is surrounded by three-
and four-storey buildings which retain the medieval
character and domestic scale of the town.

The Piazza della Cisterna is connected by narrow
passageway to the other important square, the Piazza

4.43

4.44

Figure 4.40 Market, Lucca
Figure 4.41 Market, Lucca
Figure 4.42 Church
façade, Lucca
Figure 4.43 Market, Lucca
Figure 4.44 Market, Lucca

4.45

4.46

4.47

Figure 4.45 Piazza
Cugnanesi, San Gimignano
Figure 4.46 Piazza della
Cisterna, San Gimignano
Figure 4.47 Porta San
Giovani, San Gimignano
Figure 4.48 Becci arch
and Cugnanesi tower, San
Gimignano
Figure 4.49 Ardinghelli
tower and Loggia del
Popolo, San Gimignano

4.48

4.49

Figure 4.50 Piazza del Duomo, San Gimignano

del Duomo. Because of its triangular shape the space is squeezed towards the passageway which, overshadowed by the Ardinghelli Tower, draws the observer through the gap and into the parvis before the cathedral. A grand staircase leads to the plain façade of the Cathedral, below it there is the Loggia del Popolo which forms the junction with the Piazza della Cisterna. The Piazza del Duomo leads on finally to the small and less important square, Piazza Ugo Nomi or Piazza delle Erbe then on to the town fortress. The Piazza del Duomo appears to be surrounded on all sides by great defensive towers; facing the cathedral is the Mayor's Old Palace surmounted by the Scabby Tower, to the right the Torre Grossa or Tower of Comune, to the left, and also overlooking the Piazza Ugo Nomi, stand the Salvucci or twin towers of the Ghibelline family. In San Gimignano the tower and the enclosed square are used in a single urban composition, the one contrasting with the other in scale and form. Through their grouping, however, they form a unified composition from a distance and also as the urban scene unfolds to the observer.

QUEEN'S SQUARE, THE CIRCUS AND THE CRESCENT, BATH

Much of what is seen in Bath today was built during a century when architectural taste changed little (Figures 2.2–2.5). Bath is a one-building-material town, another reason why it presents a great unity of expression. The architectural pattern was set largely by John Wood (the Elder) and his son and successor also John Wood (the Younger). Queen's Square, the Circus and the Crescent is the centre piece of the eighteenth century development in Bath and it is possibly Britain's most notable contribution in the field of urban design.

Two other men, 'Beau' Nash and Ralph Allen, are associated with Bath's rise to pre-eminence as a fashionable spa. 'Beau' Nash, as Master of Ceremonies in Bath from 1804, developed the town from a place visited for health reasons into a resort for leisure and social contact. For this purpose accommodation was needed for as many as 8,000 visitors. Ralph Allen, the richest citizen of Bath, and a dominant political figure, owned Combe Down quarries. He wished to exploit Bath stone using the town as its showpiece. According to Tim Mowl and Brian Earnshaw, John Wood, son of a local builder, returned to his native town in 1727 at a time when money was flowing into Bath making it ripe for rapid expansion.[82] For this small, medieval town lying in a provincial backwater John Wood, at the age of 21, proposed a master plan of great imagination. He returned to ancient Rome for his inspiration intending to build in Bath, a Royal Forum, a Grand Circus and an Imperial Gymnasium.[83]

John Wood in addition to being designer was also, for much of the work in Bath, the financier, developer, builder and estate agent. His method of working is interesting as he first obtained a lease on the land then designed the overall shape of the buildings, including front elevations. Parts of the development were subleased to individuals who met their own internal requirements but conformed with the public façade – a style of architecture fondly known locally as 'Queen Anne front with a Mary Ann backside'.

Queen's Square was the first part of the group completed. Wood treated three sides of the square, the north, south and east, each as one palatial composition. The north side is particularly monumental having a symmetrical arrangement of seven houses with central pediment. The west side was equally monumental having two broad corner houses and central house with portico and giant pilasters set back from the street line. The square was completed by 1736 though the west side was ruined in 1830 by filling in the space between the two houses.[84]

Despite the square having crossroads at each corner, it retains the sense of enclosure through the detailing of the corner or the closure of views with a building or tree. For example, in the north-west corner, Queen's Parade, a long terrace, is placed diagonally across the opening forming a further small space and closing the view. From Queen's Square, Gay Street rises up the hill to The Crescent. Gibberd suggests that the street is too long and the terraces not articulated to fit the ground contours.[89] For others, the walk against the contours adds greatly to the expectation and surprise of the arena formed by The Circus. Summerson describes The Circus as being both simple and remarkable: 'The Circus at Bath is a monumental conception, based on the Colosseum inverted, simplified, and enormously reduced in scale, and made to be the frontispiece of thirty-three standard town houses of moderate size. It has three superimposed orders, their entablatures richly carved, and its effect is quaintly beautiful – as if some simple-minded community had taken over an antique monument and neatly adapted it as a residence.'[86]

John Wood the Elder died in 1754 the year work began on The Circus. The work was completed by his son who went on to build Brook Street which connects The Circus to the last great space in the group, The Crescent, built between 1767 and 1775 and designed by John Wood, the Younger.

The Crescent is set out from three centres, a long radius curve in the centre and two short radii at the ends. The terrace with its unbroken line, a sweeping curve of bold, two-storey Ionic columns on a plain ground floor encloses the space it reaches out to encircle. The terrace set the style for many other such crescents throughout Britain in the years following. None surpass Bath for elegant proportions, fine details and majestic rhythm of columns.

Here the royal palace or the country mansion has been converted into a graceful, domestic terrace juxtaposed with parkland; a grande finale in a procession of spaces from Queen's Square through the long climb of Gay Street to the broad Circus which in turn is connected by Brook Street, a short shaft of space, to the open Crescent and its fine landscaped views. The composition to some extent has been marred by the group of trees in the middle of The Circus which destroy the simplicity of its volume. Wood's original scheme of simple

Figure 4.51 Place Stanislas, Place de la Carrière and Hemicycle, Nancy

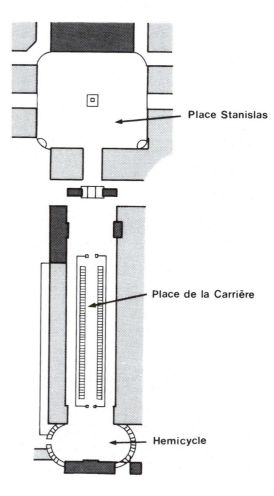

Place Stanislas

Place de la Carrière

Hemicycle

cobbled pavement would have provided a perfect foil to the enclosed garden with the obelisk of Queen's Square and the natural landscape of The Crescent.

PLACE STANISLAS, PLACE DE LA CARRÈRE AND THE HEMICYCLE, NANCY

The sequence of spaces designed in 1757 by Here de Corny in Nancy are related to each other symmetrically along an axis (Figures 4.51-4.56). This highly formal arrangement is in distinct contrast to John Wood's work at Bath. Wood though using architectural forms in the mainstream of Classical tradition adopted a less monumental and more romantic organization of spaces.

Stanislas Leszcyzynski, one time King of Poland, on taking up residence in Nancy planned to trans-

4.52

4.53

4.54

Figure 4.52 Corner detail, Place Stanislas, Nancy
Figure 4.53 Place Stanislas, Nancy
Figure 4.54 Place Stanislas, Nancy
Figure 4.55 Place de la Carrière, Nancy
Figure 4.56 The Hemicycle, Nancy

4.55

4.56

form it into a city worthy to be a European capital. As part of this plan he built a new north-south artery through the Ville Newe. On this route the architect Here de Corny set up an axis at right angles to it, extending from the Ville Newe into the Ville Vieille. It is along this axis that the three major spaces are arranged.[87]

The rectangular Place Stanislas (formerly Place Royale) is dominated by the Hotel de Ville, the main unifying element in the composition marking the point of change in direction of axis. Identical façades

complete the shorter sides and enclose the square. On its eastern edge the axial movement is confined within a narrow, elongated space lined by lower, arcaded buildings. It is a transition space between Place Stanislas and Place de la Carrière; the transition being completed with a triumphal arch. The space widens in Place de la Carrière, but the central axis is emphasized again by four rows of regularly trimmed trees. The movement is stopped by the transverse axis of the third space, an ellipsoid square, The Hemicycle, which meets the main axis at right angles. The Hemicycle is enclosed by colonnades which continue the ground-floor theme of the government buildings which terminate the axis.[88]

The rhythmic alternation of smaller and larger buildings and the unfolding of the diverse spatial forms along the main axis of movement make this a great work of urban design, a superb example of formal axial planning.

Figure 4.57 Boston, Lincolnshire
Figure 4.58 Boston, Lincolnshire
Figure 4.59 Boston, Lincolnshire

4.57

4.59

4.58

SPACES LINKED BY AN EXTERNAL REFERENCE POINT

Individual squares can fall into a coherent pattern in the mind of the observer by their strong relationship to the same building. In the case of Boston in Lincolnshire the two town squares, though connected physically by a street, establish a strong visual connection through their relationship to the mass of the church tower, known locally as The Stump (Figures 4.57–4.59). The Stump is the dominant feature in the flat fenlands of Lincolnshire. It heralds the presence of Boston to visitors at many miles distance and reconfirms the town centre by its dominant presence in both squares.

THE AMALIENBORG, COPENHAGEN

A similar relationship can be created in a formal planned layout, for example, the Amalienborg and Frederikskirke in Copenhagen (Figure 4.60). Amalienborg was designed by Nicolas Eigtved for King Frederik V of Denmark. It was first planned in 1749 and by 1754, when the architect died, the whole of the quarter was entirely laid out and many of its fine buildings completed. The reason for the project was to stimulate development on crown lands. Those willing to erect houses were given land as freehold provided they built within five years and adhered to the details of the plans approved by the King. The King reserved for himself the land on which the main square and the four palaces were to be built.[89]

The main square is an octagon enclosed by four palace buildings. Each palace consists of a large, dominant central block connected originally by single-storey wings to pavilions which punctuate the exits from the space. In the centre of the square is an equestrian statue of King Frederik V. The Classical, three-part design of the palaces, with main central block flanked by two pavilions, is mirrored in the two, fine corner houses which terminate Frederik's Street as it connects with the church square. The church, which Eigtved also designed, was to repeat the triple compositional treatment

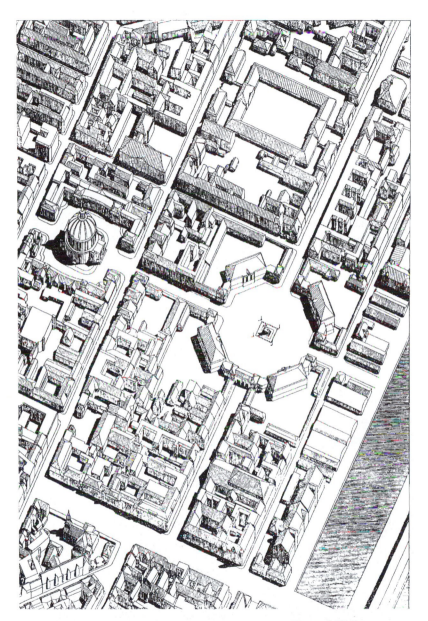

Figure 4.60 The Amalienborg, Copenhagen

having a colossal dome flanked by twin towers. Unfortunately the dramatic crescendo through the square along Frederik's Street to the massive marble church was not completed quite as planned. The scale of each main stage in Eigtved's church elevation was to be doubled from a 6 m (20 ft) ground floor to 12 m (40 ft) second storey to 24 m (80 ft) cylinder for the dome rising finally a further 48 m (160 ft) to the cross. The church, completed late in the nineteenth century, though not following the same uncompromising and highly disciplined architectural theme designed by Eigtved nevertheless by its sheer bulk still dominates the composition.

The tripartite subdivision of architectural masses is repeated in the handling of space along the main axis of Fredrik's Street. The great open space of the port, the main palace square and the space encircling the church, are connected by smaller scale streets, narrow shafts of space which articulate the major elements of the spatial composition.

OTHER SPACES

Zucker in his classification of squares lists two further types so far not discussed here; they are the

nuclear square and the amorphous square.[90] A public square, plaza or piazza, the precise nomenclature is unimportant, for the purpose of this analysis presupposes a high degree of physical enclosure leading to a feeling of being enclosed. From the point of view of this text neither the nuclear nor the amorphous square, using Zucker's definitions, qualify for inclusion in the category public square. Such features of urban structure may indeed be important places in their own right but their design requires considerations of a different order.

Busy metropolitan traffic junctions such as New York's Times Square are squares in name only and should be designed bearing in mind their primary function, the efficient movement of city traffic. A large square such as New York's Washington Square is framed by buildings on all sides - yet being too large for the surrounding heterogeneous structures it lacks enclosure. Its enlarged proportions are such that it has become something other than a city square. In Nottingham a brave attempt is being made to 'improve' Maid Marian Way, itself a road improvement of the 1960s. In the north, Maid Marian Way terminates in a roundabout and connects with three other important roads, Derby Road, Toll House Hill and Upper Parliament Street (Figure 4.61). The latest developments to the east of the roundabout, pleasant but uninspiring 'modern traditional' buildings have been designed to give a high degree of enclosure. However, while traffic remains at the ground level the enclosure of this particular space is only likely to increase traffic noise and pollution. For this space to fully justify the present form of city square, some thought has to be given to carrying the traffic below ground level, an expensive and complex prospect, or to the reduction in traffic volume through traffic management.

Zucker defines a nuclear space in the following manner: 'The spatial shape of the nuclear square is of definite order, although not so tightly knit . . . an entity, even without the frame of a continuous row of buildings or without the domination of a frontal

Figure 4.61 Junction, Maid Marian Way, Derby Road, Toll House Hill and Upper Parliament Street, Nottingham

structure. As long as there is a nucleus, a strong vertical accent – a monument, a fountain, an obelisk – powerful enough to charge the space around with a tension that keeps the whole together, the impression of a square will be evoked.' He quotes the example of the pyramid as creating 'an aesthetically impervious space around it'. Within this definition, Zucker cites as an example, the Piazza di Ss Giovanni e Paolo in Venice, In this case it is Verrochio's Colleoni sculpture which acts as a strong focus holding together an otherwise amorphous shape as a recognisable spatial unit[91] (Figure 4.62). The design procedures necessary to form such a space seem unclear, that is, apart from the centralizing feature being big or bold enough to dominate its surroundings. Predicting an observer's perception of the spatial envelope from a given design appears hazardous. Clearly the positive element being designed is the centralizing element be it sculpture, column or building and not the space. The idea of the size, shape and location of such a space as formed in the mind of the observer, if indeed it is so formed, is the result of designing a three-dimensional object around which the observer can move and not the design of an enclosed space through which the observer moves.

CONCLUSION

The public square is probably still the most important element in city design; it is the chief method by which a town or city is both decorated and given distinction. It is the natural setting for the most important civic and religious buildings, a place for fine sculpture, fountains and lighting and, above all else, a place where people meet and socialize. When such public places are designed according to some fairly basic principles and are imbued with a sense of place, they take on an added symbolic meaning. The most important physical quality of such spaces is enclosure. The methods of enclosure are many though the principles are few.

Figure 4.62 Piazza di Ss Giovanni e Paolo, Venice

NOTES

1 Hegemann, Werner and Peets, Elbert. *The American Vitruvius, An Architect's Handbook of Civic Art*, Benjamin Blom, New York, 1922, p.29

2 Vitruvius. *The Ten Books of Architecture* (trns by Morris Hicky Morgan), Dover Publications, New York, 1960, Book V, Chapter 1, p.132

3 Alberti, Leon Battista. *The Ten Books of Architecture* (The 1755 Leoni edn), Dover Publications, New York, 1986, Book IV, Chapter VIII, p.81

4 Ibid, Book VIII, Chapter VI, p.173

5 Collins, G.R. and Collins C.C. *Camillo Sitte: The Birth of Modern City Planning*, Rizzoli, New York, 1986, p.154

6 Scruton, Roger. *The Aesthetics of Architecture*, Methuen, London, 1979, p.44

7 Ibid, p.144

8 Le Corbusier. *The Radiant City*, Faber & Faber, London, 1967, p.141

9 Yeats, W.B. The Second Coming. In *Yeats Selected Poetry*, Pan Books, London, 1974, p.99

10 Norberg-Schulz, Christian. *Existence, Space and Architecture*, Studio Vista, London, 1971, p.19

11 Lynch, Kevin. *The Image of the City*, MIT Press, Cambridge, Mass., 1960

12 Ibid, p.47

13 Ibid, p.102

14 Alexander Christopher. *A New Theory of Urban Design*, Oxford University Press, Oxford, 1987, p.92

15 Ibid, p.93

16 Unwin, Raymond. *Town Planning in Practice*, T. Fisher Unwin. London, 1909, p.176

17 Collins, G.R. and Collins, C.C. Op cit, p.181

18 Murray, Peter. *The Architecture of the Italian Renaissance*, Thames and Hudson. London, (revised 3rd edn), 1986, p.124

19 Ibid, p.140

20 Summerson, Sir John. *The Classical Language of Architecture*, Thames and Hudson, London, 1963, p.69

21 Ibid, p.68

22 Zucker, Paul. *Town and Square*, Columbia University Press, New York, 1959, p.151

23 Alberti, Leon Battista. Op cit, Book IV, Chapter VIII, p.80

24 Rasmussen, S.E. *Experiencing Architecture*, MIT Press, Cambridge, Mass., 1959, p.38

25 Unwin, Raymond. Op cit, p.171

26 Alexander, Christopher, et al. *A Pattern Language*, Oxford University Press, Oxford, 1977, p.28

27 Alberti, Leon Battista. Op cit, Book VIII, Chapter VI, p.172

28 Quoted from Ashby, Thomas and Pierce, S.R. The Piazza del Popolo: Rome, Its History and Development. In *Town Planning Review*, Vol XI, No 2, December 1924, pp.74-99

29 Ibid

30 Morris, A.E.J. *History of Urban Form*, George Godwin, London, 1972, p.130

31 Rasmussen, S.E. *Towns and Buildings*, The University Press of Liverpool, Liverpool, 1951, p.50

32 Giedion, Sigfried. *Space, Time and Architecture*, Harvard University Press, Cambridge, Mass., 3rd edn, enlarged, 1956, p.152

33 Bacon, E.N. *Design of Cities*, Thames and Hudson, London, revised edn, 1975, p.155

34 Giedion, Sigfried. Op cit, p.152

35 Zucker, Paul. Op cit, p.8

36 Collins, G.R. and Collins, C.C. Op cit, p.177

37 Ibid, p.171

38 Palladio, Andrea. *The Four Books of Architecture*, Dover Publications, New York, 1965, p.72

39 Zucker, Paul. Op cit, p.7

40 County Council of Essex, *A Design Guide for Residential Areas*, County Council of Essex, The Anchor Press, Essex, 1973, p.65

41 Alberti. Op cit, p.173

42 Hegemann, Werner and Peets, Elbert. Op cit, p.40

43 Ibid, pp.42-44 and Spreiregen, P.D. *Urban Design: The Architecture of Towns and Cities*, McGraw-Hill, New York, 1965, p.75

44 Collins, G.R. and Collins, C.C. Op cit, p.182

45 Ibid, p.183

46 County Council of Essex. Op cit

47 Collins, G.R. and Collins, C.C. Op cit, p.181

48 Krier, Rob. *Urban Space*, Academy Editions, London, 1979, p.9

49 Vitruvius. Op cit, p.131

50 Alberti. Op cit, p.173

51 Palladio, Andrea. Op cit, p.72

52 Collins, G.R. and Collins, C.C. Op cit, p.182

53 Zucker, Paul. Op cit, p.9

54 Chambers, Isobel M. 'Piazzas of Italy.' In *Town Planning Review*, Vol XI, No 4, February 1926, p.225, also the drawings of Lim Y. Ng, *An Historical Analysis of Urban Space*, unpublished dissertation, School of Architecture, University of Nottingham, 1979

55 Bacon, Edmund N. Op cit, p.107

56 Baroero, Claudio, et al (eds). *Florence Guide to the City*, Univis Guide Series: Italy, Mario Gros, Tomasone & Co, Torino, 1979, p.8.1

57 Gibberd, Frederick. *Town Design*, Architectural Press, London, 2nd edn, 1955, pp.133-135

58 Bacon, Edmund N. Op cit, pp.108-109

59 Zucker, Paul. Op cit, p.11

60 Collins, G.R. and Collins, C.C. Op cit, p.177

61 Ibid, p.178

62 Ibid, p.182

63 Spreiregen, P.D. Op cit, p.19

64 Alberti. Op cit, p.173

65 Vitruvius, Op cit, p.132

66 Alberti. Op cit, p.172

67 Ibid, p.81

68 Ashby, Thomas. The Capitol, Rome, Its History and Development. In *Town Planning Review*, June, 1927, Vol XII, No 3, pp.159-173

69 Morris, A.E.J. Op cit, p.129

70 Vasari, Giorgio. *The Lives of the Artists*. A selection translated by George Bull, Penguin, Harmondsworth, 1965, pp.388-389

71 Bacon, Edmund, N. Op cit, p.115

72 Ashby, Thomas. Op cit. p.167

73 Dougill, W. The Present Day Capitol. In *Town Planning Review*, June 1927, Vol XII, No 3, pp.174-183

74 Bacon. Edmund, N. Op cit, p.118

75 Norberg-Schulz, Christian, Op cit, p.48

76 Cullen. Gordon. *The Concise Townscape*, Architectural Press, London, 1971, p.9

77 Collins, G.R. and Collins, C.C. Op cit, p.197

78 Zucker, Paul. Op cit, p.15

79 Gibberd, Frederick. Op cit, p.130-132

80 Baroero, Claudio. Op cit, p.16.2

81 Bacon, Edmund, N. Op cit, p.112

82 Mowl, T. and Earnshaw, B. *John Wood Architect of Obsession*, Millstream Books, Bath, 1988, p.10

83 Summerson, John. *Architecture in Britain: 1530-1830*, Penguin, Harmondsworth, 3rd edn, 1958, pp.222-225

84 Pevsner, Nikolaus. *The Buildings of England, North Somerset and Bristol*, Penguin, Harmondsworth, 1958, p.121

85 Gibberd, Frederick. Op cit, p.274

86 Summerson, John. Op cit, p.224

87 Bacon, Edmund, N. Op cit, p.177

88 Zucker, Paul. Op cit, pp.187-189

89 Rasmussen, S.E. *Towns and Buildings*, op cit, pp.126-132

90 Zucker, Paul. Op cit, p.8

91 Ibid, p.14

STREETS

5

Figure 5.1 The tragic scene

INTRODUCTION

Any classification of streets must start with Vitruvius and his description of the three street scenes for use as the backdrop in a theatre. Though the names and symbolism have changed, the general formal qualities still retain a powerful image for the European urbanist: 'There are three kinds of scenes, one called tragic, second, the comic, third the satyric. Their decorations are different and unlike each other in scheme. Tragic scenes are delineated with columns, pediments, statues, and other objects suited to kings; comic scenes exhibit private dwellings, with balconies and views representing rows of windows, after the manner of ordinary dwellings; satyric scenes are decorated with trees, caverns, mountains. and other rustic objects delineated in landscape style.'[1] It was Serlio who interpreted these three street types in his publication, *The Five Books of Architecture*, published between 1537-1545.[2] The scenes depicted by Serlio, using geometric perspective, are a Classical form of architecture for the tragic scene, Gothic for the comic scene and a landscape outside the city for the satyric (Figures 5.1-5.3). Anthony Vidler maintains that these three street types 'comprised the paradigmatic

Figure 5.2 The comic scene

Figure 5.3 The satyric scene

environments of the Renaissance, the public realms within which the dramas of city and country life were to be acted out; dramas of state and public ritual in the tragic street, of boisterous merchant and popular life in the residential street of comedy, and of bucolic manners and country sport in the forest path'.[3] Even today we still think of the grandeur of the formal, straight street being associated with public exhibition and parade, the charming medieval street so admired by tourists as the pedestrianized

mall of the older European city and the bucolic avenue made manifest in the vast areas of suburbia, the retreat of the many to Arcadia.

Both Alberti and Palladio distinguish two main types of streets, those within towns and those that run between towns. In speaking of streets that connect towns Alberti says: 'Highways in the country receive their greatest beauty from the country itself through which they lie, from its being rich, well cultivated, full of houses, and villages, affording delightful prospects, now of sea, now of a fine hill . . .'[4] Palladio takes up this theme suggesting that 'the ways without the city ought to be made ample, commodious, having trees on either side, by which travellers may be defended from the scorching heats of the sun, and their eyes receive some recreation from the verdure'.[5] He particularly commends the Via Portuense as having 'the utmost beauty and conveniency, which led from Rome to Ostia; because . . . it was divided into streets; between the one and the other of which there was a course of stones a foot higher than the remaining part of the way, and which served as a division: by one of these ways people went, and by the other they returned'.[6] This then, is the model for our great highways that sweep through the landscape, a subject outside the scope of this present work.

When Alberti turns to discuss streets within the town or city he again distinguishes two broad categories that follow on from the Vitruvian tragic and comic theatre scenes. Alberti recommends that streets when they enter a town should, 'if the city is noble and powerful' be 'straight and broad, which carries the air of greatness and majesty'. Though if the town is small he suggests that 'it will be better and safe to have them wind about' and, in the heart of the town, 'it will be handsomer not to have them straight, but to have them winding about several ways . . . by appearing longer they will add to the idea of the greatness of the town'.[7] Palladio's ideal for the town or city street is quite clearly the straight, regular, Classical model: 'A straight street in a city affords a most agreeable view, when it is ample and clean; on each side of which there are magnificent fabrics'.[8] The streets are the formal, military routes - an extension of the regional roads leading to the city. Palladio concentrates on military routes, and as for the other city streets, '. . . the more they shall be like them, the more they'll be commended'.[9]

DEFINITIONS

So far in this chapter several terms such as, street, path, avenue, highway, way, route, have been used almost interchangeably. It would be possible to extend this list to include other words such as, road, boulevard, mall and promenade, which have similar meanings. Without going into too great a discussion of definitions, for the purpose of this chapter the main distinction to be made is between road and street. Road is at once an act of riding on horseback and an ordinary line of communication between different places, used by horses, travellers on foot or vehicles. Or it is any path, way or course to some end or journey. The emphasis is on movement between places, the principle lines of communication between places - a two-dimensional ribbon, running on the surface of the landscape, carried over it by bridge or beneath by tunnel. A street may have these attributes, but its more common meaning is a road in a town or village, comparatively wide as opposed to a lane or alley. More importantly it is a road, that is the linear surface along which movement occurs between the adjacent houses - 'it runs between two lines of houses or shops,' says a dictionary definition.[10] For the purpose of this analysis the street will be taken as an enclosed, three-dimensional space between two lines of adjacent buildings.

One particular feature of the road or the thoroughfare which is incompatible with the street is the movement of fast-moving or heavy traffic, with all its engineering requirements. It was probably the elevation of the functional needs of vehicular traffic

to a design dogma by avant-garde members of the Modern Movements in architecture and city planning which contributed to the neglect of the street and its architecture. Le Corbusier is one of the main offenders: 'Our streets no longer work. Streets are an obsolete notion. There ought not to be such a thing as streets; we have to create something that will replace them.' Later he said: 'No pedestrian will ever again meet a high-speed vehicle.'[11] It is possible to agree with the latter statement without accepting the former. The conception of the city as a product of urban functions dominated by transport deprives the street of its role, or meaning and such functional analyses leave the urban street without an existence or a reason for being. When traffic moves at speed it cannot be accommodated within a street but that does not eliminate the utility of the street nor does it necessarily preclude the use of the street for vehicular traffic.

FUNCTIONS OF THE STREET

The Athens Charter, resulting from the Congres' Internationaux d'Architecture Moderne (CIAM) meeting in Athens in 1933, crystallized the theory of the Modern Movement in architecture and town planning. The ideas of the great men of the first half of the twentieth century - Le Corbusier, Gropius, Jacobus Oud and others - were revealed to the urbanist as the dogma of rationalism. In the 1950s this preoccupation with function, structure, standardization was challenged and ideas about human association and the softer social aspects of urban planning and architecture given greater emphasis. Peter and Alison Smithson were among those in the forefront of this movement usually associated with Team 10, a group within CIAM. One outcome of this change in thinking among some architect-urbanists was the rehabilitation of the street as a legitimate element of civic design. The Smithsons wrote: 'In a tight knit society inhabiting a tight knit development such as the Byelaw Streets there is an inherent feeling of safety and social bond which has much to do with the obviousness and simple order of the form of the street: about 40 houses facing a common open space. The street is not only a means of access but also an arena for social expression.'[12] Unfortunately the analysis led to the idea of streets in the air: 'The principle of identity we propose is the basis of the Golden Lane Project – a multi-level city with residential street-in-the-air.'[13] As an idea it failed in Britain: as a concept the street-in-the-air was not within the cultural norms acceptable to the general population in this country. An example of this type of housing at Radford in Nottingham was demolished after only twenty years in use. A street in the British tradition is firmly anchored to the land and still conforms, in the mind, to one of the three generic street scenes described by Vitruvius about 2,000 years ago.

Jane Jacobs is an important critic of the urban forms resulting from the application of design principles developed by CIAM and other like-minded groups of urban theorists. She is a great apologist for the street: 'Streets and their sidewalks, the main public places of a city, are its most vital organs. Think of a city and what comes to mind? Its streets. If a city's streets look interesting, the city looks interesting; if they look dull, the city looks dull.'[14] Jacobs sees the breakdown of law and order in cities partly, at least, as a consequence of the rejection of the street by modern planners and its replacement by large building blocks set in a sea of amorphous, unowned space – the ideal setting for the mugger and the thief. It is an assertion supported by the writings of Newman and the research carried out in Britain by Coleman.[15] There may, indeed, be a relationship between the pattern of crime and environmental form. However, showing that there is a causal relationship between these two variables is quite another matter. Nevertheless, it seems to strike a note of common sense when Jacobs asserts: 'The first thing to understand is that public peace – the sidewalk and street peace – of cities is not kept primarily by the police, necessary as police are. It is kept primarily by

an intricate, almost unconscious, network of voluntary controls and standards amongst the people themselves and enforced by the people themselves.'[16] She goes on to specify how the streets can be made self regulating: 'There must be eyes upon the street, eyes belonging to those we might call the natural proprietors of the street . . . and . . . the sidewalk must have users on it fairly continuously, both to add to the number of effective eyes on the street and to induce the people in buildings along the street to watch the sidewalks in sufficient numbers.'[17]

In analysing the utility of the street as an element of city design for the twenty-first century, sentimentality cannot be permitted to colour judgement. It is not possible to affirm with any degree of certainty how or to what extent the physical environment affects the way people behave. For example, in the 1940s and 1950s it was thought by the planners that through the manipulation of land-use patterns and the design of small neighbourhoods that somehow 'community' would result. The thinking in Britain immediately after the Second World War about this concept of community was a genuine desire to reproduce in new towns the cosiness of the English village or the co-operative unity of a working class street. The friendliness of the street was wrongly analysed as a product of the pub, the corner shop and the church hall. No account was taken of the deep roots of the inhabitants of the working class streets or of the close family and economic ties of the street system.[18] As Robert Gutman points out: 'The charming spaces Cullen describes came about because of the prior existence of a coherent community; they did not then, nor could they now, by themselves bring about such a community.'[19] Amos Rapoport's work seems to indicate that designers' rules of composition may not have the effect they believe.[20] While Herbert Gans asserts that 'the physical environment has much less effect than planners imagine. . . . The social environment has considerably more effect.'[21] He goes on to point out that Jacobs in her analysis of the lively city is engaged in repeating the fallacy of physical determinism just as the planners she attacks in her book *The Death and Life of Great American Cities*. In Gans' words: 'The last assumption, which she shares with the planners whom she attacks, might be called the physical fallacy, and it leads her to ignore the social, cultural and economic factors that contribute to vitality or dullness.'[22] It is, therefore, necessary to examine the function and role of the street within the urban fabric so that the designer is better able to understand and give form to this important element of city design.

The street in addition to being a physical element in the city is also a social fact. It can be analysed in terms of who owns, uses and controls it; the purposes for which it was built and its changing social and economic function. It also has a three-dimensional physical form which, while it may not determine social structures, does inhibit certain activities and make others possible. The street provides a link between buildings, both within the street, and in the city at large. As a link it facilitates the movement of people as pedestrians or within vehicles and also the movement of goods to sustain the wider market and some particular uses within the street. It has the less tangible function in facilitating communication and interaction between people and groups – 'thus serving to bind together the social order of the *polis*, or what in current parlance would be called the local urban community. Its expressive function also includes its use as a site for casual interaction, including recreation, conversation, and entertainment, as well as its use as a site for ritual observances.'[23] The suburban street reinforces people's social aspirations: movement 'up market' to a larger house, bigger garden. A 'better' street is all important and so the new street address becomes the symbol of self-esteem. The street, however, is also a common area which serves a group not just one family: the type of neighbours are important in this quest for self-esteem. As a space serving a group it is to some extent a closed social system. It has distinct boundaries despite acting as a communal thoroughfare to other areas.

Many changes have taken place recently in the social patterns of life in large western cities. Thirty years ago, for example, many housewives would walk to the shop, they would also walk the children to school. Now the housewife's role has changed and she may be the breadwinner and head of a single parent family or a co-working family partner. More trips are now made by car to the supermarket, the school and leisure outings. Whether male or female, young or old, a greater number of social interactions occur at the destination rather than during the trip, and the telephone call to some extent replaces the chat on the doorstep. In the design of cities it would be unwise to ignore these changes which have occurred. It would also be a brave person who would predict the direction of future social change. Environmental, or green issues, the problem of the ozone layer, the increasing cost of irreplaceable fossil fuel and so on would indicate a possible change to mass transport systems and a return to a more compact urban form. This may indeed be the future, but despite brave words and good intentions there seems little unequivocal political will to allocate funding to the development of public transport in this country. Perhaps environmental conditions must deteriorate further before the general public is weaned away from the car. In this unclear future what role, if any, has the street?

For the purpose of this study it is assumed that for the next 10 or 20 years the private car will remain an important means of urban transport and that city planning must come to terms with that prospect. The rapid movement of traffic in large volumes requires large roads. Unless some limit is placed upon traffic volume and its freedom of movement the destruction of streets and squares as places of social contact will continue, a process that will be accompanied by the degradation of local environmental quality. Some form of city structuring based upon the Buchanan model of environmental areas may be essential to limit the intrusive effect of the motor car on urban living areas. 'A convenient term is required to convey the idea of a place, or an area, or even a street, which is free from the dangers or nuisances of motor traffic. The expression that immediately comes to mind is to say that the area has a good "environment", but this would convey to most people familiar with town planning terms a good deal more than just freedom from the adverse effects of traffic. It would for instance, certainly convey the idea of a place that was aesthetically stimulating.'[24] Detailed consideration of the primary distribution network of roads necessary to serve town and city is beyond the scope of this study, nevertheless a plea is made for such a network to take the form of the tree-lined boulevard rather than the highly engineered urban motorway favoured in the 1960s. In the environmental areas within the interstices of the major routes the needs of the pedestrian dominate, and the creation of a sense of place is paramount. In such a situation the street, the square and the public façade of buildings are the dominant design elements. As Colin Buchanan points out: 'Walking is also an integral part of many other matters, such as looking at shop windows, admiring the scene, or talking to people. In all, it does not seem to be far from the truth that the freedom with which a person can walk about and look around is a very useful guide to the civilized quality of an urban area.'[25]

In the planning of a street the physical factors that appear most to influence street use are, according to Schumacher, user density, land-use mix, pedestrian-vehicular interaction, configuration and context.[26]

It appears that most street activity occurs when it is convenient for large numbers of pedestrians to use the street in a variety of ways. Activity in streets increases when densities are high enough to inhibit the use of the motor car and to support a range of facilities such as shops and schools which are within walking distance from a sustainable catchment area. It also appears that a variety of land uses stimulating many activities is a prerequisite of a lively street. The elimination of all 'non-conforming' uses from the residential area reduces the propensity for social contact and interaction in the street. Both these propositions, that is, the linking of street activity with high density and a mix of land uses, may be true in a very general way. There is, however, a need to examine both propositions more carefully with regard to the function of the street. In Britain, for example, few families would be willing to live close to a noisy public house, an all-night disco or a business operating long hours. In the study of the street it may be necessary to adopt a notion used to analyse Islamic cities. There the city is organized along a spatial continuum ranging from private, semi-private/semi-public to public space.[27] The public streets that function as the main pedestrian and vehicular networks or 'paths' within an environmental area require a different design approach to the quiet residential streets where greater consideration should be given to the need for privacy and defensible space.

The precise form of pedestrian-vehicular interaction is conditioned by the function of the street. While total separation of vehicles and pedestrians can be harmful to the development of a lively and active street, many pedestrianized town centres in Britain and in Continental Europe are extremely successful. The success of pedestrian areas is dependent on the variety of attractions they offer so that pedestrians in large numbers have reason for remaining. It is also conditional on good access for both private and public transport. One problem for the designer of the pedestrian precinct is the integration of car parking within the surrounding urban fabric. Separation of high-speed traffic movement from pedestrian traffic is obviously necessary: this occurs in a most civilized manner in the Paris boulevard. It has wide pedestrian pavements separated from the road with trees and in some cases lanes for parked or slow-moving vehicles.

In residential neighbourhoods dominated by the motor car there is a danger that the car itself becomes the sole link between the home and the world outside. This may further isolate each home and reinforce the remoteness associated with a high level of privacy for the individual dwelling. The results of this lifestyle are those deserted streets associated with the wealthy North-American suburb where meeting a dog on a Sunday morning stroll is a welcome event for the solitary user. Empty streets, as Jacobs points out, can lead to the public domain being donated to the thug, mugger and rapist. In turn this leads to the reaction, a plea for the privatization of the public street and its policing by the private security force: a policy leading to the city being compartmentalized into unfriendly, highly defended private estates where the normal writ of public law does not run. Institutionalizing 'no-go' areas, on the lines of Northern Ireland, is the death knell of the city.

In the design of the residential street a proper balance is required between privacy, defensible space, access for the car and safe pedestrian use of the street. As Coleman points out, in Britain, we have found the answer to this problem - the ubiquitous semi-detached house, a solution much despised by architect and planner alike.[28] For a rational solution to the planning of some residential areas we may also have to return to some of the ideas of Unwin and others in the early Garden City Movement. Family security is served well by the home on a plot enclosed on three sides by neighbouring plots with just one access point from the road for pedestrians and the family car. The street scene is completed with small front gardens, low hedges and protruding bay windows. The overlooked street becomes the 'owned' semi-public domain of the local community - a driveway with wide, tree-lined verges, the satyric scene of Serlio and still the ideal of the home-owning British population (see Figures 3.7 and 3.10). However, close to public transport corridors, it may be necessary to consider increased densities having the more urban character of the 'comic scene'.

THE FORM OF THE STREET

The configuration, shape or form of the street has not received the detailed consideration given to the design of the public square. Certainly many great streets have been designed and built, many others have been admired, described and photographed, but little work on the analysis of form has resulted. Scholars such as Sitte and Zucker have preferred to concentrate their efforts on the high points of urban structure, the nodes, where major activities occur, where civic buildings are concentrated and where the community lavishes most of its surplus wealth in the form of prestigious development and artistic creation. Although the street accounts for most of the urban public realm, in practice, particularly modern practice, the street is what remains after private planning of individual properties is considered satisfactory.

As seen in Chapter three, there are two quite distinct physical conceptions of a European city. In the first conception it appears that the streets and public squares are carved from an original block of solid material. This is the city Sitte knew and loved; his visual analysis is based on this concept. The other main conception of a city that has the form of an open parkland into which buildings have been introduced as three-dimensional objects sitting on and within the landscape.[29] This is the concept associated with developments like the Ringstrasse in Vienna or the ideas formulated by Le Corbusier and others in the Modern Movement of architecture and planning (Figure 5.4). Both main concepts exist side by side in the real world of the city and, indeed, as far as the street is concerned, both concepts are of ancient origin being documented by Serlio and Vitruvius in their descriptions of the tragic, comic and satyric scenes.

The form of the street can be analysed in terms of a number of polar qualities such as straight or curved, long or short, wide or narrow, enclosed or open, formal or informal. Street form can also be analysed in terms of scale, proportion, contrast, rhythm or connections to other streets and squares. No matter which analysis is followed the street has two main characteristics directly related to form; it is, at one and the same time, both path and place. It is such common practice to regard the street as a

Figure 5.4 A contemporary city

route (road) for motor vehicles that its function as a place has been quite overlooked. For many generations the street has provided urban communities with public open space right outside their homes. Says Jonathon Barnett: 'A second element basic to any public open space plan is to recognize the importance of streets as the framework of public open space.'[30] The modern city street has become in some cases a place of danger for citizens or so unattractive that it forces people to stay within the privacy of their homes and move about in the relative sanctuary of the private motor car. Alexander wishes to see an end to this situation: 'Streets should be for staying in, and not just for moving through, the way they are today.' Therefore he suggests, 'make a bulge in the middle of the public path, and make the ends narrower, so that the path forms an enclosure which is a place to stay, not just a place to pass through'.[31]

Defining a street as a road for vehicles is not the same as designing it as a 'path'. The traffic route designed by the engineer to serve so many passenger car units (PCUs) per hour relegates the street to the level of a sewer, a conduit which facilitates the efficient movement of effluent. This is far removed from Norberg-Schulz's symbolic definition of a path: 'On the plane man chooses and creates paths which give his existential space a more particular structure. Man's taking possession of the environment always means a departure from the place where he dwells, and a journey along a path which leads him in a direction determined by his purpose and his image of the environment. . . . The path, therefore, represents a basic property of human existence, and it is one of the great original symbols.'[32] Nor does a street conforming to traffic engineering standards necessarily fulfil Lynch's requirements for a memorable path. Such a path has both a beginning and an end, definite places or nodes along its length - places of special use and activity; such paths can be scaled, have contrasting elements but above all else, they must present to the observer a stimulating and memorable image of connected places.[33]

A sense of place in street design is best achieved if the spatial volume defined by the frontages is perceived as the positive form, the figure seen against the general ground of the surrounding architecture. According to Gibberd: 'The street is not building frontage but a space about which dwellings are grouped to form a series of street pictures; or alternatively the street is a space that may be expanded into wider spaces such as closes or squares.'[34] For a street to function as a place or exterior room in the city it must possess similar qualities of enclosure as the public square: 'The ideal street must form a completely enclosed unit! The more one's impressions are confined within it, the more perfect will be its tableau: one feels at ease in a space where the gaze cannot be lost in infinity.'[35] The absolute dimensions of the street must therefore be kept within reasonable proportions: 'When the street is long and wide with houses on a common frontage, it is most difficult to obtain a sense of enclosure.'[36] There have been a number of suggestions for terminating an overly long street:

'The ancients have . . . thrown an arch over the street so as to interrupt over-long perspective effects' (Figure 5.5).[35] The Essex design guide suggests that the apparent length of the street can be reduced by offsets in the building frontage.[38] If a street or a section of a street is to possess the quality of enclosure then it must be considered to have three main elements, an entrance, the place itself and a termination or exit. Since the street is also a path, and a path is two directional, the place must terminate or close in two directions.

STREET LENGTH

Sitte recommends that the plan of a public square should not have dimensions where the length of its enclosing walls are greater than the ratio 3:1. Beyond this limit insistent, converging rooflines vanishing towards the horizon suggest movement, the dynamic urban space most suitable to the path.[39] This upper limit for the proportion of the square may indeed define the lower limit for the street.[40] The confusion between street and square is exemplified by Market Square, Nottingham. Here 'Slab Square', as it is dubbed by locals, is attenuated north-westwards and finally squeezed through Angel Row to Chapel Bar. The dynamic movement is terminated by a distant view of Pugin's St Barnabas. In reverse direction the street gradually widens to the full width of the square before the Council House. Such lack of clarity in the articulation of form may give offence to the purist and cause problems for the urban analyst but it compensates by adding charm and richness to the real world in which we live and move (Figures 5.6–5.9).

The upper limit for uninterrupted length of street is probably in the order of 1,500 m (1 mile). Beyond this distance human scale is lost. Even with vistas considerably shorter than 1,500 m, the closure of the view causes considerable difficulty. According to Hegemann and Peets the distance to the terminal building should not be too far; they suggest that

Figure 5.5 Assisi

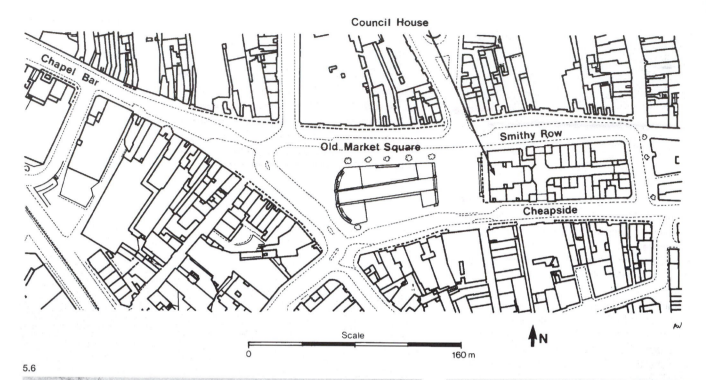

Scale

0   160 m

↑N

5.6

5.7

5.8

below an angle of 18° even a prominent building
will lose its dominance and begin to merge into a
silhouette with the surrounding neighbourhood.[41]
The condition is exacerbated when tall buildings are
ranged on either side of the vista. Jean-Louis
Garnier's Opera House in Paris is just such an
example of loss of scale. The Opera House, an
otherwise massive and imposing terminal building

5.9

5.10

Figure 5.6 Market Square, Nottingham

Figure 5.7 The Council House, Market Square, Nottingham

Figure 5.8 Market Square, Nottingham

Figure 5.9 Market Square, Nottingham, view towards St Barnabas

loses value from the high buildings ranged along the Avenue de l'Opera (Figures 5.10–5.11). Seen along this axis the building is overpowered by the insistent perspective of the six- and seven-storey apartment blocks on either side of the street. In contrast the view along the Rue Royale leading to the Madeleine is successful, the building at the terminus of the vista gaining dominance from its position on higher ground (Figure 5.12). The Champs Elysées terminating in the Arc de Triomphe also takes advantage of the ground form to close an important vista effectively. The width of the Champs Elysées and the avenue of trees climbing the contours ensures the dominance of the triumphal arch.

The long vista is reserved for special streets, great ceremonial routes, the public pathways used on state occasions. Such grand avenues may be used to adorn a capital city; the work of Haussmann in Paris, Sixtus V in Rome or l'Enfant in Washington are such glorious celebrations of the state. The more usual case throughout long periods of urban history has been the humble street of small proportion, conforming more closely to Hegemann and Peets' strictures on scale: 'The effective placing of terminal features is an important part of street design. In medieval cities which as a rule are supposed to have "grown" without a preconceived plan, it is almost uncanny how many times the curving streets manage to secure in their axis line, over the roofs of low houses, glimpses of the highest monuments which often do not stand in the same street from which the

5.11

5.12

Figure 5.10 Opera House, Paris

Figure 5.11 Avenue de l'Opera, Paris

Figure 5.12 The Madeleine, Paris

view is enjoyed.'[42] Norberg-Schulz holds much the same viewpoint: 'In the towns of the past, oblique angles and curved lines created a "closed perspective" enlivening the prospect.'[43] Even Alberti, that strict Classical thinker, extols the virtue of the small-scale, twisting street: 'Moreover, this winding of the streets will make the passenger at every step discover a new structure, and the front door of every house will directly face the middle of the street; and whereas in larger towns even too much breadth is unhandsome and unhealthy, in a small town it will be both healthy and pleasant, to have such an open view from every house by means of the turn of the street.'[44] The supreme example of the medieval street in Britain is The Shambles at York (Figure 5.13). Here the street is narrow, the buildings three-

storey but small in scale. The sense of enclosure is heightened by successively overhanging upper floors. The Shambles in York is at one extreme of the street continuum which ranges from this small-scale, medieval street to the gigantic scale of the Champs Elysées with its elegant esplanade separating vehicle from pedestrian.

The street is something more than a simple pathway, it is a series of connected places, somewhere for staying in and not just for moving through. In the words of Norberg-Schulz the street, 'in the past . . . was a "small universe" where the character of the district and of the town as a whole was presented in condensed form to the visitor. The street represented, so to speak, a section of life - history had shaped its details.'[45] In Lynch's terms the street is a path enlivened by a series of nodes where other paths meet it or where activities intensify to such an extent that place and rest vie for dominance with function of pathway and movement.[46] Such places or nodes should be at intervals of 200 to 300 m. As we saw, Alexander instructs us to 'make a bulge in the middle of a public path'.[47] A delightful example of the street widened along its length to form a place is to be found in Perugia where midway along the Corso Vannucci connecting the Piazza Italia and the cathedral the street widens into a subsidiary public space which at the same time remains an integral part of the street (Figures 5.14-5.17).

A number of techniques have been suggested for the design of comfortable streets. The Essex design guide recommends that the apparent length of a street can be reduced using offsets, while Hegemann and Peets commend the use of gates: 'The strong Gothic and Renaissance gates with their deep shadowed arches formed effective terminating features . . .'[48] Such an effect occurs in Assisi where an arched structure crosses the street and frames a distant view of the cathedral dome; or again in San Gimignano where the gateway terminates the town street and announces the start of the world beyond (Figure 4.47).

Figure 5.13 The Shambles, York

5.14

5.16

5.15

5.17

The last words on street length will be left with Sitte: 'The ideal street must form a completely enclosed unit! The more one's impressions are confined within it, the more perfect will be its tableau: One feels at ease in a space where the gaze cannot be lost in infinity'.[49] Sitte illustrates his ideal street system using part of the plan of Bruges (Figure 5.18). He was of the opinion that such picturesque results developed from the application of some practical reasons such as, fitting the development to the terrain, avoiding an existing structure, squaring up the junction by curving the road both to facilitate circulation and to form well-shaped building plots. Sitte, though having a distinct personal preference for the curved street, did not rule out the use of the straight street in city planning: 'If the meandering street is more picturesque, the straight one is

Figure 5.14 Cathedral square, Perugia
Figure 5.15 Corso Vannucci from Cathedral square, Perugia
Figure 5.16 Corso Vannucci, Perugia
Figure 5.17 Corso Vannucci, Perugia

Figure 5.18 Bruges

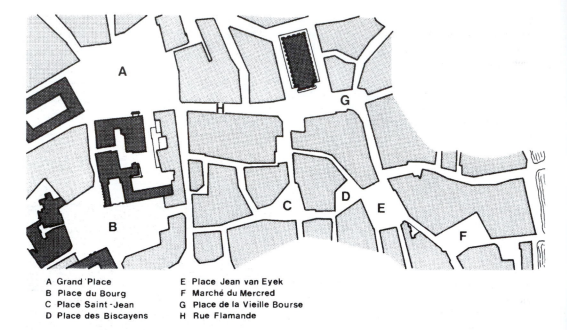

A Grand Place E Place Jean van Eyek
B Place du Bourg F Marché du Mercred
C Place Saint-Jean G Place de la Vieille Bourse
D Place des Biscayens H Rue Flamande

Figure 5.19 Arrangement of city streets

monumental; but we cannot subsist on monumentality alone, and it would be desirable that the builders of modern cities do not abuse the one or the other, but make use of them both as appropriate, in order to give to each district which they lay out an aspect in conformity with its purpose.'[50] The principle he wished to apply to the design of all streets was enclosure. In the straight street enclosure could be achieved through the use of the arch which he illustrated with a drawing of the Portico degli Uffizi, Florence. A less elegant and more contrived method he illustrated with a diagram for a modified rectangular layout of city blocks: here each straight short street is terminated by a street façade at right angles (Figure 5.19).

STREET PROPORTION

If proportion includes, within its definition, the idea of symmetry as used in the times of Hellenic

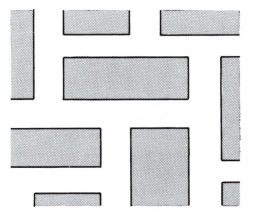

Greece, then the term when used in street design goes beyond an understanding of the crude ratio of length to width to height: the concept is broadened to include the relationship of the parts of the street to each other and to the proportions of the total composition. It may even include some notion of classical tripartite subdivision into introduction, development and climax.[51] Such formal melodic structuring is more important for the design of the straight street than its picturesque counterpart modelled on the medieval example. 'It, *the straight street*, offers us a more restricted field of study, its perfection being primarily dependent on a good proportion between its length and width, on the kind of edifices of which it is composed, and on its monumental termination.'[52] Many would take issue with Sitte in his dismissal of the classical straight street on the grounds of its restricted field of study, while agreeing with the remaining sentiments in the statement.

The ratio of width of street to height of enclosing buildings is critical for good street design. When, for example, a street is long and wide with two-storey houses ranged along a common frontage all sense of space enclosure is lost. Without dense planting and an avenue of trees such streets do little to lift the spirit and relieve monotony. Gibberd's recommendation for street design is '. . . to reduce the width of the road itself . . . But if the verges and front gardens are reduced and the dwellings brought reasonably close together, then it is possible to recapture that urban quality which characterizes our best town planning.'[53] These remarks of Gibberd refer to the domestic street but could equally refer to the traditional British shopping street. The wide street so favoured by the road engineer is most unsuitable for shopping. The narrow pedestrianized city street with continuous enclosing walls slightly higher than street width are most successful for their purpose as well as being an attractive place. They are still to be found, despite traffic engineers' best attentions, in cities like Nottingham as well as smaller towns such as Stamford or King's Lynn (Figures 5.20-5.22). When streets are narrow, 6-9 m (20-30 ft) and flanking buildings three or four storeys it gives 'the sense of completeness and enclosure to the pictures in the streets . . .'[54] The Essex design guide suggests that a ratio, height to width, of 1:1 is not too tight for comfort but that

Figure 5.20 Pedestrian street, Tours
Figure 5.21 Ironmonger Street, Stamford
Figure 5.22 Broad Street, Stamford

5.20

5.21

5.22

1:2.5 is as open as can be tolerated.[55] Narrow streets also facilitate shopping: movement from side to side for window gazing has no impediment and indeed is invited by the physical form of the development.

Aesthetic factors such as scale and proportion are by no means the only considerations in street design, other factors may of necessity be of greater significance. One such practical consideration conditioning street form is climate. Palladio, for example, says: 'For those of a temperate and cool air, the streets ought to be made ample and broad; considering that by their breadth the city will be much wholesomer, more commodius and more beautiful . . .' He adds however: 'The more the city therefore is in a cold place, and has subtile air, and where edifices are very high, so much the wider the streets ought to be made, that they may, in each of their parts, be visited by the sun . . . But the city being in a hot country, its streets ought to be made narrow, and the houses high, that by their shade, and by the narrowness of the streets, the heat of the site may be tempered; by which means it will be more healthy.'[56] Alberti, too, contains passages which discuss climate and its effect on built form. He recounts the sad tale of Nero's unsuccessful 'modernization' of Rome and its disastrous effects on the micro-climate of the city: 'Cornilius Tacitus writes, that Nero having widened the streets of Rome, thereby made the city hotter, and therefore less healthy; but in other places, where the streets are narrow, the air is crude and raw, and there is continual shade in summer. But further; in our winding streets there will be no house but what, in some part of the day, will enjoy some sun; nor will they ever be without gentle breezes, which whatever corner they come from, will never want a free and clean passage; and yet they will not be molested by stormy blasts, because such will be broken by the turning of the streets.'[57] These two long passages from Alberti and Palladio have been included to counter the ideas inherited from the 1950s and 1960s which resulted for example in the windswept plaza and sunless underpass.

Figure 5.23 Ghadaia, Algeria

Though much has been written about climate, urban form often seems to have been designed in ignorance of even the common-sense statements made by early theoreticians.[58] Such practical considerations as climate, however important, do not eliminate the need to consider scale, proportion and street composition, they simply set the parameters for their proper consideration. For example, the desert town of Ghadaia in Algeria clusters densely around hilltops penetrated by narrow, overshadowed streets kept cool in scorching heat by proportions in public spaces which are far different from those found in moderate climates (Figure 5.23).

UNITY IN STREET DESIGN

There are a number of factors which contribute to a unified street design, possibly the most important being that the form of the buildings should appear as surfaces rather than as mass. When buildings take on strong three-dimensional form the mass of the buildings dominates the scene and the space loses its importance. When the buildings ranged along a street have varied forms, styles and treatment the space loses definition. The result is development like Maid Marion Way in Nottingham[59] (Figures 2.39-2.41). Unified street design in contradistinction elevates the spatial volume to figural position against a background of two-dimensional planes, walls, pavement and sky above. Gibberd makes a similar point stating: 'The street is not building frontage but a space about which dwellings are grouped to form a series of street pictures; or alternatively the street is a space that may be expanded into wider spaces such as closes or squares.'[60] The main street in Chipping Camden is a good example of a unified street where the volume of the public street dominates the composition. The street frontages are continuous with but a few small breaks for incoming paths, roof heights vary only slightly. Although the architectural styles span two or three centuries they form a single composition constructed from the same building materials, using a few elements and incorporating similar details. Contrast there is,

though variety occurs within a disciplined theme. One fine contrasting element is the market building which stands within the street, it is a piece of sculpture contrasting with the spatial volume but, being

5.25

Figure 5.25 Chipping Campden, Gloucestershire

5.26

Figure 5.26 Chipping Campden, Gloucestershire

5.24

5.27

Figure 5.24 Chipping Campden, Gloucestershire
Figure 5.27 Chipping Campden, Gloucestershire

open, is also at the same time part of it (Figures 5.24–5.27).

There are cases where buildings having properties of mass, that is, those seen in three dimensions, are successfully integrated into an urban scene dominated at ground level by enclosed streets and squares; the prime example being San Gimignano. In San Gimignano the main public spaces are enclosed by three- and four-storey façades with one space leading to another in the 'fully approved' Sitte picturesque manner (Figures 4.45–4.50). For the main part the lower floors of the town consistently follow a pattern where the public space profile is punctuated dramatically by the group of medieval towers which rise to great competing heights above the general roofline adding a sharply contrasting dimension to both the internal ever-changing perspectives and to the more distant prospect.

Clearly, the use of common materials, details and architectural elements strengthen the unity in many street scenes. More important, however, is the imposition of a common roofline and the repetitive use of similar bay sizes for development. The roofline establishes the lid for the space and the greater the variation in its height the more unstable

the volume. This general statement is not to be read as a rigid prescription for uniform building heights in street design; indeed, some of the most charming medieval streets are composed of façades which are quite irregular. Such irregularities, however, often vary between part of a storey to two storeys at the outside. When kept within this range of difference the unity of the street scene is maintained and monotony avoided. In the same way the repetition of similarly sized building bays, which may originally have been dictated by ancient plot subdivisions, sets up a rhythm and establishes a grain for the street that forms a disciplined framework within which variety can be contained and ordered. When the scale of such a grain is violated as in Smithy Row, Nottingham, the result is not one of contrast but the disfiguration of the street (Figure 5.28).

The great problem with street architecture, as Hegemann and Peets point out, is 'the difficulty of combining the large amount of individuality required by the difference of taste and practical needs of the individual owners with the necessary element of harmony and even unity without which a street turns into a disagreeable hodge-podge of contradictory assertions'.[61] The informal nature of the curved street has certain in-built advantages, whereby the needs of individual property owners can be married to the larger requirements of social unity expressed, according to John Ruskin, as 'the great concerted music of the streets of a city'.[62] Techniques such as the use of a limited range of materials, colours, details and the repetition of a constant bay or plot width already mentioned for the successful design of the curved street apply with equal force to the design of the straight street. However, the straight street, by its nature, is formal in character and its successful design demands a more precise consideration and definition of parts. Alberti suggests that city streets will be 'rendered much more noble, if the doors are built all after the same model, and the houses on each side stand in an even line, and none higher than the other'.[63] The Classical ideal of the well-ordered and proportioned street is described by

Figure 5.28 Smithy Row, Nottingham

Palladio: 'A straight street in a city affords a most agreeable view, when it is ample and clean; on each side of which there are magnificent fabrics, made with those ornaments, which have been mentioned in the foregoing books.'[64] Alberti and Palladio using the Classical language of architecture, present a model for the straight street; it is of necessity formal and organized in a regular manner.

Absolute similarity of the individual buildings that comprise a straight street is not necessarily essential. It is often sufficient to have one strong motif at ground level which pulls the group together. The classic way of achieving this is by the introduction of colonnades or arcades at the lower floor levels. Behind or above this unifying element individual developments occur in the upper storeys. The remains of colonnades in such places as Miletus, planned it is said by Hippodamus, or the records of ancient Rome by way of the *Forma Urbis* no doubt influenced Renaissance architects like Palladio who recommended 'that the streets were divided, that on the one and on the other part there were porticoes made, through which the citizens might, under cover, go and do their business without being molested by the sun, by the rains and snow'[65] (Figures 5.29-5.30). In Britain this idea was taken up by architects such as Nicholas Hawksmoor who in 1735-6 was planning 'an arcaded Parliament Street, 110 ft wide, as the approach to the projected Westminster Bridge for which he had also made a design'.[66] Nash's early designs for the Quadrant and indeed for the whole of Regent Street envisaged a regular frontage with continuous colonnades.[67] The glass arcade running the full length of Lord Street, Southport, serves a similar purpose as the more formal colonnade; it protects the shoppers from rain and functions as an architectural element which holds together an otherwise motley collection of buildings. The arcade in Southport elevates ordinary street architecture to the level of fine urban design and in the process creates one of the loveliest shopping streets certainly in Britain and possibly Europe (Figures 5.31-5.32).

Figure 5.29 Arcaded street, Bologna

Figure 5.30 Arcaded street, Bologna

Figure 5.31 Lord Street, Southport
Figure 5.32 Lord Street, Southport

When both sides of a street are designed by one architect working for a single client great control can be exercised by the designer over the form of the architecture and the modelling of the space. Giorgio Vasari was in this position when he built the Uffizi, Florence, for the Medici between 1560-74. The architectural unity of the short street, originally known as the Piazza degli Uffizi is a model of Classical treatment (Figures 4.34-4.37). The pavilion of the Uffizi projects out into the street along the banks of the Arno, thus, in the words of Bacon,

giving the 'effect of seizing the flow of space along the river's course and pulling it into the Piazza della Signoria'.[68] The cross-section of the street approximates to the Golden Section, while the symmetrical composition of the street with three cornices and continuous projecting roof makes this 'a masterpiece of perspective in depth'.[69] The eye is led inevitably by the horizontal lines of the Uffizi falling insistently to the Piazza della Signoria and continued by the plane established by the line of sculpture from Hercules and Cacus. the copy of Michelangelo's David, on to Ammanati's Neptune fountain finally terminating in the equestrian statue of Cosimo I. In the distance is the cathedral dome while the verticality of the Vecchio tower acts as a perfect foil stabilizing the horizontal movement. Vasari in the Uffizi has given a model street design, a complete unified composition. It is a spatial sequence with an introduction, development of the idea and a concluding statement.

It was shown in Chapter four how, at Bath, John Wood the Elder developed techniques for land leasing which enabled him to control the design of individual properties so that long terraces of many units could be formed into unified compositions. The three great spaces in his composition, Queen's Square, The Circus and The Crescent are connected by short streets where the main elements on both facing elevations are related almost like reflections in a mirror. There may not always, however, be the opportunity to engage in such rigorous and disciplined street design. In these circumstances it is important not to lose sight of the main principle and accept that it is the street façades that are being designed, so placing emphasis on the complete street scene rather than individual buildings. Gaps at either end of a building façade where possible should be closed, service roads entering the street from the side should be as narrow as possible and bridged over. Architectural features that set up a strong axial line in the opposite direction to the street should be avoided unless there is a corresponding element on the opposite side of the street to pick it up and reflect it. Such reflection of major elements in the street scene is termed 'inflection'. Where possible, both sides of the street should progress in unison rather like a complex dance routine where the detailed choreography of the group recognizes and follows the movements of the others. In this way it becomes possible to think in terms of visually literate streets governed by a recognizable grammar where inflection is important for achieving unity.

It is a pleasure to admire the informal charm of the meandering street or to be carried long in excited anticipation of picturesque views unfolding round each corner and through unexpected alleyways to left or right. After further study it is possible to distinguish some important factors that have conditioned the development of the scene as presented. Many of these factors are of a thoroughly practical nature such as the form of the land, the order of development, evolving exploitation of the local environment, changing social stratification and patterns of population distribution. Knowledge of these practical factors does not however detract from an aesthetic appreciation of present physical structure, but enhances understanding by relating form with function - using function here in the widest meaning of that term. Many of the lovely Italian hill towns are ideal subject matter for such a study and would be amply rewarding for the researcher's efforts. For present purposes only the development of two small Italian hill towns, San Giorgio Morgeto in the province of Calabria and Montepulciano will be outlined briefly to show the relationship between street form and some of the formative influences that have contributed to the present delightful streets that capture the imagination of the visitor. It is maintained here that only by a study of this nature can the designer fully appreciate the present structure and that appreciation is necessary before any valid proposals can be made for its change and development.

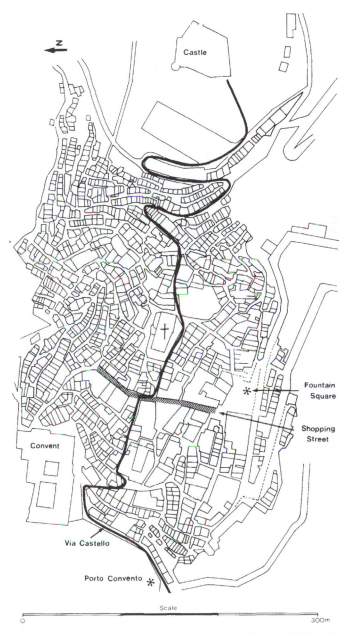

Figure 5.33 San Giorgio Morgeto

5.34

5.35

5.36

Figure 5.34 San Giorgio Morgeto
Figure 5.35 San Giorgio Morgeto
Figure 5.36 Via Castello, San Giorgio Morgeto
Figure 5.37 Shopping street, San Giorgio Morgeto
Figure 5.38 Fountain square, San Giorgio Morgeto

5.37

5.38

SAN GIORGIO MORGETO

San Giorgio Morgeto is a small town sited on the brow of a hill 500 m above sea level (Figures

5.33-5.38). The town descends in layered terraces from which are magnificent views of distant surrounds. The town is characterized by its hilltop site, tiled roofs and narrow, deeply overshadowed streets. The streets ascend and descend the hillside as if incised into the rock from which they rise; they tumble from contour to contour using the easiest practical grade.[70]

The town developed in four phases over several centuries. The first phase of growth is related to the founding of the castle by the Normans in the tenth century. The castle was built at the highest point on the hill for defensive purposes and around it clustered the first settlement. The second phase of growth is related to the convent built in the fourteenth century. The convent was an important centre of philosophical and theological learning for the Dominican Order. The convent is located approximately 1 km downhill from the castle and around it grew a second twin settlement. Between the two centres there developed an important route-way, the Via Castello. This path starting at the Porto Convento, the main entrance to the town, provided a strong axis for further development. The third phase involved development around what was to become the central area dominated by the main church built in the late fourteenth century. The fourth phase of development dates from the seventeenth century. The town became an important centre for the bourgeoisie - its wealth being dependent upon the surrounding good agricultural and grazing land; the skilled artisan work in chestnut and orangewood; for the production of bergamot perfume, local spirits, and a fine pure mineral water. The new, wealthy inhabitants during the seventeenth century built small, but well-proportioned Baroque palaces of which, unfortunately, only four remain.

The present town form has been affected by the earthquakes of 1659, 1783 and 1908. Redevelopment, however, took place following the old medieval street pattern using traditional building materials and plan types. From the street pattern it is still possible to distinguish the four quarters of the town. The convent quarter, in the lower western part of the town, is warmed by the sun and offers good views of the surrounding territory. The northern quarter is a maze of alleyways, there is little exposure to the sun and in the past disease was prevalent. The area contains many derelict houses, buildings used for storage and it is generally occupied by the poorer sections of the community. The eastern quarter, adjacent to the castle, has good views, a pleasant exposure to the sun and is probably the area with the most interesting street pattern. The central quarter is characterized by small shops, two piazze, one of which has a lovely fountain, a church and is the site of the weekly market.

San Giorgio Morgeto illustrates perfectly the type of hill town with which Alberti would have been familiar at the time of writing his seminal work on architecture. It is not inconceivable that towns like this one gave him ideas about streets that 'turn about' providing protection from the extremes of climate while permitting the penetration of sun and light for all buildings. Three of San Giorgio's quarters do meet these conditions, the fourth and northwestern quarter is built in an area with a poor prospect, probably for the expanding town during its period of greatest prosperity. It is to be contrasted with the buildings of the more affluent members of society who managed to design spacious and more formal structures within the medieval street pattern.

The form of San Giorgio Morgeto lends itself to a Lynch-type analysis.[71] The town sits distinctly in the landscape with the hard edge of building mass rising clearly from the hillside. The town, divided into easily recognizable and named quarters, is held together by a web of paths. The main paths lead directly from the two portals, Porto Convento and Fountain Square to the central business spine then up to the former political centre, the castle. Along the paths at important junctions lesser nodes form around bars and other public facilities. Dominating the skyline is the castle, a distant landmark, from

Figure 5.39
Montepulciano, Via di
Gracciano

within, the main church is an important feature
while from below the convent announces the
town's presence. For the purpose of this chapter it
is the street pattern, or the arrangement of paths to
fit contours which is of greatest interest. In the case
of San Giorgio Morgeto, however, these paths must
be seen as part of the greater whole, the form of
the town itself.

MONTEPULCIANO
Montepulciano, another of Italy's many lovely hilltop
towns, still today resembles a medieval walled town
(Figures 5.39-5.44). It is comprised of brick, tufa
and stone-built houses sitting astride a hilltop which
dominates the valleys of the Chiana and the Orcia.
The street pattern follows the contours in similar
fashion to San Giorgio Morgeto but here the architecture is much more imposing.

The Via di San Donato and its continuation the
Via Ricci run the length of the ridge. Where the two
streets meet at the Piazza Grande is the centre of
the town dominated by the Palazzo Comunale. The
Palazzo Comunale was begun in the second half of
the fourteenth century but not completed until the
middle of the fifteenth century. Its final design is by
Michelozzo in the Florentine style and has a notable

Figure 5.40 Montepulciano

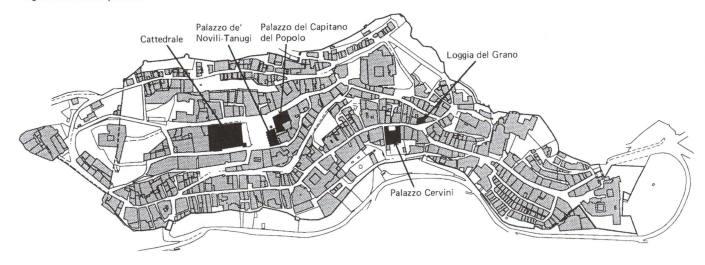

5.41

5.42

5.43

Figure 5.41 Montepulciano
Figure 5.42 Palazzo Novilia
Taruqi, Montepulciano
Figure 5.43 Via Di San
Donato, Montepulciano
Figure 5.44 Piazza Grande,
Montepulciano

5.44

resemblance to the Palazzo Vecchio in Florence.
The other main buildings in the Piazza Grande are
the Palazzo del Capitano del Popolo, one of the few
remaining examples of Gothic architecture in the
town; next to it is the Palazzo Tarugi designed by
Sangallo; facing the town hall is the Palazzo
Contucci also by Sangallo, and finally the square is
completed by the unfinished wall of the Duomo.

The main square of Montepulciano epitomizes
architectural development for the whole town.
Montepulciano's first authenticated mention is in a
parchment dated 715 AD. It seems to have been at
that time an independent town with its own laws.
At first self-governing, Montepulciano then became
embroiled in struggles between more powerful
neighbouring communes. The town being in a
strategic position and because of its wealth was
forced to ally alternatively with Siena and Florence.
Finally it became permanently allied to Florence,
and in 1511 came under the control of the Signoria
dei Medici.

The long period of wars was also a time of intense rivalry between the powerful noble families of Montepulciano to control the local government. One result of this rivalry saw the great families endow the town with wonderfully rich buildings for both public and private use. These buildings of Montepulciano aspire to compete with those of both Florence and Siena.

Most of these architectural monuments were built between 1300 and the 1500s, a testimony to the economic, social and political power of the families; a power based on wealth from the surrounding countryside. The buildings of Montepulciano, though great pieces of individual design, nevertheless fit into the basic medieval street scene, most are two-dimensional façades seen only obliquely as part of the greater street elevation, Among the architects

working in Montepulciano were the Sangallos, elder and younger, Michelozzo, Vignola and Andrea Pozzo which gives some idea of the influence of the patrons sponsoring development in this town during the early Renaissance through to the Baroque.

Designing a building as street architecture is no easy task and in the case of Montepulciano it engaged the skills of some of the great designers of the time. Two or three examples from Montepulciano are sufficient to illustrate this point. At the T-junction of Via di Gracciano Nel Corso, Via di Voltaia Nel Corso and Via delle Erbe the narrow streets open out into a small square, the Piazza delle Erbe, to display the Logge del Grano or del Mercato (the old granary) designed by Vignola. Here the narrow street is terminated on its axis by a fine structure which expands the space at ground level

Figure 5.45 Tempio di San Biagio, Montepulciano

using the device of an open loggia. Further on up the Via di Voltaia Nel Corso is the Palazzo Cervini designed by Guiliano da Sangallo. Sangallo, while maintaining the general roof height and the idea of the street frontage, incorporates a small courtyard into the street scene with a cleverly designed 'U'-plan for the palace.

In Montepulciano street architecture is raised to an art form. The individual buildings, while great designs in their own right, nevertheless respect the urban context of the general townscape. In doing so, they contribute to a greater unity where the enclosed three-dimensional space of the street is the main design consideration. For variety and contrast the street is widened to form small piazze at important nodal points, the spatial composition dominated by Piazza Grande at the top of the hill. All streets circulate from this centre like the skins of an onion. In the main square of the town Sangallo completes the enclosure with controlled elevations conforming with the general profile of the town where enclosure of the public realm is of greater significance than individual display. It is only on ascending the tower of the Palazzo Comunale that the full experience of the magnificent landscape can be appreciated.

In contrast to the tight urban structure of the town architecture and outside the defensive walls can be found the Tempio di San Biagio designed by Antonio da Sangallo the elder (Figure 5.45). In complete contrast to an architecture designed to enclose public space, the Tempio sits in the landscape isolated in space, a three-dimensional sculpted mass. Its design is based on a central square with an inscribed cross, a model of design much favoured at the time. While successful in isolation, as Sangallo demonstrates, it is an unsuitable form for urban architecture in high-density development.

Figure 5.46 The High Street, Oxford

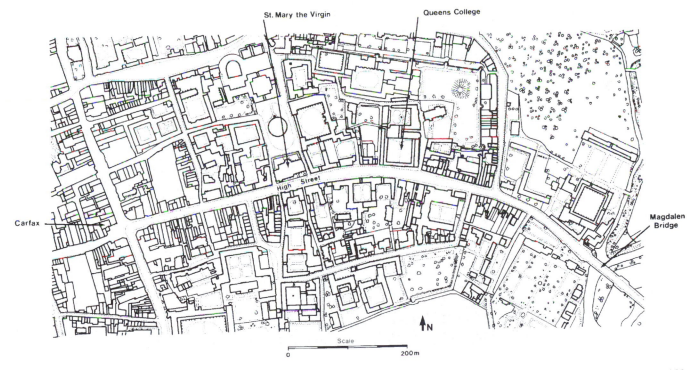

153

Figure 5.47 The High Street, Oxford (Photograph by Bridie Neville)
Figure 5.48 The High Street, Oxford
Figure 5.49 The High Street, Cupola, Queen's College, Oxford
Figure 5.50 The High Street, Oxford
Figure 5.51 The High Street, Tower at Magdalen College, Oxford

5.47

5.48

5.49

5.51

5.50

THE HIGH STREET, OXFORD
The curved street need not necessarily be confined to the hilly site where contours dictate road gradient and alignment - Oxford High Street is a case in point

(Figures 5.46–5.51). The basic landform in Oxford does not immediately suggest itself as the reason for the fine curve of the High Street. It has even been suggested that when King Edward took possession of London and Oxford in 912 he not only built the stronghold to the west of the town but, 'that at a definite moment the king laid out and created Oxford'.[72] This may or may not be so but there appears in Oxford, within part of the old walled settlement the remains of what may originally have been a grid plan. Its principal streets, the High Street being one of them, meet each other at right angles at Carfax. This is the sort of preconceived town layout often associated with colonial settlements. From Carfax, for part of its length, the High Street is straight but from St Mary the Virgin it sweeps round to Magdalen Bridge.

The wonderful curve of Oxford's High Street may result from the convenient connection between the termination of a planned development and an important river crossing or, more simply, the threading of a route through existing properties along an ancient right of way. No matter what the reason for its present form the result is a series of beautiful street pictures where spires and towers keep rising into view above lower buildings. Thomas Sharp goes so far as to suggest that this street 'is the greatest and most typical work of art England possesses . . .'.[73]

The visual sequence opens from Magdalen Bridge, High Street is seen curving away to the left past the pinnacled Magdalen College Tower. Moving along the High Street the sweep of the north side reveals Hawksmoor's Queen's College.[74] From Queen's College the steeple of St Mary's Church rises above All Souls College. From the footpath close to Queen's yet another view is revealed with the spire of All Saints Church visible beyond St Mary's and All Souls. Further on and across the street the fine curve of the street flattens and the street frontage produces a monumental effect. The panorama ends dramatically at Carfax with the tower of St Martin's. The progression of views in the opposite direction, starting at Carfax, is equally picturesque. The street curves to the right and at all points gives the feeling of enclosure and completion though hinting at further surprise just round the corner. The wall of the street façade appears continuous with entrances small and disguised by building mass. In the view from St Mary's looking to Queen's, the façade is completed by the tree between All Souls and Queen's. This tree which Sharp described as 'one of the most important in the world', adds an essential contrasting form to the street scene.[75] Below Queen's the same sweep of the street continues to reveal the first glimpse of Magdalen. The view then opens out to the bridge and tower signalling the end of this particular visual sequence.

Unwin warns about the temptation facing the planner in merely copying the outward form of streets such as the High Street, Oxford, and ending with, 'aimlessly wandering lines in the hope that happy accidents may result therefrom'.[76] Oxford High Street may have resulted from a series of 'happy accidents' but nevertheless produces an effect of completeness which is subject to analysis. This completeness or unity depends only marginally on the architectural quality of the individual buildings – by international standards few if any are top quality. The street, however, is outstanding. The first characteristic of the street is its completeness with a beginning and end at Carfax and Magdalen. The second important characteristic is the street's subdivision into easily identifiable and small-scale, enclosed spatial units which unfold as the observer moves along its length. A further important quality is the relationship between the buildings; the harmony of similar materials, forms and details juxtaposed with complementary elements, the towers at Carfax, All Saints, St Mary's and Magdalen. Finally, the street scene is enlivened along its length by exquisite detailing, the Baroque porch of St Mary's, Hawksmoor's cupola at Queen's and the lovely medieval gateway at Magdalen. In any part of the street there are decorative features, oriel windows, pinnacled roofs, ornamental chimneys or Magdalen's grotesque gargoyles to catch and eye and uplift the spirit. Despite Unwin's timely warning against the use of curved streets as a panacea for avoiding monotony, there is still much for the designer to learn from this high street, not least in how to decorate the city.

Figure 5.52 Priene

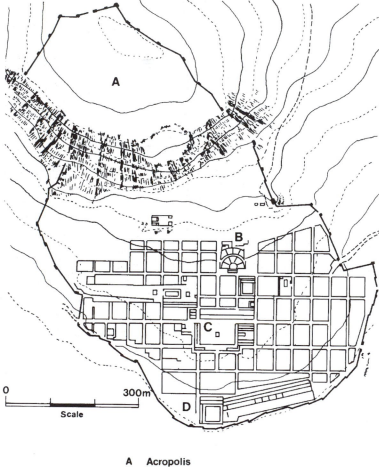

A	Acropolis
B	Theatre
C	Agora
D	Gymnasium and Stadium

LANDSDOWN CRESCENT AND SOMERSET PLACE, BATH

Curves may, of course, be as formal as straight lines. John Wood the Elder and his son at Bath, as seen earlier, developed the curved terrace for extremely formal compositions. Later, during the last quarter of the eighteenth century, John Palmer built the sweeping curves of Landsdown Crescent and Somerset Place in Bath. In parts, the development was designed to fit into the contours. The design consists of four segmented blocks of four-storey houses arranged alongside a landscaped depression. Landsdown Crescent is a symmetrical composition; the central block, on the highest point of the site follows the contours and is linked by bridges to crescents on each side which reverse the curve of the main block. The land falls steeply on each side of the main block requiring the side crescents to step down the slope. Somerset Place, the last block in the composition, reverses the direction of the curve again echoing the shape of the central crescent in the Landsdown group. The undulating wall of the composition manages to convey the feeling of monumentality and formality in distinct contrast to the general informality of High Street, Oxford.

There are a number of practical reasons for designing curved as opposed to straight streets; in addition to the need to arrange for the road surface to follow the contours in a hilly site, it may be necessary to follow ancient rights of way, to avoid significant structures, pay respect to ownership boundaries or design a convenient link between fixed points. At times even aesthetic reasons may have suggested a curved street alignment to give a view of a distant prospect or important landmark.

PRIENE

In Landsdown Crescent, Bath, the form of the hill and its contours may have suggested the initial point of departure for the development but the contours in no way dictated the final undulating form of the group. Similarly, the straight street, though most appropriate for a flat site has, nevertheless, on many occasions been employed in the most uncompromising manner on steeply sloping sites. A prime example of this form of development is Priene in the foothills of Mykale, Turkey (Figure 5.52).

Priene was a small provincial town of about 4,500 inhabitants founded in its present location in 350 BC.[77] It is probably typical of many other Hellenistic settlements of the time, but few could boast such a magnificent site. On to this steep site a gridiron layout was imposed. The east-west streets were more or less level, but the north-south connections were steep stairways. The gridiron plan is often dismissed as a dull, unimaginative, two-dimensional planning concept, but in Priene it was given full architectural treatment where the third dimension is fully exploited. The rock of the acropolis rises 300 m (985 ft) between two deep gorges. The town 210 m (690 ft) below the acropolis is arranged on four main terraces. On the uppermost terrace is the temple of Demeter, below it the temple of Athene Pollas, the theatre and upper gymnasium. The third terrace contains the main agora and the temple of Zeus, while on the fourth and lowest terrace is the stadium and lower gymnasium. These four great terraces are connected by steep north-south stairways. The rest of the town consists of the normal insulae between the grid; each insulae containing four plots measuring 24 m × 18 m (78 ft × 59 ft) for domestic buildings.[78]

The agora in the centre of the town covered two insulae and was surrounded on three sides by stoai; the north side remaining open. Along this side of the agora the main east-west road passed the square bordered on its north by a long stoa which closed the whole composition. The agora in Priene presents a clear architectural programme where the adjoining streets are subservient and are adapted to its form. The main street does not lead on a continuous axis through the centre of the space and the agora is not an extension of the street but a square bordered tangentially by a street. In this way the street retained its own functional integrity as a traffic route and the square remained undisturbed, a quiet meeting place.

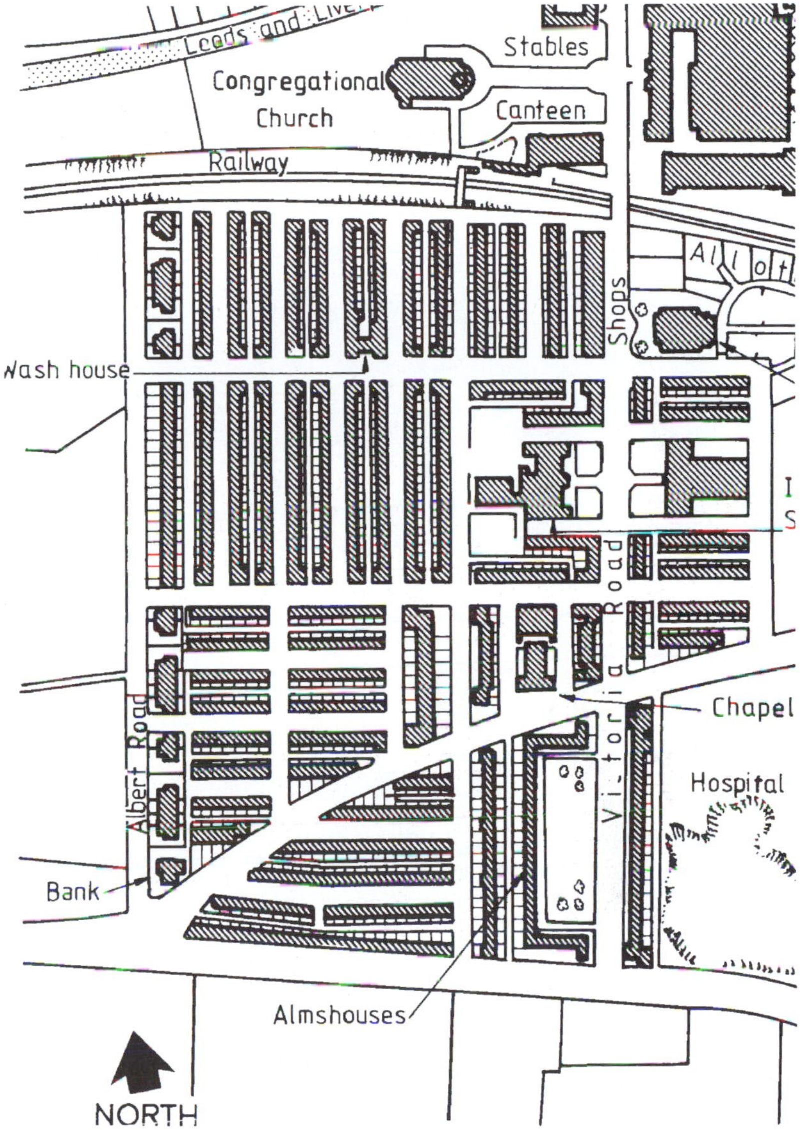

Figure 5.53 Saltaire

SALTAIRE

Saltaire, a small, planned, nineteenth-century settlement close to Bradford in Yorkshire, has many features in common with Priene on the Turkish

5.54

5.55

5.56

Figure 5.54 Saltaire
Figure 5.55 Saltaire
Figure 5.56 Saltaire

coast developed 2,000 years before (Figures 5.53-5.56). Like Priene, Saltaire's population was just under 4,500 and its size, 20 ha (49 acres), is similar to the built-up area of Priene but not including the acropolis. Both Priene and Saltaire were based on a gridiron plan and both imposed this layout type on to a sloping site. In the case of Saltaire, the site has none of the landscape drama of the Mykale foothills, nevertheless to the north it is still flanked by some very pleasant countryside.

Saltaire was begun in 1851 when Titus Salt decided to move his business out of a growing and congested Bradford. Inspired by one of Disraeli's novels, *Sybil*, published in 1845, Titus Salt employed architects Lockwood and Mawson to build his new town four miles from Bradford on the River Aire between the Leeds-Liverpool canal and the main railway line from Scotland to the Midlands. The choice of site was not fortuitous, being outside Bradford it was cheaper to build and it was not subject to the borough's rates nor its restrictions on building which would have prevented the more novel aspects of the scheme. The site was excellent for the location of a manufacturing town; the factory being sited between the canal and railway line made the handling of goods cheap, while the general location gave direct connections, both with the sources of raw materials and market outlets for finished articles.

In order to determine the type and quantity of housing required for the town, Salt commissioned a sort of social survey among his workers. From this he was able to estimate the various housing needs for different family sizes. According to Robert Dewhurst this was 'the first time that it had occurred to anyone that a workman with 10 children needed more rooms than a workman with one child'.[79] The variety in house type in the programme gave to his architects the possibility of articulating the long street elevations. Large houses were placed at the ends of terraces or at strategic points along the 60-90 m (197 ft × 295 ft) length where emphasis was required. Long street frontages stepping down the contours were judiciously broken up with pavilions of larger houses which accommodated the change in roofline in an architecturally controlled manner. Though the gridiron plan was similar to the one used for much of nineteenth-century, working-class housing, in Saltaire it did not plumb the same depths of monotony. This may be due in part to the small scale of the development but more probably because of the thought given to the architectural detailing.

The main street, Victoria Road, is the spine of the development. Along Victoria Road are arranged the public buildings. Entrance to Saltaire is through the little square enclosed on one side by the hospital and on the other three sides by the almshouses. As in Priene, the road passes down one side of the square, leaving the remaining space for a private communal garden attached to the almshouses. From the entrance square the road narrows between terrace blocks then opens out into a square enclosed by the school and the institute. From here it narrows again between terrace blocks, and crosses the railway to the works and the chapel. Here made physically manifest are the Protestant values of Salt and so many others in Victoria's reign - the key to life was hard work and prayer. The axis from factory door to chapel door is at right angles to the main movement down Victoria Road terminating the main street, a constant reminder of the Protestant work ethic.

Walking down Victoria Road is a delightful aesthetic experience. The spaces are architecturally modulated, buildings are arranged on either side of the route, in mutually reflecting projections or axially composed elevations. The whole street is an exercise in inflection, that is, the echo of feature with feature across the space, the 'minuet of street architecture' as A. Trystan Edwards would describe it.[80]

AXIAL PLANNING

The straight street is associated with axial city planning in addition to gridiron planning. Two outstanding examples of axial planning are Rome, as laid out by Sixtus V, and Paris, as planned by Haussmann for Napoleon III. Sixtus V was concerned to develop a structure of paths along which pilgrims could move freely from church to church.[81] The great processional routes established by Sixtus V set the pattern for much later architectural development and heritage which remains today. Haussmann, too, was concerned with

movement, but in this case it was a concern for the rapid movement of troops to keep order in the city. The plans Haussmann prepared have also left a great heritage of city street design.[82] The Parisian boulevard is a model of city street design which has been neglected by urban designers and city planners in the past decades. Its revival is necessary if the art of city design is itself to revive.

PULTENEY BRIDGE AND GREAT PULTENEY STREET, BATH

Alberti, Palladio and Serlio, in their writings, devote a great deal of attention to bridge design.[83] For them, particularly Palladio, the bridge was an architectural problem, subject to the same kind of analysis as a building, defensive structure or town square. Partly as a response to traffic increases, the main function of the street, in recent years, has been seen as enabling the free movement of vehicles. This emphasis on movement has resulted in the neglect of the street as a place with three-dimensional properties. The street once reduced to a two-dimensional, metalled road becomes the province of the road engineer. The bridge carrying this two-dimensional ribbon of tarmacadam is also reduced to an engineering problem. There are of course many wonderful bridges designed in this way and for this purpose. For example, there is Darby's first cast-iron bridge over the River Severn or Maillart's elegant reinforced concrete bridges, such as the one at Schandbach-Bruke, Canton Berne, constructed in 1933. Clearly, bridges carrying a pavement across a river or gorge predate Darby and the Industrial Revolution. They have, however, not been the only bridge form used, particularly in towns and cities. The old London Bridge carried not only the pavement but also shops and perhaps more importantly, from an architectural viewpoint, the enclosed space of the street. The Ponte Vecchio, which crosses the Arno in Florence at its narrowest point, and the Rialto in Venice are surviving examples of the bridge designed to carry a street rather than a road across an opening (Figures 5.57-5.61).

Figure 5.57 Ponte Vecchio, Florence
Figure 5.58 Ponte Vecchio, Florence
Figure 5.59 Rialto Bridge, Venice
Figure 5.60 Rialto Bridge, Venice
Figure 5.61 Rialto Bridge, Venice

5.57

5.58

5.60

5.59

5.61

Following on from this tradition, Robert Adam built a bridge across the Avon at Bath using the Ponte Vecchio as his architectural model. As a first step in opening up the land in Bathwick Estate to the east of the Avon, the owner Sir William Pulteney commissioned Adam to design the bridge which was built between 1769 and 1774. Much of the Adam detailing has been lost through repeated alterations, but fortunately the main enclosed street form remains. The Adam bridge is a wonderful, and in this country, unique example of urban street architecture; it is not simply a river crossing, but also a visual junction connecting two parts of eighteenth-century Bath and a fine entrance to one of the great streets of Europe (Figures 5.62–5.64).

5.62

5.63

5.64

Figure 5.62 Pulteney Bridge, Bath

Figure 5.63 Pulteney Bridge, Bath
Figure 5.64 Pulteney Bridge, Bath

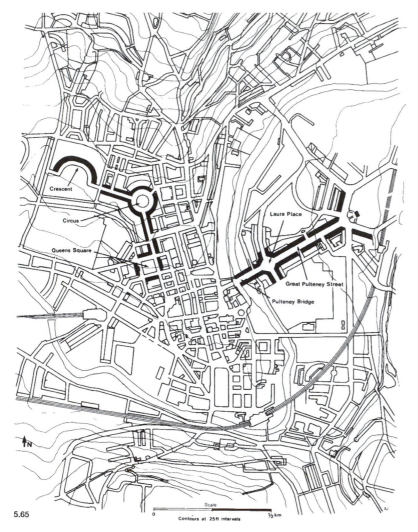

5.66

5.67

5.68

Figure 5.65 Bath
Figure 5.66 Great Pulteney
Street from Laura Place,
Bath
Figure 5.67 Laura Place,
Bath
Figure 5.68 Great Pulteney
Street, Bath

Adam also prepared plans for the development of a new town at Bathwick. His first and most imaginative scheme for the estate 'linked the bridge by a wide road to a great circus from which five other streets led off. These in turn were crossed by streets converging on a semi-circular open space at the bridge entrance.'[84] Neither this nor the later amended version

of the scheme were adopted and the final plan for Bathwick was drawn up by Thomas Baldwin (Figures 5.65–5.69). Baldwin, in his plans, incorporated Adam's wide street but omitted both the semi-circular space in front of the bridge and the circus, the focal point of the original design. Baldwin's plan for the project consists of a short street, Argyle Street, which leads to a diagonally placed square, Laura Place, with streets into it at the other three corners. Two of these streets

lead nowhere. The continuation of Argyle Street, Great Pulteney Street, leads into Sydney Gardens which is an elongated hexagonal designed as a pleasure garden.[85] Great Pulteney Street enters the hexagonal of Sydney Gardens at the apex of the space as indeed it does in Laura Place. The project was started in 1788 but Baldwin and a number of other builders went bankrupt. When work ended only one block, Sydney Place, of the hexagon was completed. The Sydney Hotel at the head of the plan on the axis of Great Pulteney Street was completed later by Harcourt Masters following closely the ideas of Baldwin. The Sydney Hotel was drastically remodelled by Sir Reginald Blomfield and is now the Holburn and Menstrie Museum.

Great Pulteney Street, 300 m long by 30 m wide (984 ft × 98 ft) and three storeys high is an elegant and well-proportioned street even though in its architectural detailing it has little of the authority of the Woods nor the charm of Adam. The vista from the bridge, in all 600 m (656 yd) long, is effectively stopped by the mass of Sydney Hotel reinforced as it is by dense planting. Along its length the variety of spaces – the small scale of the bridge, the short Argyle Street, the widened space of Laura Place, the elongated Great Pulteney Street stopped by the hotel but connected to the park beyond – are a model of architectural control which distinguishes this area of Bath as a great work of urban design. It contrasts greatly with the early composition of the two Woods but in its own way is equally important as a generic model for development.

REGENT STREET, LONDON

John Nash, together with a firm of developers, Leverton and Chawner, was instructed to make plans for Marylebone Park and also for a new street to facilitate communication between north and south London in that part of the city (Figures 5.70-5.75).

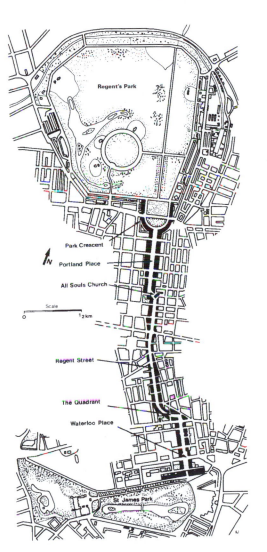

Figure 5.69 Sydney Hotel, Bath

Figure 5.70 Regent Street, London

5.71

5.72

5.74

5.75

Figure 5.71 Park Crescent, London
Figure 5.72 The Quadrant, Regent Street, London
Figure 5.73 All Souls' Church, London
Figure 5.74 Lower Regent Street, London
Figure 5.75 The York Column, London

5.73

After dissecting the problem Nash identified the line for the new street which to him seemed inevitable. He observed that at a certain time the morphology and character of the town changed abruptly. He proposed that this clear edge in development should form the route of the new street, to provide 'a boundary and complete separation between the Streets and Squares occupied by the Nobility and Gentry, and the narrow Streets and meaner Homes occupied by mechanics and the trading part of the community'. Nash explained later that his purpose 'was that the new street should cross the eastern entrance to all the streets occupied by the higher classes and to leave out to the east all the bad streets, and as a sailor would express himself, to hug all the avenues that went to good streets'.[86] This may not sit comfortably with the more social ideas of early twentieth century planning but it proved a perfectly good strategy for realizing improved land values from a property speculation.

Portland Place by the Adam brothers and the finest street in London at the time was the northern-most starting point for the new street. The street, Nash continued southwards crossing Oxford Street through a circus. The line of the new street was to continue southwards passing Golden Square entering on the north-west side of a proposed new square containing a free-standing public building. The street left the square in the south-east corner then further south it turned another corner at Piccadilly Circus. From here there was a straight vista to the palace of Carlton House.[87]

Nash planned the street from Oxford Circus to Pall Mall to be lined on both sides with a continu-ous covered colonnade. This was a far more formal and imaginative design for a street than any other built in Britain. The length, however, of the new street was cleverly articulated at important junctions or where a change of direction became necessary. At these critical positions a circus or square was introduced so that no length of street was uninter-rupted for more than 600 m (656 yd).

Once his report and plan were approved in principle, Nash was asked to reconsider the new street in greater detail. He prepared two additional plans. The one that was finally adopted for the development introduced, instead of the square, a portion of curving street 'resembling in that respect the High Street at Oxford'.[88]

The development from Regent's Park to St James's Park then along the Mall to Buckingham Palace is one of the masterpieces of European urban design. Park Square and Park Crescent function as a powerful connection between Regent's Park and Portland Place. The semicircular sweep of the Ionic colonnaded crescent directs the movement to Portland Place and heralds a magnificent opening to the street sequence. At the end of Portland Place Nash was obliged, for practical reasons, to change the direction of the street. In the hands of a lesser designer this could have resulted in an awkward kink. Nash resolved the problem with masterly precision; All Souls' Church with its adroitly placed, circular spired vestibule acts as a terminal feature at the awkward junction neatly turning the corner. The church and its spire have been criticized for the lack of architectural articulation, nevertheless, the siting of the circular drum shows a fine appreciation of urban form.

At the crossing with Oxford Street, Nash utilized the circus shown in the earlier plan. The circus not only dignified an important junction, but also facili-tated another directional change. Bacon remarking on the 'sinuosity of Regent Street' comments on 'the superb handling of the changes in direction of the street by cylinders and flat domes of the bordering buildings'.[89] The major change in direction was achieved using The Quadrant, which took Oxford's High Street as the model. The architectural treat-ment of Regent Street and the High Street however had very little in common. Regent Street, unlike its model in Oxford, was a formal composition with covered, colonnaded walkways down its whole length and its uniform architectural treatment was in complete contrast to the picturesque and largely medieval street scenes in Oxford. From The Quadrant the street turned sharply through 90° and down the axis to Carlton House, first passing through a circus at Piccadilly and then a new square at Waterloo Place.

Since its completion by Nash, the street has undergone many changes. Carlton House was demolished when King George IV built Buckingham Palace to replace it in the late 1820s. The axis along Lower Regent Street was stopped by the York Column and an imposing flight of steps to the park. Nash built Carlton Terrace at the edge of the park, extending the new route to Buckingham Palace. The first major change to the street itself was in 1848 when the arcades of The Quadrant were removed. The major changes, however, occurred in the early decades of the last century when many leases fell due. The changes wrought on the street were architectural in nature involving a change in scale to suit the new shopping needs. Nash's stucco buildings, or those built with his approval, were replaced by larger and, on the whole, more ponderous buildings. Despite these changes and the despoiling of Piccadilly Circus, the route from Regent's Park to Buckingham Palace retains, in the main, its original line and urban form. It illustrates that good urban design is not solely dependent upon the quality of the surrounding architecture, though if an opportunity ever arises for the rebuilding of part of this street it would be well to reconsider a return to its original scale and character.

CONCLUSION

There are two main generic forms for the European city street. In the first, streets appear to be carved out of an original block of solid material. In this conception, the spatial volume of the street defined by the frontages is perceived as the positive form, or the figure seen against the general background of the surrounding architecture. The other concept lays stress on the buildings as three-dimensional objects, in this case the city is a parkland in which buildings stand as isolated sculptural forms. Space including streets flows without shape around buildings and other landscape features. This last concept in its purer manifestations such as Frank Lloyd Wright's

Broadacre requires for its implementation large areas of low-density development, decentralization of functions, complete and unrestricted freedom of movement for the car.[90] In effect, it is the very antithesis of place formation with its notion of centrality. Both main concepts of the city and its streets exist side by side in the real world. They may, indeed, represent the poles of a continuum rather than a simple dichotomy. Indeed in the High Street, Oxford, classified as an enclosed form, much of its interest is achieved from the contrasting three-dimensional forms of its towers and spires.

The chief quality of a street is due mainly to the handling of volume, but the mood or character of the street is created by its architecture. The main types of street scenes were captured by Serlio with his drawings of the tragic, comic and satyric backdrops for theatre productions. The tragic scene is the formal classic interpretation of the street typified by the monumentality of the Parisian boulevard. Here in Britain this is not the most common interpretation of street architecture; it is the exception rather than the rule. Development in Edinburgh and Bath comes close to this generic street form, particularly in the case of Great Pulteney Street. As a rule, monumentality in street design fits most comfortably with the straight street. The sinuous development of Regent's Street by Nash, however, particularly The Quadrant with its continuous porticos, falls firmly within the monumental Classical tradition which Serlio would define as tragic.

The comic scene of Serlio fits most appropriately within the British, particularly English, tradition. The slow, meandering medieval street of small-scale architecture, preponderance of whimsical detail and warm, weathered material is the picturesque delight of the British small town. High Street, Oxford, though not residential, retains a domestic scale. Even Classical buildings, such as Queen's, conform with the overall uniformity of the scene.

The satyric street scene is another common feature of the British town. The Englishman's ideal home, his miniature castle surrounded by garden, is the driving force, the motive power for suburbia. This return to the country and escape from the horrors of city life was given credence and aesthetic form by Ebenezer Howard and his architects Parker and Unwin in their Garden City Movement. Low-density housing, the landscaped street and resulting garden suburb represents an attainable ideal environment for a vast majority of British people. It is also an urban form which, by its nature, is highly participatory in a property-owning democracy. There is, of course, a price to pay for this freedom for all to build a personalized dream house. Those who cannot afford the mortgage down payment or monthly repayments cannot participate in the building of this brave new suburbia; they become the underclass, the permanently disenfranchised. Sustaining this expansive and expanding suburban dreamland presupposes free movement of individualized transport. With constant political turbulence in the Middle East and the knowledge that fossil fuels have a limited lifespan, the development of another form of motor power for individual travel will be needed to sustain suburbia. Assuming that another form of private vehicle will be developed it seems clear that unrestrained vehicular movement on a massive scale is incompatible with cities and their streets as we know them today.

NOTES

1 Vitruvius. *The Ten Books of Architecture* (trns. Morris Hicky Morgan), Dover Publications, New York, 1960, p.150

2 Serlio, Sebastiano. *The Five Books of Architecture*, unabridged reprint of the English edn of 1611, Dover Publications, New York, 1982, Second Book, The Third Chapter, Fol. 25 and Fol. 26

3 Vidler, Anthony. The scenes of the street: transformations in ideal and reality. In *On Streets* (ed. Stanford Anderson), MIT Press, Cambridge, Mass., 1986, pp.29, 30

4 Alberti, Leone Battista. *Ten Books of Architecture* (trns. Cosimo Bartoli (into Italian) and James Leoni (into English) Tiranti, London, 1955, Book VIII, Chapter 1, p.162

5 Palladio, Andrea. *The Four Books of Architecture*, Dover Edition, New York, 1965, Third Book, Chapter III, p.60

6 Ibid, p.61

7 Alberti, Leone Battista. Op cit, Book IV, Chapter V, p.75

8 Palladio, Andrea. Op cit, Third Book, Chapter I, p.58

9 Ibid, Third Book, Chapter I, p.59

10 For definitions see *The Shorter Oxford Dictionary*, Clarendon Press, Oxford, 1933 onwards

11 Le Corbusier. *The Radiant City*, Faber & Faber, London, 1967, pp.121 and 123

12 Smithson, A. and Smithson, P. *Urban Structuring*, Studio Vista, London, 1967, p.15

13 Ibid, p.22

14 Jacobs, Jane. *The Death and Life of Great American Cities*, Random House, New York, 1961, and Penguin Books, Harmondsworth, 1965, p.39

15 Newman, O. *Defensible Space*, Macmillan, New York, 1972, and Coleman, Alice. *Utopia on Trial*, Hilary Shipman, London, 1985

16 Jacobs, Jane. Op cit, p.41

17 Ibid, p.45

18 Moughtin, J.C. *The Planters Vision*, The University of Nottingham, Nottingham, 1978, p.5

19 Gutman, Robert. The Street Generation. In *On Streets*, op cit, p.259

20 Rapoport, Amos. *House Form and Culture*, Prentice-Hall, Englewood Cliffs, New Jersey, 1969, *Human Aspects of Urban Form: Towards a Man Environment Approach to Urban Form and Design*, Pergamon Press, New York, 1977

21 Gans, Herbert. *People and Plans*, Basic Books, New York, 1968, p.19

22 Gans, Herbert. *People and Plans*, abridged edn, Penguin, Harmondsworth, 1968, p.34

23 Gutman, Robert, Op cit, p.250

24 Buchanan, C. *Traffic in Towns, The Specially Shortened Edition of the Buchanan Report*, Penguin, Harmondsworth, 1963, p.55

25 Ibid, pp.56-57

26 Schumacher, T. Buildings and streets: notes on configuration and use. In *On Streets*, op cit, p.133

27 Rapoport, Amos. *Human Aspects of Urban Form*, op cit

28 Coleman, Alice. *Utopia on Trial*, Hilary Shipman, London, 1985

29 Ellis, W.C. The spatial structure of streets. In *On Streets*, op cit, p.115

30 Barnett, J. *An Introduction to Urban Design*, Harper & Row, New York, 1982, p.168

31 Alexander, C. et al. *A Pattern Language*, Oxford University Press, Oxford, 1977, pp.590-591

32 Norberg-Schulz, C. *Existence, Space and Architecture*, Studio Vista, London, 1971, p.21

33 Lynch, K. *The Image of the City*, MIT Press, Cambridge, Mass., 1960, pp.47-56

34 Gibberd, F. *Town Design*, Architectural Press. London, 2nd edn, 1955, p.230

35 Collins, G.R. and Collins, C.C. *Camillo Sitte: The Birth of Modern City Planning*, Rizzoli, New York, 1986, p.199

36 Gibberd, F. Op cit, p.230

37 Collins, G.R. and Collins, C.C. Op cit, p.202

38 County Council of Essex. *A Design Guide for Residential Areas*, Essex County Council, Chelmsford, 1973, p.71

39 Sitte, Camillo. *Der Stadte-Bau*, Carl Graeser, Wien, 1901

40 County Council of Essex. Op cit, p.65

41 Hegemann, Werner and Peets, Elbert, *The American Vitruvius, An Architect's Handbook of Civic Art*, Benjamin Blom, New York, 1922, p.154

42 Ibid, p.152

43 Norberg-Schulz, C. Op cit. p.83

44 Alberti, L.B. Op cit. Book IV, Chapter V, p.75

45 Norberg-Schulz, C. Op cit, p.81

46 Lynch, K. 1960. Op cit

47 Alexander, C. Op cit, p.591

48 County Council of Essex. Op cit, p.71: and Hegemann, Werner and Peets, Elbert. Op cit, p.152.

49 Collins, G.R. and Collins, C.C. Op cit. p.199.

50 Ibid, p.205.

51 Lynch, K. Op cit, p.99.

52 Collins, G.R. and Collins. C.C. Op cit. p.204

53 Gibberd, F. Op cit, p.231

54 Unwin, Raymond. *Town Planning in Practice*, Fisher Unwin, London, 1909, p.245

55 County Council of Essex. Op cit

56 Palladio. Op cit, Third Book, Chapter II, p.59

57 Alberti, L.B. Op cit. Book IV, Chapter V, p.75

58 For example see Koenigsberger, O. et al. *Manual of Tropical Housing and Building*, Part 1: *Climatic Design*, Longman, London, 1974; or Moughtin, J.C. *Hausa Architecture*, Ethnographica, London, 1985, Chapter 6, Climate and built form

59 An apocryphal statement allegedly made by Professor Arthur Ling, first Professor of Architecture, University of Nottingham

60 Gibberd, F. Op cit. p.230

61 Hegemann, Werner and Peets, Elbert. Op cit, p.187

62 Ibid, p.169

63 Alberti, L.B. Op cit, Book VIII, Chapter VI, p.172

64 Palladio, A. Op cit, Third Book, Chapter 1, p.58

65 Ibid, p.60

66 Downes, Kerry. *Hawksmoor*, Thames and Hudson, London, 1980, p.86

67 Summerson, John. *John Nash, Architect to King George IV*, Allen and Unwin, London, 1935, p.219

68 Bacon, Edmund N. *Design of Cities*, Thames and Hudson, London, 1975, p.112

69   Giedion, S. *Space, Time and Architecture*, Harvard University Press, Cambridge, Mass., 1954, p.39

70   For this analysis of the town I am indebted to the work of my students: David Armiger, Raphael Cuesta, Alison Gee, June Greenway, Persephone Ingram and Christine Sarris. See for example Cuesta, J.R. et al. *Appraisal and Proposals for San Giorgio Morgeto, Programa Erasmus*, Universita di Reggio Calabria, and University of Nottingham, unpublished report, March 1989

71   Lynch, K. Op cit

72   Quoted in Gutkind, K.A. *Urban Development in Western Europe:* Volume VI, *The Netherlands and Great Britain*, The Free Press, New York, 1971, p.392

73   Sharp, Thomas. *Oxford Replanned*, Architectural Press, London, 1948, p.20

74   The sources of the design of Queen's, 'are complex and are associated with the architects Wren, Aldrich, Hawksmoor, Clark and the mason-contractor Townsend'. This is according to Kersting, A.F. and Ashdown, John. *The Buildings of Oxford*, Batsford, London, 1980, p.141. Sherwood and Pevsner appear to suggest that Hawksmoor was probably responsible for the Front Quad that faces onto the High Street, 'Whoever designed the Front Quad knew his Wren precidents. But the details of the N. range are not Wren at all; they - and those of the W and E ranges - go more with Hawksmoor, Wren's principal pupil, than anybody else.' Sherwood, Jennifer and Pevsner, Nikolaus. *The Buildings of England, Oxfordshire*, Penguin, Harmondsworth, 1974, p.188

75   Sharp, Thomas. Op cit, p.23

76   Unwin, Raymond. Op cit, p.260

77   Morris, A.E.J. *History of Urban Form*, George Godwin, London, 1972, p.28

78   Gutkind, E.A. *Urban Development in Southern Europe*, Volume IV: *Italy and Greece*, The Free Press, New York, 1969, pp.579-583

79   Dewhurst, R.K. Saltaire. In *Town Planning Review*, Vol XXXI, No 2, July 1960, pp.135-144

80   Edwards, A.T. *Architectural Style*, Faber and Gwyer, London, 1926, pp.106-107

81   Giedion, S. *Space, Time and Architecture*, 3rd edn, Harvard University Press, Cambridge, Mass., 1956, pp.75-106

82   Bacon, Edmund N. Op cit, p.193

83   Alberti, L.B. Op cit, Book VIII, Chapter VI, pp.172-173. Palladio. Op cit, Third Book, Chapters IV to XV (see particularly plates IX and X). Serlio. Op cit. Third Book, Chapter 4, Fol.41

84   Gadd, David. *Georgian Summer*, Adams and Dart, Bath, 1971, p.120

85   Pevsner, Nikolaus. *The Buildings of England: North Somerset and Bristol*, Penguin, Harmondsworth. 1958. p.135

86   Summerson, John. Op cit, 1935, p.124

87   Hobhouse, Hermione. *History of Regent Street*, Macdonald and Jane's, London, 1975 (see map on p.30)

88   Ibid. p.34

89   Bacon, Edmund N. Op cit, p.209

90   Wright, Frank Lloyd. *The Living City*, Horizon Press, New York, 1958, pp.81-83

SEAFRONT, RIVER AND CANAL 6

It will rise, in a time after times,

After swallowing death and the pit
It will return stainless

For the delivery of this world.
So the river is a god

Knee-deep among reeds, watching men,
Or hung by the heels down the door of a dam

It is a god, and inviolable.
Immortal. And will wash itself of all deaths.

River by Ted Hughes

INTRODUCTION

The city is structured by four types of water feature. The first is the water point or fountain. It has magical connotations associated with the grotto, the life giving spring and bottomless well. The urban descendent of the spring, the drinking fountain, is a centre of activity, a gathering place for the community often located at its heart, in the market square. The second is the pool, a place of reflection, contemplation and recreation. Together with the 'green', it is at the centre of the English village. In a more formal setting the pool mirrors, Narcissus-like, the leisure pursuits of indolent actors against a backcloth of city structures. The exemplar of the reflective pool is of course the Alhambre (Figure 6.1). The third type is the linear water course which runs through cities in the form of either a river or a canal. A river out of control is an awesome sight, a source of great destruction. A river, therefore, is controlled as it passes from a natural landscape into the town or the city. The power of the river to cause damage to life and property is tamed as it passes through the city: it is canalized, dammed, regularized with weir or set within an ample flood plain. The river may also be canalized and controlled with a complex system of lock gates so that the water course is better able to serve the requirements of water transportation. The fourth and last type of water feature associated with the city is the coast. Like the river or canal this is a linear feature which structures urban form: it is the edge of the city, a place where another world begins. It is a place where both dangers and possibilities abound. It is here where the docklands are located, where prostitution, drink, drugs and crime abound but also the place which presages a new beginning in a new world.

Figure 6.1 The Alhambre

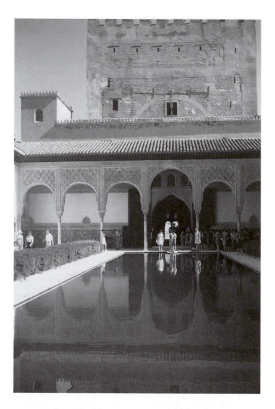

A discussion of the decorative implications for urban design, of the fountain and reflective pool, appears in *Urban Design: Ornament and Decoration*.[1] This chapter will therefore concentrate upon the function of river, canal and waterfront in urban design, paying particular attention to their relationship to street and square.

THE NATURE OF WATER

Water has always been imperative for life. It is the genesis of settlement, controlling the birth, location and development of cities. Without water human settlement is impossible. Water is, therefore, protective of life, many cities being sited within the defensive loop of a river, a symbol of the city's freedom and its *raison d'être*. Flooding in Bangladesh is witness to the destructive and dangerous power of water in full flood. With flooding also comes renewal, of which the great Biblical myth of Noah is an archetype. Embodiments of this power of water for renewal are the annual floods of the Nile, the life blood of a long and sustained city culture in Pharaonic Egypt. Water is, therefore, both protective and dangerous. Until controlled and managed, it poses a threat to those who live in close proximity and who depend upon its bounty for existence. The power of water has sculpted many of the world's unique landscapes: they have been eroded by rain, by glaciers, or by seas and mountain torrents. Landscapes moulded by the action of water are a constant source of inspiration for architects and urbanists. The dynamic force of water gives vitality to those built structures designed to contain it, or to those structures designed to harness its great power for sustaining development and for improving the well-being of the community. Water also imbues with quality those buildings, streets and city squares which incorporate the audiovisual effects of moving water or the calm and tranquillity of its reflective mood (Figures 6.1 to 6.3).

Water as a structuring element is central to the art of city building. The creative act of developing city form which expresses the needs and aspirations of its citizens is predicated on an appreciation and understanding of the myths we associate with water and of the symbolic meaning we attach to it.[2] Water is the essence of the universe made real. It is at the heart of the great myths of creation: 'God at the beginning of time, created heaven and earth. Earth was still an empty waste, and darkness hung over the deep; but already, over the *waters*, stirred the breath of God . . . God said too, Let a solid vault arise amid the *waters*, to keep these *waters* apart from those; a vault by which God would separate the *waters* which were beneath it from the *waters* above it; and so it was done. This vault God called sky . . . And now God said, let the *waters* below the vault collect in one place to let dry land appear. And so it was done; the dry land God called Earth, and the *water*, where it had collected, he called the Sea.'[3] Water is seen in this and other myths of creation as a source of life. In the Judaeo-Christian world water is also seen as a source of re-birth: baptism in water is associated with a washing away of sins and part of the initiation process of re-birth into a purer welcoming community. Water is the mirror of the world but it disturbs present certainties and extends the possibilities of a brighter and better future. Water in the world of Ancient Greece was seen as one of the four main elements which comprise the universe in which we live. The myths associated with the rivers Styx, Ganges and Nile signified the crossing place to the underworld, the world of the dead, where the body cannot follow. Water has these two opposing and contradictory properties: it arouses fear and dread but it is also a symbol of bounty and of life itself. In practical terms these opposites manifest themselves in the life that water can bring to the desert and the death and destruction which results from the power of the uncontrolled deluge.

FUNCTION OF WATER AS A DESIGN ELEMENT

Clearly the most important and the most obvious function of water for city development is sustaining life in the city. The continued existence of the city depends upon an adequate supply of potable drinking water together with water for industrial and agricultural purposes. It is not the intention here to discuss this aspect of the subject; nevertheless, it is apparent that the consumption of water to sustain large urban centres is expanding at an alarming rate. It may be some comfort to know that, in Britain, our own domestic, industrial and agricultural use of water, though wasteful, compares favourably with other developed countries. In global terms the result

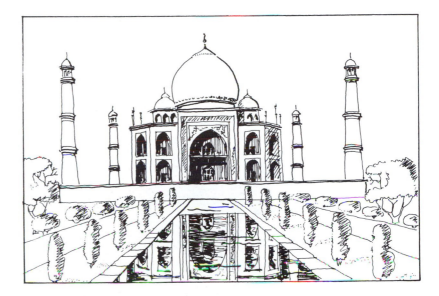

Figure 6.2 The Taj Mahal
Figure 6.3 Mogul Gardens, Srinagar, Kashmir, India

of the overindulgent use of this not inexhaustible resource could seriously affect water tables and water courses in and around the world's great cities. Developing a civilized and balanced strategy for the design of water areas in cities may require a more frugal attitude to the use of this most vital of the earth's resources. The attitudes and values necessary for sustainable development and a 'greener city' are discussed more fully in *Urban Design: Green*

173

6.5

6.6

Figure 6.4 The Landing Stage, The Pier Head, Liverpool
Figure 6.5 The Grand Canal, Venice
Figure 6.6 Amsterdam

Dimensions.[4] Since the book's publication in 1996 there have been a number of alarming reports and political decisions, particularly in the United States of America, which taken together, paint a bleak future for Planet Earth. *The Global Environmental Outlook*, compiled by the UN, prepared by 1,100 scientists charts the environmental degradation of the last 30 years and looks forward to how the world might appear in 2032. The report estimates that unless cultures change their current 'markets first' approach to development, then more than half the world will be affected by water shortages, with 95 per cent of people in the Middle East and 65 per cent of people in Africa and the Pacific, having severe problems.[5]

Many towns and cities owe their existence to water, developing around a port or being located at a major crossing point on a navigable river. The water frontage became the focus of commerce, industry and transport. 'The rapid decline of traditional industry over the last 30 years together with technological change has released large areas of land for redevelopment. This has made it possible to re-use waterside locations to promote regeneration.'[6] Regeneration,

however, depends upon finding new uses for the land and buildings adjacent to the water frontage. More importantly, it also means finding a new function for the water itself which may provide the impetus or *raison d'être* for regeneration. Regeneration of the water frontage may indeed derive from an older or former use being given new emphasis or direction.

The traditional function for the water frontage is one associated with the transportation of goods and people. The movement of goods by water transport has decreased significantly since the heyday of the canal in the nineteenth century; nevertheless, it remains an important function of many inland waterways and port cities. Water transport, where it is still operating, adds colour and life to the canal as in the cities of Bruges, Venice and Amsterdam or to the harbour of many great sea ports (Figures 6.4 to 6.6). Clearly the movement of people to and from work and for other city journeys is and will remain largely land based. The relative ease of building bridges and tunnels connecting opposite banks of major cities has reduced the need for and the use of ferry crossings. The use of the ferry in cities such as Hong Kong, Auckland, or in Britain at Southampton and Liverpool, illustrate the potential for this form of urban transport. It endows the city waterfront with life and movement, an opportunity which can be seized by retaining and developing public and private water transport.

The development of leisure activities holds out a viable prospect for the regeneration of redundant docks and for sites along canals and rivers. Such activities associated with disused water frontages are becoming popular for leisure users. 'A direct view of water from the window or terrace of an hotel, restaurant or pub adds to its attractiveness and hence value. The light is better, and often reflected upwards; the surface is changeable; there is little or no traffic. One may have a more distant view, or the glimpse of people in boats.'[7] There are, however, many leisure pursuits which can only be associated with a waterfront. These specific leisure pursuits requiring location close to a waterfront include pleasure cruising, boating and fishing. Marinas and other facilities which serve this expanding water industry are in themselves attractions for

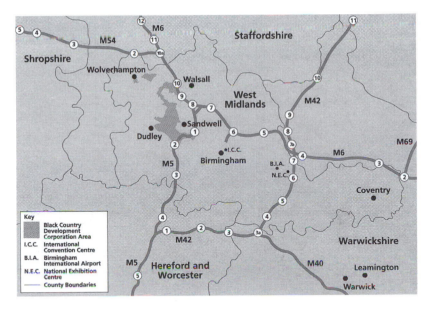

Figure 6.7 Black Country Development Corporation Area

the public, and, along with rowing, canoeing and power-boating, generate on-shore activities. Shops associated with fishing including fish sales and aquaria, and museums such as the Maritime Museum in Liverpool, may also thrive from close proximity to water and the activity it can generate. For leisure activities to be successful, 'A company or group of companies have to be persuaded to create a complex leisure business which is large and exciting enough to be an attraction ... and if it is not well-designed and well-managed it may never succeed ... So the waterfront leisure zones have to be managed and must be large and busy enough for this to be worthwhile.'[8] The days, however, of the large single-use zone are no longer appropriate. The movement towards sustainable development together with ideas about making all parts of the city interesting and lively indicate the adoption of a policy of mixed uses for urban areas. Therefore the notion that leisure alone can regenerate redundant docklands is an idea requiring some qualification.

Regeneration of waterfronts is more likely to be successful if a policy is adopted which plans for the

Figure 6.8 Residential
Development, Birmingham
Canal
Figure 6.9 Marina,
Nottingham Canal

6.8

6.9

Figure 6.10 Evening Post
Building, Nottingham Canal

introduction of a group of compatible and mutually
supportive uses. A function of water not so far
considered is its aesthetic appeal. It is a most attractive setting for residential purposes. A number of
recent waterside developments have introduced
housing fronting onto canals and former industrial
docks. Tividale Quays, West Bromwich is an interesting development of this type. The Black Country
Development Corporation, now disbanded, was
charged, in 1987 when it was set up, with the regeneration of a swathe of land, 25 square kilometres in
extent, ranging from Darleston in the north down to
Langley in the south.[9] The task included the upgrad-
ing of the Black Country canals. Part of this canal
improvement included the development of groups of
residential properties designed as frontages along the
canal; the one at Tividale encloses a large water mass
(Figures 6.7 and 6.8).

The regeneration of rundown and under used
sites adjacent to the Nottingham Canal is a good
example of successful mixed use development.
Twenty years ago the banks of the Nottingham
Canal were derelict, dirty, an unpleasant eyesore in
the city. Since then a whole series of developments
has been built including housing, a marina, museum,
shopping, office developments, the prestigious
Inland Revenue Building by Michael Hopkins and
Partners, several courts and a leisure complex with
bars, pubs, and restaurants. The length of the canal

6.10

6.11

has been cleaned and landscaped; it is now a pretty place to walk, admire the buildings and observe the boat traffic (Figures 6.9 to 6.11).

Rivers, canals and urban coastline perform a crucial role in terms of environmental protection. Waterways, particularly river marginal wetlands, are ecosystems of particular value in urban areas. They are important wildlife corridors, often connecting isolated and vulnerable habitats. While waterways perform this function of maintaining biodiversity through environmental protection they also serve more selfish requirements of the human community: they are essential links in the landscape network which act as lungs for the city and provide recreation outlets for the urban population. As House, Ellis and Shutes point out, these ecosystems have suffered major losses, 'as a result of flow regulation and speculative land-take, despite the growth of control legislation.'[10] There is a strong possibility of conflict between the aims of environmental conservation along waterways and the understandable desire to regenerate disued water frontages. 'Even recreational activities have had adverse effects on the ecology of rivers and streams by affecting both wildlife and their habitats . . . Swimming, canoeing, boating and angling all have a tendency to clash significantly with wildlife conservation. In addition, the perceived desire of the public for intensively managed river corridors is in direct opposition to

nature conservation objectives'[11] Being aware of this potential clash of interests between development objectives and environmental concerns is the key to developing a strategy for waterfront development which is sensitive to all concerns. The Environmental Statement, a requirement for most major urban developments, containing an assessment of environmental effects, is a useful tool in the search for a reasonable balance between these conflicting aims.

WATERFRONT AND FORM

There are seven generic waterfront forms. The first takes its form from the vertical cliff edge. It comprises buildings rising sheer from the water's edge. The second main type is derived from the

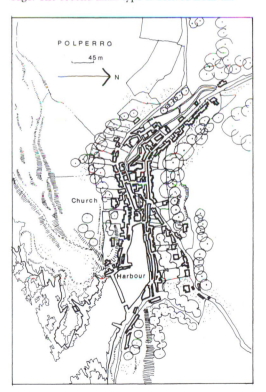

Figure 6.11 Rehabilitated Warehouse, Nottingham Canal

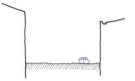

Figure 6.12 Waterfront forms: the vertical cliff edge

Figure 6.13 Waterfront forms: the fishing village

177

Figure 6.14 Waterfront forms: the bank or beach
Figure 6.15 Waterfront forms: the dockside quay
Figure 6.16 Waterfront forms: the bay or open square
Figure 6.17 Waterfront forms: the pier

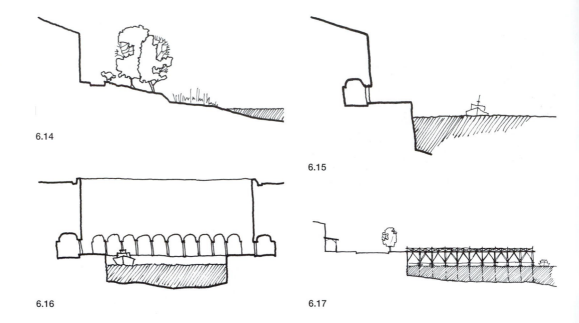

6.14

6.15

6.16

6.17

fishing village where the development is sheltered from the driving coastal winds. Access to the sea is along narrow ginnels or passageways. Owen calls this type the 'perforated wateredge'.[12] The third type is the bank or beach where the water meets a soft, natural bank or gentle slope rather than the hard formal constructed edge of the dockside quay, the fourth type. The fifth type of wateredge envelops or encloses the water in the form of a bay or open square. The sixth type is the pier jutting out into the water at right angles to the shoreline. The final type follows the convenient tradition of 'turning a back' to the water, treating it as sewer, dumping ground or, at best, a culvert. This last type of watercourse is one which has been prevalent for much city development in many parts of the world (Figures 6.12 to 6.17).

The 'cliff edge' waterfront treatment is most commonly associated with the nineteenth century canal lined by the sheer faces of multi-storied warehouses. The warehouse has a private ownership of the frontage onto the canal. Openings in the canal façade of the warehouse are for the purpose of loading and unloading goods into and out of the building. For the length of the warehouse there is no public access to the waterside. The Waterways Building on the Nottingham Canal is typical of the cliff edge waterfront (Figure 6.11). As a canal frontage this building type has a long history. Many of the fine canal frontages in Venice, for example, are lined with palaces with views over the canals and private access from them. In Bruges the canals in parts, are given a similar treatment, in some cases fronted by buildings and properties founded by religious organizations (Figures 6.18 to 6.20). This type of frontage which limits access to the water's edge for the general public would now be used only in exceptional circumstances. Reasons for a continued use of this wateredge treatment would be the conservation of a building of architectural note such as the Waterways

Building in Nottingham or if private ownership of the water frontage prevented public access.

The 'perforated edge', as suggested, has for its model the traditional fishing village, having fingers of narrow public pathways leading to the quay and seafront. This is Thomas Sharp's description of the English seaside village: 'It would almost seem from the planforms of these villages, that their builders deliberately refused to recognize the existence of the great natural element close to their doors. The houses generally turn their backs to the sea, or actually hide out of sight of it under the shelter of a cliff . . . But this apparent lack of recognition is really recognition of a very respectful kind: a recognition that a situation in full face of an element which may seem to be benign in the few calm months of summer can be very far from satisfactory in the roaring days that are apt to occupy a large part of the rest of the year. The buildings of a fishing village huddle tightly together on narrow tortuous streets for mutual warmth and shelter.'[13] Clearly, the functional necessity which governs the form of the traditional fishing village does not apply to the frontage of a canal, urban riverside or seafront today. Nevertheless, the form when used for a stretch of waterfront does secure good access to that waterfront for the public. Frequent ginnels leading to the waterfront would, in the terms of Bentley *et al.*, increase the 'permeability' of the

6.18

6.20

6.19

Figure 6.18 Bruges, The Beguinage Convent
Figure 6.19 Canal scene, Bruges
Figure 6.20 Canal scene, Bruges

Figure 6.21 The Avon, Stratford
Figure 6.22 The Avon, Stratford
Figure 6.23 The waterfront, Lamu, Kenya

6.21

6.22

district.[14] The long narrow Piazza Degli Uffizi, Florence can be classified under this category of the perforated water's edge. The long narrow gallery of the Piazza connects the banks of the River Arno with the central place of the Piazza Della Signoria, in addition to giving access to the Palazzo degli Uffizi (Figures 4.34 to 4.36 on pages 112 and 113).

The natural bank or beach is the condition of the waterfront we usually associate with a river as it meanders lazily through the countryside or the condition of many parts of the coastline. It is also found in city watercourses where the main function is associated with environmental pollution control or more often simply as the soft recreational landscape of a city park or green corridor. The delights of rivers such as the Avon in Stratford or the Dee in

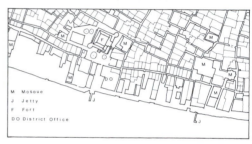

6.23

Chester appear to be popular with the general public (Figures 6.21 and 6.22). House *et al.* report on a survey which measured the public's perception of the qualities of a number of river corridor

Figure 6.24 The waterfront, Lamu, Kenya

6.25

features and found that the results: '. . .indicate that the public has some very definite ideas of what they perceived to be their ideal river setting and some strong preferences for both river and vegetational characteristics . . . In particular there was an overwhelming desire for trees either lining or overhanging the banks of a river. There was a strong preference for diversity of vegetation in terms of plants, trees and grasses and for varieties of these suggesting an inclination towards a more natural environment and a move away from uniformity.'[15] The paper by House *et al.* goes on to suggest that far from desiring intensively managed and manicured landscapes, often assumed by the

National Rivers Authority and designers in some local authorities, the public show a strong preference for a natural landscape along rivers in towns.

Buildings arranged along a dockside quay is a common wateredge treatment for a port settlement in a sheltered location. The treatment of the water's edge comprises a sea wall surmounted by a quay running parallel to the line of the sea. At the rear of the quay are located the buildings. Public access between the buildings which lead to the inner districts of the town or city. Typical of this form of development is the small town of Lamu on the Kenyan coast (Figures 6.23 and 6.24). Pier Head, the entrance to the city of Liverpool, together with, but on a much grander scale, the great city waterfronts in New York and Hong Kong, are examples of this fourth model for the water front (Figures 6.4 and 6.25). Many of the elegant canal frontages in Amsterdam follow this pattern, having a quayside along each side of the canal beyond which are arranged rows of four or five storied terraced developments (Figures 6.26 to 6.28). The canal in Amsterdam is often in the form of a curved street, with its enclosing frontages reflected in the water and its length punctuated by a series of bridges spanning the canal: it is an elegant use of a double quayside along both sides of the watercourse.

Figure 6.25 The waterfront, New York

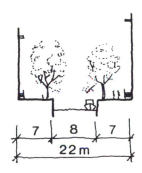

Figure 6.26 Amsterdam, Achterburgval (from Thorne, 'Streets Ahead', *The Architectural Review*, March, 1994)

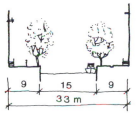

Figure 6.27 Amsterdam, Reguliersgracht (from Thorne, 'Streets Ahead', *The Architectural Review*, March, 1994)

Figure 6.28 Canal scene, Amsterdam

Figure 6.29 Reston, USA

6.28

6.29

Figure 6.30 The Albert Dock, Liverpool

Figure 6.31 Canal, Westport, County Mayo, Republic of Ireland

The fifth model for waterside treatment is the bay. A particularly good example is the natural setting for Belfast in Northern Ireland. The city stands at the head of Belfast Lough at the mouth of the River Lagan. The city is surrounded and enclosed by hills on both sides of the lough. This is a wonder-

ful setting for a city. Fortunately, the fine landscape was protected by a green belt policy which strictly limited the expansion of the built-up area. The policy of urban containment was imposed by the 'Matthew Stopline', a planning tool named after Sir Robert Matthew, the planner for the Belfast region in the 1960s. This model for enclosing water has been used, more formally and, on a smaller scale in the new town of Reston in the USA (Figure 6.29). The Albert Dock, Liverpool is a fine example of the way to use buildings for the enclosure of a large mass of water, now a setting for leisure activities. In this case the ground floor of the enclosing buildings is the arcade which unifies the composition. If the canals in Venice are the equivalent of a water street, then Albert Dock is the equivalent of the piazza or square where water forms a reflective ground plane (Figure 6.30).

Thorburn suggests that the use of piers or jetties and building out onto water in the form of floating structures, are two of the fundamental methods for the planning and design of waterside structures, particularly for leisure use.[16] The fun character of a pier such as the one in Blackpool enlivens the waterfront of many British seaside resorts. The cost of maintenance does raise doubts about the survival and continued utility of this type of pier which is part of the great tradition of nineteenth century structural innovation. The pier with its cafés, boutiques and stalls is an extension of the seaside street: a parade for the relaxed holiday maker, where he or she can be in closer contact with, and gain a different experience of, the sea. The jetty for small boats, however, seems to be in great demand, increasing the available water frontage and hence the value of land and property along its bank (Figure 6.9). The building of floating structures competes favourably for cost with building on land.[17] Floating structures, according to Thorburn, can be used in sheltered water, falling and rising with the tide. Clearly, the building of such a structure offers an opportunity to create a unique experience of water.

Many urban waterways have been channelled into a concrete culvert or an open storm drain. They follow the engineering tradition of neatness with the laudable aim of improving public health and sanitation. This follows a long tradition for urban development where town buildings back onto the river using it as a sewer rather than an environmental amenity. The lovely canalized river in Westport, County Mayo, Republic of Ireland, part of the planned town, is in sharp contrast to the more usual procedure for integrating town and rivers in Ireland (Figure 6.31).

The watercourse is one of the main elements of urban design. It may be a feature of the street as in the canals at Westport (Figure 6.31), Venice (Figure 6.32) and Amsterdam (Figure 6.28) or it may be enclosed by buildings taking on the form of a piazza as in Albert Dock (Figure 6.30). The *Piazza Navona* in Rome, as described earlier, was adapted occasionally to fulfil the function of an urban lake. See pages 107 to 108 and Figures 4.23 to 4.25. The entire pavement of the *Piazza Navona* could be flooded by plugging the drains so that it became an enormous pool in which churches and palaces were mirrored. Onlookers on the raised sidewalks or from upper floor windows could observe this spectacle of the water festivals. Together with the street, the square, the park, and the major public buildings, water features are the components used by the urban designer to create a visually exciting city. The categories or types of treatment of the edge and surrounds to water are not a series of formal alternatives but rather a broad continuum of ideas: the designer, while being aware of this conceptual range has the opportunity to use water-side treatments in creative combinations to suit his or her particular purpose. One aim of urban design is to create stimulating city spaces for public use. Water offers the designer an opportunity to introduce a reflective and aural dimension to the city landscape, together with light and colour. Venice is the exemplar for those concerned with studying the ways of

introducing water into the spatial composition of the city (Figures 6.5 and 6.32).

The watercourse has a role to play in another aim of urban design which is to structure cities which have perceptual clarity or 'imageabilty.'[18]

Figure 6.32 The Grand Canal, Venice

Figure 6.33 River Seine, Paris

Figure 6.34 Notre Dame, Isle de France, Paris

Figure 6.35 Thames Strategy by Ove Arup Partnership (Figures 6.35–6.47 taken from Lowe, M., 'The Thames Strategy', *Urban Design*, 55, July, 1995)

Water can be used to strengthen the five perceptual structuring elements: the path, the node, the edge, the district and the landmark. The navigable river

and canal have served in the past as important routes into the city, often being the main approach to towns and cities. Rivers and canals still perform this role but to a lesser extent, being replaced first by rail, then by road connections. The footpaths along the edges of urban watercourses, however, do act as major links in the network of pedestrian and cycle routes. Where they and other paths meet at bridging points for river crossings, a node is formed. At the points of embarkation by ferry a terminal or transportation node of some significance forms. Towns located at 'break of bulk' points on transportation networks have always been important locations for markets, or places of rest and recuperation after a long journey. The highest navigation point on the river or at important river crossing

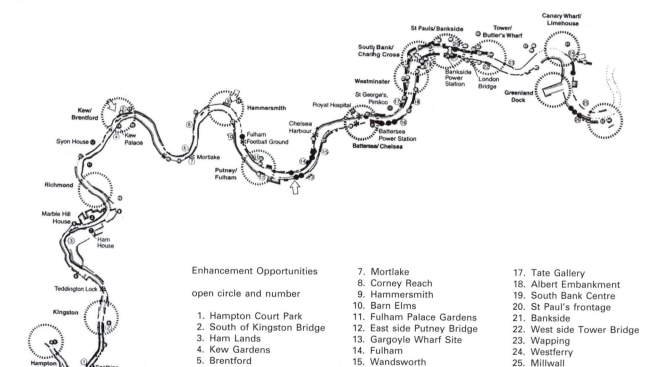

Enhancement Opportunities

open circle and number

1. Hampton Court Park
2. South of Kingston Bridge
3. Ham Lands
4. Kew Gardens
5. Brentford
6. Duke's Meadow
7. Mortlake
8. Corney Reach
9. Hammersmith
10. Barn Elms
11. Fulham Palace Gardens
12. East side Putney Bridge
13. Gargoyle Wharf Site
14. Fulham
15. Wandsworth
16. Nine Elms
17. Tate Gallery
18. Albert Embankment
19. South Bank Centre
20. St Paul's frontage
21. Bankside
22. West side Tower Bridge
23. Wapping
24. Westferry
25. Millwall
26. Deptford Creek

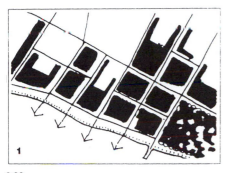

6.36

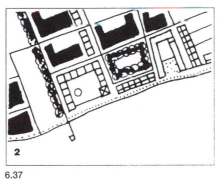

6.37

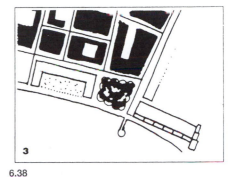

6.38

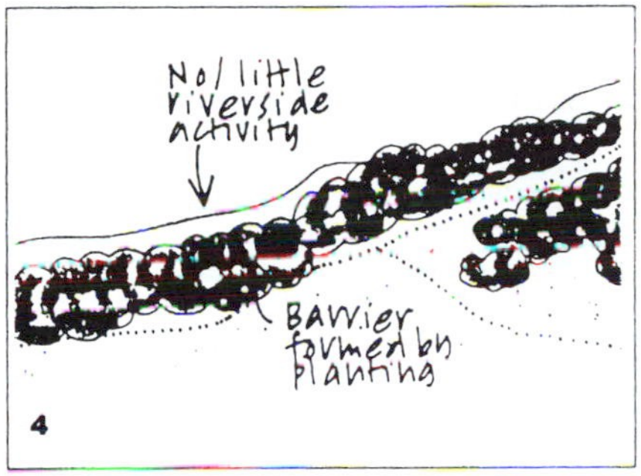

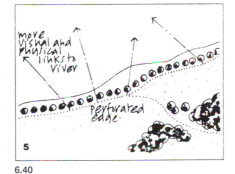

6.39

6.40

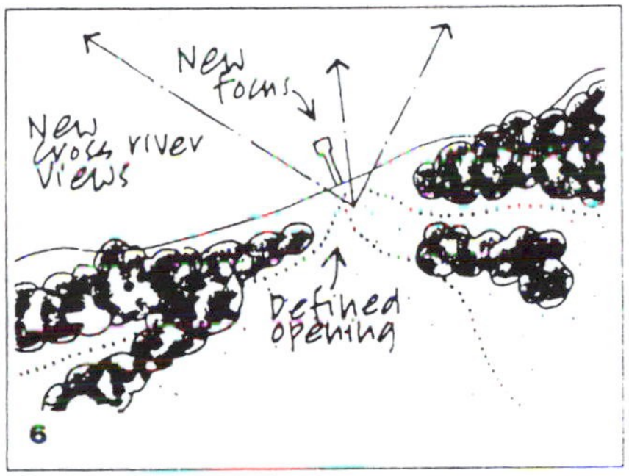

6.41

points are places of significance. Water in cities, even today, can evoke these historic memories and give emphasis to some places or nodes within the urban fabric. Water defined the edge of most formerly fortified towns which depended for their continued existence and the safety of their citizens on the protective mantle of a nearby river. This role as edge to an urban area remains one of the functions of the watercourse, though the need for defence against aggression may no longer take on quite the same meaning. This role as a visual edge to urban development is still performed by rivers such as the Thames in London or the Seine in Paris (Figure 6.33). A particular treatment of a watercourse and the architecture along its banks can imbue a city quarter or district with unique quali-

ties, distinguishing it from adjacent areas. The Isle de France in Paris is such a distinctive district forming another world, quite distinct from neighbouring areas on both the left and right banks of the Seine (Figures 6.33 and 6.34). Water, when it reflects a beautifully composed building such as the Taj Mahal, lends it greater power and visual significance, magnifying the building's potential to perform the role of memorable landmark (Figure 6.2).

THE THAMES STRATEGY

The core area of urban design is the design of public space in cities and in particular the structuring of

Figure 6.36 Permeable layout
Figure 6.37 Creating a positive relationship with the river
Figure 6.38 Reinforcing the form of the river's edge
Figure 6.39 Barrier planting
Figure 6.40 Perforated edge
Figure 6.41 Activity points

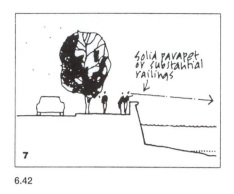

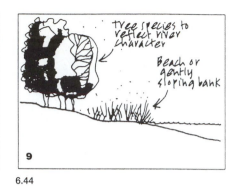

6.42

6.43

6.44

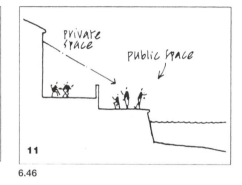

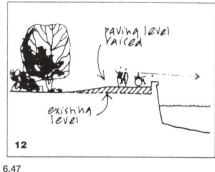

6.45

6.46

6.47

Figure 6.42 Masonry wall for urban areas

Figure 6.43 Battered masonry water's edge

Figure 6.44 Natural edge treatment

Figure 6.45 Arrangements for cycle and pedestrian routes

Figure 6.46 Separation of public and private space

Figure 6.47 Raised promenades for viewing

city quarters. The urban designer may be and should be involved in projects with a wider remit than the local design study. This is true for river frontage design. The Thames Strategy illustrates the need for urban design skills in the development of a planning strategy for a component of an extensive sub-region of Greater London.[19] The Ove Arup Partnership was commissioned by the Government Office for London in 1994 to undertake a detailed analysis of the Thames, prepare overall design principles, and make recommendations for draft planning guidance. The underlying aim was to prepare a visionary document, promoting high quality design and landscape along the River Thames. In addition to specialists in town planning, landscape architecture, transport planning, economics and tourism, the team assembled by Ove

Arup included professionals with skills in urban design. The study was strategic in nature, aiming at an overview of opportunities arising within a 30-mile stretch of the river, rather than considering the development potential in isolation of particular sites along its length.

As expected the analysis included studies of the history of development along the Thames, the decision-making bodies affecting development, river management and the planning context. Information was also assembled in map form on the distribution of riverside land uses, accessibility along the banks, the river's hinterland traffic, traffic use of the river itself together with qualitative studies of the environment, including areas of heritage and ecological importance, key landmarks, building heights, urban form and landscape character. In addition to the records in map form, 1500 images of riverside development and environmental conditions were recorded as a continuous photographic account of the river corridor.

Figure 6.35 summarises the proposals made by Ove Arup for the improvement of the environment along this 30-mile length of the Thames. A series of focal points are suggested to give articulation and visual punctuation. Arup considered that there is an opportunity to strengthen existing focal points and establish new places at meeting points of routes where activity is generated. Figures 6.36 to 6.47 illustrate Arup's detailed design concepts as developed in the report. Figure 6.36 illustrates a permeable development and Figures 6.37 and 6.38 illustrate a recommendation for a 'positive relationship' between the urban fabric and the river front. In particular, an urban form emphasizing orthogonal development parallel to the river front, with an appropriately scaled architecture is recommended. Mixed uses are suggested for sites close to the river front with ground floors devoted to public uses in order to generate activity. Figures 6.40 and 6.41 illustrate some features of the landscape qualities being proposed: 'Good planting design should be used to perform the function of formalising and strengthening the edge, particularly in urban conditions and where roads abut the River ... Strong landscape treatment is recommended to establish continuity and coherence where there is discordant and visually disruptive architecture. The River Seine in Paris and the Rhone in Lyon are two examples where formal tree planting is used to give an appropriate civic quality.'[20] Barrier planting as shown in Figure 6.39, according to the design team, should be discouraged in most locations.

Figures 6.42 to 6.44 illustrate suggested edge treatment for stretches of the river. A varied river edge is proposed in the study: treatments include a masonry edge for urban locations, a battered masonry wall for the upper reaches of the Thames, and a more natural treatment in rural areas. The wateredge treatment is also related to the demands made by the types of movement along the river bank. The requirement for pedestrian traffic is quite different from that of cyclist or motorist. The relationship of these various forms of transport with the adjacent land use and any potential conflict can sometimes be resolved by sensitive riverside treatment (Figures 6.45 to 6.47).

CONCLUSION

The Ove Arup study brings together, in a practical way, the theoretical concepts outlined in the earlier part of the chapter. The strategic context is of paramount importance in the field of urban design: It sets the parameters for the development of detailed proposals for components, such as streets and squares, of which the city and its quarters are composed. Water is one of the elements in urban design: it has a number of functions and can take a number of specific forms. An understanding of the potential of water in the planning and design of cities, in particular its use in street and square, is based on an analysis of the set of generic forms which it can take and the suitability of those forms in serving the functional and aesthetic requirements of any given situation.

NOTES

1   Moughtin, J.C., Oc, T. and Tiesdell, S A. *Urban Design: Ornament and Decoration*, Butterworth-Heinemann, Oxford, 1995

2   Betsky, A. Take Me to the Water: Dipping in the History of Water in Architecture, *Architectural Design*, Volume 65, No. 1/2 Jan-Feb, 1995, pp. 9-15

3   *The Holy Bible: The Book of Genesis* (Trns from the Latin Vulgate), Burns and Oats Ltd, London, 1963

4   Moughtin, J.C. *Urban Design: Green Dimensions*, Butterworth-Heinemann, Oxford, 1996

5   United Nations, *The Global Environmental Outlook*, The
    United Nations, 2002.

6   Falk, N. UK Waterside Development, *Urban Design*, Volume
    55, 1995, July, pp. 19-23

7   Thorburn, A. Leisure on the Waterfront, *The Planner*,
    Volume 73, No. 13, 1990, pp. 18-19

8   Ibid

9   Black Country Development Corporation. '*Before and After*',
    Oldbury, West Midlands, Black Country Development
    Corporation, undated report

10 House, M.A. et al. Urban rivers: ecological impact and
    management. In *Urban Waterside Regeneration: Problems
    and Prospects* (ed. K.N. White et al.), Ellis Horwood Ltd,
    Chichester, 1993, p. 312.

11 Ibid, p. 317.

12 Owen, J. The Water's Edge: The Space Between Buildings
    and Water, in *Urban Waterside Regeneration: Problems
    and Prospects*, Ibid.

13 Sharp, T. *The Anatomy of the Village*, Penguin,
    Harmondsworth, 1946

14 Bentley, I. et al. *Responsive Environments*,
    Butterworth-Heinemann, Oxford, 1985

15 House, M.A. et al. Op cit

16 Thorburn, A. Op cit

17 Ibid

18 Lynch, K. *The Image of the City*, MIT Press, Cambridge,
    Mass., 1972

19 Lowe, M. The Thames Strategy, *Urban Design*, Volume 55,
    July, 1995, pp. 24-29

20 Ibid

SUSTAINABLE URBAN FORM

7

INTRODUCTION

This chapter examines in outline the theory of sustainable development as it affects urban form and in particular its relationship to the design of street and square as elements of the city quarter. It should be read in conjunction with *Urban Design: Green Dimensions,* where the subject matter of sustainable development is discussed more fully.[1] This chapter concentrates upon the notion of sustainable transport, examining how such a system, if implemented, would affect the streets and squares of the city. A city not dominated by the motorcar but one where movement is largely by public transport, or on foot, or by bicycle, opens up a whole new prospect for the design of public space. The last part of the chapter concentrates on the architectural setting for the tram or light train, beginning with an examination of older examples of towns where the tram is an important part of the urban infrastructure. Finally, a review of more recent developments in Britain and the rest of Europe, where the tram is central to the remodelled transport network, is discussed. This section of the chapter will also include a case study of current proposals in Nottingham for the development of a network of lines for a light city train.

> Any discussion of the design of public space which does not address environmental issues has little meaning at a time of declining natural resources, ozone layer depletion, increasing pollution, and fears of the greenhouse effect.

This statement was made in 1996 in *Urban Design: Green Dimensions.*[2] It still holds true, despite the arguments presented by Lomborg in his thought-provoking book *The Skeptical Environmentalist.*[3] In the field of environmental science, most reputable scientists have rebutted the optimistic, almost complacent, view of the state of the global environment, which was presented by Lomberg (see, for example, *Scientific American,* January 2002[4]). Nevertheless, Lomberg's assessment that conditions on earth are generally improving for human welfare has encouraged those advocating an 'environmental free for all' and in particular those to the right in American politics. Fortunately, here in Britain and indeed in Europe, sustainable development and environmental protection still seem to be goals of urban planning. Lord Faulkner in his response to some of the criticisms of the Green Paper, *Planning: Delivering a Fundamental Change,* promised to give more weight to sustainability as a goal of development in the future reorganization of Planning.[5] Here it is intended to advocate 'the precautionary principal' as a guide for environmental design: this principle is fundamental to the theory of sustainable development, which advocates a cautious approach to the use of environmental resources. Until the Scientific Community, acting on its research findings, advises otherwise, it would seem prudent to propose development strategies, which reduce, as far as possible, the pressures on a fragile global environment.

Why should we pursue policies of sustainable development? Why is it important to design sustainable urban structures? What, if anything, can such an approach to city design contribute to an improved global environment? Convincing answers to these questions are necessary to persuade sceptical multinational companies and other global power brokers, primarily concerned with profit margins, that serious consideration should be given to the Earth's environmental problems: answers are also important if national and local administrations are to pursue policies sustaining the global environment, sometimes against opposition from vested interest groups who fear they might suffer a possible economic loss from the pursuit of such policies. The structure and the construction of the built environment both have a vital role to play in limiting the damage we do to this fragile planet on which we live. Those involved in city building are engaged in the use and consumption of scarce resources such as land, building materials, energy, etc., together with the control and management of waste production and its by-product pollution. These impacts of the local built environment on the global environment are considerable, though they pale into insignificance when compared with the need for international political agreements such as the Kyoto Accord which attempts to set the agenda for worldwide action.

THE NATURE AND EXTENT OF ENVIRONMENTAL PROBLEMS

Caution is necessary when discussing the environmental problems faced by humanity. There is great uncertainty when assessing the future of global or regional conditions whether it is population forecasting, climate change, energy sources, biodiversity or pollution. Indeed, this attitude of caution is the one adopted by natural scientists when reporting research findings in their specialist fields: it was also the approach adopted in *Urban Design: Green Dimensions.*[6] How far the authors of *The Limits to Growth,* and others following a similar path, progressed the aims of the Green Movement is problematical.[7] *The Limits to Growth* attempted to plot the depletion of resources and to warn of the danger of exponential growth, leading, it was argued, to the ultimate destruction of a global environment fit for human occupation. It has been criticized for overstating the case, damaging the environmental cause, and giving credence to Lomborg and others like him who hold the Panglossian view that this 'is the best of all possible worlds' and furthermore that it is getting better daily.[8]

Those who predicted widespread famine caused by rapid population growth often overstated their case. However, according to Bongaarts, Lomborg's assertion that the number of people on this planet is not the problem, is simply wrong'.[9] One important contributory factor affecting the deterioration of the environment is population. The global population growth rate may have declined slowly in recent years but absolute growth remains nearly as high as levels observed in the last decades of the last century, simply because the population base keeps expanding. In 1960, world population was three billion: it now stands at six billion and is expected to rise to ten billion by 2050. However, these global figures mask details of unprecedented demographic change, which are highly significant for the impact they may have on the environment. The world's poorest nations in Africa, Asia and Latin America have rapidly growing and young populations, while in the wealthy nations of Europe, North America and Japan, growth is zero or in some cases negative. People, on the whole, are living longer and are healthier; women are bearing fewer children, increasing numbers of people are moving to cities; or across national borders, seeking a better life. In Europe, including Britain (according to some commentators), we are at the receiving end of this much needed migration of younger people in order to sustain the services and so maintain an ageing population. Cities in this country are likely to see a continuing influx of either legal or illegal immigrants.

Demand for feeding this extra population, most of which will be located in the poorest countries of the world, will be a great challenge: 'The ability of agriculturists to meet this challenge remains uncertain'. Bongaarts believes that 'the technological optimists are probably correct in claiming that overall food production can be increased substantially over the next few decades'. This agricultural expansion will be costly. Some expansion will probably take place on soils of poor quality, located in areas less favourable for irrigation, than existing intensively farmed land. Water is in increasingly short supply, while demand grows so the environmental cost of this increase in food production could be severe. 'A large expansion of agriculture to provide growing populations with improved diets is likely to lead to further deforestation, loss of species, soil erosion and pollution from pesticides and fertilizer runoff as farming intensifies and new land is brought into production'.[10] It would seem wise for countries like the UK to maintain its potential for food production and limit the extent to which its cities encroach upon agricultural land. Such thinking would support the idea of the compact city and the reuse of 'brownfield sites' wherever practical.

Global environmental problems, including the greenhouse effect, are closely linked to the abundance of energy used to sustain our civilization: much of the atmospheric pollution is caused by the burning of fossil fuels in the creation of energy to support city life. This energy is used in the building of city structures (energy capital); during the lifetime of the structure; and in the transportation of people and goods between and within cities (energy revenue). The design of cities and the ways in which they are used therefore have a great impact on the natural environment. Few serious environmental scientists believe that we are running out of energy to sustain our civilization. 'The energy problem' – and there is an energy problem – 'is not primarily a matter of depletion of resources in any global sense but rather of environmental impacts and sociopolitical risks – and, potentially, of rising monetary costs for energy when its environmental and socio-political hazards are adequately internalized and insured against'.[11] Oil is the most versatile and most valuable of the conventional fuels that have long provided for all our city-building energy needs: today it remains the largest contributor to world energy supply, accounting for nearly all the energy used for transport. But the bulk of recoverable conventional oil resources appear to lie in the Middle East, a politically unstable part of the world: much of the rest of the recoverable resources lies offshore and in other difficult or environmentally fragile locations. Nuclear energy, which currently contributes about 6 per cent of global energy production, has long-term problems of pollution and the storage of waste material. There are other problems with nuclear energy. Breeder reactors produce large amounts of plutonium that can be used for weapons production: a security problem so significant that it may preclude the use of this technology. Problems with both oil and nuclear power presents urban designers with the challenge of developing urban structures less dependent on these conventional sources of energy for their continuing existence.

Almost every week we read in the press that climate change is upon us and that matters can only get worse. Scientists are, however, more circumspect. In his rebuttal of Lomborg, Schneider stressed the uncertainty surrounding this whole vexed question of climate change in his rebuttal of Lomborg. He said: 'Uncertainties so infuse the issue of climate change that it is impossible to rule out either mild or catastrophic outcomes'. Temperatures in the year 2100 may have increased by 1.4°C or by 5.8°C. The first temperature would mean relatively adaptable change; the second would induce very damaging changes. Schneider goes on to say that: 'It is precisely because the responsible scientific community cannot rule out such catastrophic outcomes at a high level of confidence that climate mitigation policies are seriously proposed'.[12]

SUSTAINABLE DEVELOPMENT

There seems to be widespread agreement, particularly in Europe and here in Britain, that solving global environmental problems means the adoption of policies and programmes that lead to sustainable development. One generally accepted definition of sustainable development is from the Brundtland Report: 'Sustainable development is development that meets the needs of the present generation without compromising the ability of future generations to meet their needs'.[13] Building on the ideas of Brundtland, Elkin suggests four principles of sustainable development: futurity, environment, equity, and participation.[14] The first principle, that of futurity, is seen as maintaining a minimum of environmental capital, including the major environmental support systems of the planet together with the conservation of more conventional renewable resources, such as forests. The second principle is concerned with costing the environment. The true cost of all activities, whether they take place in the market or not, should be paid for by the particular development through regulation and/or market-based incentives: the environmental cost should not be deferred for future generations to pay. The third principle is

inter and intra-generational equity, as indeed it is advocated by many others writing on the subject. The fourth, and final, principle which Elkin includes is that of participation. He notes: 'The problems of economic development without democratic participation have been made manifest time after time. Unless individuals are able to share in decision-making and in the actual process of development, it is bound to fail'.[15]

URBAN DESIGN AND SUSTAINABLE DEVELOPMENT

The objectives for a framework of urban design in a regime of sustainable development would emphasize conservation of both the natural and built environments. Firstly, there is a need to use already developed areas in a more efficient way while making them more attractive places in which to live and work. Principles of sustainable urban design would place priority on the adaptation and reuse of buildings, infrastructure and roads, together with the recycling of materials and components. There would be a presumption in favour of conservation: the onus for proof of development would be placed squarely on the developer. The concept of a conservation area, so successful in the recent past, could well be applied in the less noteworthy urban districts, while whole cities could follow the example of Barcelona and benefit from a regeneration based on the innate advantages of location and historic legacy. Secondly, sustainable development places a premium on the conservation of natural resources, wildlife and landscape. Thirdly, where new development is necessary the patterns and construction should minimize the use of non-renewable energy sources, including the energy consumed in travel between activities and also in the operation of the buildings. New buildings to meet the requirements of sustainability would have to be flexibly planned so that they could be adapted for different uses over their lifespan. The transport system serving future urban systems would not only have to serve economic development, but also protect the environment and sustain future quality of life. Such a transport system would probably give priority to public transport, cycling and walking, with reduced dependency on the private car.

The requirements of sustainable development closely mirror the current agenda of urban design. Applying the principles of good urban design at the scales of the quarter, city and region, supports the notion of sustainable development, though action in the field of urban design is not sufficient to achieve this end. Clearly, National and International action in the fields of politics and economic development is vital for achieving long-term sustainable settlements. The focus of this book, however, is on the ingredients that comprise good urban design, and in particular, how the amalgam of ideas that make up the theory of post-modern urban design affect the design of street and square. The rest of the chapter, therefore, will focus on the design of street and square within a framework of sustainable development. *Towards an Urban Renaissance* summarizes very clearly current thinking on urban design:[16] the following paragraphs owe much to that summary.

The sustainable city, or more correctly, a city that approximates to a sustainable form, is a compact and flexible structure in which the parts are connected to each other and to the whole, with a clearly articulated public space. The public realm connects the different quarters to each other across the city, while also linking individual homes to workplaces, schools, social institutions and places of recreation. Figure 7.1 shows a possible structure for such a compact city, and Figure 7.2 illustrates the linkages for the structure. Lord Rogers' Task Force describes the compact city in this way: 'Urban areas are organized in concentric bands of density, with higher densities around public transport nodes (rail, bus and underground stations) and lower densities in less connected areas. The effect of this compact layout is to establish a clear urban boundary, contain urban sprawl and reduce car use'.[17]

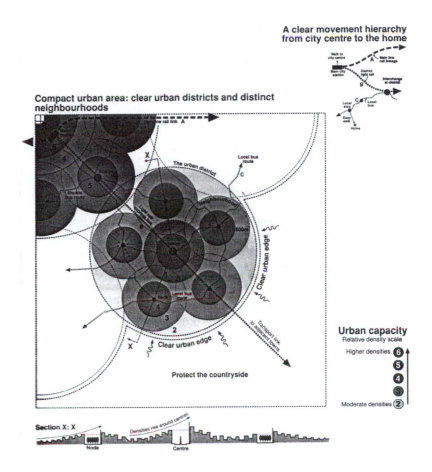

Figure 7.1 Urban structure: the compact city

Sustainable urban forms require densities much higher than the 20-30 dwellings per hectare currently widely used in suburban developments in the UK. Developments where densities are in the region of 70-100 dwellings per hectare would use significantly less land, and consequently, reduce the distance between home and local centre with its transport hub. For example, a neighbourhood of about 7,500 people could be housed at densities of about 70 dwellings per hectare on a piece of land where the furthest distance from the centre is just over 500 metres, a reasonable walking distance. The

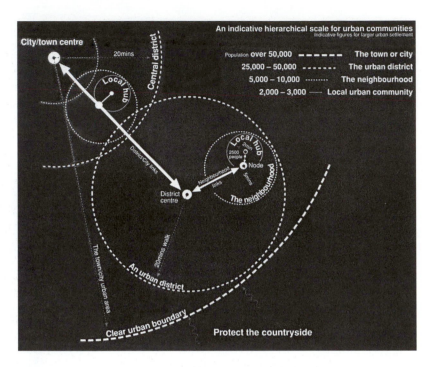

An indicative hierarchical scale for urban communities
Indicative figures for larger urban settlement

Population	over 50,000	------	The town or city
25,000 – 50,000	······	The urban district
5,000 – 10,000	········	The neighbourhood
2,000 – 3,000	——	Local urban community

Figure 7.2 Circulation in the compact city

population of 7,500 people would support a viable core of activities at its centre (Figure 7.3). Grouping such neighbourhoods, as also shown in Figure 7.3 would support a larger and more vibrant range of social facilities and warrant a more extensive bus service.

The same density can be expressed in a number of quite different architectural forms. The accommodation can be arranged as a single tall pavilion in the middle of the site, dispersed in parallel rows of two-storey terraced blocks or arranged as four-storey perimeter development around the edge of the site (Figure 7.4). This kind of perimeter development mirrors many continental European cities (Figures 7.5 and 7.7), and is a model that may prove useful for some new developments in the British context.

There is no reason why densities should be uniform throughout the city. For example, there is a sound argument for increasing densities in areas close to important transport interchanges. Such nodes of activity could support higher population densities, and a mix of diverse land uses becoming pyramids of intensity within the urban scene. This idea of mixed uses, rather than large areas within the city devoted entirely to a single land use is a suggestion, which is a common feature of many books written on sustainable development and urban design. 'One of the main attractions of city living is proximity to work, shops and basic social, educational and leisure uses. Whether we are talking about mixing uses in the same neighbourhood, a mix within a street or urban block, or the mixing of uses vertically within a building, good urban design should encourage more people to live near to those services which they require on a regular basis'.[18] Many activities can exist in close proximity: most businesses and urban services can live harmoniously in a residential area. There are, of course, exceptions: noxious industries, and those generating high traffic volumes or noise, will need careful location. Notwithstanding, these important exceptions, mixed land-use in neighbourhoods, assist in creating and maintaining a self-sustaining city community. A further requirement of the self-sustaining, or autonomous neighbourhood is a population drawn from families with a wide range of incomes, occupying properties of mixed tenure. Such mixed-income neighbourhoods are able to support viable neighbourhood facilities and there is a possibility that spending is recycled within the neighbourhood by the purchase of local goods and services. Community stability is enhanced if the neighbourhood is one with a variety of house types and where there is a mix of tenures. A mix of house and tenure types also gives more flexibility for families to change properties to meet changing needs, without necessarily having to move out of the neighbourhood.

As stated previously, the theme of this book is the design of street and square. The street and the square are both important elements of the public realm: each street and each square has its own

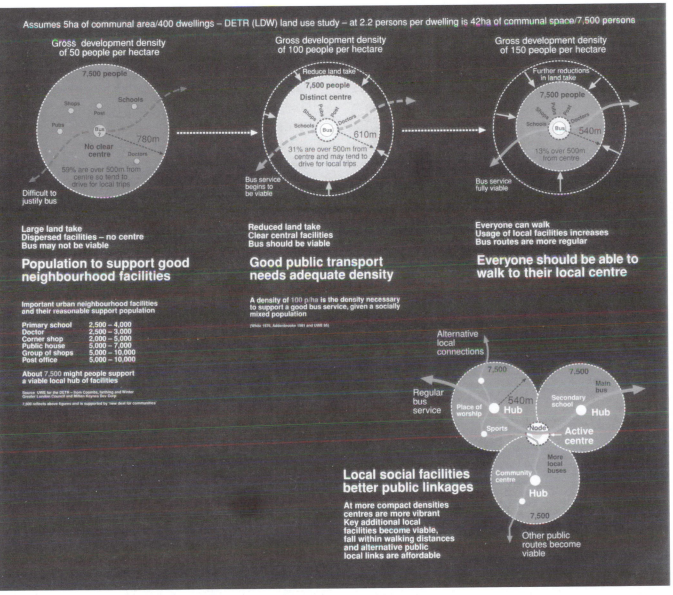

Assumes 5ha of communal area/400 dwellings – DETR (LDW) land use study – at 2.2 persons per dwelling is 42ha of communal space/7,500 persons

Gross development density of 50 people per hectare

7,500 people

Shops
Schools
Post
Pubs
Bus?
No clear centre
Doctors

780m

59% are over 500m from centre so tend to drive for local trips

Difficult to justify bus

Large land take
Dispersed facilities – no centre
Bus may not be viable

Population to support good neighbourhood facilities

Important urban neighbourhood facilities and their reasonable support population

Primary school	2,500 – 4,000
Doctor	2,500 – 3,000
Corner shop	2,000 – 5,000
Public house	5,000 – 7,000
Group of shops	5,000 – 10,000
Post office	5,000 – 10,000

About 7,500 might people support a viable local hub of facilities

Source UWE for the DETR – from Coombs, farthing and Winter Greater London Council and Milton Keynes Dev Corp

7,500 reflects above figures and is supported by 'new deal for communities'

Gross development density of 100 people per hectare

Reduce land take
7,500 people
Distinct centre
Shops Pubs Post Doctors
Schools Bus
610m
31% are over 500m from centre and may tend to drive for local trips

Bus service begins to be viable

Reduced land take
Clear central facilities
Bus should be viable

Good public transport needs adequate density

A density of 100 p/ha is the density necessary to support a good bus service, given a socially mixed population

(White 1976, Addenbrooke 1981 and UWE 95)

Gross development density of 150 people per hectare

Further reductions in land take
7,500 people
Shops Pubs Post Doctors
Schools Bus
540m
13% over 500m from centre

Bus service fully viable

Everyone can walk
Usage of local facilities increases
Bus routes are more regular

Everyone should be able to walk to their local centre

Alternative local connections

7,500
Regular bus service
Place of worship
Sports
Hub
540m
Node
7,500
Secondary school
Main bus
Hub
Active centre
More local buses
Community centre
Hub
7,500
Other public routes become viable

Local social facilities better public linkages

At more compact densities centres are more vibrant
Key additional local facilities become viable, fall within walking distances and alternative public local links are affordable

Figure 7.3 Land requirement: Communities of 7,500 and 22,500 people

Figure 7.4 Relationship between density and urban
form

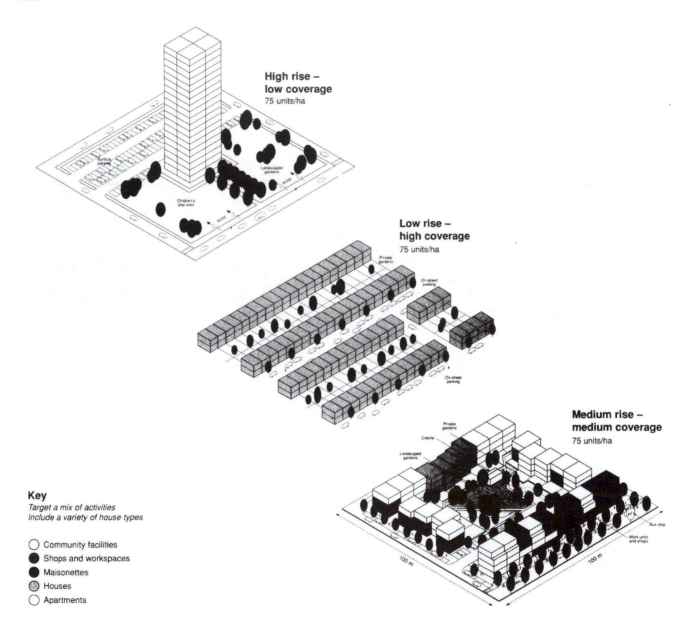

**High rise –
low coverage**
75 units/ha

Surface
parking

Landscaped
gardens

Children's
play area

**Low rise –
high coverage**
75 units/ha

Private
gardens

On-street
parking

On-street
parking

**Medium rise –
medium coverage**
75 units/ha

Private
gardens

Crèche

Landscaped
gardens

Bus stop

Work units
and shops

100 m

100 m

Key
Target a mix of activities
Include a variety of house types

○ Community facilities
● Shops and workspaces
● Maisonettes
◉ Houses
○ Apartments

7.5

7.6

Figure 7.5 Perimeter
development: Amsterdam,
Hembrugstraat, by de Klerk
Figure 7.6 Perimeter
development: Amsterdam,
Hembrugstraat, by de Klerk
Figure 7.7 Perimeter
development: Amsterdam,
Hembrugstraat, by de Klerk

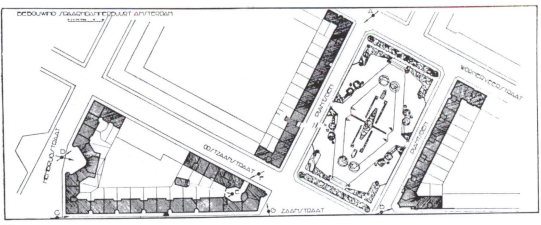

7.7

Figure 7.8 Linear city by
Soria y Mata

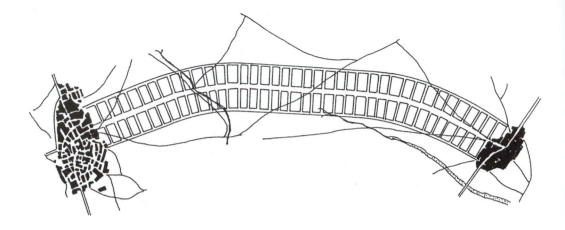

individual identity and design requirements.
Nevertheless, as features of a linked public realm
they take on added significance, as indeed Camillo
Sitte noted in his studies of medieval towns in
Europe.[19] A city served by an integrated transport
system, where the tram, light rail, metro or bus
serves the bulk of the population, is able to develop
within the interstices of the transport system; a
parallel network of public spaces designed for
pedestrian use, which link the home to the centre
and to the countryside through a series of streets,
squares and green corridors.

Rail travel within cities began in the nineteenth
century. On Merseyside, for example, the most
comprehensive local rail network outside London,
was developed in the 1850s. In 1886, the Mersey
Railway opened, providing a passenger service
under the river from James Street Station in
Liverpool to Green Lane in Birkenhead. The line
was later extended to serve other areas in the Wirral
including from James Street Station to Central
Station and so linking to the national rail network.
At its peak in 1890, the Mersey Railway carried 10
million passengers. In 1903 the system was electri-
fied - the first rail electrification in the world -
preceding the process in London. Other electrification schemes followed, with lines from Exchange

Station to Southport, Aintree and Ormskirk being
built. The network was completed in 1974 linking
the four main city stations.[21]

A network of tram and bus services complements
suburban rail systems, such as the one in Liverpool
and the more extensive rail and underground
systems in London. The tramway is an efficient and
environmentally friendly method for carrying many
people around the city. The electric tram has a long
history dating back to the end of the nineteenth
century. One well-known example is the electric
tram route planned by Soria y Mata to serve a linear
suburb in Madrid (Figure 7.8). The linear suburbs of
Soria y Mata ran between two major radials of the
city. Unlike other suggestions for urban development, such as Garnier's *Cite Industrielle*, the Madrid
project was actually built and then operated by the
designer's family, until the 1930s.[22] The tramways
were intended to circle the whole of Madrid and
were originally designed to service areas of cheap
housing for the middle classes. The main feature of
the development was a tree-lined boulevard, along
which ran a private 'street car'. The 'street car'
connected the linear arrangement of house plots
with radial transport routes to the city centre.

The first-generation trams in the UK were phased
out after the Second World War: the 'last tram' in

7.9

Figure 7.9 The tram, Lisbon, Portugal
Figure 7.10 The metro, Manchester

Liverpool, for example, was phased out in the mid-1950s. One pleasant reminder, however, of those first-generation tramways, and which is still run as a public service, though mainly as a tourist attraction, is in Blackpool. In cities such as Prague and Lisbon in mainland Europe, and in San Francisco in the USA trams have survived from the early part of the last century (Figure 7.9).

France is a country with a great deal of experience in developing the new generation of rapid transit systems for medium-sized cities. In this area of city planning it is a country from which Britain has learned much. The planning of rapid transit systems in France began in the 1970s. New interest in public transport was stimulated by the growth of urban populations and by the increasing road congestion within cities. For example, in major cities such as Marseille and Lyon, the Metro was the favoured solution to urban congestion. Then around 1975, the French Government began to look at less-expensive systems than the Metro for use in medium-sized cities. The result was a new generation of tramways: the first opened in Nantes in 1985, then in Grenoble in 1987; others were to follow in the 1990s. It was the urbane and highly stylish French Tramway systems that influenced many similar developments in Britain in cities like Manchester, Sheffield, and Nottingham's installation of the Express Transit System (Figure 7.10).[23]

7.10

Figure 7.11
Plan of Salford
Quays
Figure 7.13
Waterside
development,
Salford Quays

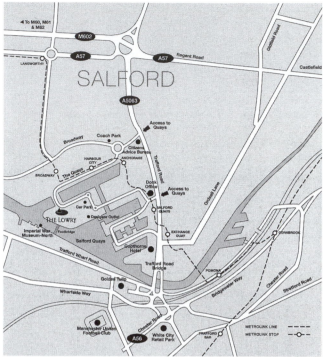

7.11

7.12

In Manchester, there was no connection between the two main line stations of Victoria and Piccadilly. A number of schemes for connecting these stations had been suggested but the one that was finally adopted was a light rail carrying trams. This connection was to be part of a six-route system, radiating from the city centre, totalling about 100 km of line. The initial phase, dating from the early 1990s comprised lines to Bury and Altringham, using mainly existing British Rail lines. It also included important on-street sections in the city centre. A later route to Salford Quays is of particular interest for the urban designer, because of the way in which the line has assisted in generating development potential. The whole area of Salford Quays, served in part by the Metro, provides an opportunity to develop a whole district of mixed land uses comprising squares, streets, prestigious buildings, all arranged around a system of inter-connected water basins: sustainable development of the highest environmental quality (Figures 7.11-7.13).

THE NOTTINGHAM EXPRESS TRANSIT

The main concern of this case study is the visual impact of the proposed tram and its infrastructure on the streets and squares of Nottingham. This is only a small section of the environmental analysis undertaken as part of the design of the system.

The Nottingham Express Transit (NET) system is designed to provide a key contribution towards the future public transport needs of Greater Nottingham. The first line of NET is currently under construction and is part of an integrated transport system which links public transport services and the national rail network with tram and bus routes. The first line of the NET will be completed by November 2003 and will be serviced by 15 trams. Figure 7.14 shows the position of Line One, which is under construction, while Figure 7.15 shows the position of the proposed future routes.

Figure 7.13 The Lowry
Centre, Salford

The main reason for investment in the express transit for Nottingham is the expected growth in the number of cars using city roads. Every year the city roads get a little more congested. This congestion, it is thought, will eventually stifle the city's vibrant economy from growing further. The vehicles congesting Nottingham's roads also cause pollution, which can damage the health of the people of Nottingham and harm the city's environment. Providing a first class public transport service that is integrated into the life of the city together with other forms of transport, including cycling and walking, tackles the twin problems of congestion and pollution by reducing the number of vehicles on the road. It also gives people a choice of trans-port options, where dependence upon the private motorcar is not so overwhelming.

Elsewhere in Britain, and the rest of mainland Europe, new tram systems have helped to regenerate the economy of urban areas, through which they pass. This was an important consideration in deter-mining the route chosen for Line One of the project in Nottingham, which runs from Hucknall through Bulwell, Baseford and Hyson Green to the city centre, with a branch to the M1 motorway. These are some of the most run-down areas in the city, including former coalfields: they should benefit from new businesses and people relocating to areas close to the new public transport service. Therefore, in addition to an estimated reduction of 2 million car journeys in

Figure 7.14 Nottingham, NET Line One, central area

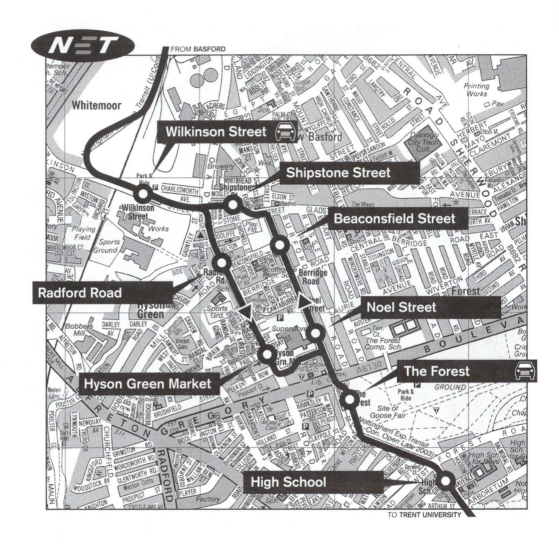

the city every year, Line One of the NET should boost run-down local economies because of this better link with the growing and stronger economy of the city.[24] It should also bring back life to the public realm in the areas through which it runs, which will mean more vibrant streets and squares.

The project was the subject of an Environmental Assessment Process, a technique dealt with more fully in *Urban Design: Method and Technique*.[25] Environmental Assessment is a procedure for evaluating the environmental impacts of major projects. Analysis of the project's characteristics and their impact on the existing environment provides the basis for the evaluation.

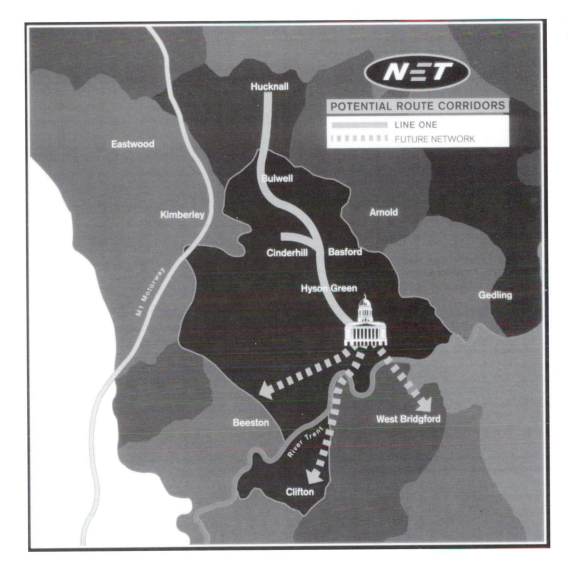

Figure 7.15 Nottingham,
NET future extension

The full visual impact, however, of the tram on the streets and squares of Nottingham can only be judged when the Express transit has been installed and is fully working. Figure 7.16a/b is a summary of the expected environmental impact of the tram on the different sections of Line One in Nottingham: it shows, under the heading 'Visual Intrusion/Landscape', that the tram system will have moderately positive results in four of the seven sections of the line; one section where the benefits

Figure 7.16 Nottingham,
NET environmental impacts

Traffic

Land Use / Planning

Noise and Vibration

Ecology / Water Quality

Visual Intrusion / Landscape

Community

Contaminated Land, Spoil and Waste

Air Quality

(a)

Traffic

Land Use / Planning

Noise and Vibration

Ecology / Water Quality

Visual Intrusion / Landscape

Community

Contaminated Land, Spoil and Waste

Air Quality

(b)

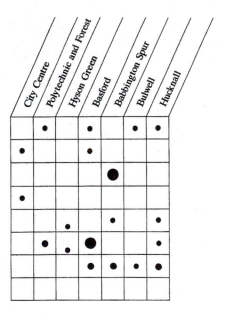

Figure 7.17 Tram. Christchurch, New Zealand

and drawbacks cancel each other out, and two sections where there are environmental disadvantages. In Baseford, for example, there is concern about the visual quality of the replacement footbridges, while in Bulwell there is concern over the effect on a nature reserve and the loss of amenity for a number of families living close to the track. In both cases, mitigation in the form of additional security to prevent vandalism and tree planting for screening have been suggested.[26] Going beyond the bland statements in the Environmental Assessment, requires a leap of imagination and an attempt to try to recapture the excitement of the vision that lies behind this expensive but necessary project. A study of the effect of the trams in Manchester, Sheffield or in other cities where they

are currently running, is probably the best way to get some idea of the probable result in Nottingham (Figures 7.17-7.20).

There is little doubt that the introduction of new forms of transport running on the streets in the city centre will transform the look of Nottingham. This is not a minor adjustment in the urban scene. The presence of such a vehicle in Market Square, for example, will bring life right into the heart of the city. If it mirrors similar developments in France, it can only improve the image of the city. The development of the infrastructure for the tram is to be accompanied by new landscaping of pavements, new road surface materials, some bold street furniture and facilities for cyclists and pedestrians.

Figure 7.18 The Tram
Museum, Derbyshire
Figure 7.19 The Tram
Museum, Derbyshire
Figure 7.20 Tram in
Amsterdam

7.18

7.19

7.20

The tram is an urbane solution to transport problems in the city. Its size and scale is compatible with the street scene. Where the modern tram is operating, it has a positive effect upon the townscape, often associated with a European-style café culture. The tram will replace a litter of untidy parked cars that degrade the townscape in many city squares and streets. The resulting pedestrian-friendly and pollution-free environment is ideal for better appreciation of the streets and squares that adorn our cities. The installation of the Express Transit System as part of a wider and integrated network of public transport is a move in the direction of a more sustainable city of environmental quality.

NOTES

1   Moughtin, J.C. *Urban Design: Green Dimensions,* Architectural Press, Oxford, 1996

2   Ibid

3   Lomberg, B. The *Skeptical Environmentalist,* University of Cambridge Press, Cambridge, 2001

4   Science Defends itself Against the Skeptical Environmentalist, *Scientific American,* January 2002

5   Department of Transport, Local Government and the Regions, *Planning Green Paper, Planning: Delivering a Fundamental Change,* DTLR, 2002. See also *Planning,* 22 March 2002

6   Moughtin, J.C. op cit

7   Meadows, D.H. et al., *Beyond the Limits,* Earthscan, London, 1992

8   See Voltaire, *Candide or Optimism,* (trans Doctor Ralph), Penguin, Harmondsworth

9   Bongaarts, J. Population, ignoring its impact. *Scientific American,* January 2002, pp. 65-67

10 Ibid

11 Holdren, J.P. Energy: asking the wrong question. *Scientific American,* January 2002, pp. 63-65

12 Schneider, S. Global warming: neglecting the complexities. In *Scientific American,* January 2002, pp. 60-62

13 World Commission on Environment and Development, *Our Common Future: The Brundtland Report,* Oxford University Press, Oxford, 1987

14 Elkin, T. et al., *Reviving the City,* Friends of the Earth, London, 1991

15 Ibid

16 Department of the Environment, Transport and the Regions, *Towards an Urban Renaissance: Final Report of the Urban Task Force Chaired by Lord Rogers of Riverside,* DETR, London, 1999

17 Ibid

18 Ibid

19 Sitte, C. *Der Stadte-Bau,* Carl Graeser and Co, Wien, 1901

20 Walmsley, D. and Perrett, K. *The Effects of Rapid Transit on Public Transport and Urban Development,* HMSO, London, 1992

21 Hall, P. and Hass-Klau, C. *Can Rail Save the City?* Gower, Vermont, 1985

22 Wiebenson, D. *Tony Garnier: The Cite Industrielle,* Studio Vista, London, undated

23 Nottingham City Council, *Nottingham Express Transit, Construction Countdown,* NCC, Nottingham, 2001

24 Mott MacDonald, *Greater Nottingham Light Rapid Transit Project, Environmental Statement in Support of the Bill,* Mott MacDonald, Croydon, 1991

25 Moughtin, J.C. et al., *Urban Design; Method and Technique,* Architectural Press, Oxford, 1999

26 Mott MacDonald, Op cit

VISUAL ANALYSIS

Miguel Mertens and Cliff Moughtin

8

INTRODUCTION

The main purpose of this chapter is to demonstrate the procedure used to analyse the form, function and significance of the street and square as elements within a given urban context. The second aim is to make concrete the practical significance of the book's main content, which has been written largely from a theoretical perspective. Finally, the chapter introduces the idea of urban design survey techniques.

The case study for this chapter is Tavira, a town in the Algarve, Portugal, comprising a number of lovely squares connected by narrow traditional streets set within an historic core, structured around a series of named quarters. The first part of the chapter deals with an analysis of the history and development of Tavira. Such a study is important for an understanding of the town and its *genius loci*. The study of the town's history also forms a basis for conservation policies and is an instrument for the promotion of ideas for development compatible with local traditions.

The second part of the chapter discusses townscape analysis, permeability, land use and visual analysis, particularly in relation to the squares and streets of the historic core of Tavira. The chapter will conclude by illustrating how such an analysis can be used to inform the urban design process.

TAVIRA AND ITS REGION

The administrative district of Tavira is situated on the coastal belt in the south of the Algarve and to the east of Faro, the region's capital (Figure 8.1). The district of Tavira occupies about 12.2 per cent of the region's land area: it has a population of approximately 24,000 people, which is about 7.2 per cent of that of the region. This population doubles in the summer months with an influx of tourists from the rest of Portugal, in addition to those visitors from Britain and the rest of Europe. It is this influx of people, which supports the tourist industry, one of the main economic activities of Tavira.

The town of Tavira is in the south of its district lying astride the River Sequa which becomes the River Gilâo as it passes under the Roman Bridge at the heart of the town and then heads for the sea. Tavira is also on the main road and rail routes that traverse the Algarve connecting Vila Real de Santo Antonio on the River Guadiana and the Spanish

Figure 8.1 The Algarve

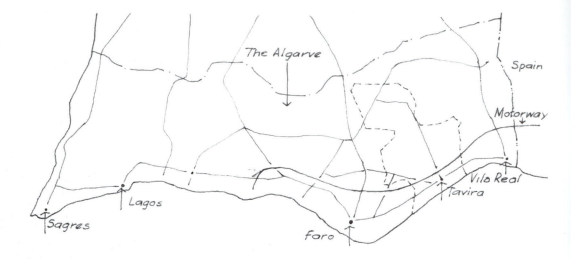

border in the east, to Lagos and the Atlantic coast in the west. The region is connected to Lisbon, the capital, to Spain by motorway, and to the rest of Europe via the busy airport at Faro. Locally, Tavira's influence extends to the mountain area to its north, competing with such towns as Sâo Bras de Alportel and Loulé. Closer to Tavira there are a group of subsidiary small settlements, also in the coastal zone, comprising Luz de Tavira, Santa Luzia, and Cabanas. Figure 8.2 shows the administrative district of Tavira.

The location of Tavira within its regional setting and in its relation to the transportation network has implications for the role, function and significance of the streets and squares of this small town. Figure 8.3 is a schematic map of Tavira showing the town's main quarters. For most of the year the town serves the needs of the people of Tavira and the population of its rural hinterland. For eight months of the year Tavira is a small market town with an urban infrastructure that performs a purely local function. In the bustling tourist season that same infrastructure, and in particular the towns streets and squares, take on quite a different role: they become sources of entertainment and places of

relaxation for the many visitors. Tavira, to date, has combined these two functions without losing its character and without losing too much of the environmental quality that is one of the town's main attractions.

The development pressures arising from both a rapidly expanding tourist industry and the wealth created by membership of the EU, are increasing at a rate never before experienced in the eastern Algarve. These pressures are manifest in many factors: growing car ownership with its associated road congestion; movement of local populations from the countryside to Tavira and its suburbs; increased demand for retirement and holiday homes; the building of more hotels and other accommodation for tourists; and the growing demand for development such as supermarkets that are associated with growing prosperity. Can those planning for the future of Tavira and its satellite settlements avoid the environmental destruction that has often accompanied tourist development in, for example, some parts of Spain or in some places in the western Algarve? Can this small but attractive town capitalise on its great tourist potential without destroying those very qualities that make it a desirable place in

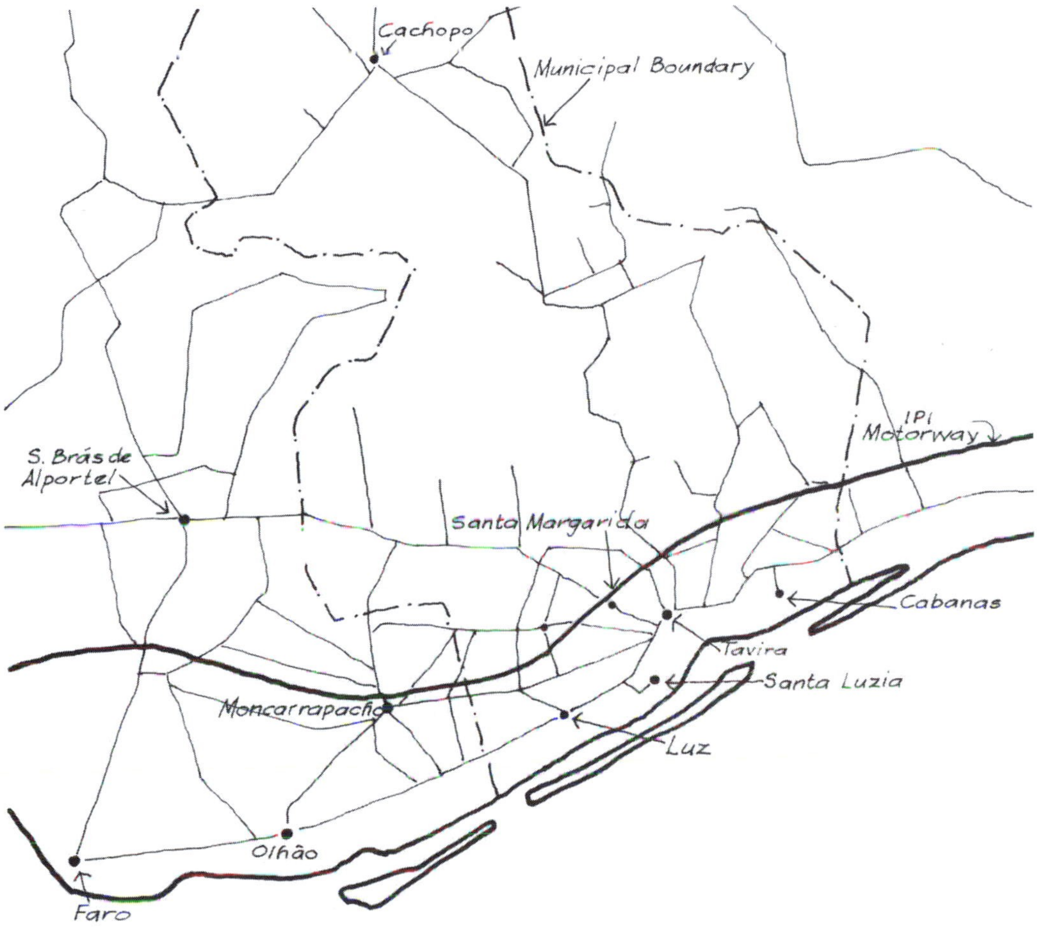

Figure 8.2 Tavira and its region

which to live, work or visit? These are the difficult questions that have to be addressed by those responsible for the future of the town.

DEVELOPMENT OF *TAVIRA*

THE ORIGINS OF THE TOWN

Little is known about the origin and early history of Tavira. Some writers have referred to the area as having once been occupied by the Greeks, the Phoenecians and the Cartheginians. Recent excavations in the oldest part of Tavira have uncovered Phoenecian ruins, which indicate that this is indeed an ancient foundation. The remains of a Roman port have been discovered on the coast between Santa Luzia and Luz de Tavira while there is evidence of a Roman road connecting Castro Marim, (Baesuris) near the Guadiana on the Spanish border and Faro (Ossonoba). The Romans also constructed bridges

Figure 8.3 Tavira and its
quarters

Figure 8.4 The Roman
bridge

Figure 8.5 The Arab town

Figure 8.6 Town walls

Figure 8.7 Town walls

across the Almargem and the Gilâo. The bridge connecting both parts of Tavira across the Gilâo is known locally as the Roman Bridge though its present structure appears to date from much later (Figure 8.4). It is thought that the Romans occupied the highest part of Tavira but no archaeological evidence has been found to confirm this assumption.[1]

THE ARAB OCCUPATION OF THE TOWN

Figure 8.5 shows the probable extent of the Arab occupation of the town. Most of the urban development was within the fortress walls, which also contained two Mosques. Figures 8.6 and 8.7 show the remains of the town walls. The port and farm areas were located beyond the walls. During the Christian re-conquest of Portugal Tavira was liberated in 1242. In the ensuing peaceful times the town began to expand beyond the walls outside the gates, taking advantage of its important location on the lowest crossing point on the river and also of its port facilities. The port continued to grow with

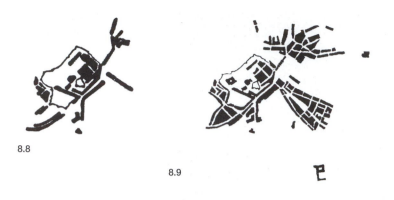

8.8

8.9

8.10

Figure 8.8 *Tavira* after the Christian re-conquest
Figure 8.9 *Tavira* at its commercial peak
Figure 8.10 *Tavira* in the sixteenth century

development along the riverfront. There were also developments around the hill on which the Convent of Sâo Francisco is located and on the eastern bank of the river. It was also at this stage in its development that the defensive walls were strengthened. This bears witness to the town's growing prosperity and strategic importance. See Figure 8.8, which shows the extent of the town after the Christian re-conquest.

TAVIRA DURING THE FOURTEENTH CENTURY
Tavira's close trading links with North Africa and its commercial connections with other countries led to the town's growth, particularly during what is known in Portugal as 'the Century of Discovery'. This great century of development is still reflected in the town's morphology. There was a consolidation of the development in quarters such as Ribeira, Alagoa, Malforo, and the heights around Sâo Fransisco. New quarters such as Sâo Lazaro and Sâo Bras were founded at this time. Tavira merged into a series of towns within a town (Figure 8.3). Each town district had its own identity and to some extent was self-sufficient or autonomous. This structure is very much in evidence today, though the degree of self-sufficiency of each district is much reduced. Figure 8.9 shows Tavira at the height of its commercial activity during the middle ages.

DECLINE AND REVIVAL
In the sixteenth century, Tavira lost much of its commercial base. The port declined and many of the traders moved to Seville. It was a period of decline and stagnation with a general movement of population from the town back to the countryside. Figure 8.10 shows the town at this time. It wasn't until the middle of the eighteenth century that commerce once again revived. Commercial activity in the eighteenth century was exclusively associated with fishing and coastal trade along the Algarve. The earthquake of 1755 caused great damage - the Ribeira district, in particular, being affected most. Parts of the Hospital, the Convent of Sâo Fransisco and the church of Santa Maria were also destroyed. Economic recovery in the wake of the earthquake was given impetus by the founding of a factory making tapestries and the development of the salt trade. The salt industry is still an important component of Tavira's economy and a prominent feature of its landscape (Figure 8.11). With economic recovery in the latter part of the eighteenth century, new urban areas were developed and existing ones rehabilitated and extended.

The second half of the nineteenth century was another period of growth and development: the urban core of the town centre was transformed with the construction of a garden by the riverside

8.11

Figure 8.11 The salt pans
Figure 8.12 The waterside
park

and the municipal covered market. The old market
has now been converted into a covered public
square surrounded by cafés and boutiques (Figures
8.12 and 8.13). The river was regularized with
stone-retaining walls, as it passed through the town.
These pleasant riverside walks are still a feature of
the town centre. Tavira faces directly onto its river,
which is an important visual feature, giving the
town much of its character (Figures 8.14 and 8.15).

TAVIRA IN THE TWENTIETH CENTURY
In 1904 the railway line was opened, heralding the
start of another period of growth and expansion for
Tavira. A new avenue was built from the railway
station in the south-west of the town to the centre.
Along this avenue new residences and a primary
school were built, while on the access roads into
the town newly established canning factories were
located. For the first seventy years of the twentieth
century Tavira expanded, much of the development
being at a lower density and quite different in form
from the tight urban streets and squares of the older
parts of the town. The land subdivision was largely
unplanned, with scattered development bearing little
visual relationship with the older, attractive core of
the town. Meanwhile, parts of the historic core of

8.12

Figure 8.13 The former
municipal market
Figure 8.14 The waterfront

8.13

8.14

Figure 8.15 The waterfront

Figure 8.16 Early twentieth century development

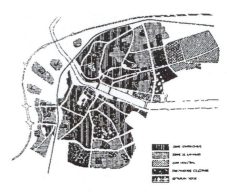

8.18

Figure 8.17 Modern frontage in a traditional street
Figure 8.18 Plano Geral de Urbanização
Figure 8.19 Urban decay

the town itself went through a process of demolition and reconstruction. Consequently parts of the older town have been destroyed, weakening its character and image (Figures 8.16 to 8.17).

A plan was made for Tavira in 1981: the Plano Geral de Urbanização (Figure 8.18). This plan attempted to control and direct spontaneous development and, where possible, to reverse some of its worst effects (Figure 8.19). Unfortunately, the plan was not formally approved until 1992, during which time the town continued to expand and grow, without any real consideration being given to the impact on the environment. In 1997, the town boundary was extended to permit the suburban extension of the town. This suburban expansion was caused both by an influx of population from the surrounding countryside into the town, and by a movement of population out of the town where pressure to meet the growing needs of commerce and administration proved irresistible.

The traditional settlement pattern of Tavira is structured around streets, squares, quarters, fine public buildings, sculpture, and street furniture of quality. The new suburbs are quite different. These new developments are no longer clearly defined self-sufficient quarters; rather, they are a series of amorphous single-use zones with little urban design quality. They are not built for the benefit of the pedestrian, but primarily to serve the motor car, which has now become the main cause of traffic and parking problems in the historic core.

The development of Tavira in the late twentieth century mirrors similar developments in towns and

8.19

cities across Europe. This development has come late to Tavira and pressures have not been as great as in other places. This presents the town authorities with the opportunity to learn from the mistakes of others. The twin aims of seeking environmental excellence and sustainable development may yet inform the planning and design process for the coming decades of the new millennium in this still fine town. There are positive signs that these concerns are being addressed. Some important buildings in the historic core have been restored; a town bus service linking various parts of the town to the centre has been launched; a planning study has been prepared, which advises on ways to ameliorate the worst features of the faceless developments of the twentieth century and to suggest the direction of new development in the town (Figure 8.20).

TOWNSCAPE ANALYSIS

This section of the chapter will discuss four aspects of townscape analysis. The first is legibility. That is, the ways in which people perceive, understand and react to the urban environment: it concerns those qualities of place that give the town a distinct identity, one which is easily grasped and perceived by its users. The second aspect of this townscape analysis is concerned with the permeability of the environment. That is, the choice of movement the environment presents to the user. The third aspect is the vitality of the environment, particularly in terms of the variety and mix of land uses and the activity thereby generated. The fourth aspect of the analysis is the visual study. This study conforms more to the traditional meaning of townscape analysis as used, for example, by Cullen.[2] The visual analysis includes a study of town spaces and their connections: it will focus on a selection of streets and squares in the historic core of Tavira, examining the treatment of façades, pavements, rooflines, sculpture and street furniture.

Figure 8.20 Restored buildings: used now as town's main exhibition gallery

PERCEPTUAL STRUCTURE OF TAVIRA

This section of the chapter is based on the work of Kevin Lynch.[3] He developed a technique for analysing legibility and suggested ways in which the concept can be used to structure new urban development and strengthen the legibility of existing areas where the environment has been degraded by inappropriate modern development. In order to appreciate the function and form of a street or a square it has to be viewed, initially, as an element in this perceptual structure. Lynch demonstrated with his studies in mental mapping that a legible environment is one that is capable of being structured by people into accurate images. With this

Figure 8.21 Main Paths in Tavira

Figure 8.22 Street decoration

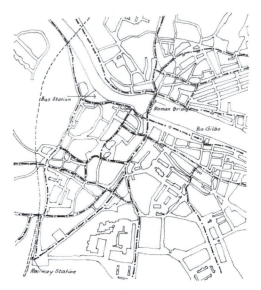

8.21

8.22

clear perceptual image of the town the user can react to the environment more effectively. Lynch also found evidence that individuals share features of a common image with other members of the same community. It is this common or shared image that is important for urban design. Some of these structuring features of the image have been discussed earlier in the book - they are: paths, nodes, districts, landmarks and edges.

The path

The path is probably the most significant structuring element in image building. Most people relate other imaging features to their main network of paths. The main paths in the historic core of Tavira are shown in Figure 8.21. The main paths in the historic core of the town radiate from the Roman Bridge, the ancient crossing point of the river. The bridge has now been pedestrianized, thereby enhancing its image as a meeting point. The paths link the main public buildings, usually located

within important public squares. The main paths are the routes taken by processions at times of public festivals and together with the main public squares such as Praça da Republica, Praça Dr Padinha and Largo de São Bras they become richly decorated and form the backcloth for public display (Figure 8.22).

Nodes

Nodes are focal points of activity such as the junction of paths, meeting places, market squares, or places of transport interchange. A town may have nodes, which serve a purely local purpose, and others that have a wider significance in the region. This is true of Tavira. The main local nodes are shown on Figure 8.23: also indicated are those nodes that are of particular significance. For example, the Praça da Republica is the symbolic town centre: it is here that the Câmara, the Local Government Office, is located and it is here that the Mayor has his office. The Praça Dr Padinha is an important square, the centre of a thriving restaurant

Figure 8.23 Main Nodes in
Tavira
Figure 8.24 The Quarter of
Santa Maria

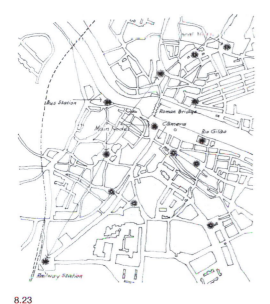

8.23

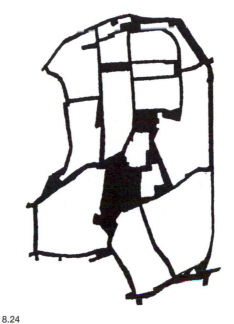

8.24

complex serving the resident population and visiting tourists; there is an important group of spaces surrounding the churches of Santa Maria and Santiago. In former times this was probably the town centre but is now a major tourist attraction, soon to be given added importance with the proposed conversion into a Pousada of the Convento Nossa Senhora da Graça, the third major religious building of the group (see later, Figure 8.30). These spaces are not the only ones in Tavira associated with churches or other former religious foundations; indeed, most squares, in addition to their modern function of meeting places and centres of activity, are also the setting for one of the many churches that decorate the town.

Districts

The city, according to Lynch, is divided into quarters or districts, each having some identifying characteristic. The quarter or district is a medium to large section of a city, such as the well-known areas in London like Soho and Mayfair. Following Lynch's categorization, Tavira can be viewed as divided by the river into two quite distinct parts; the connecting link between the two main areas is the Roman Bridge. However, Tavira is miniscule in scale when compared to a large city. This is reflected in the size of the town's main quarters, shown on figure 8.3. These quarters have their roots in the history and development of the town: they are named and usually built around a church and square which acts as the quarter's main node or centre (Figure 8.24). It is from this focus that the main paths radiate, connecting the quarter to the rest of the settlement.

Landmarks

Landmarks are points of reference that are experienced at a distance. They are three-dimensional sculptural objects in contrast to nodes, which are places to be entered and experienced from within.

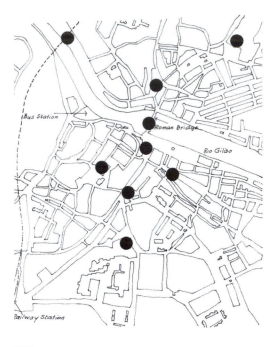

8.25

8.26

The most significant landmark in Tavira is the group of towers belonging to Santa Maria and Santiago. Together with the town's water storage tank the towers mark the hilltop at the centre of the historic core of the town. Other important landmarks are the great auracaria trees that mark the position of important squares in the town (Figures 8.25 and 8.26). The Roman bridge is an important meeting point for young and old alike: for that reason, it is a point of reference and landmark for local people and indeed for tourists.

Edges

The fifth major structuring element for the perceptual image of the town is the edge. Edges are two-dimensional elements where the function of pathway is of less importance than the role of boundary. The most obvious edges in Tavira are the river and the old town walls. In Tavira the main pathways, together with the enclosing street façades, perform the dual function of path and dividing edge between adjacent town quarters. These are the type of 'fleshy' boundaries that Alexander recommends.[4] 'Fleshy' boundaries, which permit the movement of goods and people, reflect the complexities of modern urban life where activities overlap in numerous combinations. This is particularly necessary for the boundaries between town quarters. Figure 8.27 shows the position of important edges in Tavira. It includes both the hard edge such as the river, town walls and railway line, in addition to the more 'fleshy', and less distinct boundaries of the quarters.

Paths, nodes, landmarks, districts or quarters, and edges all play a significant role in structuring Tavira and determining the town's legibility, this being particularly true of the older parts of the town. Some suburban developments in the town dating from the late twentieth century do not possess this clarity of structure, being planned as single use dormitories and designed primarily for the efficient use of the car.

PERMIABILITY AND LAND USE

We all live public and private lives. A function of urban government is to ensure the safe use of the public realm. A second role of urban government is to guarantee its citizens the level of privacy required by its culture. A third role is to provide suitable conditions for social and economic exchange. These, sometimes contrary, requirements are resolved at the interface between the public realm and the private or semi-private domains of home, shop or office. The nature of the design of the interface between the public spaces of street and square, and the more private areas of individual properties in Tavira, is the concern of this section of the chapter.

According to Bentley et al. 'Both physical and visual permeability depend on how the network of public space divides the environment into blocks: areas of land entirely surrounded by public routes'.[5] Clearly an area divided into small blocks gives the user a greater choice of routes and therefore greater flexibility of movement than one divided into large blocks. This fine grain of land subdivision is evident in many areas of the historic core of Tavira (Figure 8.28), a quality that has been lost in the larger scale developments of the last century (see Figure 8.16). Where street blocks vary between half to one hectare in size, street junctions occur at about 70 to 100 metres giving a wide variety of routes in moving from place to place on foot and therefore, according to Bentley et al., a high degree of permeability. This is the experience for most of central Tavira, which is a town of great environmental

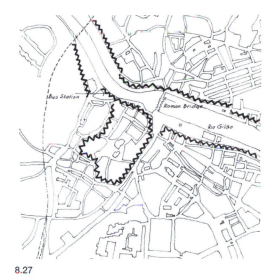

8.27

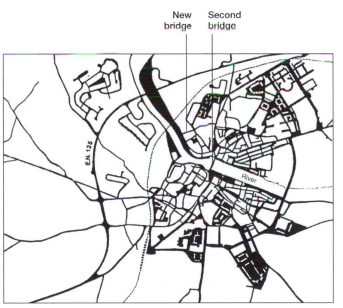

8.28

Figure 8.27 The edge in Tavira
Figure 8.28 Main public spaces in Tavira

Figure 8.29 Street scene

cial buildings have been introduced with little thought being given to the quality of the urban environment. It is the ground floors of the buildings in a town that act as the zone of social and commercial exchange generating the activity which makes streets both safe and lively, with the frontage between public and private space being the mechanism of ensuring privacy. In Tavira privacy is not maintained by the ubiquitous front garden often found in the British residential street. In Tavira the terrace frontage of the street is built right up to the pavement. Narrow windows light and ventilate the interior of the building, permitting a view of the outside world but keeping the dark interior private, out of public view (see Figures 8.35, 8.36). Current ideas about the planning of residential areas in Britain and the rest of Europe advocate mixed land use as a method of achieving a degree of self-sufficiency in city quarters and a move towards sustainable urban development: in Tavira this practice is common, but under threat from pressures for redevelopment, particularly if future developments in the town are permitted to follow short-sighted market trends. Such developmental pressures would destroy a fine urban environment while in the long term reducing the town's sustainability.

VISUAL STUDY

The visual study presented here is in two parts: a three-dimensional study of the main public spaces and a study of the two-dimensional surfaces that enclose public space, together with their architectural details, which give the town much of its character. Figure 8.30 shows the area of the study: it includes the spaces around Santa Maria and Santiago in the oldest part of the town: they are connected to Praça da Republica via the main street of the town Rua da Liberdade. Off the Praça da Republica is the lovely green riverside park abutting the Rua do Cais. The Praça da Republica – the centre of the town – is connected across the Rio Gilâo via the Ponte Romana to the Praça Dr. Padinha. These main public spaces are connected to

quality in no small measure due to the variety – almost maze – of lovely pathways through the urban structure.

To some extent, public safety in streets is related to the intensity of their use and the activity they generate. Streets are safer if they are heavily used, and if they are overlooked by occupants in the surrounding buildings. Busy streets by both day and night are in the words of Jane Jacobs: 'self policing'.[6] In Tavira old town the pattern of land-use is mixed. It still retains a large residential population giving life to the town, but even residential streets contain numerous shops, bars, restaurants and small offices (Figure 8.29). It is only in those areas that were redeveloped in the last half of the twentieth century that this particular pattern has been broken. In some places largescale administrative or commer-

8.30

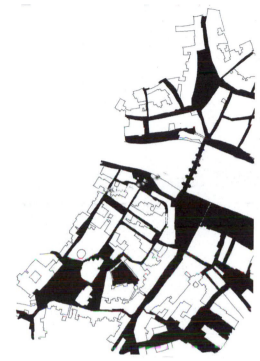

8.31

Figure 8.30 The main squares in Tavira
Figure 8.31 The main squares in Tavira. Ground study

further visually important public spaces, which punctuate and structure the rest of the town. It is only for convenience and brevity that they are excluded from the study.

In Figure 8.31 the spaces are shown in black and the surrounding buildings in white: it is a reversal of the presentation technique used in the previous figure. It follows an idea from Gibberd for alternating the way form and ground, building and space, are presented.[7] This change of perspective concentrates the mind, not on the buildings and their forms, but upon the spaces and the volumes between buildings. It is this anti-form which is so distinctive in Tavira, where narrow passageways twist and turn, finally to open out onto the larger space of a public square or more formal commercial street. Figure 8.32a–g shows a series of perspective

drawings illustrating this feature of Tavira's townscape form. This way of illustrating movement through spaces in a town is based on Cullen's suggestion that we see and appreciate a town as a series of unfolding pictures.[8] Cullen called this way of seeing, serial vision. Serial vision is most memorable in picturesque landscapes like Tavira. The route taken for the illustration of a typical spatial sequence through the town is shown on Figure 8.30: it follows the path from Santa Maria through to the Praça da Republica, which is the main town square, its heart both politically and socially. This, the main square of the town is triangular in shape, apparently small, being about 100 metres by 100 metres, with a war memorial at its centre. The square, however, expands along the length of the river in the form of a garden with

Figure 8.32(a)-(g) Townscape in Tavira

8.32a

8.32b

8.32c

8.32d

8.32e

8.32f

8.32g

bandstand, places for dancing, concerts and outdoor eating. The Praça da Republica is enclosed on two of its sides by buildings. The third side extends beyond the river's edge expanding across the Rio Gilâo, terminating visually on the frontage of Rua Jacques Pessoa. In this way the river is enclosed as part of the very heart of Tavira; along with the Ponte Romana; it successfully connects both halves of the town.

The building height in the historic core of Tavira is generally two storeys, about 8 metres high, though there are both single and three-storey buildings. This height is disrupted only in the areas where rebuilding was carried out during the last century and where a church tower punctuates the roofscape. Roofs are constructed throughout the town of clay tiles, which weather a rich brown colour. A distinctive feature of the town is a pyramid roof: a long rectangular space being roofed by a series of small square gabled roofs where ridge and valley alternate along the length of the building. This highly decorative roofline, brought to Tavira from Goa in India, is at times partly hidden behind a balustrade but generally it is the pyramid roof that dominates the urban scene making it one of the most memorable features of Tavira (Figure 8.33).

Figure 8.33 Roofscape

Building plan forms are based on a variety of court-yard designs following Arab and Mediterranean traditions (Figure 8.34).

Façades tend to be white throughout the historic core of the town: they are divided into bays about 3 metres wide comprising a window and doorway aligned vertically. This bay is surmounted by the pyramid roof and gives a small, intimate scale and insistent rhythm to the town. The façades are usually edged in classical detailing, formed either in stone or decorative plasterwork. In addition to these classical details of plinth, end pilasters and cornice, the windows and doorways are edged with decorative surrounds. This simple and satisfying urban terrace architecture still retains traces of Arab influence: shuttered windows, latticed balconies and solid ground floor doors with 'spy holes' permit views of the world outside and act as a source of ventilation but retain privacy for the occupants - an important requirement for the Muslim family (Figures 8.35-8.36).

Figure 8.34 Building plans
Figure 8.35 Architectural detail

TORRE

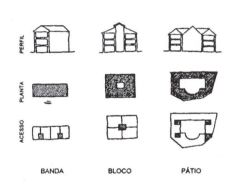

PERFIL   PLANTA   ACESSO

BANDA   BLOCO   PÁTIO

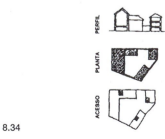

PERFIL   PLANTA   ACESSO

8.34

8.35

8.36

8.37

Figure 8.36 Door detail
Figure 8.37 Balcony detail
Figure 8.38 Floorscape

Pavements for pedestrians are constructed from small limestone and basalt blocks about 8 centimetres square. The granite blocks vary in colour from off-white to dark grey and are used to create delightful mosaic-like patterns, which in some cases take the form of largescale complex geometric shapes. Street furniture is simple, dignified and functional: railings to enclose the river, street lighting and fountains. The decoration of the town is completed by a series of small gardens with shade trees, flowering shrubs, scented flowers and small-scale sculptures to honour local people of distinction (Figures 8.38 to 8.40).

8.38

Figure 8.39 Garden square
of Dr Padinha
Figure 8.40 The new
galleries – a local landmark

8.39

8.40

TAVIRA IN THE FUTURE

There are clear indications that the degeneration of
the urban environment, which was a feature of
Tavira in the last decades of the last century, may
have been arrested. Several old buildings in the core
of the town have been rehabilitated while others are
in the process of reconstruction. In some cases the
buildings have been completely revitalized, taking
on a completely new function. For example, the
town has just refurbished a large domestic property,
converting it into a fine set of galleries (see Figure
8.20). The former Convento de Nossa Senhora da
Graca at the centre of the old walled town is being
converted into a Pousada, or state-run hotel. A
number of small-scale sites now have buildings that
follow the pattern set by the traditional vernacular
architecture of the town. When they are renewed,
roofs throughout the old town keep the original
shape and are constructed in local tiles to match the
existing colour; and most building façades are
painted white giving the town a great sense of
unity. Not all recent developments in Tavira
maintain the human scale of the town's urban grain.
While, for example, the new hotel by the riverside
is generally three storeys high, the building's
footprint or ground coverage is such that it restricts
easy pedestrian movement. Generally, buildings
maintain a height that is compatible with the traditional streets and squares of the town. Nevertheless,
developments such as the new hotel reduce easy
access and impede pedestrian movement (Figure
8.37).

Figure 8.41 shows a plan for the extension of
Tavira, which is designed to cater for an expected
increase in demand for housing. This planned extension of the town, Plano de Pormenor de Pêro Gil, is
based on the concept of the quarter.[9] Four quarters
are planned, each with its own quite distinct architectural character: a firm edge or boundary; a mix
of land uses, which will include shops, schools,
public buildings; green areas; and work places in
addition to residential properties. The design of
each quarter is based upon a highly structured

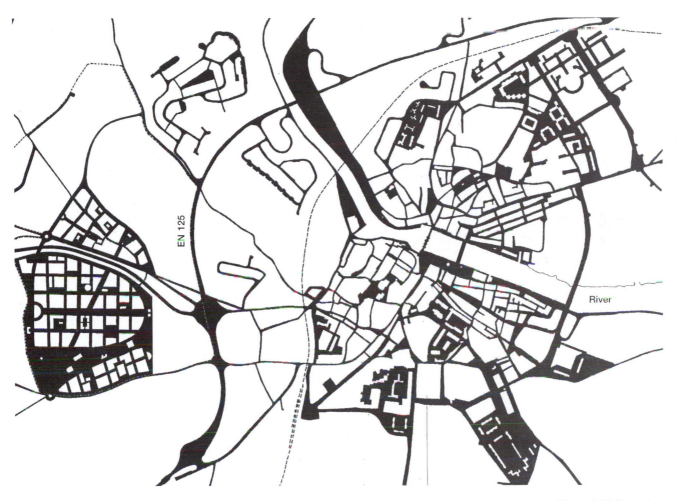

EN 125

River

Figure 8.41 Plano de Pormenor de Pêro Gil

public space taking the form of streets and squares, along which, and around which, the buildings will be arranged. The design and ideas for the structure of the new neighbourhoods are the result of a detailed urban design study prepared for the Camara, the planning authority for Tavira.[10]

NOTES

1 For a brief history of Tavira see Mertens, M., *Plano de Pormenor de Pêro Gil*, Camara Municipal de Tavira, Tavira, 2001

2 Cullen, G., *Townscape*, Architectural Press, London, 1961

3 Lynch, K., *The Image of the City*, MIT Press, Cambridge, Mass., 1960

4 Alexander, C., et al., *A New Theory of Urban Design*, Oxford University Press, Oxford, 1987

5 Bentley, I., et al., *Responsive Environments: A Manual for Designers*, Architectural Press, London, 1985

6 Jacobs, J., *The Death and Life of Great American Cities*, Penguin, Harmondsworth, 1965

7 Gibberd, F., *Town Design*, Architectural Press, London, 2nd edn, 1955.

8 Cullen, G., Op cit

9 *Mertens*, M., Op cit

10 Duarte, C., et al., *Plano de Reabilitacão e Salvaguarda do Centro Historico de* Tavira, Direccão Geraldo Equipamento Regional e Urbano, Tavira, 1985

CASE STUDIES IN URBAN DESIGN

9

Urban design is the art of arranging buildings to form unified compositions. The main medium of this design process is the urban realm. There are a number of ways in which buildings can be arranged to form single compositions, but the one advocated here is the discipline of forming outdoor or external space. The two main components of this discipline are the street and square in all their manifestations. When this discipline is applied to urban design, context is the paramount concern for building design. Architectural design is the art of designing the transition between the internal and mainly private spaces within the building and the external spaces of the public realm: it is also the difficult task of designing an appropriate, largely two-dimensional façade which forms the interface between these two zones.

Five case studies will be presented to illustrate the main scales at which urban design operates. The first case study is the planning of Paternoster Square, that is, the area surrounding St Paul's Cathedral, London. The analysis of the development of Paternoster Square is centred on a discussion of the ways in which the public realm surrounding a great cathedral should be treated. The second case study is the planning and development of the Isle of Dogs in the London Docklands. This area corresponds to the approximate size of the quarter that

some writers suggest as the main concern of urban design. The third case study outlines the planning of a small neighbourhood in Belfast. It is concerned with public participation in urban design and illustrates that the lay person is capable of producing design ideas and that those ideas conform in a general way with the theories put forward in this text. The fourth case study deals with the regeneration of the river frontage in Newark in Nottinghamshire. It raises two particular concerns: the design of public space along an urban watercourse and the design process seen in its temporal dimension, time scale being, possibly, the most critical dimension of urban design. Urban design is a long-term process. It takes many centuries for the development of a great urban design composition such as the spaces around St Mark's in Venice. The fourth case study tries to capture the nature of this ongoing process, or the temporal scale of urban design. The fifth case study is Barcelona. The recent planning of Barcelona is an example of the techniques of urban design being applied to the large-scale planning problems of the city and in particular to the regeneration of a great waterfront. While the chief concern of this book is the design of street and square, these important elements of city structure can only be fully appreciated as part of a wider study of morphology. In addition, a study

Figure 9.1 St Paul's Cathedral, London

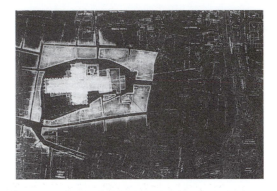

Figure 9.2 Hawksmoor's plan for St Paul's precinct, London

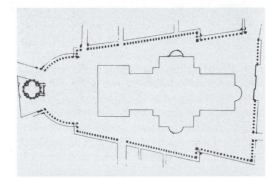

Figure 9.3 War damage around St Paul's, London

of Barcelona provides an opportunity to examine the nature of the public realm and in particular the street and square in the context of a major seafront.

ST PAUL'S AND PATERNOSTER SQUARE

The axis of the old Gothic cathedral replaced by Sir Christopher Wren's Baroque cathedral of St Paul's, London, was at an angle to the main approach up Ludgate Hill. Wren had the perfect opportunity to realign the axis of the cathedral with the approach. But, instead he tilted the axis of the cathedral a further 6.5° so that the line of Ludgate Hill met the west front more obliquely than before[1] (Figure 9.1). Following the rejection of Wren's plan for London after the Great Fire, the area immediately surrounding St Paul's was planned as a series of small-scale, linked spaces with a continuous arcade at ground-floor level. The scheme for the churchyard probably dates from 1710 after the completion of the cathedral. The plans and elevations were drawn by Hawksmoor, though Wren may also have participated in the design[2] (Figure 9.2).

Large areas around St Paul's, particularly to the north, were damaged during the Second World War which presented a great opportunity to rebuild the surroundings of the cathedral as a great work of urban design (Figure 9.3). Walter Bor considers that: 'The saga of the redevelopment of the St Paul's Precinct and Paternoster Square is symptomatic of our approach to much post-war reconstruction of historic parts of our cities'. In his view it was a 'muddled and unhappy compromise'.[3]

There were two early post-war plans for St Paul's precinct. There was the unofficial plan by the Royal Academy. It epitomized the views of the 'Classical' lobby by being rigidly symmetrical and much more grandiose than the scheme Wren and Hawksmoor had in mind. There was another, rather pedestrian plan prepared as part of the City of London Plan (Figure 9.4). This was rejected by Duncan Sandys, the then Minister of Housing and Local Government. He appointed William Holford as consultant to St Paul's and established his own advisory committee which was strongly influenced by the Classicist Professor Richardson. Holford's first design was indeed Classical (Figure 9.5). It still disappointed the minister who wanted something on the scale of St Peter's in Rome. Holford, however, considered that: 'It was too late to attempt for St Paul's what Bernini did for St Peter's in Rome, and it would in any case be out of character at the top of Ludgate Hill.'[4] He was also of the opinion that the Classical forecourt to his first design was 'wrong in principle'.[5] Instead, Holford designed a rectangular layout of informal spaces revealing significant views of parts of the great cathedral rather on the lines suggested by Camillo Sitte[6] (Figure 9.6).

From the outset the Holford plan was subject to the conflict of counter requirements. There was a need to maximize the area of public domain and also to restrain the scale of the buildings while at the same time meeting the requirements of a plot ratio of 5:1. Most of the land was owned by the Church Commissioners who insisted on their maximum entitlement of office space. Office layout was restricted at the time to the depth achieved with natural daylighting. This is a point to which we may have to return, if society is to pay any attention to energy saving and a green architecture.

The result of the conflicting programme in part determined the form of the slab blocks that surrounded the cathedral. Holford aimed to retain the imposing views of the dome from the river and concentrated much of the office space in one large slab to the north of the cathedral (Figures 9.7-9.9).

9.4

Figure 9.4 City of London plan for St Paul's, London
Figure 9.5 Holford's first design for St Paul's precinct, London
Figure 9.6 Holford's final design plan for St Paul's precinct, London

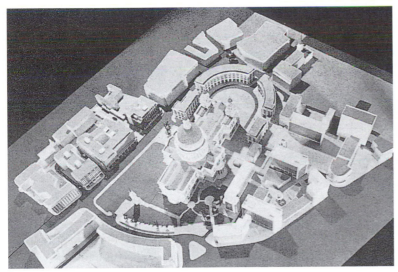

9.5

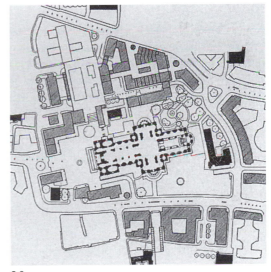

9.6

9.7

Figure 9.7 St Paul's
precinct, London
Figure 9.8 St Paul's
precinct, London
Figure 9.9 St Paul's
precinct, London
Figure 9.10 Competition
site
Figure 9.11 Rogers' plan
for St Paul's, London
Figure 9.12 SOM plan for
St Paul's, London

9.8

9.9

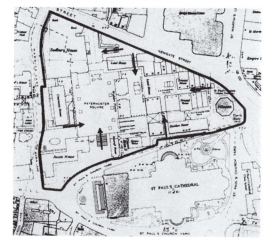

9.10

Much justified criticism was levelled at the now
demolished block which had obscured the view of
the cathedral's west front from Ludgate Hill. This
unloved block had been placed so as to conform,
according to Holford, with Wren's intention to form
an oblique approach to the cathedral. However, as
one ascended the hill, the view of the great cathedral front became obscured by the former Juxon
House. This is the type of scenic device, unsuccess-
fully implemented by Holford, which was advocated
by Sitte and his followers: its aim was to concentrate
the attention of the viewer on the cathedral. The
remaining buildings were designed to retreat into the
background, thereby not competing with the cathedral. The architecture of the buildings surrounding
the cathedral was certainly dull, even if the buildings

were not invisible: many would agree that Holford's development around the cathedral deserved the criticism it received as an example of faceless modernism. However, the proportion of the spaces and their arrangement were effective within Sitte's informal tradition. Clearly, buildings of quality are a prime requirement of the 'picturesque', which was sadly lacking in Holford's St Paul's precinct.

The decision of developers to sweep away the dull architecture of the Holford development was, according to critic Maev Kennedy, 'A heaven-sent second opportunity – an opportunity to see St Paul's rising up from surrounding low roof tops'.[7] The development of the site was the subject of an architectural competition in 1988 (Figure 9.10). The brief called for 100,000 m² of office space and between 9,300 and 14,000 m² of commercial retail space

giving a plot ratio of 6.5:1, a higher density than Holford worked with. A number of entrants in the competition limited the plot ratio to 5:1, which they thought more appropriate to the site. However, Leon Krier among others, believed that even this

Figure 9.13 Isozaki plan for St Paul's, London
Figure 9.14 MacCormac plan for St Paul's, London

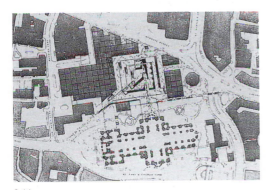
9.11

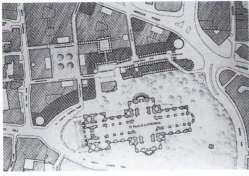
9.12

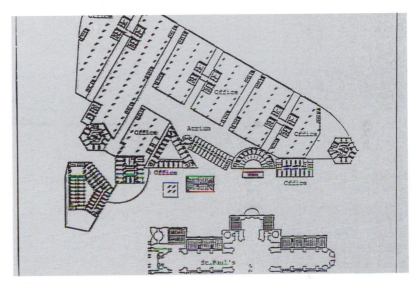
9.13

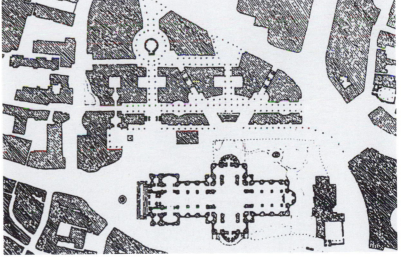
9.14

237

Figure 9.15 Arup plan for St Paul's, London

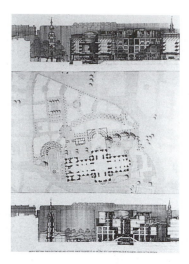

Figure 9.16 Simpson plan for St Paul's axonometric
Figure 9.17 Jencks's composite plan for St Paul's, London

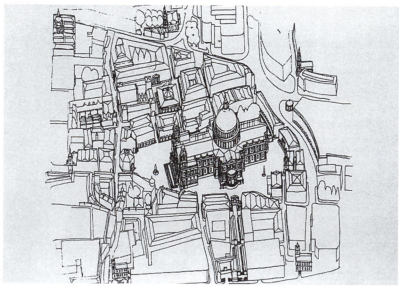

9.16

figure was too high a density for the site, suggesting a need for 35-40 per cent of the ground area to be given over to the public realm[8] (Figures 9.11 to 9.15).

In assessing the competition results Charles Jenks had this to say: 'These architects have all produced a mediaevalesque plan in Big Bang terms. For me Rogers has produced a mediaeval High-Tech, whilst Norman Foster produces something like ten Burlington Arcades all in a row, all in a very tightly networked field of alleyways. All of these schemes are Post-Modern classical plans in a general typological sense, no-one has seen slabs in a park'.[9] No longer were office blocks the slab-like form dictated by natural lighting requirements. Perhaps more important, the street and street block were once again back in favour as elements of city design.

The winning design, by Arup and Associates, contained many of the features beloved by Prince Charles and probably by the general mass of the public. In this scheme there were colonnades, squares, rooftop gardens, arcades and four-storey buildings roofed in lead and slate. Like the other entries, the weakest aspect of the winning design was the treatment of the cathedral's immediate surrounds where there was a lack of enclosure. It

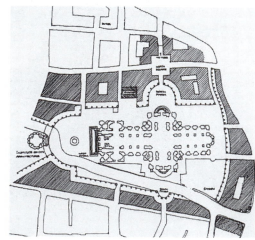

9.17

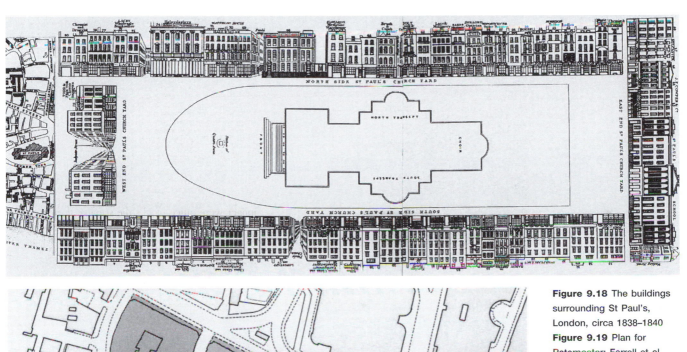

Figure 9.18 The buildings surrounding St Paul's, London, circa 1838–1840
Figure 9.19 Plan for Paternoster: Farrell et al

could be argued that this perhaps is the main design problem to be solved.

Two plans not submitted in the competition attempted to solve the problem of encircling the cathedral with appropriate enclosed spaces: John Simpson's beautifully scaled and detailed 'Classically inspired composition' a design very much to the taste of the Price of Wales, and Jencks's composite plan (Figures 9.16 and 9.17). Both echo the features of Wren and Hawksmoor's layout for St Paul's. The pattern of streets and street blocks were of human scale, a perfect foil and contrast to the monumentality of the cathedral.[10] The building blocks were also similar in scale to the buildings that surrounded the cathedral in 1838-1840 when John Tallis made his record of London streets[11] (Figure 9.18).

PROPOSALS FOR PATERNOSTER DURING THE 1990S

An exhibition in the summer of 1991, displaying the redevelopment of Paternoster Square, was mounted by a consortium of British, American and Japanese developers (Paternoster Associates) working with a team of Post-Modern and neo-Classical architects from Britain and the United States who had liaised with Prince Charles. The architects, a talented group by any standards, included Terry Farrell, Thomas Beeby, John Simpson, Robert Adam, Paul Gibson, Allan Greenberg, Demitri Porphyros and Quinlan Terry.[12]

The aim of this proposal was to 'revitalize the area, restoring vibrancy and architectural excellence to improve the quality of the environment for those

Figure 9.20 Whitfield's masterplan: Paternoster

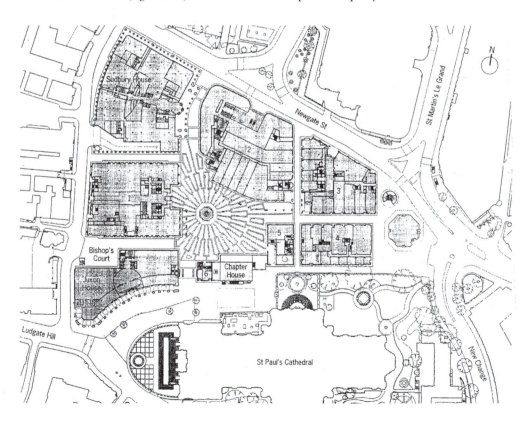

who visit and work in the area'.[13] The specific aesthetic objectives were: to restore views of St Paul's Cathedral; to create buildings in harmony with the cathedral; to restore the traditional alignment of St Paul's churchyard; to re-establish a traditional street pattern; to create new traffic-free open spaces and to build in a traditional Classical style of architecture. Figure 9.19 is the ground-floor plan of that proposal; it gives some idea of the ways in which it was proposed to meet the scheme's objectives.

The proposal consisted of a number of street blocks varying between five and nine storeys, though most were to approximate to the height of St Paul's main wall. The street blocks were designed as beefy office blocks above wine bars and boutiques. The blocks were arranged to form a group of relatively short streets, which to some extent, reflected the mediaeval pattern pre-dating the Holford development. There was also to be a public plaza, Paternoster Square. The architecture of the square, and indeed the whole development, was to be decked out in a revived late Classicism, reminiscent of Lutyens but in technicolour. Judging by the drawings, Paternoster Square, if built as planned, may have taken on the appearance of a set for an epic film, rather than a dignified plaza nestling under the shadow of Wren's great dome. Fortunately St Paul's was saved from the indignity of having neighbours, as Glancy put it at the time, painted 'in kinder-garden colours'.[14]

Though this project, which incorporated the classical vision of the Prince of Wales, received planning permission in 1993, it too was found to be unviable and was abandoned in 1996, to be replaced by a more flexible design.[15] The public exhibition for this particular scheme was no substitute for effective public participation, another of Prince Charles' interest. Unfortunately, the opportunity for public input was minimal – far less than the former Holford scheme which had involved detailed ministerial interjections and wide public debate, even some public acclaim, for what at the time was considered a fine development.

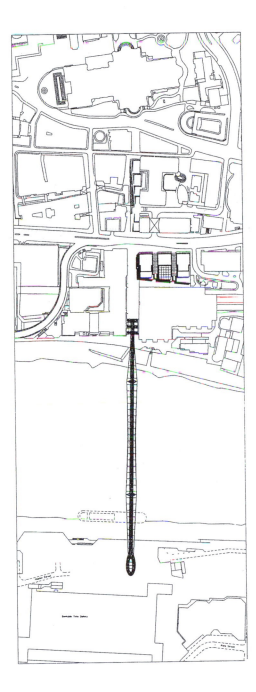

Figure 9.21 Millennium Bridge: connection between St Paul's and the Tate Modern

Sir William Whitfield was appointed by Mitsubishi to devise a workable masterplan for Paternoster Square and the area to the north of St Paul's Cathedral with less emphasis on style. As Sir William Whitfield wisely said: 'You look for quality, for merit, you are not preoccupied with style. Style is something you identify after you've got it'.[16]

Figure 9.20 illustrates Whitfield's masterplan. Sir William Whitfield was one of the assessors for the 1988 architectural competition and his masterplan incorporated contributions from some of the competitors in that competition.[17] At the time of writing, the buildings are under construction but should be completed and occupied within months, so it still remains to be seen just how successful the development around St Paul's will be, but early signs appear to be promising. The public space is now at ground level: there is a restored street pattern, central to which is the new Paternoster Square fronted by colonnades and dominated by a ventilation shaft, disguised as a replica of a Corinthian column used by Inigo Jones in the portico of old St Paul's.

While it is still only possible to imagine the effect the Whitfield development will have on St Paul's,

one completed addition to the public realm which has a direct bearing on the cathedral, is the delightful Millennium Bridge designed by Foster and Partners with sculptor Anthony Caro and Engineers Ove Arup and Partners. The Thames is one of the least impressive city rivers in Europe. Along much of its banks drab Victorian buildings and even more gross modern hulks have replaced delicately scaled Georgian buildings. The gentle curve of the Millennium Bridge is a welcome relief from much dross: it connects the powerful mass of Giles Gilbert Scott's Bankside Power Station, now the Tate Modern with the south transept and towering dome of Wren's great cathedral[18] (see Figures 9.9 and 9.21). Such connections are the lifeblood of a vibrant city: it is by the quality of a civilized extension of the public realm in and around St Paul's Cathedral that Sir William Whitfield's masterplan will be judged.

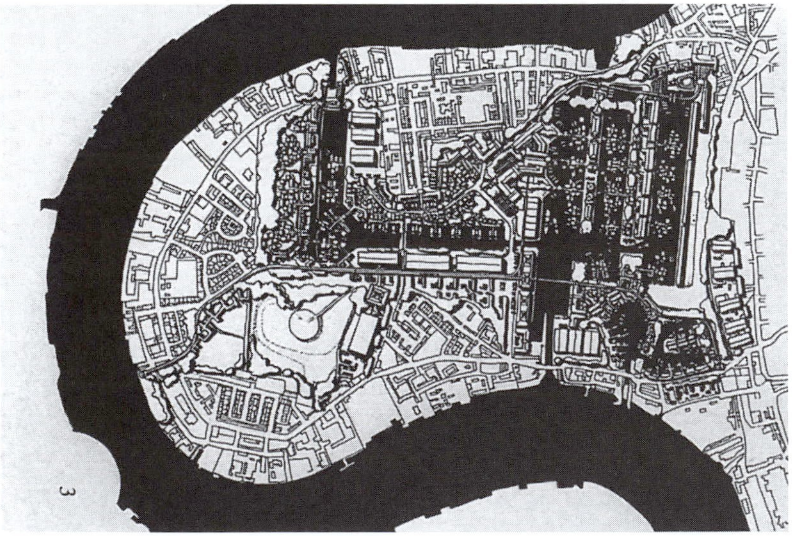

ISLE OF DOGS

The Conservative Government of the 1980s considered planning a bureaucratic instrument inhibiting development and in particular that planning had been one of the important constraints on the process of revitalization of the decaying inner city. As a result a number of strategies were invented to circumvent this blockage in the development process; these included Urban Development Corporations (UDCs), Enterprise Zones (EZs), and Simplified Planning Zones (SPZs). Some members of the architectural profession entered this argument usually on the side of the government. Their case was that planning controls resulted in mediocre architectural development where innovative designs were suppressed by unimaginative planners with little or no design training and poor aesthetic judgement.[19]

The Isle of Dogs was part of the land overseen by the London Docklands Development Corporation (LDDC) between 1985 and 1991: it is an area where planning procedures have been circumscribed. It

Figure 9.22 Preliminary study, Isle of Dogs

was also the flagship of market enterprise where free reign was given to the private sector and where non-interventionist, free-market economics ruled the day. Has it produced the brave new aesthetic world where imaginative urbanism creates a city of the quality of a Bath, York, Florence or the visual excitement of the waterfront at Barcelona? The short answer, in my view, is no.

An urban design study was made for the LDDC by David Gosling Associates, working with Edward Hollamby, chief architect of the corporation[20] (Figure 9.22). A number of alternative options were presented (Figure 9.23). The most interesting one explored the structural implications of the Greenwich axis. At the tip of the peninsula, Island Gardens, there is a magnificent view towards Wren's hospital with Inigo Jones's Queen's House at the head of the vista (see Figures 2.43 and 9.24). In the other direction there is a direct axial view of St Ann's Church, Limehouse, by Hawksmoor. While the axis is just over 3 km (2 miles) in length and beyond the normal visual scale for such features, some recognition of Queen's House and Greenwich Hospital is demanded. Gosling was prepared to see the axis as a structuring element taking on 'the mystical form of a ley-line with a significance beyond the linking of two monuments, and provides a series of reference points which enhance the visual structure'[21] (Figure 9.25). Gordon Cullen also joined the design team. His townscape analysis is a valuable tool for study of the existing development and a method for suggesting environmental improvements. However, as a method, it fails to provide a strong and coherent morphological framework for development[22] (Figure 9.26).

The final plan adopted by the LDDC for development purposes is a pragmatic one incorporating all the planning constraints and decisions, plus the alternative schemes put forward by developers. The only strong visual framework for the plan is the retention of the existing dock basins. It is the strength of this framework which holds together an otherwise amorphous collection of architectural monuments (Figure 9.27).

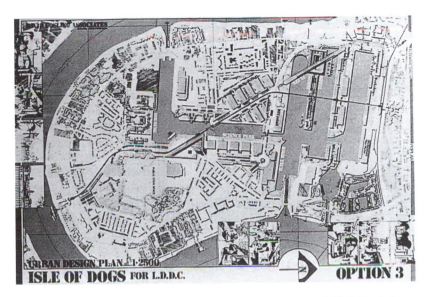

Figure 9.23 Option 3, Isle of Dogs
Figure 9.24 Greenwich

243

The scale of the dock basins, the main area of planned public realm is such that the surrounding large-scale buildings, probably even including Canary Wharf, are unified by the landscape - the gigantic water basins donated by former generations (Figures 9.28-9.29). No thought has been given to the problem of changing scale from the monumental water frontage to the public realm behind, where buildings are ranged along the road like eating houses in an American suburb (Figures 9.30-9.32). Along the spine road, decorated with inset red bricks

allegedly costing more per mile than a motorway, amorphous blocks are separated from each other by ill-shaped, car-parking lots and boundary fences. Buildings along the 'Red Brick Road' are tightly packed next to each other with no thought being given to their overall arrangement. This is no street, no clearly defined volume linking development, it is a two-dimensional road surface, a mere spine for traffic. Where the public realm is planned at Canary Wharf, the monstrous scale is broken down into some small-scale pleasant places and internally the private spaces of the malls are well detailed. But this is no substitute for a public realm of linked streets, squares and parks, which give form and structure to the whole development (Figure 9.33).

Another major element of the public realm - the rail system - initially consisted of the Docklands Light Railway's single spur line, which penetrated into the Isle of Dogs and which was far too small in scale for the expected size of the development (Figure 9.34). The connections of the peninsula to the rest of London have been much improved by

Figure 9.25 The Greenwich Axis

Figure 9.26 Cullen study, Isle of Dogs
Figure 9.27 Approved plan, Isle of Dogs

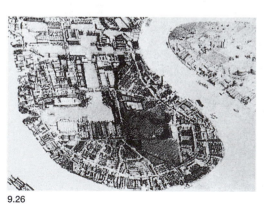

9.26

9.27

the extension of this light rail across the Thames to Greenwich, then on to Lewisham, linked by the extension of the Jubilee line through Canary Wharf.[23]

A great opportunity has been lost in this canalized peninsula, the Isle of Dogs, where water pervades the landscape: this could have been a Venice, a Bruges or an Amsterdam. A fine public heritage, the dock basin has been squandered in the name of free enterprise. More prosaically, in the region of £2 billion of public and £12 billion of private investment have been poorly directed on lumpy - in some cases even - obese buildings symbolizing nothing more than corporate power and greed. With the present Labour administration toying with ideas of 'simplifying' and 'freeing-up' the planning system to better serve the business world, it may be pertinent to look once again at the Isle of Dogs development: it may act as a salutary reminder

9.28

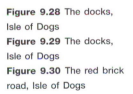

Figure 9.28 The docks, Isle of Dogs
Figure 9.29 The docks, Isle of Dogs
Figure 9.30 The red brick road, Isle of Dogs

9.29

9.30

9.31

9.32

9.33

Figure 9.31 The red brick road, Isle of Dogs
Figure 9.32 Bird Cage Walk, London
Figure 9.33 Old and new, Isle of Dogs

Figure 9.34 The light railway, London

of the weakness of privatizing the provision of the public realm. According to Edwards 'what is most remarkable on reflection about the Docklands experiment was the assumption by the Conservative Government that a collection of private interests could create an acceptable urban environment. Contrary to what many architects claim, the effect of removing controls and abandoning urban structuring plans has resulted in visual chaos and social disorder'.[24] Edwards goes on to admit, as indeed is the case, that among much dross some fine buildings have resulted from the Docklands experiment. This, however, is no substitute for a structured well-connected public realm.

9.34

There is an urgent need for public intervention in the Isle of Dogs. One that develops a strategy for structuring and landscaping the public realm - a system of streets, squares and parks connected internally to the great docks and linking via elegant bridges to Rogers' Millennium Dome and to Wren's Greenwich Complex with its elegant climax, Jones' Queen's House. Nothing less than a public structuring exercise can be expected to civilize and unify this peninsula so full of history, a monument to London's great past.

PARTICIPATION IN PLANNING: THE MARKETS AREA, BELFAST

The late 1960s and early 1970s in Belfast offered a unique opportunity to work with community groups in the field of planning and development. Belfast was the perfect laboratory for experiments in participation and planning. Inner-city, working-class groups were cohesive and organized on defensive lines; they possessed political muscle and were both willing and able to use such power in the pursuit of community ends. In the late 1960s community activists were presented with a golden opportunity, the proposed Belfast Urban Motorway, BUM as it was colourfully known, to marshal the communities' action. Both Protestant and Catholic local inner-city communities, the demolition of whose territories was necessary for building the motorway, joined forces to defeat the project at a public inquiry. Working for one such community opposing the motorway, I was able to observe the development of a tentative co-operation across the religious divide. For a short while many deep-rooted differences were forgotten in the joint effort to beat a common enemy, the hated motorway.[25] The planners, it seemed, had by chance been able to unite communities where the politicians had failed!

The original plan for the motorway was defeated, or rather delayed, only to return in diluted form later. It is difficult to assess the reason for the withdrawal of the original proposal. Was it, indeed, the strength of argument presented by the communities at the inquiry, or simply the power and weight of generalized public opposition? Or was it the threat by paramilitary forces to demolish any motorway built? There was, at the time, a change of attitude towards urban motorways among professionals in Britain, and, of course, the enormous cost of building such pieces of infrastructure in cities throughout the country must have given much food for thought and reflection. Irrespective of the reasons for the change of policy, community action where powerful groups have the ability to stop developments if extended over the whole range of urban government could make cities ungovernable. If there is any lesson to be learned from this and other similar anti-motorway action, then, it is the long-term futility of such negative and confrontational procedures. An important function of urban government since the founding of cities in the great valleys of rivers such as the Nile and Tigris-Euphrates is the provision of urban infrastructure - the control of flooding, the building of defensive structures or the provision of water supplies. Where anarchy prevails or where there is no consensus on essential infrastructural development then the city may be brought to a standstill in impotent stalemate.

At the then Department of Town and Country Planning of The Queen's University of Belfast in the early 1970s a Planning Projects Unit was established to provide planning aid to communities by assisting them to articulate their own needs and aspirations. The idea was to replace confrontational community policies where the emphasis was on saying 'No', or in Belfast terms 'Not an inch', to a constructive process whereby the ideas of local residents could be formulated and presented as viable, grass-roots solutions to a community's problems as perceived and analysed by themselves. One such study under-

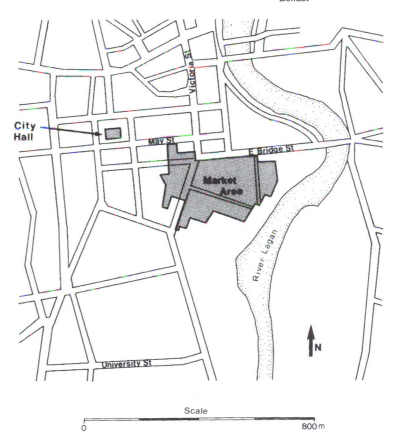

Figure 9.35 Markets Area, Belfast

Figure 9.36 Typical housing, Markets Area, Belfast

Figure 9.37 Courtyard housing, Markets Area, Belfast

Figure 9.38 Fine Victorian terrace, Markets Area, Belfast

Figure 9.39 Early redevelopment project for the Markets Area, Belfast

taken by the Planning Projects Unit was the preparation of a plan for the Markets Area in Belfast and it is this case study which is presented below.

THE AREA

The Markets Area in a loop of the River Lagan is within two or three minutes' walk of the city centre. The land on which the Markets people live was reclaimed from the estuarine flats of the Belfast Lough in the late eighteenth century. The community grew with the expansion of the Market and its allied trades: 'Old people still remember vividly the cattle being driven over the Albert Bridge to the Shankill for sale, then back again to the abbatoir for slaughtering.'[26] The Markets community was entirely working class, of one religion - Catholic, attended one church - St Malachy's - and the children attended the same school. The community was highly homogenous and very like an urban village.

At the time of the study there were 624 families with an average family size of 3.5, close to the then Belfast norm. However, within these statistics there were great differences; the community comprises many one- and two-person households in addition to families having 10 and more persons. The housing conditions in the Markets were poor and both the community and the planners were agreed on immediate redevelopment.[27] While most of the property was in poor condition there were some very fine Georgian and Victorian houses which the community wished to keep as a link with the past[28] (Figures 9.35-9.38).

9.37

9.38

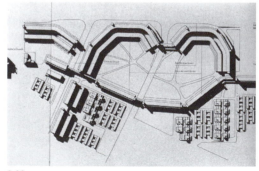

9.39

9.36

Before redevelopment took place in the late 1970s and 1980s there was a high proportion of buildings with non-residential uses in the Markets Area. These small firms were either the older established ones connected with the market or late arrivals dependent upon connections with the garages and motor-sales rooms in nearby areas. A further group of industries was located in the Markets Area simply to benefit from the availability then of cheap accommodation.[29]

The Markets Area was and still is divided by Cromac Street, a major traffic route in the city. Cromac Street divides the Markets Area into the Lower and Upper Markets which developed as separate groups within the greater Markets community. The street before redevelopment tended to act as the focus for the whole community and at that time was not the physical barrier it now has become. It was along this street and the associated Cromac Square that most of the 45 shops and service establishments were located. Many of the shops before redevelopment were closing down due to lack of business. The level of shopping provision required to serve the community was an issue that separated the thinking of the Northern Ireland Planning Executive and the community. The planning executive, bearing in mind the plans to rationalize city shopping into a series of district shopping centres, suggested a group of four shops while the community envisaged a much larger group of 15-20. The approved plan compromised with 10 in a precinct in the Lower Markets. The centre never materialized. In 1976 the planning executive's commercial department carried out a further study which found the proposals excessive; eventually one shop was built to facilitate the shopping needs of the community.[30]

ACTION PLANS

Early in 1973 the city planning department prepared two alternative action plans for the Markets Area. The first scheme, which was preferred by the planners and the city council, consisted of a ground

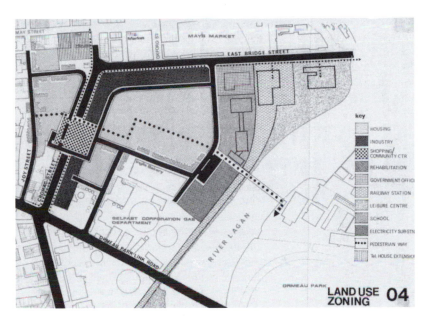

Figure 9.40 Residents' plan, land use, Belfast

floor for roads, industry and car parking covered by a concrete deck acting as a platform for four-storey maisonettes. The second scheme was more conventional and consisted of about four acres of land for industry with the housing arranged in four-storey maisonettes in the Lower Markets – it was entirely on land to the east of Cromac Street. The plans were presented to the community at a public meeting and the deck solution was rejected outright. The city planning department then prepared an amended version of the traditional maisonette scheme by introducing some two-storey housing in an attempt to meet the community's requirements. This last solution was still not acceptable to the community so the management committee of the Redevelopment Association then commissioned the Planning Projects Unit to assist them in preparing a plan of their own (Figure 9.39).

All the residents of the Markets Area were members of the Redevelopment Association, which was therefore fully representative of all shades of opinion in both the Lower and Upper Markets. In order to facilitate the organization of the work required in preparing for development, a management committee was elected. ThIs management committee and the Planning Projects Unit jointly prepared the residents' plan for the Markets Area of Belfast.[31] The ideas were provided by the residents while the professionals in the projects unit advised on method and presentation.

PLANNING GOALS

The management committee and the Planning Projects Unit first drew up a brief for the preparation of the plan, then through a process of many discussions arrived at a hierarchy of planning goals which was followed by a detailed breakdown of those goals into specific objectives. The most important goal was to provide a pleasant residential environment for the existing people of the Markets, This goal was ranked above all others and on its achievement rested the success of the plan. In specific terms it meant the rehousing of 2,200 people on at least 9.5 ha (21 acres) of land in two- and three-storey terrace housing. During the plan-making process the original brief was expanded and redefined to include, for example, the retention of the 'Markets culture'. It was felt by the management committee that the Markets community had a very distinctive way of life which should not pass into oblivion after redevelopment.

This way of life was thought more likely to survive redevelopment if the existing population were to remain in the area and if redevelopment were to proceed in a series of small phases, with whole street blocks rehoused together. It was also proposed that many of the original terraces should be retained and that existing street lines and their names should be a part of the new development. The street was an important part of the local way of life. The residents insisted that it should form the basis of future planning.

Other goals included the rehabilitation of some of the better-quality housing, to relocate small industries in the area, to minimize pedestrian-vehicular conflict and the physical separation of the Upper and Lower Markets; to provide a shopping community centre to act as a focus and, finally, to provide a primary school campus.

THE RESIDENTS' PLAN

The plan was based essentially on the primary goal of rehousing the existing population in two- and three-storey terrace housing, and is illustrated in the plan shown (Figures 9.40-9.44). The aim to retain the identity of the Lower and Upper Markets areas as an expression of the heritage of the community while at the same time ensuring that they do not suffer physical separation, led to the decision that Cromac Street should be sunk 6 m (20 ft) as it passes through the Markets Area. Across part of the lowered Cromac Street it was proposed to build a platform on which was to be sited the new Cromac Square containing an open market surrounded by shops and community buildings. East Bridge Street runs along the northern boundary of the area and is another major traffic route which poses a serious threat to environmental standards. Along this road it was decided to locate a 30 m (100 ft) strip of small industries to act as a barrier between the housing and the traffic. The two schools serving the area were planned to occupy one campus of three acres sited on the derelict abattoir adjacent to the railway line. Car parking was considered by the residents to be a luxury which should be provided within the curtilage of each home and only at the request of the individual. Therefore, the plan was designed to provide the opportunity of accommodating one car-parking space in the yardspace of each home if required. The type of housing preferred by the community was dual-aspect terrace housing with a small private yard at the back, a communal garden or paved area at the front and road access to the yard. This type of housing was chosen from a range of house types and layouts discussed with the management committee which finally decided that the first layout shown in Figure 9.42 was most suited to their purposes. An important consideration in planning the area was a conscious attempt to link it with the surrounding areas. Pedestrian routes link the housing, the shops and community buildings with St Malachy's Church and the city centre in the west and across the Lagan to Ormeau Park in the east. Finally, the plan was devised bearing in mind that this is an inner-city location and that the term 'a pleasant residential environment' in such a situation requires a different interpretation from a suburban context. Thus the plan purposely encouraged a mixing of land uses which it was believed to be in character with the Markets.

ANALYSIS OF PLAN FORM

The residents' plan for the Markets as described and illustrated here is the result of ideas developed by lay people without professional knowledge of architecture, urban design or planning. The finished plan for the area, however, demonstrates that the residents involved in this exercise clearly understand and subscribe to the norms of good design outlined in

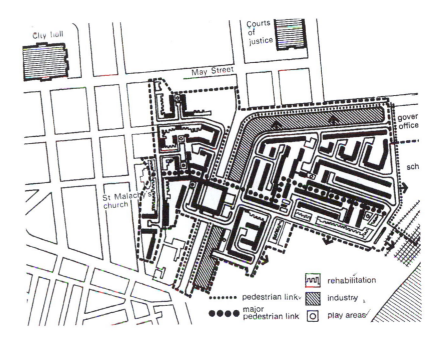

Figure 9.41 Residents' plan, layout, Belfast
Figure 9.42 Housing options

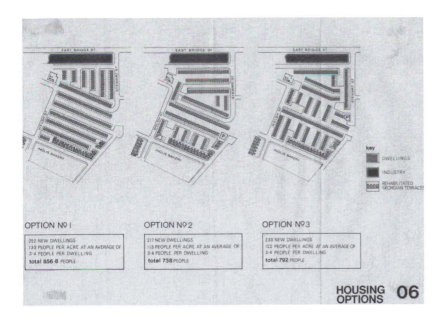

Figure 9.43 Phasing plan

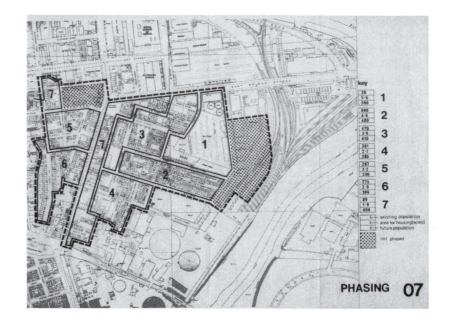

Figure 9.44 Residents' plan: axonometric

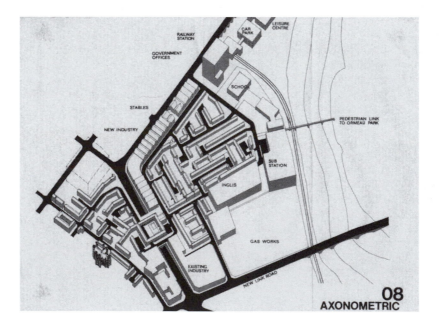

this text. How far the principles of good design are simply the codified common-sense behaviour of a long tradition is impossible to determine. Nevertheless it is worth noting that the aim of the plan was to make this one area and to mitigate the worst effects of dividing it by a traffic route – in other words, to form a unified development. Secondly, the residents wished to establish a clear centre as a focus for the community. The creation of a centre, as both Alexander and Norberg-Schulz attest, is a primary aim for any development and a significant act in the quest for unity.[32] The community was determined to create a strong boundary, or, in Lynch's terms, edge, to the development.[33] Industrial sites in the south, the railway and river to the east were continued in the north and north-west by a narrow barrier of industry. Entrance to the housing areas was restricted to few clearly defined portals ensuring privacy for the community or perhaps, more importantly in Belfast, security; a perfectly defensible space. At the most secure place was located the school with its back to the railway line and river and faced at the front by friendly housing. Finally, the community's choice of urban design forms for the development were the street and square, the main spatial elements of the traditional city. Of course the plan is not a complete unity but this is rarely achieved in practice and for most projects it remains an ideal never quite achieved.

IMPLEMENTATION

The residents' plan for the Markets was unanimously adopted by the community at a public meeting in the area where it was exhibited and explained using slides, models, axonometric and other drawings.

Implementation of the plan, however, was dependent on the agreement of many agencies in addition to the local community. Those agreements were required speedily. Without early agreement on an acceptable plan, housing conditions would have deteriorated further and the community would have become disheartened so triggering a further popula-

tion emigration. A significant emigration of families from the area would have reduced the strength and viability of the community, leaving the way free to develop the land for other purposes. A further pressure for speedy action was thought, by this Catholic community, to be the fragile state of the experimental power-sharing government with its Catholic and Nationalist Minister of Development. This was thought by the leaders of the Markets community to be a window of opportunity, a time when they might expect sympathetic treatment.

Members of the planning executive were invited to meet key residents and the planning projects teams to discuss the rebuilding of the Markets. After a presentation of the residents' plan the government team accepted the general goals of the plan with the exception of the sunken Cromac Street. Since it was calculated that the sinking of Cromac Street would have cost about £1.5 million (1973 prices) more than its simple widening at ground level – a decision in favour of this aspect of the plan would have required central government approval in London and this would have involved further time-consuming negotiations. The community leaders were told that if they accepted this amendment to the plan then an architect would be appointed immediately to work with them in an attempt to achieve the remaining planning goals.

The full committee of the residents' association met to discuss the implications of the views expressed by the planners from Stormont. A long and lively discussion ensued. The general mood of the meeting was to press on with their own plan but the worry about the need for speed was a constraint on their natural inclinations. The argument was finally resolved by one of the wise old men present. He said: 'Sure, Cromac Street won't be widened for years. We should say yes to the present proposal, get the houses built, then later say no to the widening of Cromac Street.' This bit of lateral thinking won the day.

An architect was appointed to work with the community on a revised plan for the Markets Area.

Figure 9.45 Markets Area:
approved plan

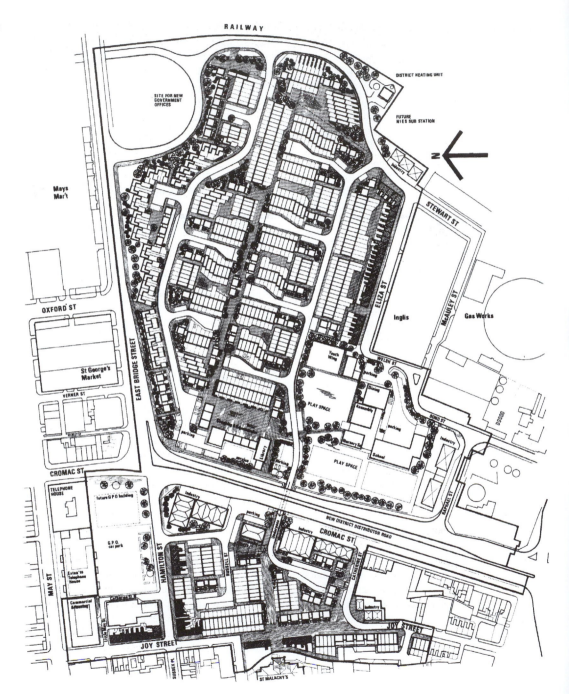

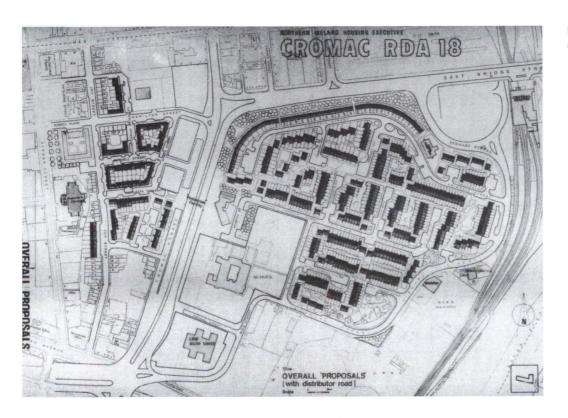

Figure 9.46 Markets Area: amended plan

When completed the plan was presented to a public inquiry on 12 September 1974. The community did not object to the proposals which were approved and formed the basis of the present development. The plan, however, was amended during implementation in a number of significant details (Figures 9.45-9.46).

Looking at the development so far completed it is clear that the main goal of the community has been achieved, those families wishing to remain in the area have been able to do so. They have also been accommodated in terrace housing, an important requirement of the community. During the later stages of redevelopment, because of community pressure the house type was changed for the better. The original plan employed narrow-frontage housing

with small bedrooms in order to achieve the high densities necessary to rehouse the total population. However, additional land was acquired when a local bakery closed and there was a slight fall in the number of families to be rehoused which made it possible in later phases to build at slightly lower densities using wide-frontage housing (Figure 9.47).

The plan, as built, isolates the Upper from the Lower Markets by a proposed six-lane dual carriageway; this is no longer one physical neighbourhood. The centre for the neighbourhood was never completed nor is there any intention to do so in the future. The defensive screen of industry has been replaced by a housing shield, a reasonable substitute if as appears there is no demand for small-scale workshops. Only half of the houses proposed by the

Figure 9.47 Completed
Markets Area

community for conservation have been preserved, the rest were demolished. It is interesting to note that the buildings retained are only those listed by the Historic Buildings and Monuments branch of the Department of the Environment. The Victorian buildings described by the occupants as good homes to live in and designated by the community for conservation were not retained. The houses that have been built, though a vast improvement on the previous housing stock, are suburban in character. They do not preserve the idea of the street architecture of Belfast so loved by the community. It will be interesting to see how the residents adapt to this new housing form. A school campus is part of the development but it now occupies a non-defensible space with a frontage to Cromac Street. Since the school population will not be drawn entirely from the Markets this is probably a reasonable change from the residents' plan.

The Markets community has achieved, after lengthy negotiation and much hard work, its main aim. The community still exists and is housed in the sort of dwellings it demanded, The disappointing feature of the whole process is the end product which has few of the urban design qualities and ideas which the residents were able to inject into their own plan. This is not a criticism of the architects of the project; they had a difficult job reconciling the views of the residents with the planners at City Hall and Stormont.

REGENERATION OF THE RIVERSIDE: NEWARK IN NOTTINGHAMSHIRE

Since the early 1970s the riverside in Newark has been undergoing a process of renewal and regeneration. Before the process of regeneration began, the River Trent and its associated canal and locks in Newark were largely unused, unkempt and very obviously unloved. The industrial buildings along its length were rundown and dilapidated. Even the hulk of the twelfth century Castle, the site of much activ-

Figure 9.48 Town Hall, Newark, by Carr of York

Figure 9.49 Rehabilitation, Market Square, Newark

ity in the Civil War, was relatively unknown to the tourist and ignored by much of the local population. With the death of canal trade the town again turned away from the river and shrank back to its centre. Viability and commercial life was centred on Market Square overlooked by Carr's Town Hall and dominated by the 87 metre high spire of St Mary Magdalene. This was the core of Newark and it was from here that the spark of regeneration was kindled. Many buildings of architectural and historic interest, some dating back to medieval times, have been restored using a combination of private and public finance. The confidence shown by such belief in the fabric and future of the town is an essential backcloth to successful regeneration (Figures 9.48 and 9.49).

Regeneration is a long-term incremental process. The development of Newark's riverside is no exception to this general rule. Regeneration is an expensive undertaking: it requires the organization, structuring and husbanding of a multitude of resources. These resources include capital, land and, most critically, human resources. Maintaining community interest and commitment in a long-term project is one key to a successful outcome. There will be times over the life-span of a project, particularly during an economic downturn, when activities cease, 'Financial plans for the project should explicitly recognize the cyclical nature of private investment. While planners cannot be expected to accurately forecast the duration and timing of a recession, it seems foolish to assume that a 20-year project will not encounter one . . . An agency should have plans for infrastructure and social housing ready for a down cycle, in order to keep busy and maintain momentum.'[34] Keeping the interest of key actors in the regeneration process during periods of slowdown is possibly as important as making the necessary financial plans, so that coalitions and initiatives are rebuilt when the economy revives. Regeneration is a collaborative venture, a partnership involving public and private finance. Community, as used here, is therefore an all inclusive concept. Successful regeneration involves many sections of the community; it includes those directing the political process, innovative public officials, those driving the private development process; it also includes the large body of lay people who form the backbone of bodies such as civic societies concerned with conservation and the protection of the local environment.

Newark has a strategic location in relation to transport networks originating at the junction of the Roman Fosse Way and the north-south crossing point of the Trent. The later developments of inland waterways strengthened the importance of the river and with it Newark's trading position. The building of the London-Edinburgh railway line gave a further boost to Newark's centrality. London which is only just over one hour away by high-speed train is fast becoming within reasonable commuting range. The A1 Motorway, which has replaced the Great North Road, by-passes the town. Together with the east-west by-pass opened in 1990, the A1(M) has eased congestion in the town while increasing accessibility for those with business there. The growing accessibility of Newark from London and from the surrounding region places the town in a strong position to capitalize on development pressures in the East Midlands. Channelling some of those developmental pressures into riverside regeneration will itself increase Newark's attraction for tourists, new business and as a location for commuters.

The regeneration of the River Trent is a tale of two contrasting styles of development. To the west of the Castle is the Millgate river frontage and the scene of late 1970s style regeneration, while around the Castle area and to its east, is regeneration in the manner of the late 1980s and 1990s. The plan for Millgate was adopted by the Planning Committee of the then Newark District Council in January 1975. The plan, however, was based on surveys and planning studies dating back to the early 1970s. The plan for Millgate was drawn up after twenty years' neglect of this potentially attractive gateway into the town of Newark. The neglect consequently led to a lack of confidence in the area by both the community and those wishing to invest in the town. The plan aimed at reinstating the area as a lively, pleasant place in which to live, work and enjoy unique riverside amenities. A further aim was to restore Millgate's architectural and environmental quality.[35]

Although run down, the area around Millgate Street had many advantages. Amid the vacant plots and broken frontages there were, even in the mid

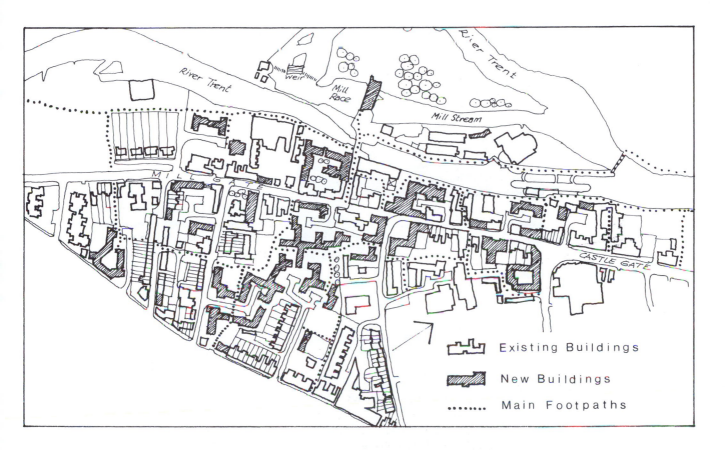

Existing Buildings

New Buildings

······ Main Footpaths

1970s, areas of picturesque townscape with red brick Georgian and Victorian housing. Because of its architectural qualities Millgate received Outstanding Conservation Grading from the Department of the Environment. Much of the fine property located in the area was capable of improvement and it has, indeed, been upgraded. The plan envisaged river walkways on both sides of the Trent and the refurbishment of old warehouses for use as museums, restaurants, bars and craft-based workshops (Figures 9.50 and 9.51).

Millgate was fortunate in two other ways. It had a strong community willing to work with the Council and its planners in order to improve the

Figure 9.50 Early proposals for Millgate, Newark
Figure 9.51 Rehabilitation of warehouse, Millgate, Newark

Figure 9.52 Millgate, Newark

Figure 9.53 Access to the canal, Millgate

local area. One experiment in public participation which occurred in Millgate is described in Chapter 4 of *Urban Design: Method and Techniques*.[36] That particular participation exercise was only one small

part of a much wider programme of collaboration by the Council which has resulted in a fine example of urban design. Millgate was also fortunate in the innovative planners and other professionals who worked on the project for the Council. The planning approach used in the regeneration of Millgate was, for that time, highly unconventional. Middle management planners of the Council responsible for Millgate were encouraged to experiment with techniques of participation and supported in their deployment of entrepreneurial skills.

This is how Aspbury and Harrison describe the approach: 'Middle management immersed itself in the community, relying on personal contact with residents, employers, landowners, builders, and developers, to generate the "nuts and bolts" of the project. They became quasi-social workers, helping individuals solve problems in other areas of central and local government, and with the statutory undertakers. By stepping outside narrow professional roles, the officers eased residents through the transition, and helped them overcome the inertia and remoteness of the bureaucratic machine where it was adversely affecting the project. This strengthened the bond between the local authority officers and the people of the area, forming the basis of genuine public participation.'[37]

Securing finance for the regeneration of Millgate was critical for the project's success. Both financial and human resources were strictly limited. There was no specific budget for Millgate so public investment became, 'an amalgamation of existing departmental budgets, outside subsidies and grant aid – such as the housing programme, industrial investment, general improvement area works, home improvement grants, town scheme, and section 10 grants. Selected buildings and sites were tackled by these means in the hope that private sector investment would be rekindled, following the lead set by the local authority.'[38] The dedication and skill of the officers of the council, sustained by the political will of the elected members of the council and supported by popular consent, has been the platform for continued private sector investment in Millgate. As in many regeneration projects the first to invest in the area were small developers. It was not until the later stages of regeneration that the larger developers became interested in making a serious commitment to the project: 'Most waterfront implementation agencies should expect that their first private investments will come from small builders rather than big developers, who often pursue larger opportunities on less risky sites.'[39]

Figures 9.52 and 9.53 illustrate the results of this phase of the riverside in Newark. The development along the Millgate water's edge is small-scale sensitive infill of sites between existing buildings of architectural merit or historic importance. The existing buildings, many of which are warehouses, have been rehabilitated and used for leisure purposes. The waterfront is a delightful mixture of residences, restaurants, public buildings and craft workshops. The original river frontage was privately owned and comprised warehouses rising sheer from the canal. An aim of the plan for the area was to obtain increased public access to the water. This has been achieved in a number of different ways. Sites for housing have been designed as open ended squares facing onto the water; the waterfront elevations of former industrial buildings have been opened up using large widows from which diners can view the passing water traffic; existing ginnels and newly formed passageways have been landscaped and lead naturally down to the water's edge, opening occasionally on to a small open space; a footbridge leads to a riverside walk and to the Island site between the canal and the River Trent. The aims of the original plan dating from the early 1970s have been fully achieved in a most elegant and civilized manner.

The focal point of riverside opportunity for development in Newark since the late 1980s has been the area around the bridge over the Trent and beneath the walls of the twelfth century Castle. The site of the former cattle market and the adjacent Castle Station Site, both overlooked by the Castle,

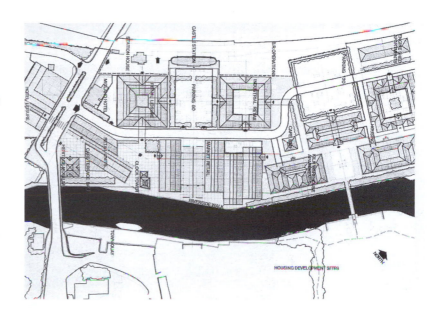

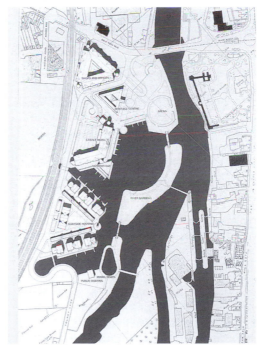

Figure 9.54 Design study for canal development, Newark (Brock and Scoffham)
Figure 9.55 Winning competition entry for Canal Development, Newark (Brock and Scoffham)

Figure 9.56 Newark Castle, centre piece of regeneration proposals
Figure 9.57 Riverside walk, Newark

were unused and derelict, presenting developers with extensive open areas, a wonderful opportunity for the development of lucrative real estate. The area was the subject of a design study by Brock and Scoffham, a consultancy associated with the University of Nottingham (Figure 9.54). A two stage competition for developers elicited a number of viable development proposals. The project, however, fell into abeyance, which according to Scoffham, was because of: '. . .high interest rates and the understandable unwillingness of a developer to enter into a necessarily prescriptive Section 52 Agreement. . .'[40] (Figure 9.55).

The site of the former Cattle Market became derelict in 1989 when the market was relocated to a new site on the edge of Newark. After a process of decontamination, the site was landscaped and has become a much needed town park, another feature of successful regeneration. The river frontage of Castle Station Site has been developed by Nottingham Community Housing Association. The site accommodates a 176-unit social housing scheme comprising: 83 flats for rent, 58 of which are refurbished accommodation; 28 units of new sheltered accommodation;

46 family homes for rent; and 18 shared ownership flats. Inland from the riverfront, Waitrose, a member of the John Lewis Partnership chain of departmental stores, has developed a site for a 40,000 square feet store.[41] Former industrial buildings on the site which were identified as being worthy of conservation have been refurbished and reused in an imaginative way (Figures 9.56 and 9.57).

The Newark and Sherwood District Council together with other institutions in the Partnership, successfully lodged a Single Regeneration Budget Challenge Fund Bid and a Capital challenge Bid to raise further capital for regeneration.[42] Twenty million pounds was raised for the completion of the landscaping schemes, to refurbish former industrial buildings and to build a marina. The regeneration

programme for the Northgate riverside in Newark was not entirely a matter of physical developments but included many actions of a social, economic and educational nature, enabling residents to gain access to employment, developing community based training schemes and even providing childcare facilities.[43]

This successful regeneration of a fine country town is the result of sound management structures being in place serviced by people with the ability to assemble the necessary resources. The 'spin-offs' from the riverside regeneration have filtered through to the rest of Newark; small developments in scale and in keeping with Newark's traditional built form, have extended the town centre, creating a number of new shopping streets; the old core of the town no longer has that faded appearance of impover-

ished gentility which was the hall-mark of this fine old town 30 years ago (Figures 9.58 and 9.59). When the rail link with Europe is complete and the journey from Newark to Paris takes only four hours, Newark will have in place an urban structure ready to capitalize on the inevitable development pressures.

BARCELONA, THE REGENERATION OF THE SEAFRONT

Barcelona has much to teach urban designers: it has a very fine old medieval city, 'Barrio Gotico' with areas of which have been pedestrianized. The planned nineteenth-century expansion, the

'Eixample', is a model of its type: as is the imaginative regeneration of the waterfront completed in the late twentieth century, which is the main concern of this case study. Barcelona has recently won accolades normally reserved for individuals – Harvard University's Prince Charles Award in 1993 and the RIBA Gold Medal in 1999.

With the death of Franco in 1975, nearly 40 years of dictatorship and isolation ended. The restoration of democracy stimulated whirlwind changes: as a result of joining NATO and the European Union, the country looked out beyond its borders, so that by the mid-1980s the economy was on a dramatic upswing. Within Spain there was a resurgence of regional identities. Regional self-government was given to Barcelona in 1980: it was given control of domestic trade, regional economic development, planning, housing, public works, transport and public space. This autonomy was the decisive factor in Barcelona's physical transformation, as it aimed to

be a city worthy of being the capital of Catalunya. This transformation of the city and its regeneration was given added impetus by the selection of Barcelona in 1986 to host the 25th Olympic games in 1992.[44]

Barcelona is located on Spain's northern Mediterranean Coast. For centuries, the ancient rivers Besos and Llobregat formed the western and eastern boundaries of Barcelona: they also determined the position of access routes into the city. The sea and the coastal strip are to the south of the city, while to the north is the Sierra of Collserola, a natural mountain barrier to urban development; the plain on which the city has been built is confined within these natural barriers of the sea, rivers and mountains: it is punctuated by the foothills of the Collserola and the two hills near the sea, Montjuic and Mons Taber, a crest overbuilt by earlier settlements (Figure 9.60). The piercing of the Sierra Collserola and the building of other major highways

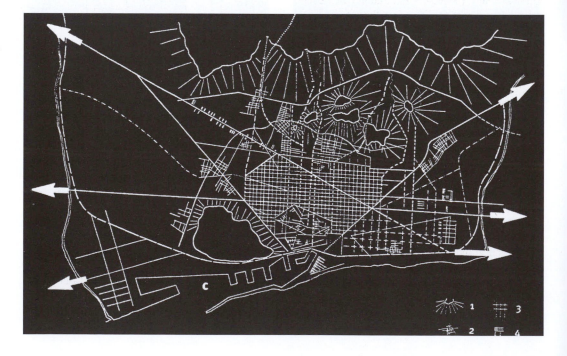

Figure 9.60 The Barcelona Plain. (Taken from Map C on the 2nd illustration in the introduction to *Barcelona* by Guasa)

in Valles, Llobregat and the littoral has stimulated new urban growth beyond the historical confines of the Barcelona plain.[45]

Barcelona's distinct urban form originated some 2,000 years ago as a compact Roman *oppidum*. The walled medieval centre expanded from that core, supported by an economy linked closely to maritime activities. By the nineteenth century, growth stimulated by industrialization necessitated the demolition of the city walls to permit its expansion. This expansion was based upon a grid plan by the engineer urbanist Ildefons Cerda. The Eixample, which is Catalan for expansion, is composed of 550 square blocks set out on an 113 metre module. The plan by Cerda covered the alluvial plane between sea and mountain incorporating outlying independent towns, increasing the city footprint to ten times its original size. The most central part of the Eixample straddling the Passeig de Gracia became the context in which modernist architects such as Lluis Dominech i Montaner and Antoni Gaudí built ostentatious homes for the turn-of-the-century nouveaux riches. It was here too in *Eixample* that Guadi started the building of his still unfinished masterpiece, Sagrada Familia[46] (Figures 9.61 and 9.62a/b).

The World Expositions of 1888 and 1929 brought about further development in two large districts. The 1888 Fair transformed the Cuitadella - the military fort bordering the old city to the north - into parkland. The 1929 Exposition, in which Mies van der Rohe built his Barcelona Pavilion, was the stimulus for the taming of Montjuic, the hilly outcrop that dominates the city on the southwest. Barcelona has a long tradition of hosting major international events and in using those events to further the aims of city growth and development. The celebration of the Olympic games in 1992 created yet another pretext for achieving planning objectives that under more normal circumstances may not have been possible. Very ambitious urban projects have been achieved in Barcelona in a short time.[47] Barcelona has been transformed in little more than a

decade, built on the impetus derived from the organization of a venue to host the Olympic games. An event that in itself had no urban planning goals: this experience that derives from Barcelona's recent history, provides a valuable lesson for other cities.

The transformation of Barcelona in the 1990s had its roots in the early nineteen eighties. A team of professionals in the City Planning Department, led by Oriol Bohigas, followed an aggressive policy of buying unused land and obsolete factories for transfer into public ownership.[48] This enlightened policy permitted Barcelona to tackle problems such as the lack of public space in a very dense urban structure. Between 1980 and 1992 many spaces were created for public use, a number being in the old city, Ciutat Vella. In the process of creating small public spaces in the urban fabric, large areas of the Ciuta Vella have been pedestrianized and to some extent, the movement of traffic has been tamed. James and

Figure 9.61 Casa Mila La Pedrera by Gaudí.

Figure 9.62 Sagrada Familia by Gaudí

Anne Thomas have described the control of vehicles in three-interconnected squares in Barcelona.[49] Below are passages from their paper illustrating the lessons to be learned from sharing public space with the motor vehicle, a requirement for the planning of any successful neighbourhood of high density and mixed land use, and a favoured solution to urban living by those advocating sustainable development here in Britain. '...Plaza del Pi, had a floorscape of rectangular blocks, some in marble, no kerbs or steps, and six trees – the trees shaded pedestrians and those seated at the two restaurants. Bollards... limited car parking to the perimeter... Pedestrian movement flowed through the space, enclosed by the dominant fourteenth century Church of Santa Maria del Pi to the east...'. The rest of the buildings – 'were tall, mainly five and a half to six storeys high, so there was an intense sense of enclosure... Here, in the centre of medieval Barcelona, the public space is where the citizen lives – from early morning to very late at night. The pedestrians, who walk about the streets and plazas are still supreme, and the motor vehicle becomes just a tool to be used, part of the service industry,' (Figure 9.63). The pedestrian controls the centre of the spaces in the old city following the example of the Ramblas Boulevard, the main street of Barcelona: here, the central area of the street is given over to market stalls, exhibitions and cafés, forming a pedestrian mall for parade and leisurely display, while the vehicles are restricted to side lanes.

Barcelona seized the possibilities offered by the Olympic games to forge links between the city and the sea. The Moll de Fusta along the old Barcelona docks was the first attempt to tackle mobility in a city paralysed by heavy traffic and at the same time renew contact between the city and its waterfront. The thoroughfares were repositioned below ground level to permit easy access to the waterfront for pedestrians. This idea became a major objective of waterfront developments for city planning officials. The culmination of this policy is the redevelopment of the Port Vell Marina, planned by Pinon and

Figure 9.63 Plaza del Pi, sketch by Thomas, J. and A. *Urban Design Quarterly*, no. 71

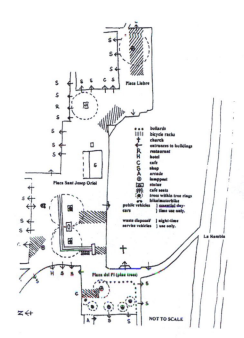

Figure 9.64 Rambla de Mar

Viaplana. An elegant bridge connects the Ramblas with the island-like Port Vell Marina with its shops, restaurants and multiplex. The maritime footbridge is set slightly off-centre to the Placa del Portal de la Pau and the Columbus statue, which marks the end of the 2-kilometre long historic Ramblas. This long and elegant boulevard is extended via the footbridge onto the Rambla de Mar which is part bridge, board-walk and plaza, a public realm that has been extended into the port as a recreational promenade – a quite different experience from its urban counterpart (Figures 9.64 to 9.66).

The Olympic Village, Nova Icaria, was another opportunity for Barcelona to enhance contact between city and sea. The masterplan for Nova Icaria by Martorell, Bohigas, Mackay and Puigdomenech is, in some ways, exemplary in its attempt to integrate the new areas of the Olympic Village with the rest of the city (Figure 9.68). Land was made available for the project by demolishing redundant industrial buildings and railway tracks that had previously blocked Barcelona off from the sea. The tracks have been realigned and sweep north; they have been buried below-ground in front of an arc of housing that faces onto a landscaped area extending far into the city, and linking the new village into the existing urban fabric.[50] The Cinturon, running parallel to the old railway, has been sunk and bridged by parks: the boulevard above it has been tamed by realigning the lanes so that pedestrians encounter each lane separately, while the road along the seaside winds in a snake-like fashion to aid traffic calming and is screened with yet more landscaping (Figure 9.69). Moreover, the roads and the traffic they carry do not intrude upon the seafront, which connects visually with the edge of properties that face out onto the Mediterranean.

Figure 9.65 Rambla de Mar

Figure 9.66 Rambla de Mar

Figure 9.67 Rambla de Mar

Figure 9.68 Plan of Nova Icaria, taken from Buchanan, *Urbane Village*, *Architectural Review*, August 1992

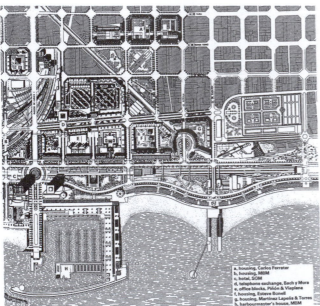

a, housing, Carlos Ferrater
b, housing, MBM
c, hotel, SOM
d, telephone exchange, Bach y Mora
e, office blocks, Piñón & Viaplana
f, housing, Esteve Bonell
g, housing, Martínez Lapeña & Torres
h, harbourmaster's house, MBM

The Cerda grid is extended into Nova Iscaria. The Passeig de Carles 1 extends from Gaudí's Sagrada Familia through Nova Iscaria, terminating on the broad pier edging the new harbour. As a gateway, and to mark the meeting of city and sea, is a pair of towers of identical dimensions but different designs. The rather boring towers are no fit frame for Gaudí's great church which, even when the mighty central tower is complete, will appear to be dwarfed by these lesser pillars. The 2.5 kilometres or 1.5 mile axis to Sagrada Familia deserved a more subtle and appropriate treatment (Figure 9.69).

The collection of apartment blocks which infill the Cerda grid of the Olympic Village were each designed by an award-winning architectural team: it is a demonstration of the way in which peripheral blocks can maintain a continuity of massing and façade. Like the older buildings that line the water-side of the old port, these buildings form a neutral backcloth for the activities along the quays and jetties: they also provide a permeable edge permit-

Figure 6.69 Seafront landscaping

Figure 9.70 Twin Towers, Nova Icaria.

Figure 9.71 Olympic
Harbour

Figure 9.72 Olympic
Harbour

Figure 9.73 Olympic Harbour

ting movement through to the development behind the waterside frontage. In front of this development is the Olympic Harbour, a great enclosed public space with a myriad moored boats and many lively quayside cafés, bars and restaurants: it is buzzing with activity (Figures 9.71 to 9.73).

Using the Olympic games as catalyst, Barcelona has developed 4 kilometres of exciting waterfront where the pedestrian is given priority and where public space in the form of streets and squares is of the highest environmental quality. Part of this waterfront is the old dockland that has been remodelled and revitalized; part has been imaginatively created on a site formerly occupied by derelict industries; and part of this wonderful recreation facility

includes the creation of beaches for the residents of the city. In addition to the waterfront development, Barcelona has embarked upon a process of improving urban space in the older parts of the city where streets and squares have been given back to the pedestrian and where the motor vehicle has been tamed.

CONCLUSION

Five case studies have been discussed in this chapter. The area around St Paul's after the Second World War was planned by Holford with advice from a special committee of experts. The minister himself took a particular interest in the subject. The resulting development was the subject of much public debate and criticism. The second post-war attempt at redesigning St Paul's precinct has again, after an architectural competition and two exhibitions, been the subject of debate. It remains to be seen if the results will live up to expectations.

The developers of the Isle of Dogs in the early days of the project were oblivious to public opinion. The sole concerns were profitability and efficiency of operation. The results are there for all to see and warrant no further comment.

In the third case study, Belfast Markets Area, genuine attempts were made to involve the general public in the planning and development process, and with some notable success. The failures in design occurred when the views of the residents were given low priority. Perhaps it may be time to listen more carefully to the people. There seems enough evidence elsewhere to show that people know best about the problems that beset them and can formulate common-sense solutions to these problems which work out not to be outrageously expensive.

The catchphrase in a democracy is - 'The people know best' - applying this in the field of urban design might let some light into the closed world of architectural theory.[51]

The fourth case study, the development of the riverside in Newark, examines the process of urban regeneration. It has a particular concern with the temporal dimension of urban design. Unlike the other three case studies which examine the different spatial scales of urban design, this case study gives emphasis to the timescale of urban design, giving a reminder that our cities are the result of an incremental process which involves many actors for many years.

The fifth case study is an account of the developments in Barcelona that are associated with the Olympic Games held there in 1992. The case study examines the creation of streets and squares as part of a large-scale urban restructuring process, a reminder that the role of the urban designer can involve work at a metropolitan scale, while at the same time being deeply engaged in the detailed design of street and square where the effect of the urban designer's work is immediate and most apparent.

NOTES

1   Holford. William. St Paul's report on the surroundings of St Paul's Cathedral in the City of London. In *Town Planning Review'*, Volume XXVII, No 2, July 1956, pp.58-98

2   Downes, Kerry. *Hawksmoor*, Thames and Hudson, London, 1969, p.88

3   Bor, Walter. The St Paul's precinct saga. In *The Planner*, Volume 74, No 5, May 1988, pp.26-28

4   Holford, W. Op cit, p.68

5   Ibid, pp.69-70

6   Sitte, C. *Der Stadte-Bau*, Carl Graeser and Co., Wien, 1901.

7   Kennedy, Maev. Paternoster's piazzas fit for a prince. In *The Guardian*, 19 November 1988, p.3

8   Krier, Leon and Jencks, Charles. Paternoster Square. In *Architectural Design*, Volume 58, No 1/2, 1988, pp.VII-XIII

9   Ibid. p.IX

10 Simpson, John. Paternoster Square redevelopment project. In *Architectural Design*, Volume 58, No 9/10, 1988, pp.78-80

11 Tallis, John. *London Street Views, 1838-1840*, introduced by Peter Jackson, Nattali & Maurice. London, 1969

12 Glancey, Jonathan. Is this fit company for St Paul's? In *The Independent*, 29 May 1991

13 Paternoster Associates. *Paternoster Square*, Paternoster Associates, London, 1991

14 Glancey, J. Op cit

15 Architects Journal, Thumbs down from city for Prince's dream of Paternoster. *Architects Journal*, 21 December 1995, p. 11

16 Architects Journal, What's right for St Paul's? *Architects Journal,* 2 May 1996, pp. 18-19

17 Architects Journal, Third time lucky with Whitfield masterplan, *Architects Journal,* 27 November 1997, pp.10-12

18 Architects Journal, Queen Victoria Street, *Architects Journal,* 10 June 1999, p. 55

19 Pawley, Martin. Final act of the Fawcett saga. In *The Guardian,* 5 February 1990

20 Hollamby, E., Gosling, D., Cullen, G. et al. *Isle of Dogs: Urban Design Plan: A Guide to Design and Development.* London Docklands Development Corporation, November 1982

21 Gosling, D. and Maitland, B. *Concepts of Urban Design,* Academy Editions, London, 1984, p.149

22 Wilford, M. Off to the races, or going to the Dogs? In *Architectural Design,* Volume 54, No 1/2, 1984, pp.8-15

23 Aldous, T. Crossing the river from a different angle, *Architects Journal,* 12 March, 1998, pp.10-11

24 Edwards, B. Deconstructing the City: London Docklands, *Urban Design Quarterly,* 69, January 1999, pp. 22-24

25 See for example, Sandy Row Redevelopment Association, *Sandy Row at the Public Enquiry,* Sandy Row Redevelopment Association, Belfast, 1972

26 McKay, Kathy, Gryzmek, Brian and Holden, Jo. *The Markets,* Gown (Belfast), 9 May 1972

27 County Borough of Belfast, City Planning Department. *The Markets - Redevelopment Area 18,* County Borough of Belfast, Belfast, August 1971

28 Ulster Architectural Heritage Society. *Survey and Recommendations for the Joy Street and Hamilton Street district of Belfast,* Ulster Architectural Heritage Society, Belfast, 1971

29 Belfast County Borough, City Planning Department. *Industry and Commerce in Redevelopment 18,* Belfast County Borough, Belfast, February 1971

30 Taggart, W.D.R. and Taggart, R.T. *Cromac RDA 18, Planning Appraisal,* W.D.R. & R.T. Taggart, Belfast, 1985, p.15

31 Markets Redevelopment Association and The Planning Projects Unit, *The Markets Area of Belfast, The People's Plan* (Preliminary Report), Queen's University, Belfast, November 1973

32 Alexander, Christopher, et al. *A New Theory of Urban Design,* Oxford University Press, Oxford, 1987 and Norberg-Schulz, Christian. *Existence, Space and Architecture,* Studio Vista, London, 1971

33 Lynch, Kevin. *The Image of the City,* MIT Press, Cambridge, Mass., 1960

34 Gordon, D.L.A. Financing Urban Waterfront Redevelopment, *APA Journal,* Spring, 1997

35 *Newark Advertiser,* 25 January 1975.

36 Moughtin, J.C. et al. *Urban Design: Method and Technique,* Butterworth-Heinemann, Oxford, 1999

37 Aspbury, A. and Harrison, R. Newark-Millgate Revival, *Planner,* Volume 68, February, 1982

38 Ibid

39 Gordon, D.L.A. Op cit

40 Scoffham, E.R., Balancing Community and Commercial Interests in Newark-on-Trent, in White, K.N., et al., *Urban Waterside Regeneration: Problems and Prospects,* Ellis Horwood Ltd, Chichester, 1993

41 Nottingham Evening Post: *Notts Commercial Property Weekly,* 22 October 1996

42 Newark and Sherwood District Council, 'Capital Challenge Bid for Newark Riverside Regeneration', internal publication of Newark and Sherwood District Council, undated report

43 Newark and Sherwood District Council, 'SRB Challenge Fund Bid for Newark Riverside Regeneration, internal publication of Newark and Sherwood District Council, undated report

44 Cole, R. Homage to Barcelona. *Urban Design,* Issue no. 69, 1999, pp. 11-13

45 Guasa, M. et al. *Barcelona: A Guide to its Modern Architecture, 1860-2002,* Actar, London, 2002

46 Nonell, J.B. *Antonio Gaudí: Master Architect,* Abbeville Press, London, 2000

47 Guasa, M., et al., op cit

48 Canogar, S., Major events in Spain, *Urban Design Quarterly,* Issue no. 58, April 1996, pp. 29-31

49 Thomas, J. and A. Three squares in Barcelona, *Urban Design Quarterly,* Issue no. 71 July 1999, pp. 38-39

50 Buchanan, P. Urbane village, *Architectural Review,* August, no. 1146, 1992, pp. 30-31

51 See for example, Moughtin, J.C. et al. *The Nottingham Experiments, Towards Positive Participation in Planning.* Institute of Planning Studies, Nottingham, 1979, and Moughtin, J.C. and Bone, Daniel *The Building of a Community, Second Experience at Millgate in Newark, Nottinghamshire,* Institute of Planning Studies, Nottingham, 1981

CONCLUSION

10

The twentieth century was not known for the building of wonderful streets or squares. This is of course a gross oversimplification, a generalization of almost heroic proportions. Not all twentieth century streets are as ugly as Nottingham's Maid Marion Way (Figures 2.39-2.41). Nevertheless, the statement does contain some truth. Most commentators on architecture, of whatever aesthetic predisposition, could point to examples of twentieth century buildings, which they would consider to be as great as the Taj Mahal, the Parthenon or one of the great Gothic Cathedrals. Moreover, there probably would be much overlap and agreement between the various lists produced. Could such commentators or critics find examples of twentieth century squares to equal or rival the spaces around St. Mark's in Venice, or even the less imposing medieval squares that can be found in many European cities? Or could those critics name twentieth century streets to rival the main street in Chipping Campden or the arcaded streets of Bologna? (Figures 5.24-5.27 and 5.29-5.30). The answer to both these questions, I suspect, is: 'with great difficulty!' If there is any truth in the statement at the beginning of this paragraph, then why is it so? And what can be learnt from this apparent failure?

This concluding chapter will be confined largely to a discussion of the poverty of design in twentieth century street and square in Britain. The planned centres of the British new towns, or the rebuilt centres of older cities such as Coventry, which were destroyed by bombing during the Second World War, exhibit few of the qualities of the traditional British town or city centre such as Lincoln or York. Gibberd who wrote a fine book on urban design, failed to reproduce a decent square or street in his new town at Harlow. Harlow has other features that are commendable, but the public spaces in the town centre do not compare with the great European public squares and streets that Gibberd knew so well, and which he analysed with such clarity in his book.[1]

The unproductive and unrewarding task of cataloguing the urban design disasters committed in the name of good planning is not the aim of this chapter: its purpose is to try to discover why the street and square in the twentieth century received such little attention from those building towns and cities. This is particularly puzzling when one considers that from the time of Sitte in the late nineteenth century, there has been a body of literature setting out a theory for the design of public space. This literature seemed to have little effect on the outcome, either in the sphere of public development in new towns, social housing, or in private developments such as the vast shopping centres and business parks.

The theoretical legacy of Sitte was particularly strong in Britain with writers such as Unwin, Gibberd and Cullen, following quite clearly the spirit of his writing.[2] However, there was an alternative view of urbanism that proved more influential as far as architectural education was concerned. This other view of urbanism came from Le Corbusier and those in the 'avante guarde' of the Modern Movement in architecture. Siegfried Giedion, as we saw earlier, dismissed Sitte's ideas as palliatives, and instead, he advocated mass housing, vast engineering road works and comprehensive city centre redevelopment.[3] Le Corbusier wrote: 'Our streets no longer work. Streets are an obsolete notion. There ought not to be such a thing as streets; we have to create something to replace them'.[4] Gropius expressed similar views: 'Instead of the ground floor windows looking on to blank walls, or into cramped and sunless courtyards, they command a clear view of the sky with a broad expanse of grass and trees which separate the blocks and serve as playgrounds for children'.[5] With a philosophy like this being presented as the designer's guide, it is not surprising that streets in the twentieth century were considered unworthy of study by designers. The design agenda outlined by Le Corbusier, Gropius and others was realized, in part, by high rise housing developments that were so common in Britain: some like 'The Piggeries' in Everton Heights, Liverpool, were demolished as unsuitable for human occupation.

Architects and town planners can only work within the parameters set by the structure and culture of any given society. Therefore, it would be both unfair and inaccurate to attribute to the professionals all the blame for badly designed public space. The nation's long and unsatiated love affair with the motorcar has been instrumental in the destruction of town centres as attractive places in which to live, work and shop. The last century witnessed a growing flight to the suburbs, where the use of the car is both a necessity and where it is most effective as a means of moving from place to place: it is here too, in the suburbs where property prices for first-time home buyers tend to be cheapest, where schools are thought to be best, and where addresses assume, by popular consensus, a status of being 'up-market'. Low-density suburbia is not the ideal type of development to support public transport, which to be effective, requires a densely populated catchment area within walking distance from the transport corridors. The consequent disadvantage imposed on public transport by extensive suburban development further strengthens the need for private transport and in many cases, even a need for individuals within a family to have his or her own car.

Shopping and other services, previously associated with a thriving town centre, followed the pull of the suburban population locating in out-of-town sites, having good road connections and space for car parking. Some town authorities, in an effort to save a traditional centre and compete with out-of-town shopping, improved urban roads, built multi-storeyed car parks and massive shopping malls, so destroying fine streets and squares, the very lifeblood of a lively sustainable town centre. Massive investment in development to facilitate both the moving as well as the stationary car is partly responsible for the destruction of the fabric of the public realm in many traditional towns and cities of this country.

Architects and town planners are aware of the problems that are associated with the unbridled growth in car use. Members of both professions have given clear warnings about the consequences of not making an adequate public response. Probably the most thorough study of the effect on the environment of increased car use, together with an account of the alternative methods for dealing with the phenomenon, was given in the report *Traffic in Towns*.[6] In that report, the author,

Buchanan, demonstrated quite clearly the implications for towns and cities of planning for the expected growth in car use: without massive, expensive investment in road infrastructure the result predicted was gridlock and chaos, a state of affairs which grows daily closer. Clearly, at the other extreme, building the infrastructure that was required to meet the demand for car use imposed an unacceptable burden on the urban environment. Other writers have pointed out that building additional urban roads and improving others merely increases the demand for more cars, so hastening eventual gridlock.[7] Such writers affirm that it is impossible to satisfy the demand for free car movement in Britain without destroying our urban environment and its culture of streets and squares. In Britain, we now have the worst possible situation: a run-down public transport system, a road network incapable of dealing with increasing car usage and a vast suburbia, which, because of its low density, is dependent upon the car for the movement of goods and people and unsuitable for service by public transport. Clearly, an effective public transport system is the basic requirement for the development of compact, fine-grained sustainable cities of mixed land use, and the foundation for a network of urbane streets and squares. Anything short of this holistic urban design agenda is superficial, merely treating the symptoms of the ills that beset our cities.

The structure of the building industry is also a factor that militated against the creation of civilized streets and squares in the twentieth century. The building industry is most cost-effective and most profitable when large construction firms are engaged in the development of cleared sites for large-scale projects. In addition, the economies of scale for shopping developments inevitably result in out-of-town shopping malls or in-town developments such as the Victoria and Broadmarsh Centres in Nottingham. Such developments have been built on tracts of land formerly occupied by a warren of public streets, which have since been replaced by private spaces, closed to the public at times determined by the private landowner. This is privatization of public space by 'the back-door'; it emphasizes the lack of value placed upon public space in the last century, an attitude that must be challenged if we wish to build vibrant cities. Furthermore, large sites of single use, whether for housing, offices or shopping, are the very antithesis of the public square or the public street, each with its myriad interconnected land uses.

The political system in Britain does not support the development of compact sustainable cities. Cities of streets and squares served by an effective public transport system where car use is discouraged require long-term support and nurture. As we have seen, during the Renaissance the Papacy in Rome performed the role of guardian of the urban environment, being responsible for the many fine public squares in Rome so admired today (see pages 90-97). Can our system of democratic government perform a similar function to that of the Papacy in Renaissance Rome? The jury is still out! Development of the vibrant city of streets and squares as we have seen is, today, dependent upon an effective public transport system. The development of an integrated public transport system for the towns and cities of this country requires long-term commitment, spanning several Parliaments. In effect, it means the transfer of resources from private to public transport, followed by a process of converting car use to the use of public transport. This transfer of resources would take two main forms. Firstly, it would mean higher costs for the motorist in terms of petrol prices, road taxes and road pricing: this will make motoring more costly, particularly in towns and cities. Secondly, the transfer of resources would take the more direct form: development of costly public transport facilities at the expense of road improvements; it may also mean a direct subsidy to public transport fares.

The development of an effective public transport system may take up to 20 years, which is four or five Parliaments. Competition between our political parties means that no Government, of whatever political persuasion, can afford to alienate too many voters. Most of us living in Britain today own, use and love our cars. How many voters in so-called 'Middle England' will accept the undoubted pain accompanying any restriction in car use? One simple and effective way in which the car user in this country was asked to pay for the environmental damage caused by too much petrol consumption was through the mechanism of a petrol price 'accelerator': the policy was introduced by the Conservative Government in the early 1990s as a clever procedure to increase the price of petrol annually at each budget by an amount greater than inflation. In 1997, the incoming Labour Government accepted the 'accelerator' but, as a policy, it floundered with the threatened petrol strike and blockading of petrol stations in 1999. The Conservative Opposition Party then denounced the 'accelerator policy' despite having introduced it themselves during their period in office. The public anger over petrol prices threatened the Government's commanding lead in the polls, which caused a re-think of petrol taxing policy. Since then, the Government's ten-year transport plan, a weak but welcome initiative in this field, has met with much opposition. It will be interesting to see how far suggestions like road pricing will be implemented throughout the country. It is difficult to see how this and other contentious policies can be made palatable for the motorist.

As far as the local environment in this country is concerned, it seems that conditions may get worse before there is a public will to make the necessary cultural change in attitudes towards the use of the private car, waste management and energy consumption in general. In Britain one or more of the main political parties has to find the courage and the political will to combat the road lobby and other powerful vested development interests in addition to educating the public about the necessity for sustainable living styles.

In the last years of the twentieth century there were signs of a change of attitude towards development and towards urban design both in Britain and in Continental Europe. There is a growing body of literature, some of it in official government documents, which advocates sustainable development and which sees environmental quality in terms of vibrant streets and squares. There are now many building projects following a design agenda, which minimize the use of non-renewable energy sources. Projects, such as those mentioned earlier in the case studies, others described in *Urban Design: Green Dimensions*,[8] together with many more, point the way forward to a more urbane and civilized city environment in the future.

Many of the finest squares and streets of the past have been developed over many generations. Perhaps, in the future, we should be measuring success in urban design, not simply in terms of the streets and squares we develop in total but by those judicious small-scale additions to the many fine streets and squares that still exist in our towns and cities. It may now be a good time to replace some of those inappropriate, out of scale twentieth century additions to streets and squares by development in tune with and inspired by this country's great city building traditions, though not necessarily by slavishly copying the best we have inherited from former generations.

NOTES

1. Gibberd, F. *Town Design*, Architectural Press, London, 2nd edn. 1955

2. Unwin, R. *Town Planning in Practice*, London, 1965, Gibberd, F. op cit., Cullen, G. *Townscape*, Architectural Press, London, 1961

3. Giedion, S. *Space, Time and Architecture*, Harvard University Press, Cambridge, Mass. 3rd edn. 1956

4. Le Corbusier, *The Radiant City*, Faber and Faber, London 1967

5. Gropius, W. *New Architecture and the Bauhaus* (trans P.M. Shand and F. Pick), Faber and Faber, London, 1935

6. Buchanan, C. D. *Traffic in Towns*, HMSO, London, 1963

7. Jacobs, J. *The Death and Life of Great American Cities*, Penguin, Harmondsworth, 1965 and see also Moughtin, J.C.

Urban Design: Green Dimensions, Architectural Press, Oxford, 1996

8. Moughtin, J.C. *Urban Design: Green Dimensions*, Architectural Press, Oxford, 1996

BIBLIOGRAPHY

Abercrombie, P. The fifty years' civic transformation. In *Town Planning Review*, Vol 1, No 3, October 1910, pp.220-234.

Abercrombie, P. Vienna as an example of town planning. In *Town Planning Review*, Vol 1, No 4, January 1911, pp.279-293.

Abercrombie, P. The era of architectural town planning. In *Town Planning Review*, Vol V, No 3, October 1914, pp.195-213.

Abercrombie, P. *Town and Country Planning*, London, 1944.

Abercrombie, P. *Greater London Plan*, HMSO, London, 1945.

Alberti, L.B. *Ten Books on Architecture* (trns. Cosimo Bartoli (into Italian) and James Leoni (into English)), Tiranti, London, 1955.

Alexander, C. A city is not a tree, *Architectural Forum*, New York, April 1965, pp.58-62 and May 1965, pp.58-61.

Alexander, C. *Notes on the Synthesis of Form*, Harvard University Press, Cambridge, Mass., 1974.

Alexander, C. *A Pattern Language*, Oxford University Press, Oxford, 1977.

Alexander, C. *A Timeless Way of Building*, Oxford University Press, New York, 1979.

Alexander, C. *The Oregon Experiment*, Oxford University Press, Oxford, 1979.

Alexander, C. et al. *A New Theory of Urban Design*, Oxford University Press, Oxford, l987.

Allsopp, B. *A Modern Theory of Architecture*, Routledge & Kegan Paul, London, l977.

Ambasz, E. Plaza Mayor, Salamanca. In *Architectural Design, Architectural Design Profile, Urbanism*, Vol 54, No 1/2, 1984, pp.44-45.

Anderson, S. (ed.) *On Streets*, MIT Press, Cambridge, Mass., 1986.

Anderson, S. (ed.) Studies toward an ecological model of the urban environment. In *On Streets*, ibid.

Appleyard. D., Lynch, K. and Myer, J. *The View from the Road*, MIT Press, Cambridge, Mass., 1964.

Appleyard, D. *Livable Streets*, University of California Press, Berkeley and London, 1981.

Aristotle, *The Politics* (trns. T.A. Sinclaire (revised by Trevor J. Saunders)), Penguin, Harmondsworth, 1986.

Archives d'Architecture Moderne. The battle for corner properties in Brussels. In *Architectural Design, Architectural Design Profile, Urbanism*, Vol 54, No 1/2, 1984, pp.69-74.

Arnstein, S.R. A ladder of citizen participation. In *Journal of the American Institute of Planners*, Vol 35, No 4, July 1969, pp.216-224.

Ashby, T. and Pierce Rowland, S. The Piazza del Popolo: its history and development. In *Town Planning Review*, Vol XI, No 2, 1924, pp.74-99.

Ashby, V. The Capitol, Rome: its history and development. In *Town Planning Review*, Vol XII, No 3, 1927, pp.159-181.

Ashdown, J. *The Buildings of Oxford*, Batsford, London, 1980.

Aspbury, A. and Harrison, R. Newark-Millgate Revival. In *The Planner*, Vol 68, February, 1982

Averlino, Antonio di Piero (known as Filarete) *Treatise on Architecture* (vol trns. John R. Spencer), Yale University Press, New Haven and London, 1965.

Bacon, E.N. *Design of Cities*, Thames and Hudson, London, revised edn., 1975.

Baker, G.H. *Le Corbusier, An Analysis of Form*, Van Nostrand Reinhold, Wokingham, 1984.

Banham, R. *Theory and Design in the First Machine Age*, Architectural Press, London, 1960.

Banham, R. *Megastructure: Urban Futures of the Recent Past*, Thames and Hudson, London, 1976.

Banz, G. *Elements of Urban Form*, McGraw-Hill, San Francisco, 1970.

Barnett, J. *An Introduction to Urban Design*, Harper & Row, New York, 1982.

Baroero, C. et al. (eds.) *Florence: Guide to the City*, Univis Guide Series: Italy, MarioGros, Tomasone and Co, Torino, 1979.

Beazly, E. *Design and Detail of Space Between Buildings*, Architectural Press, London, 1967.

Beer, A.R. Development control and design quality, part 2: attitudes to design. In *Town Planning Review*, Vol 54, No 4, October 1983, pp.383-404.

Benevelo, L. *The History of the City*, Scolar Press, London, MIT Press, Cambridge, Mass., 1968.

Betsky, A. Take me to the water: dipping in the history of water in architecture. In *Architectural Design*, Vol 65, No 1/2, Jan-Feb, 1995, pp. 9-15

Black Country Development Corporation, 'Before and After', Oldbury, West Midlands, Black Country Development Corporation, undated report

Blowers, A. et al. (eds.) *The Future of Cities*, Hutchinson, London, 1974.

Blumenfeld, H. Scale in civic design. In *Town Planning Review*, Vol XXIV, April 1953, pp.35-46.

Boesiger, W. (ed.) *Le Corbusier*, Thames and Hudson, London, 1972.

Booth, P. Development control and design quality; part 1: conditions: a useful way of controlling design? In *Town Planning Review*, Vol 54, No 3, July 1983, pp.265-284.

Bor, W. The St Paul's precinct saga. In *The Planner*, May 1988, Vol 74, No 5, pp.26-28.

Braunfels, W. *Urban Design in Western Europe*, The University of Chicago Press, Chicago, 1988

Broadbent, G. and Ward, A. (eds.) *Design Methods in Architecture*, Lund Humphries, London, 1969.

Broadbent, G. *Emerging Concepts in Urban Space Design*, Van Nostrand Reinhold, London, 1990.

Browne, K. Why Isfahan? A special issue. In *Architectural Review*, Vol CLIX, No 951, 1976, pp.253-322.

Buchanan, C. *Traffic in Towns: the Specially Shortened Edition of the Buchanan Report*. Penguin, Harmondsworth, 1963.

Buchanan, P. Paternoster, planning and the Prince. In *Architects' Journal*, Vol 187, No 3, 20 January 1988, pp.26-29.

Burckhardt, J. *The Architecture of the Italian Renaissance* (ed. Peter Murray), Penguin, Harmondsworth, 1987.

Bynner, J. and Stribley, K.M. (eds.) *Social Research: Principles and Procedures*, Longman, Harlow, 1978.

Campbell, C. *Vitruvius Britannicus* (first published in three volumes, London, 1917-25), Vol 1, Benjamin Blom Inc. New York, reissued in 1967.

Canter, D. *The Psychology of Place*, St Martin's Press, New York, 1977.

Carlson, A.A. On the possibility of quantifying scenic beauty. In *Landscape Planning*, Vol 4, 1977, pp.131-172.

Chandler, E.W. The components of design teaching in a planning context. In *Education for Planning: Retrospect and Prospect* (ed. P.W.S. Batey), reprinted from *Town Planning Review*, Vol 56, No 4, October 1984, pp.468-482.

Chermayeff, S. and Tzonis, A. *Shape of Community*, Penguin, Harmondsworth, 1971.

Cherry, G.E. *Urban Change and Planning*, G.T. Foulis, Oxford, 1972.

Chambers, I. Piazzas of Italy. In *Town Planning Review*, Vol XII, No 1, 1926, pp.57-78, and Vol XI, No 4, February 1926, pp.221-236.

Church, A. Urban regeneration in London Docklands: a five-year policy review. In *Environment and Planning: Government and Policy*, Vol 6, 1988, pp.187-208.

Coleman, A. *Utopia on Trial*, Hilary Shipman, London, 1985.

Collins, G.R. and Collins, C.C. *Camillo Sitte: The Birth of Modern City Planning*, Rizzoli, New York, 1986.

Colquhoun, A. Vernacular Classicism. In *Architectural Design, Architectural Design Profile, Building and Rational Architecture*, Vol 54, No 5/6, 1984, pp.26-29.

County Borough of Belfast, City Planning Department, *The Markets Redevelopment Area 18*, County Borough of Belfast, Belfast, 1971.

County Borough of Belfast, City Planning Department, *Industry and Commerce in Redevelopment 18*, County Borough of Belfast, Belfast, 1971.

County Council of Essex, *A Design Guide for Residential Areas*, Essex County Council, 1973.

Cowan, R. It doesn't add up in Docklands. In *Architects' Journal*, Vol 188, No 39, 28 September 1988, p.17.

Crook, J.M. *The Dilemma of Style*, John Murray, London, 1987.

Crompton, D.H. Layout, chapter 7: land use in an urban environment, a general view of town and country planning. In *Town Planning Review*, Vol 32, 1961, pp.185-232.

Cuesta, J.R. et al. *Appraisal and Proposals for San Giorgio Morgeto, Programa Erasmus*, Universita di Reggio Calabria and University of Nottingham, Nottingham (unpublished report), March 1989.

Cullen, G. A square for every taste. In *Architectural Review*, Vol CII, No 610, 1947.

Cullen, G. *Townscape*, Architectural Press, London, 1961.

Cullen, G. *The Concise Townscape*, Architectural Press, London, 1986.

Danby, M. *Grammar of Architectural Design*, Oxford University Press, London, 1963.

de Daney, D. Canary Wharf: critical mass. In *The Planner*, Vol 72, No 3, March 1986, p.36.

Davidoff, P. Working towards redistributive justice. In *Journal of the American Institute of Planners*, Vol 41, No 5, September 1975, pp.317-318.

Dean, J. The inner cities and urban regeneration. In *The Planner, TCPSS Proceedings*, Vol 75, No 2, February 1989, pp.28-32.

de Bono, E. *Lateral Thinking*, Penguin, Harmondsworth, 1977.

Derrida, J. In discussion with Christopher Norris. In *Deconstruction II* (ed. Andreas C. Papadakis) Architectural Design, London, 1989, pp.7-11.

Derrida, J. *Positions* (trns. Alan Bass), Athlone Press, London, 1981.

Dewhurst, R.K. Saltaire. In *Town Planning Review*, Vol XXXI, No 2, July 1960, pp.135-144.

Dougill, W. The present day Capitol. In *Town Planning Review*, June 1927, Vol XII, No 3, pp.174-183.

Downes, K. *Hawksmoor*, Thames and Hudson, London, 1969.

Doxiadis , C.A. On linear cities. In *Town Planning Review*, Vol 38, No 1, April 1967, pp.35-42.

Doxiadis, C.A. *Ekistics*, Oxford University Press, New York, 1968.

Edwards, A.M. *The Design of Suburbia*, Pembridge, London, 1981.

Edwards, A.T. *Architectural Style*, Faber and Gwyer, London, 1926.

Eisenman, P. and Krier, L. My ideology is better than yours. In *Reconstruction: Deconstruction* (ed. Andreas C. Papadakis) Architectural Design, London, 1989, pp.7-18.

Ellis, W.C. The spatial structure of streets. In *On Streets* (ed. S. Anderson) MIT Press, Cambridge, Mass., 1986, pp.114-131.

Eversley, D. *The Planner in Society*, Faber & Faber, London, 1973.

Fagence, M. *Citizen Participation in Planning*, Pergamon Press, Oxford. 1977.

Falk, N.P. Baltimore and Lowell: Two American approaches. In *Built Environment*, Vol 12, 1986, pp. 145-152

Falk, N.P.H. Waterside renaissance: a step by step approach. In *Urban Waterside Regeneration: Problems and Prospects* (K.N. White et al., eds), Ellis Horwood Ltd, Chichester, 1993, pp. 22-30

Falk, N. UK Waterside development. In *Urban Design*, Vol 55, July, 1995, pp. 19-23

Farmer, J. *Green Shift: Towards a Green Sensibility in Architecture*, Butterworth-Heinemann, Oxford, 1996

Farrell, T. Terry Farrell in the context of London. In *The Planner*, Vol 74, No 3, March 1988, pp.16-19.

Fishman, R. *Urban Utopias in the Twentieth Century*, Basic Books, New York, 1977.

Frampton, K. The generic street as a continuous built form. In *On Streets* (ed. S. Anderson), MIT Press, Cambridge, Mass., 1986.

Frick, D. Post-Modern planning: a retreat to urban design. In *AESOP News*, No 2, spring 1988, pp.4-5.

Fyson, A. Paternoster shows the way. In *The Planner*, Vol 74, No 12, December 1988, p.3.

Gadd, D. *Georgian Summer: Bath in the Eighteenth Century*, Adams and Dart, Bath, 1971.

Gans, H. *People and Plans*, Basic Books, New York, 1968.

Gardner, J.L. et al. Urban waterside: context and sustainability. In *Urban Waterside Regeneration: Problems and Prospects* (K.N. White et al., eds), Ellis Horwood Ltd, Chichester, 1993, pp. 4-14

Guadet, J. *Elements et Théorie de L'Architecture*, Vols I-IV, 16th edn., Librarie de la Construction Moderne, Paris, 1929 and 1930.

Ghorst, T. Isle of Dogs has its day. In *Architects' Journal*, Vol 176, No 47, 24 November 1982, pp.46-49.

Ghyka, M. *The Geometry of Art and Life*, Dover, New York, 1977.

Gibberd, F. *Town Design*, Architectural Press, London, 2nd edn, 1955.

Gibson, T. *People Power*, Penguin, Harmondsworth, 1979.

Giedion, S. *Space, Time and Architecture*, Harvard University Press, Cambridge, Mass., 3rd edn., enlarged, 1956.

Glancey, J. *New British Architecture*, Thames and Hudson, London, 1989.

Gosling, D. and Maitland, B. *Concepts of Urban Design*, Academy Editions, London, 1984.

Gosling, D. Definitions of urban design. In *Architectural Design, Architectural Design Profile, Urbanism*, Vol 54, No 1/2, 1984, pp.16-25.

Grant, D.P. A general morphology of systematic space planning approaches. In *Design Methods and Theories, Journal of the DMG*, Vol 17, No 2, 1983, pp.57-98.

Grassi, G. On the question of decoration. In *Architectural Design,*

Architectural Design Profile, Building and Rational Architecture, Vol 54, No 5/6, 1984, pp.10-13 and 32-33.

Griffith, R. Listed buildings and listed building control. In *The Planner*, Vol 75, No 19, 1 September 1989, p.16.

Gropius W. *The New Architecture and the Bauhaus* (trns. P. Morton Shand with introduction by Frank Pick), MIT Press, Cambridge, Mass., 1965.

Gutkind, E.A. *Urban Development in Western Europe: Vol. VI The Netherlands and Great Britain*, The Free Press, New York, 1971.

Gutkind, E.A. *International History of City Development*, Vol I *Urban Development in Central Europe*, The Free Press, New York, 1964.

Gutkind, E.A. *International History of City Development*, Vol IV, *Urban Development in Southern Europe: Italy and Greece*, The Free Press, New York, 1969.

Gutman, R. The Street Generation. In *On Streets* (ed. S. Anderson) MIT Press, Cambridge, Mass., 1986, pp.249-264.

Habraken, N.J. *Three R's for Housing*, Scheltema and Holdema, Amsterdam, 1970.

Habraken, N.J. *Supports: An Alternative to Mass Housing* (trns. B. Valkenburg), Architectural Press, London, 1972.

Hall, E.T. *The Hidden Dimensions*, Garden City, Doubleday, New York, 1969.

Hall, P. The age of the mega project. In *The Planner*, Vol 75, No 24, 6 October 1989, p.6.

Halprin, L. *Cities*, MIT Press, Cambridge, Mass., 1963.

Hambidge, J. *The Elements of Dynamic Symmetry*, Dover, New York, 1926.

Hegemann, W. and Peets, E. *The American Vitruvius, An Architect's Handbook of Civic Art*, Benjamin Blom, New York, 1922.

Hobhouse, H. *History of Regent Street*, Macdonald and Jane's, London, 1975.

Holford, W. St Paul's: report on the surroundings of St Paul's Cathedral in the City of London. In *Town Planning Review*, Vol XXVII, No 2, July 1956, pp.58-98.

Hollamby, E., Gosling, D., Cullen, G. et al. *Isle of Dogs: Urban Design Plan; A Guide to Design and Development*, London Docklands Development Corporation, London, November 1982.

Houghton-Evans, W. *Planning Cities*, Lawrence and Wishart, London, 1975.

House, M.A., Ellis, J.B. and Shutes, R.B.E. Urban rivers: ecological impact and management. In *Urban Waterside Regeneration: Problems and Prospects* (ed. K.N. White et al.), Ellis Horwood Ltd, Chichester, 1993, pp. 312-322.

Howard, E. *Garden Cities of Tomorrow*. Faber & Faber, London, 1965.

HRH, The Prince of Wales. *A Vision of Britain*, Doubleday, London, 1989.

HRH, The Prince of Wales. Building a better Britain. In *The Planner*, mid-month supplement, May 1989, pp.4-5.

Hunt, W.P. Measured symmetry in architecture. In *RIBA Journal*, Vol 56, No 10, August 1949, pp.450-455.

Insall, D. Comments on conservation issues. In *The Planner*, Vol 74, No 3, March 1988, p.32.

Irving, R.G. *Imperial Summer, Lutyens, Baker and Imperial Delhi*, Yale University Press, New Haven and London, 1981, p.143.

Jacobs, J. *The Death and Life of Great American Cities*, Penguin, Harmondsworth, 1965.

Jarvis, B. Design language? In *The Planner*, Vol 75, No 26, 20 October 1989, p.2.

Jefferson, B. Getting better buildings. In *The Planner*, Vol 74, No 2, February 1988, pp.47-51.

Jencks, C. *Language of Post-Modern Architecture*, Academy Editions, London, 4th edn., 1984.

Jencks, C. and Silver, N. *Adhocism, The Case for Improvisation*, Anchor Press, New York, 1973.

Jencks, C. and Baird, G. (eds.) *Meaning in Architecture*, Barrie and Jenkins, London, 1969.

Jung, C. *Man and his Symbols*, Pan, London, 1978.

Katz, D. *Gestalt Psychology*, Ronald Press, New York, 1950.

Kennedy, M. Paternoster's piazzas fit for a prince. In *The Guardian*, 19 November 1988, p.3.

Kepes. G. *The New Landscape in Art and Science*, Paul Theobald and Co, Chicago, 1956.

Kersting, A.F. and Ashdown, J. *The Buildings of Oxford*, Batsford, London, 1980.

Koenigsberger, O. et al. *Manual of Tropical Housing and Building, Part 1, Climatic Design*, Longman, London, 1974.

Koffka, K. *Principles of Gestalt Psychology*, Harcourt, Brace and World Inc, New York, 1935.

Krier, L. *Rational Architecture*, Archives d'Architecture Moderne, Brussels, 1978.

Krier, L. *Houses, Palace, Cities* (ed. Demetri Porphyrios), Ad Editions, London, 1984.

Krier, L. The cities within the city, II: Luxembourg. In *Architectural Design*, Vol 49, No 1, 1979, pp.18-32.

Krier, L. and Jencks, C. Paternoster Square. In *Architectural Design* Vol 58, No 1/2, 1988, pp.VII-XIII.

Krier, R. Breitenfurterstrasse, Vienna. In *Architectural Design, Architectural Design Profile, Urbanism*, Vol 54, No 1/2, 1984, pp.80-81.

Krier, R. Typological and morphological elements of the concept of urban space. In *Architectural Design*, Vol 49, No 1, pp.2-17.

Kroll, L. Les vignes blances, Cergy-Pontoise. In *Architectural Design, Architectural Design Profile, Urbanism*, Vol 54, No 1/2, 1984, pp.26-35.

Lawson. B. *How Designers Think*, Architectural Press, London, 1983.

Le Corbusier. *Towards a New Architecture*, Architectural Press, London, 1946.

Le Corbusier. *Concerning Town Planning*, Architectural Press, London, 1947.

Le Corbusier. *The Home of Man*, Architectural Press, London, 1948.

Le Corbusier. *The Modulor*, Faber & Faber, London. 1954.

Le Corbusier. *The Chapel at Ronchamp* (trns. Jacqueline Cullen), Architectural Press, London, 1957.

Le Corbusier. *Chandigarh, The New Capital of the Punjab, India* (ed. T. Futagawa), Global Architecture, Tokyo, 1957.

Le Corbusier. *The Radiant City*, Faber & Faber, London, 1967.

Le Corbusier. *The City of Tomorrow*, Architectural Press, London, 1971.

Lee, T. The psychology of spatial orientation. In *Architectural Association Quarterly*, July 1969, pp.11-15.

Levin, P.H. The design process in planning. In *Town Planning Review*, Vol 37, April 1966, pp.5-20.

Levitas, G. Anthropology and sociology of streets. In *On Streets* (ed. S. Anderson), MIT Press, Cambridge, Mass., 1986.

Lim, Y Ng. *An Historical Analysis of Urban Spaces*, unpublished BArch dissertation, Nottingham University, 1980.

Linazasoro, J.I. Ornament and Classical order. In *Architectural Design, Architectural Design Profile, Building and Rational Architecture*, Vol 54, No 5/6, 1984, pp.21-25.

Linder, A. New thinking about urban design. In *The Planner*, Vol 74, No 3, March 1988, pp.24-25.

Little, B. *The Building of Bath*, Collins, London, 1947.

Little, B. *Bath Portrait*, The Burleigh Press, Bristol, 1961.

Llewelyn-Davies, R. Some further thoughts on linear cities, In *Town Planning Review*, Vol 38 No 3, October 1967, pp.202-203.

Llewelyn-Davies, R. Town design. In *Town Planning Review*, Vol 37, October 1966, pp.157-172.

Lock, D. The making of Greenland Dock. In *The Planner*, Vol 73, No 3, March 1987, pp.11-15.

Lowndes, M. and Murray, K. Monumental dilemmas. In *The Planner*, Vol 74, No 3, March 1988, pp.20-23.

Lozano, E.E. Visual needs in the urban environment. In *Town Planning Review*, Vol 45, No 4, October 1974, pp.351-374.

Lynch, K. *The Image of the City*, MIT Press, Cambridge, Mass., 1960.

Lynch, K. *Site Planning*, MIT Press, Cambridge, Mass., 2nd edn., 1971.

Lynch, K. *What Time is This Place?*, MIT Press, Cambridge, Mass., 1972.

Lynch, K. *A Theory of Good City Form*, MIT Press. Cambridge, Mass., 1981.

MacPherson, T. Regenerating Industrial Riversides in the North East of England. In *Urban Waterside Regeneration: Problems and Prospects* (K.N. White et al., eds), Ellis Horwood Ltd, Chichester, 1993, pp. 31-49

Maertens. H. *Der Optische Mastab in der Bildenden Kuenster*, 2nd edn, Wasmath, Berlin, 1884.

Madanipour, A. *Design of Urban Space*, Wiley, Chichester, 1996

Maitland, B. The uses of history. In *Architectural Design, Architectural Design Profile, Urbanism*, Vol 54. No 1/2, 1984, pp.4-7.

Manser, M. RIBA licks its wounds after Charlie's bombshell. In *Architects' Journal*, 6 June 1984, p.30.

Markets Redevelopment Association and the Planning Projects Unit, *The Markets Area of Belfast, The People's Plan* (preliminary report). Queen's University, Belfast, 1973.

Markus, T.A, The role of building performance measurement and appraisal in design method. In *Design Methods in Architecture* (eds. G. Broadbent and A. Ward), Lund Humphries, London, 1969.

Maver, T.W. Appraisal in the building design process. In *Emerging Methods in Environmental Design and Planning* (ed. G.T. Moore), MIT Press, Cambridge, Mass., 1971).

McKei, R. Cellular renewal. In *Town Planning Review*, Vol 45, 1974, pp.274-290.

McKay, K. Gryzmek, B. and Holden. Joe. *The Markets*, Gown, Belfast, 9 May 1972.

Moore, G.T. (ed.) *Emerging Methods in Environmental Design and Planning*. MIT Press, Cambridge, Mass., 1970.

Morgan, B.G. *Canonic Design in English Medieval Architecture*, Liverpool University Press, Liverpool, 1961.

Morris, A.E.J. *History of Urban Form*, George Godwin, London, 1972.

Moughtin, J.C. *Hausa Architecture*, Ethnographica, London, 1985.

Moughtin, J.C. *Planning for People*, Queen's University, Belfast, 1972.

Moughtin. J.C. Markets Areas redevelopment. In *Built Environment*, February 1974, pp.71-74.

Moughtin, J.C. *The Plansters Vision*, University of Nottingham, Nottingham, 1978.

Moughtin, J.C. and Simpson, A. Do it yourself planning in Raleigh Street. In *New Society*, 19 October 1978, pp.136-137.

Moughtin, J.C. Public participation and the implementation of development. In *Town and Country Summer School Report*, Royal Town Planning Institute, London, l978, pp.81-84.

Moughtin, J.C. et al. *The Nottingham Experiments, Towards Positive Participation in Planning*, Institute of Planning Studies, Nottingham, 1979.

Moughtin, J.C. and Bone, D. *The Building of a Community, Second Experience at Millgate in Newark, Nottinghamshire*, Institute of Planning Studies, Nottingham, 1981.

Moughtin, J.C. and Shalaby, T. Housing design in Muslim cities: towards a new approach. In *Low Cost Housing for Developing Countries*, Vol II, Central Building Research Institute, New Delhi, 1984, pp.831-851.

Mowl, T. and Earnshaw, B. *John Wood, Architect of Obsession*, Millstream Books, Bath, 1988.

Mumford, L. *The Culture of Cities*, Secker and Warburg, London, 1938.

Mumford, L. *City Development*, Secker and Warburg, London, 1946.

Murray, P. *The Architecture of the Italian Renaissance*, Thames and Hudson, London, revised 3rd edn., 1986.

Nairn, I. *Outrage*, Architectural Press, London, 1955.

Newark and Sherwood District Council, 'Capital Challenge Bid for Newark Riverside Regeneration,' Newark and Sherwood District Council, Newark, undated report

Newark and Sherwood District Council, 'SRB Challenge Fund Bid for Newark Riverside Regeneration,' Newark and Sherwood District Council, Newark, undated report

Newman, O. *Defensible Space*. Macmillan, New York, 1972.

Norberg-Schutlz, C. *Intentions in Architecture*, Universitetsforlaget, Oslo, 1963.

Norberg-Schulz, C. Meaning in architecture. In *Meaning in Western Architecture* (eds. Charles Jencks and George Baird), Barrie and Jenkins, London, 1969, pp.215-229.

Norberg-Schulz, C. *Existence, Space and Architecture*, Studio Vista, London, 1971.

Norberg-Schulz, C. *Genius Loci, Towards a Phenomenology of Architecture*, Rizzoli, New York, 1980.

Norris, C. *The Contest of Faculties: Philosophy and theory after deconstruction*, Methuen, London. 1985.

Norwood, H. Planning at York. In *The Planner*, Vol 72, No 3, March 1986, p.5.

The Observer. The Prince and the ten commandments. In *The Observer*, 30 October 1988. p.18

Owen, J. The water's edge: the space between buildings and water. In *Urban Waterside Regeneration: Problems and Prospects* (K.N. White et al., eds), Ellis Horwood Ltd, Chichester, 1993, pp. 15-21

Palladio, A. *The Four Books of Architecture*, Dover Publications, New York, 1965.

Pateman, C. *Participation and Democratic Theory*, Cambridge University Press, Cambridge, 1970.

Pawley, M. Prince and country. In *The Guardian*, 31 October 1988, p.38.

Pawley, M. Final act of the Fawcett saga. In *The Guardian*, 5 February 1990.

Pevsner, N. Three Oxford colleges. In *Architectural Review*, Vol CVI, No 632, 1949, pp.120-124.

Pevsner, N. *The Buildings of England: North Somerset and Bristol*, Penguin, Harmondsworth, 1958.

Pevsner, N. *An Outline of European Architecture*, Penguin, Harmondsworth, 7th edn., 1977.

Piaget, J. *The Child's Conception of the World*, Routledge & Kegan Paul, London, 1929.

Pidwell, S. Salford Quays: The urban design and its relationship with that of other wateside initiatives. In *Urban Waterside Regeneration: Problems and Prospects* (K.N. White et al., eds), Ellis Horwood Ltd, Chichester, 1993, pp. 94-105

Pirenne, H. *Medieval Cities*, Princeton University Press, Princeton, New Jersey, 1969.

The Planner, news. Canary Wharf: president urged secretary of state to intervene. In *The Planner*, Vol 71, No 12, December 1985, p.5.

The Planner, news. Time for design. In *The Planner*, Vol 74, No 3, March 1988, pp.29-31.

The Planner, news. Always a time for design. In *The Planner*, Vol 74, No 5, May 1988, p.7.

The Planner, news. Covent Garden plan: opponents lose appeal. In *The Planner*, Vol 74, No 11, November 1988, p.6.

The Planner, news. Paternoster exhibition. In *The Planner*, Vol 74, No 12, December 1988, p.6.

The Planner, news. DoE welcomes Docklands accord. In *The Planner*, Vol 75, No 21, September 1989, p.4.

The Planner, news. Government on LDDC: 'it's big and we did it'. In *The Planner*, Vol 75, No 21, September 1989, p.7.

The Planner, news. Docklands experiment: a failure rejected even by its own disciples, says Shepley. In *The Planner*, Vol 75, No 26, October 1989, p.3.

The Planner, news. Underground to Stratford via Canary Wharf. In *The Planner*, Vol 75, No 31, November 1989. p.5.

Plato. *The Laws* (trns. Trevor J. Saunders), Penguin, Harmondsworth, 1988.

Plato. *Timaeus and Critias* (trns Desmond Lee), Penguin, Harmondsworth, 1987.

Pogacnik, A.B. A systems approach to urban design. *Town Planning Review*, Vol 48, 1977, pp.187-192.

Popham, A.E. *The Drawings of Leonardo da Vinci*, Jonathan Cape, London, 1964.

Prak, Niels, Luming. *The Language of Architecture*, Mouton, The Hague, 1968.

Proshanksky, H., Ittelson, W. and Rivlin, L. *Environmental Psychology*, Holt, Rinehart and Wilson, New York, 1970.

Pugin, A.W.N. *Contrasts*, Leicester University Press, Leicester, 2nd edn, 1841, reprinted 1969.

Pugin, A.W.N. *The True Principles of Pointed or Christian Architecture*, Henry G. Bohn, London, 1841.

Punter, J. A history of aesthetic control: part 1,1909-1953. In *Town Planning Review*, Vol 57, No 4, October 1986.

Rapoport, A. and Kantor, R.E. Complexity and ambiguity in environmental design. In *Journal of the American Institute of Planners*, Vol 33, No 4, July 1967, pp.210-221.

Rapoport, A. *House Form and Culture*, Prentice-Hall, Englewood Cliffs, New Jersey, 1969.

Rapoport, A. Some observations regarding man-environment studies. In *Art*, February 1971.

Rapoport, A. *Human Aspects of Urban Form: Towards a Man-Environment Approach to Urban Form and Design*, Pergamon Press, New York, 1977.

Rapoport, A. *The Meaning of the Built Environment*. Sage, London, 1983.

Rasmussen, S.E. *Towns and Buildings*, Liverpool University Press, Liverpool, 1951.

Rasmussen, S.E. *Experiencing Architecture*, John Wiley and Sons, New York, 1959, MIT Press, Cambridge, Mass., 1959.

Rawlinson, C. Design and development control. In *The Planner*, Vol 73, No 12, December 1987, pp.25-26.

Rawlinson, C. Design and development control. In *The Planner*, Vol 75, No 19, September 1989, pp.17-20.

Rhodes, E.A. The human squares: Athens, Greece. In *Ekistics*, Vol 35, 1973.

RIBA. *Architectural Practice and Management Handbook*, RIBA Publications, London, 1965.

Robertson, H. *The Principles of Architectural Composition*, Architectural Press. London, 1924.

Rogers, R. (and Partners). Proposals for the banks of the River Arno, Florence. In *Architectural Design, Architectural Design Profile, Urbanism*, Vol 54, No 1/2, 1984, pp.62-68.

Rosenau, H. *The Ideal City*, Studio Vista, London, 1974.

Rowe, C. Collage city. In *Architectural Review*, August 1975, p.80.

Rowe, C. and Koetter, F. *Collage City*, MIT Press, Cambridge, Mass., 1978.

Rudofsky, B. *Architecture without Architects*, Doubleday and Co, New York, 1964, Academy Editions, London, 1977.

Rudofsky, B. *Streets for People*, Braziller, New York, 1969.

Rykwert, J, The street: the use of its history. In *On Streets* (ed. S. Anderson), MIT Press, Cambridge, Mass., 1986, pp.14-27.

Saarinen, E. *The Search for Form in Art and Architecture*, Dover Publications, New York, 1985.

Sandy Row Redevelopment Association, *Sandy Row at the Public Enquiry*, Sandy Row Redevelopment Association, Belfast, 1972.

Savoja, U. Turin the regular town. In *Town Planning Review*, Vol XII, No 3, 1927.

Schumacher, T. Buildings and streets. In *On Streets* (ed. S. Anderson), MIT Press, Cambridge, Mass., 1986, pp.132-149.

Schumpeter, J.A. *Capitalism, Socialism and Democracy*, Allen and Unwin, London, 1943.

Scoffham, E.R. *The Shape of British Housing*, Godwin, London, 1984.

Scoffham E.R. Balancing community and commerical interests in Newark-on Trent. In *Urban Waterside Regeneration: Problems and Prospects* (K.N. White et al., eds), Ellis Horwood Ltd, Chichester, 1993, pp. 106-115

Scruton, R. *The Aesthetics of Architecture*, Methuen and Co, London, 1979.

Scully, V. *The Earth, The Temple and The Gods: Greek Sacred Architecture*, Yale University Press, New Haven and London, 1962.

Segal, H. A psychoanalytic approach to aesthetics. In *International Journal of Psychoanalysis*, 1952, pp.196-207.

Serlio, S. *The Five Books of Architecture, An Unabridged Reprint of the English Edition of 1611*, Dover Publications, New York, 1982.

Shane, G. Contexualism. In *Architectural Design*, No 11, 1976, pp.676-9.

Sharp, T. *The Anatomy of the Village*, Penguin, Harmondsworth, 1946.

Sharp, T. *Oxford Replanned*, Architectural Press, London, 1948.

Sharp, T. Dreaming spires and teeming towers, the character of Cambridge. In *Town Planning Review*, Vol 33, January 1963, pp.255-278.

Sherwood, J. and Pevsner, N. *The Buildings of England: Oxfordshire*, Penguin, Harmondsworth, 1974.

Shute, J. *The First and Chief Grounds of Architecture*, John Shute, London, 1563.

Simpson, J. Paternoster Square redevelopment project. In *Architectural Design*, Vol 58, No 9/10, 1988, pp.78-80.

Sitte, C. *Der Stadte-Bau*, Carl Graeser and Co, Wien, 1901.

Smith, P.F. *Architecture and Harmony*, RIBA Publications, London, 1987.

Smithson, A. and Smithson, P. *Urban Structuring*, Studio Vista, London, 1967.

Sommer, R. *Personal Space: The Behavioural Basis of Design*, Prentice-Hall, Englewood Cliffs, New Jersey, 1969.

Southworth, M. and Southworth, S. Environmental quality in cities and regions. In *Town Planning Review*, Vol 44, No 3, July 1973.

Spencer, D.K. *Urban Spaces*, New York Graphic Society, Greenwich, Conn., 1974

Spreiregen, P.D. *Urban Design: The Architecture of Towns and Cities*, McGraw-Hill, New York, 1965.

Stones, R.C. Grain theory in practice: redevelopment in Manchester at Longsight. In *Town Planning Review*, Vol. 41, October 1970, pp.354-356.

Summerson, J. *John Nash, Architect to King George IV*, Allen and Unwin, London, 1935.

Summerson, J. *Architecture in Britain 1530-1830*, Penguin, Harmondsworth, 1953.

Summerson J. *The Classical Language of Architecture*, Thames and Hudson, London, 1963.

Summerson, J. *Inigo Jones*, Penguin, Harmondsworth, 1966.

Summerson, J. *The Architecture of the Eighteenth Century*, Thames and Hudson, London, 1986.

Taggart, W.D.R. and Taggart, R.T. *Cromac RDA 18, Planning Appraisal*, W.D.R. and R.T. Taggart, Belfast, 1985.

Tallis, J. *London Street Views, 1838-1840*, Nattali and Maurice, London, 1969.

Tibbalds, F. Mind the gap! A personal view of the value of urban design in the late twentieth century. In *The Planner*, Vol 74, No 3, March 1988, pp.11-14

Tibbalds, F. Planning and urban design: a new agenda. In *The Planner*, mid-month supplement, April 1988, p.4.

Tiesdell, S. et al. *Revitalizing Historic Urban Quarters*, Architectural Press, Oxford, 1996

Thiel, P. A sequence-experience notation for architectural and urban spaces. In *Town Planning Review*, Vol 32, April 1961.

Thorburn, A. Leisure on the Waterfront. In *The Planner*, Vol 73, No 13, 1990, pp. 18-19

Tunnard, C. *The City of Man*, Architectural Press, London, 1953.

Tzonis, A. and Lefaivre, L. *Classical Architecture, The Poetics of Order*, MIT Press, Cambridge, Mass., 1986.

Ulster Architectural Heritage Society, *Survey and Recommendations for the Joy Street and Hamilton Street District of Belfast*, Ulster Architectural Heritage Society, Belfast, 1971.

University of Liverpool, Recorder, *Report of the Development Committee to the Council of the University for the years 1959-1964*, The University of Liverpool, Liverpool, January 1965.

Unwin, R. *Town Planning in Practice*, London. 1909.

Vale, B. and Vale, R. *Green Architecture*, Thames and Hudson, London, 1991

Vasari, G. *The Lives of the Artists* (a selection trns. by George Bull), Penguin, Harmondsworth, 1965.

Venturi, R. *Complexity and Contradiction in Architecture*, MOMA, New York, 1966.

Vidler, A. The third typology. In *Rational Architecture*, Archives d'Architecture Moderne, Bruxelles, 1978.

Vidler, A. The scenes of the streets: transformations in ideal and reality. In *On Streets* (ed. S. Anderson), MIT Press, Cambridge, Mass., 1986, pp.28-111.

Vitruvius. *The Ten Books of Architecture*, Dover Publications, New York, 1960.

Violich, F. Urban reading and the design of small urban places: the village of Sutivan. In *Town Planning Review*, Vol 54, No 1, January 1983, pp.41-62.

Wallace, W. An overview of elements in the scientific process. In *Social Research: Principles and Procedures* (ed. John Bynner and Keith M. Stribley), Longman, Harlow, 1978, pp.4-10.

Weller, J.B. Architects and planners: the basis for consensus. In *The Planner*, Vol 75, No 22,22 September 1989, p.11.

Webber, MM. Order in diversity, community without propinquity. In *Cities and Space: The Future Use of Urban Land* (ed. L. Wingo Jr), Johns Hopkins University Press, Baltimore, 1963.

Webber, M.M. The urban place and the nonplace urban realm. In *Explorations into Urban Structure* (eds. Melvin M. Webber et al.), Oxford University Press, London, 1967, pp.79-153.

Webber, M.M. et al. *Explorations into Urban Structure*, University of Pennsylvania Press, Philadelphia, 1963.

Whinney, M. *Wren*, Thames and Hudson, London, 1987.

White, K.N. et al. *Urban Waterside Regeneration: Problems and Prospects*, Ellis Horwood Ltd, Chichester, 1993

Wilford, M. Off to the races, or going to the dogs? In *Architectural Design, Architectural Design Profile, Urbanism*, Vol 54, No 1/2, 1984, pp.8-15.

Williams-Ellis, C. *Portmeirion - the Place and its Meaning*, Portmeirion Ltd, Penrhyndeudraeth, Wales, 1973.

Wittkower, R. *Architectural Principles in the Age of Humanism*, Tiranti, London, 1952.

Wittkower, R. *Art and Architecture in Italy 1600-1750*, Penguin, Harmondsworth, 1958

Wolf, P. Rethinking the urban street: its economic context. In *On Streets* (ed. S. Anderson), MIT Press, Cambridge, Mass., 1986.

Wölfflin, H. *Renaissance and Baroque*, Collins, London, 1964.

Wotton, H. *The Elements of Architecture*, Gregg, London, 1969.

Wright, F. Lloyd. *The Living City*, Horizon Press, New York, 1958.

Yeats, W.D. *Yeats Selected Poetry*, Pan Books, London. 1974.

Zevi, B. *Architecture as Space* (trns. M. Gendel), Horizon Press, New York, 1957.

Zucker, P. *Town and Square*, Columbia University Press, New York, 1959.

FIGURE SOURCES

The author and publishers would like to thank those who have kindly permitted the use of images in the illustration of this book. Attempts have been made to locate all the sources of illustrations to obtain full reproduction rights, but in the very few instances where this process has failed to find the copyright holder, apologies are offered. In the case of an error, correction would be welcomed.

1.10–1.13	Wallace, W. *The Logic of Science in Sociology*, Aldine-Atherton, Chicago, 1971
2.1	*Amsterdam: Planning and Development in a Nutshell*, Public Works Department, City of Amsterdam, 1976
2.6, 5.1–5.3	Serlio, S. *The Five Books of Architecture*, Dover Publications, New York, 1982
2.7	Morris, A.E.J. *History of Urban Form*, George Godwin, London, 1972
2.9	Robertson, H. *The Principles of Architectural Composition*, Architectural Press, Surrey, 1924
2.28	Chitham, R. *The Classical Orders of Architecture*, Architectural Press, London, 1985
2.31	Le Corbusier *The Modulor*, Faber and Faber, London, 1951, Copyright DACS 1992
2.32	Moughtin, J.C. *Hausa Architecture*, Ethnographica, London, 1985
2.42 and 2.46	Robertson, H. *The Principles of Architectural Composition*, Architectural Press, Surrey, 1924
2.44	Kersting, A.F. and Ashdown, J. *The Buildings of Oxford*, Batsford, London, 1980
3.6	Baker, G.H. *Le Corbusier: An Analysis of Form*, Van Nostrand Reinhold, Berkshire, 1989
3.21	Gibberd, F. *Town Design*, Architectural Press, London, 1955
3.22	Scoffham, E.R. *The Shape of British Housing*, George Godwin, Harlow, 1984
3.27	Guadet, J. *Elements et Theorie de l'Architecture Volume 1*, 16th Edition, Librarie de la Construction Moderne, Paris, 1929
3.28	Groslier, B. and Arthaud, J. *Angkor, Art and Civilisation*, Thames and Hudson, London, 1957
3.33	Reprinted by permission of the publishers from *Space, Time and Architecture*, by Sigfried Giedion, Cambridge, Massachusetts: Harvard University Press, Copyright 1941, 1949, 1954, 1962, 1967 by the President and Fellows of Harvard College
4.6	Redrawn from Shalaby, T. *The Arab House*, Ed. Hyland A. D.C., CARDO, University of Newcastle, 1986
4.22 and 5.19	Sitte, C. *Der Stadte Bau*, Carl Graeser & Co, Vienna, 1901
4.60	Rasmussen, S.E. *Towns and Buildings*, Liverpool University Press, 1951
5.4	Le Corbusier *The City of Tomorrow*, Architectural Press, London, 1971, Copyright DACS 1992
5.18	Collins, G.R and Collins, C.C. *Camillo Sitte: The Birth of Modern City Planning*, Rizzoli, New York, 1986

6.7	Black Country Development Corporation, *Before and After*, Oldbury, West Midlands, Black Country Development Corporation, undated report
6.13	Based on Sharp, T. *The Anatomy of the Village*, Harmondsworth, Penguin, 1946
6.26 and 6.27	Based on Drawings in Thorne, Streets Ahead, *The Architectural Review*, March, 1994
6.35–6.47	Lowe, M. The Thames Strategy, *Urban Design*, Vol 55, July 1995 (Ove Arup Partnership - Tom Armour, Jon Carver, Michael Lowe)
7.1	*Towards an Urban Renaissance*, Urban Task Force 1999
7.2	*Towards an Urban Renaissance*, Urban Task Force 1999
7.3	*Towards an Urban Renaissance*, Urban Task Force 1999
7.4	*Towards an Urban Renaissance*, Urban Task Force 1999
	The Box Office Leaflet, What's On, *The Lowry*, May-August, 2002
7.14 and 7.15	Nottingham County Council, *Nottingbasm, Express Transit*
End picture	Tibbalds, F. *Making People Friendly Towns: Improving the Public Environment in Towns and Cities*, Longman, 1992
8.1	Morrison, T., *The Atlas of Mysterious Places*, Westwood, J. (ed.), Marshall Editions Ltd, pp. 142-3, 1987
9.1	Bor, W. The St Paul's Precinct Saga, *The Planner*, Vol 74, No 5, May 1988
9.2, 9.10–9.17	Krier, L. and Jencks, C. Paternoster Square, *Architectural Design*, Vol 58, No 1/2, 1988
9.5 and 9.6	Holford, W. St Paul's Precinct, *Town Planning Review, Vol XXVII*, No 2, July 1956
9.18	Tallis, J. *London Street Views 1838-1840*, The Bodley Head, London, 1969
9.20	Third Time Lucky with the Whitfield Masterplan, *Architects Journal*, 10th June 1999 page 55
9.21	Queen Victoria Street, *Architects Journal*, 27th November 1997 page 10
9.22, 9.23, 9.26 and 9.27	Gosling, D. and Maitland, B. *Concepts of Urban Design*, Academy Editions, London, 1984
9.24 and 9.25	Wilford, M. Off to the Races or Going to the Dogs? *Architectural Design*, Vol 54, No 1/2, 1984
9.35, 9.45–9.47	Taggart, W.D.R. *Cromac RDA 18 Planning Reappraisal*, Northern Ireland Housing Executive, Belfast, 1985
9.40 and 9.42	The Markets Area Redevelopment Association, *The Markets Area of Belfast, The Residents' Plan*, Department of Town and Country Planning, Queen's University of Belfast, 1973
9.41	Moughtin, J.C. Markets Area Redevelopment, *Built Environment*, Feb 1974
9.55 and 9.56	Scoffham, E.R. Balancing Community and Commercial Interests in Newark-on-Trent. In *Urban Waterside Regeneration: Problems and Prospects* (eds K.N. White et al.), Ellis Horwood, Chichester, 1993
9.60	Guasa, M. et al., *Barcelona: A Guide to its Modern Architecture*, ACTAR, 2002
9.68	Buchanan, P. Urbane Village, *Architectural Review*, August 1992 page 31

INDEX